Handbook of
NEW TESTAMENT
GREEK

BIBLICAL AND NEAR EASTERN LANGUAGE HANDBOOKS
by Dr. LaSor

HANDBOOK OF BIBLICAL HEBREW
HANDBOOK OF BIBLICAL ARAMAIC
HANDBOOK OF OLD BABYLONIAN
HANDBOOK OF NEW TESTAMENT SYRIAC

Handbook of
NEW TESTAMENT GREEK

An Inductive Approach Based on the Greek Text of Acts
by WILLIAM SANFORD LaSOR
with Peter Hintzoglou and Eric N. Jacobsen

VOLUME TWO
Grammar
Synoptic Paradigms
Basic Vocabulary

WILLIAM B. EERDMANS PUBLISHING COMPANY
Grand Rapids, Michigan
in cooperation with
THE WILLIAM CAREY LIBRARY
533 Hermosa St., South Pasadena

Copyright © 1973 by William Sanford LaSor
All rights reserved
ISBN 0-8028-2342-4
Printed in the United States of America

Library of Congress Cataloging in Publication Data

La Sor, William Sanford.
　Handbook of New Testament Greek.

　CONTENTS: v. 1. Reading lessons keyed to the
grammar.—v. 2. Grammar, synoptic paradigms, basic
vocabulary.
　1. Greek language, Biblical—Grammar.
I. Hintzoglou, Peter, joint author.　II. Jacobsen,
Eric N., joint author.　III. Title.
PA817.L3　　　　　487'.4　　　　　73-6951
ISBN 0-8028-2342-4　(vol. 2)

Reprinted, November 1980

TABLE OF CONTENTS
VOLUME TWO

Part II
GRAMMAR

INTRODUCTION

§01.   Greek is the language spoken by the Greeks, who called themselves Hellenes and their language Hellenic. They inhabited
what we know as Greece, the islands of the Aegean, the coastal region of
Asia Minor, and important colonies in Italy and the western Mediterranean.
There is increasing evidence that certain tribes of Asia Minor were in
some way related to the complex we call Greek.

§01.1   The Greek language, in the widest meaning, belongs to the
linguistic family called Indo-European, a family of languages
which spread to India and to Western Europe, and then to the Americas.
Greek is therefore cognate with English, the Germanic languages, the
Romance languages, etc., with which we of the Western World are most
familiar. This close relationship will be obvious in numerous words
from common origin and in similar syntactical constructions.

§01.2   In the early years of linguistic science and comparative
linguistics, the obvious relationship of the Indo-European
languages to Sanskrit led to wide study of the various stages of development of Sanskrit. The popular conception grew that Sanskrit was the
oldest form of the Indo-European languages, hence Sanskrit was looked upon
as the ancestor of all other Indo-European languages. The fallacy of this
popular view has not entirely disappeared. The importance of Sanskrit lies
in the grammatical studies of Panini, from about the 4th cent. B.C.,
which have given us considerable knowledge of the language. But grammarians often conceal important data (not intentionally) in their effort
to fit everything into a neat system. Modern knowledge of Indo-European
is based on the study of texts from many areas, some of them many centuries
older than Panini's works. Sanskrit is still important; but it must take
its place in a much larger context of linguistic data, not the least of
which is Hittite.

§01.3   Formerly, the Indo-European languages were divided into two
main groups, the centum languages, and the satem languages
(based on two forms of the word for '100'). Today, this simple division
is generally rejected for a more complex division, and one scholar finds
nine families that have developed from the parent (ultimate, not immediate)
Indo-European: (1) Indo-Iranian, (2) Armenian, (3) Greek, (4) Albanian,
(5) Italic, (6) Celtic, (7) Germanic, (8) Balto-Slavic, (9) Tocharian.
Hittite is not included at this stage, since, according to the same scholar,
it broke away from the parent stock at a much earlier date. If we group
the nine families (or sub-families) above under a heading Proto-Indo-
European, we could place them alongside another group headed Proto-
Anatolian, and bracket both groups under a heading, Proto-Indo-Hittite.
Actually, because of continual interpenetration of various languages, due
to commerce, war, etc., the solution is not so simple. (E. H. Sturtevant,
An Introduction to Linguistic Science [New Haven: Yale University Press, 1946;
paperback, 1960], 154-167.)

§02.   Formerly, four dialects of Greek were identified: Attic, Ionic,
Aeolic, and Doric. Koinē was sometimes added as a fifth dialect,
although it was generally related to Attic. Attic (classical) Greek
became prominent because of the great men of Athens from the 4th cent. B.C.,
and later. Closely akin to Attic was Ionic, and since Homer was from Ionia,
it is obvious that the earlier language (Homeric or Epic) could readily be
related to Attic. Inscriptional discoveries however have made it clear
that the picture is highly complex, and many dialects are now identified.
Koinē is placed in the sub-group of Northwest Greek by some, and in a sense,
Hellenistic Greek, or the Koinē (i.e. common) language, is one of the results
of the Hellenistic process begun by Alexander the Great of Macedon. Attic
elements in literary Koinē are to be explained as Atticisms, or deliberate
attempts to imitate the classical Attic writers. (For further study, see:
C. D. Buck, The Greek Dialects [Chicago: University of Chicago Press, 1955]
3-16; A. Wikgren, et al., Hellenistic Greek Texts [Chicago: University of
Chicago Press, 1947] xvii-xxvi.)

§02.1   The New Testament is written in Koinē or "common" Greek. Koinē
         has been variously described, between such limits as "bad Attic"
and "the language of the Holy Ghost." Today it is looked upon as the
language of Hellenism existing in different levels: literary (highly
Atticizing, hence not included under Koinē by some scholars), vernacular,
and various shades between.

§02.2   Within the New Testament there are various levels of Koinē.
         Scholars recognize the Greek of the Lukan writings and Hebrews
as the most "literary," the language of the Apocalypse as the most "common,"
and the language of Matthew as suggestive of translation from an original
Aramaic composition. Paul uses Greek as an educated Greek would use the
vernacular. The Greek of James and I Peter is considered "remarkably good,"
while that of II Peter "seems to have been learnt mainly from books." The
reason for selecting Acts as the basis of this Handbook is obvious.

§03.   It is a mistake to attempt to explain the Greek of the New
         Testament solely on the basis of the historical development of
the Greek language. The New Testament, to varying degrees but always
markedly, is developed from the religion of the Old Testament. Its Semitic
character is obvious to all except those totally ignorant of the Semitic
world. Scholars have therefore noted many "Semitisms" or "Hebraisms" in the
New Testament.

§03.1   Some of these "Semitisms" must be ruled out, since the same ideas
         or expressions can be found in Greek that has not been Semitized.
Some, however, can be explained by a more subtle process. During the three
centuries before Christ, the eastern Mediterranean was not only undergoing
a Hellenization; it was also undergoing a Semitization. These two sides of
historical process can be seen in the Greek Old Testament, or Septuagint,
where the Greek language is Semitized in order to make the translation, and
where the Hebrew religion is at the same time Hellenized. Ideas expressed
in Hebrew began to take on new dimensions as they were expressed in Greek
terms which were broader than the Hebrew expressions. At the same time,
Greek words took on new shades of meaning. The Gentile world learned from

the Jews of the Dispersion, whether directly or indirectly, willingly or
unwillingly. When the New Testament writers were ready to put their message
in written form, the Greek language was already to some extent preconditioned
for them.

§03.2   Another element may be mentioned in passing. The Roman Empire
           was beginning to effect a change which would not be completed
for two or three centuries, and which in some places would never be done:
the Latin language was spreading eastward. Since Paul, at least, had his
sights set on Rome, we may expect to find some traces of "Latinisms" in
the New Testament. They are, however, few and relatively unimportant.

§03.3   For recent bibliography, see F. Blass and A. Debrunner,
           A Greek Grammar of the New Testament and Other Early Christian
Literature; translated and revised from the 9th-10th German edition by
Robert W. Funk (Chicago: University of Chicago Press, 1961), §§1-7.

§04.   The study of any language involves the study of grammar and
           its elements. It is impossible to convey meaning if the
recipient does not recognize a difference between feud and viewed,
between was and is, or between I gave it to him and he gave it to me.
It is utterly impossible to communicate if the words are meaningless.
Language study therefore involves phonology, morphology, syntax, and
vocabulary.

§04.1   Phonology is the study of the elements of sound used to form
           words and phrases. (We include "phrases," for some sounds
occur in phrases which do not occur in words. Get eem! is meaningful,
for in this word-group eem is understandable even though by itself it
would be meaningless.) Division 1 of the grammar deals with Phonology.
All sections and paragraphs are numbered with numbers beginning with 1
in the tens-place (i.e., §10., §11., §11.1., etc.).

§04.11   Since the sounds of a language can only be studied in the
           spoken form (i.e., from a speaker, or from a recording of a

speaker) it is necessary to use some other way of studying the phonology
of historic languages. The recording of language in written form has
provided us with such materials, and therefore orthography (the study of
the method of writing) is ancillary to the study of phonology.

§04.2   Morphology, also called accidence, is the study of the forms of
         words, or the formation of inflected words. It is particularly
important in an inflected language. Division 2 of the grammar deals with
Morphology. All sections are numbered with numbers beginning with 2:
§20., §21., §22.2., etc.

§04.21   Languages are described as isolating, agglutinating, or inflecting,
          depending on their way of indicating the relationship between
words. When the relationship is shown purely by word order, without any
other indication, the language is isolating. Joe hit John and John hit Joe
are examples of the isolating kind, although English is not basically an
isolating language. Agglutinating languages tack together a number of
elements to the basic word. If we refer to a certain kind of altruism
as "do-good-ism," and then speak of a man's do-good-ism-ness, we are ap-
proaching an agglutinating method. Modification of a word root or stem--
which is never in itself a word except by accident--by prefixes, infixes,
suffixes, and other formative elements, is inflection. In English, traces
of ancient inflection remain in words such as love, loves, loved, loving,
unloved, unloving, and he, his, him. Greek is a highly inflectional
language.

§04.3   Syntax is the study of the means used to convey meaning through
         words. A vocabulary list contains many words, but it conveys
no meaning (the definitions, without syntax, simply supply substitute words).
Even the words of a sentence convey no meaning without syntax. Can you
understand the following: convey is meaning means of syntax study through
the to the used words. Rearranged according to syntax the words form a
meaningful sentence. Division 3 of the grammar deals with syntax. All
sections are numbered with numbers beginning with 3., §30., §31.4, §32.11, etc.

§04.4   With a knowledge of phonology, morphology, and syntax, we still
          cannot communicate unless the words form mental pictures, in
other words, unless we know the meaning of the words. Vocabulary control
is absolutely essential in language study.

§04.41   How much vocabulary should a student know in any given language?
          Obviously, the larger our vocabulary, the more extensively and
more rapidly we can read. But of what use is a large medical vocabulary
if we never read medical texts? Or a mythological vocabulary if we never
read mythology? Modern linguistic studies emphasize a basic vocabulary.
We have followed this approach in this Handbook.

§04.42   In the Greek New Testament, there are about 5,500 words. Of
          these, nearly 3,600 occur four times or less. This means that
we shall encounter each of these low frequency words only once in about
160 pages of the New Testament. Over two-thirds of the vocabulary of the
New Testament is of such low frequency. Only about 1,100 words occur ten
or more times. We should make every effort to learn this basic list. A
few low-frequency words are of great theological significance; these, too,
should be learned. With a vocabulary of 1,200 basic words, we can read
throughout the New Testament with facility.

§04.43   What about the other 4,300 words? Not all teachers will agree,
          but my advice is, try to guess the meaning from context. It
is not necessary to look up the meaning of every strange word in a
mashehuzebuch when you want to know what it means. If the picture comes
through in context, that is usually sufficient. However, for careful
study of a significant passage, for study of the theological content of
words, and for similar purposes, use a good lexicon. (By the way—did
you have to look up the meaning of mashehuzebuch?)

§05.   Translation is the process of transferring the thought expressed
          in one language to another language, preferably in equivalent
words and equivalent syntax. "Equivalent" does not necessarily mean an
exact word-for-word and phrase-for-phrase transfer. Only an unimaginative

literalist would translate <u>Wieviel Urh ist es?</u> as <u>How many hour is it</u>? or <u>Il fait beau temps</u> as <u>It makes good time</u>. More important than the words is the idea. The words serve to control the idea, provided they are understood in their own background. Translation therefore is an attempt to put the idea defined by the words and syntax of one language into the words and syntax of a second language that will define the same idea.

§05.1   <u>Exegesis</u>, sometimes equated with <u>hermeneutics</u>, is the process of discovering the meaning intended by the author. Since, as we have just seen, translation involves the same objective, it is necessary for us to have attempted an exegesis of a passage before the final stage of translation. It is customary to study Exegesis only after the elementary study of a language, particularly a Biblical language, has been completed. All too often Exegesis is attempted without the use of the original language, and the student therefore fails to see the close connection between the disciplines. In this <u>Handbook</u> we are seeking to make Exegesis an integral part of the language discipline, so that the student, when he goes into Exegesis will already know that linguistic knowledge is an essential part of Exegesis. When the author wrote, he expressed himself according to certain accepted rules of grammar. He could only be understood by his contemporaries by following those rules. He can only be understood by us as we seek to learn and follow the same rules.

§06.   The <u>numbering system</u> used in this Handbook is not only <u>decimal</u>, but it is also <u>logical</u>.

§06.1   Numbers are to be read as decimals, with "§14." = §14.0000, "§14.1" = §14.1000, and "§14.12" = §14.1200. Accordingly, "§14.123" is found after §14.12, but before §14.13, etc.

§06.2   The system is also logical, and subtopics are indicated by the addition of the next decimal. Accordingly §14.1, §14.2, etc., are subsections of §14. Moreover §14.11, §14.12, etc., are to be read as developments or expansions of §14.1, and §14.111, §14.112, etc., as expansions of or exceptions to §14.11. Usually, a subsection of three of more decimals (§14.124, §14.1241) must be read in the light of the section it is developing.

Division 1--Phonology

§§07--09 ARE ARBITRARILY OMITTED.

§10.   Phonology is that part of grammar which deals with the sounds and
         sound changes in a language. It includes phonetics, phonemics,
and orthography.

§10.1   Phonetics is the study of sounds. It includes the description of
          how the various sounds are produced, the classification of the
sounds, their relationship to one another, their influences upon one another,
and their shifts or alterations in the history of the language or language-
group.

§10.11   In this Handbook we use the International Phonetic Association
          alphabet, with some minor (and generally accepted) variations.
The exceptions are: [ž] for [ʒ], [š] for [ʃ], [ǧ] for [dʒ], [č] for [tʃ],
[ai] for [aɪ], [au] for [aʊ], [oi] for [ɔɪ], and [ᵉ] for [ə].

§10.12   For those not familiar with the I.P.A. alphabet, the following
          signs are explained. Others are self-explanatory. [ð] th in
there; [θ] th in three; [ǧ] g in George; [č] ch in church; [ŋ] ng in sing;
[ŋk] nk in sink; [ž] z in azure; [š] sh in ship; [ç] ch in German ich;
[x] ch in German ach; [j] y in yes; [y] German ü or French u; [i] i in
machine; [ai] i in ice; [e] a in chaotic; [ei] a in cave; [a] a in ask;
[ɑ] a in father; [æ] a in man; [ɛ] e in met; [ɔ] o in soft; [o] o in
notation; [ou] o in go; [u] oo in pool; [ᵉ] a in sofa, i in university, etc.

§10.2   Phonemics is the study of phonemes, which are the smallest
          meaningful units of a given language. It is also the study
of the history of the individual phonemes and the phonetic alterations
they may have undergone.

§10.21   Sounds which are phonetically different may, under certain
          conditions or in certain languages, be nonphonemic. For example,

B-9

[d] and [t] are phonetically different, and phonemic in English. However, in final position in German words, both d̲ and t̲ are pronounced [t]. On the other hand, sounds which are phonetically identical may represent the historical confluence of different phonemes. For example, the [ai] in Eng. light ('not heavy') is the same as in Eng. light ('not dark'); that it represents two original phonemes is indicated by the Ger. cognates leicht [laiçt] and Licht [liçt].

§10.3   Orthography is the method of writing a language. The phenomena of orthography should not be confused with the data of phonetics and phonemics. However, since orthography is the only means we have of reconstructing the sounds of languages no longer extant, we must work with the written records.

§10.31   Most systems of orthography were not invented by the people using them, and therefore do not fit the languages, either phonetically or phonemically. For example, our alphabet has no sign for [š], [č], [θ], etc., and we must use sh̲, ch̲, and th̲, respectively. On the other hand, our symbol s̲ serves for the sounds [s] and [z], our a̲ for [ei], [a] [æ], [^{e}], and many other sounds.

§10.4   Speech is communication by meaningful sounds, or the spoken form of language. Writing is language in written form, or speech reduced to a system of symbols that are meaningful to a community using the language.

§10.41   The sounds that are used to produce speech are called vowels and consonants. The vowel is the basic sound, and the consonant is an interruption or restriction of that sound. The resulting component parts are syllables. One or more syllables forming a unit that conveys an idea, is a word. We do not speak words, however, but sentences, which are formed of one or more words to convey a thought.

§10.42   A vowel is the basic sound in speech, made by vibrating the vocal cords. It can be modified by the angle of the jaw, the shape of

the mouth-opening, and the position of the tongue. Any interruption or
restriction, however, is considered as a consonant.

§10.43 A consonant is an element in speech which interrupts or restricts
the passage of breath, whether sound is being produced by the vocal cords
or not.

§10.44 A syllable is a vowel or diphthong set apart by a consonant or
    consonants from preceding or following vowels or diphthongs.
This is sometimes defined as a summit of sonority (cf. §16.).

§10.441 According to this definition, certain consonants have to be
    recognized as vowels. For example, bottle [bɔ-tl̩], chasm
[ka-zm̩], fighter [fai-tr̩], canon [kæ-nn̩], and houses [hauz-z̩], are all
disyllabic words, and [l̩], [m̩], [n̩], [r̩], and [z̩] have to be considered
as vowels.

§10.442 It is also necessary to recognize that there are consonants
    which are not indicated in writing. If two successive vowels
form two summits or syllables, a consonant has divided them. Examples:
idea either has a consonantal y-sound [ai-di-jᵉ] or a glottal stop
(or aleph) [ai-dɨ-'ᵉ] dividing the vowels; cooperate either has a
bilabial consonant [ko-wap-r̩-ret] or a glottal stop [co-'ap-r̩-ret],
depending on the speaker. Of course it is possible to fuse the two
vowels into a diphthong and reduce two syllables to one (e.g. [ai-dijᵉ]
or [ai-diᵉ]).

§11. The Greek alphabet has 24 letters. For the forms, names, and
    pronunciation, see Part III, Table A, of this Handbook.

§11.1 Certain points should be observed.

§11.11 Two styles of uncials (or majuscules, or capitals) are found
    in modern typography, hence we need to be able to recognize
both. Note particularly the different forms of alpha, delta, epsilon,
lambda, xi, sigma, and omega.

§11.12   Three styles of <u>minuscules</u> are found in modern typography.
           Note particularly the different forms of zeta, theta, kappa,
and phi.

§11.13   Minuscule <u>sigma</u> has a different form at the end of a word from
           that occurring within a word: σ, ς.

§11.14   <u>Iota</u>, whether uncial or minuscule, is not dotted.

§11.15   Certain letters <u>extend upwards</u> above the normal line of the tops
           of the letters. Those with upward extenders are: β (beta),
δ (delta), ζ (zeta), θ (theta), λ (lambda), ξ (xi), φ (phi, except in
some fonts), ψ (psi, except in some fonts). Note that κ (kappa) and τ
(tau) do not have upward extenders.

§11.16   Certain letters <u>extend downwards</u> below the line. Those with
           downward extenders are: β (beta), γ (gamma), μ (mu), ρ (rho),
φ (phi), χ (chi, both arms), and ψ (psi). In addition, ζ (zeta), ξ (xi),
and ς (final sigma) have a small tail extending downwards.

§11.17   In cursive writing, some letters can be connected with the
           following letter, others cannot. We shall not attempt to
analyze handwritten Greek here (see Table B). Note, however, that in
the printed form, sigma has a <u>connector</u> (at the top), whereas omicron
has no connector.

§11.2   The alphabet was borrowed from the Phoenicians who, according to
           many scholars, invented it, probably in the 2d millennium B.C.
All the letters of the Phoenician alphabet were consonants. For Greek,
the representation of vowels is much more essential than in Phoenician
where the consonants carry the meaning of the word. The Greeks therefore
adapted certain letters, which they did not need as consonants, to
represent vowels.

§11.21   The following were adapted as vowels: Ph. ʼaleph (a glottal
           stop) for Gk. <u>alpha</u>; Ph. <u>hê</u> (glottal fricative [h]) for Grk.

epsilon; Ph. ḥêt (emphatic glottal fricative) for Gr. ēta; Ph. yôd semiconsonant [i] for Gr. iota; Ph. ʿayin (emphatic glottal stop) for Gk.
omicron. There is some inscriptional evidence that the ḥêt was used, at
least in some regions, for the uvular fricative [h] or [x] (ch in Ger.
ach), and a modification of the sign came to be used for the rough
breathing.

§11.22   Two Phoenician letters were used by the Greeks for a time, and
          one was not borrowed at all. The Ph. waw was borrowed to serve
as digamma, Ϝ [w]. Ph. qôp was borrowed as Gk. koppa, ϙ [q] or [ḳ].
These letters came over into the Latin alphabet, which we use for English,
but fell into disuse in Greek. The Ph. ṣadê was apparently never borrowed
by the Greeks.

§11.221   One line of evidence is, the use of the alphabet as numerical
          system requires the digamma (Ϝ = 6) and koppa (ϙ = 90). On the
other hand, it does not require any representation of the Ph. ṣadê. Ph.
ṣ, q, r, š, and t, were used for 90, 100, 200, 300, and 400 respectively.
Gk. koppa, rho, sigma, and tau, were used for 90, 100, 200, and 300,
respectively.

§11.23   The names of the letters were probably borrowed from Aramaic,
          the -â at the end being the Aram. definite article. In several
instances there has been modification, e.g. gamma for gamlâ, zeta for
zêntâ (?), iota for yodtâ (?), lambda for lamtâ, mu for mîm, nu for nûn,
rho for rêš or râš, sigma for šinâ (?)

§11.24   The Greeks added to the Phoenician alphabet (at the end, notice!)
          the letters upsilon, phi, chi, psi, and omega.

§11.25   The psilon, added to e and u, was a Byzantine alteration of the
          names of these letters. Likewise, the micron and mega definitions
of o and ō were Byzantine.

§11.3   In the earliest inscriptions, Greek, like Phoenician, was written
         from right to left, and the letters were quite similar to
Phoenician forms.   Later, rows were written alternately right-to-left
(sinistrograde) and left-to-right (dextrograde), with the letters reversed
according to the direction of writing.   This method of writing was called
boustrophedon, or 'as the ox plows.'   Finally, the present system of writing
from left to right was standardized, with the letters in the reversed
position; accordingly, the early Greek letters in this system often are
mirror-images of the corresponding Phoenician letters.

§11.4   These 24 letters do not, and probably never did, represent the
         basic phonemes of Greek or the phonetic elements of the language.
The phonetics of Greek is a subject that has occupied scholars for many
years, and remains a problem.   We simply do not know how certain letters
were pronounced, and it is reasonable to assume that the pronunciation
varied according to dialect.   In the discussion of phonetics and phonetic
shifts, below, we shall touch on some of the problems.

§11.5   The earliest form of the letters was the capital, used in
         inscriptions cut in stone.   A modification of this used for
manuscripts is called uncial.   All Biblical manuscripts in Greek before
the 10th cent. A.D. were written in uncials.   The development of the
minuscules and the modification of them into a cursive or flowing form,
led to the displacement of the uncials.   With the invention of printing,
modern editorial devices, such as capital and lower case, punctuation, etc.,
were introduced.   See Part III, Table A.

§11.51   Division into words was not indicated in the earliest uncials.
         The scribes, however, were careful to break words according to
syllables, and when a new subject was introduced, they started the word on
a new line.

§11.52   Marks of punctuation used in Greek are the period (.), the colon
         (·), the comma (,), and the question mark (;).   In older manu-
scripts, the double dot (:) was used to indicate a major break, more than
a period but less than a paragraph.   Note the forms of the colon and the
question mark.

§11.521   Punctuation was not found in the earliest uncials. The single dot
            (period, semi-colon, etc.), comma, and double dot (a strong break)
were introduced around the 5th cent. A.D. The full system of punctuation
found in our Greek Testament probably began with the printed text.

§11.53   Every vowel or diphthong at the beginning of a word is marked with
            the sign of smooth breathing (') or rough breathing ('). The
rough breathing indicates that aspiration [h] precedes the pronunciation of
the vowel or diphthong.

§11.531   The mark of breathing is placed over the initial vowel, or over
            the second vowel of a diphthong. If the diphthong is written with
iota subscript (cf. §11.56), the breathing of course stands on the first
vowel. In some texts where such a diphthong is written with iota adscript
(i.e. on the line, following the α, η, or ω), the breathing is still placed
on the first vowel. Otherwise, if the breathing is written over the first
of two successive vowels, it is an indication that no diphthong is present.

§11.532   If the word is written with an uncial initial letter (or entirely
            in uncial characters), the sign of breathing and the accent (if any)
are placed before the initial letter.

§11.5321   If the initial sound is a diphthong, the provisions of §11.531 apply.
            When the word is printed entirely in uncial characters, the provision
of §11.532 applies.

§11.533   The indication of aspiration (the rough breathing) was found in
            some ancient inscriptions, where the (H)eta was used as a consonant.
Later, half of the H was used to indicate rough breathing (⊢), and subsequently the other half was used to indicate smooth breathing (⊣). From these developed (') and ('). In manuscripts, however, the earliest use of the rough
breathing was about the 5th cent. A. D.

§11.534   At the beginning of a word, in some texts, ῥ is regularly written
            with rough breathing (hence the spelling rho). When two rho's occur
together, the first is sometimes written with smooth breathing, and the second with rough breathing (hence such loan words as pyrrhoea): ῤῥ.

§11.535   Initial ὑ is generally aspirated (i.e., has rough breathing).

§11.54   <u>Accents</u> were invented in the Hellenistic Age, and used in poetic
         texts to indicate meter, and then more fully to preserve the
correct pronunciation of the language. Their use in N.T. manuscripts, however,
was a later introduction, around the 7th cent. A.D. We shall consider the
rules of accent in §17.

§11.541   The accent is written over the vowel. If the vowel is an uncial,
          the accent is written in front of it. When two vowels form a
diphthong, the accent is written over the second vowel (except when the
diphthong is written with <u>iota</u>-subscript or -adscript.) (τὴν, Ἄλλην, τοῖς, τῷ)

§11.542   When both a sign of breathing and an accent are written over
          (or before) a vowel, the sign of breathing is written first
and the acute or grave accent is placed to its right over the same letter.
However, if the accent is circumflex, the breathing is placed under the
circumflex. (ἔχων, αἶνον).

§11.55   Certain <u>other diacritical marks</u> may be mentioned here.

§11.551   The diaeresis (¨) is placed over the second of two vowels to
          show that they form two syllables and not a diphthong: Μωϋσῆς
διϊσχυρίζετο .

§11.552   The <u>corōnis</u> (᾿) is used to indicate <u>crasis</u> (cf. §15.52). It
          is placed over the contracted syllable. (κἀγώ from καὶ + εγω)

§11.553   The <u>apostrophe</u> (᾿) is used to indicate <u>elision</u> (cf. §15.53).
          It is placed after the word with the elided vowel. (ἐπ᾿ αὐτόν)

§11.56   The use of <u>iota</u> after long vowels to form diphthongs was
         indicated in early texts, where the iota was written on the
line following the first vowel of the diphthong. Later, when the diphthong
monophthongized, the iota fell out--this was before the New Testament period.
The introduction of <u>iota subscript</u> to indicate these ancient diphthongs did
not take place until the 12th cent. A.D. The iota subscript is not found
in any uncial manuscript.

§11.57   It is important for the student to keep in mind the <u>lateness</u>
         of some of the editorial devices. The earliest uncial manuscripts
were even without breaks between the words. Breathings, accents, <u>iota</u>
subscripts, punctuation marks, etc.--which often greatly influence the
translation--are later editorial additions and should be treated as such.
<u>The ultimate authority in every case is the unedited text</u>: what meaning
does the context require? If it is ambivalent, then the interpreter must
refrain from dogmatic assertion. The student is encouraged to study
replicas of the great uncial manuscripts in the library, or photographs
of them in Bible dictionaries, textbooks, etc.

§12.   The <u>consonant</u> is the element that modifies sound into units to
         form meaningful patterns, hence we start with the study of the
Greek consonants. There are 17 consonants represented in the Greek
alphabet: β γ δ ζ θ κ λ μ ν ξ π ρ σ/ς τ φ χ ψ.

§12.1   Consonants are described according to three characteristics:
         (1) the use or non-use of the voice during the production of
the consonant; (2) the interruption or restriction of the breath by the
consonant; (3) the part of the mouth or throat used in making the consonant.
See Part III, Table D.

§12.11   The classification of consonants used in many Greek grammars of
         the past is neither scientific nor satisfactory. The term <u>mute</u>
has been used to describe consonants that are voiced as well as those not
voiced. The term <u>stop</u> has been used to describe fricatives (originally
aspirates) as well as stops. And the terms <u>smooth</u>, <u>middle</u>, and <u>rough</u>
are not at all descriptive. It would be better to use modern linguistic
terms consistently.

§12.2   A consonant is described as either <u>voiced</u> or <u>surd</u>.

§12.21   A consonant is described as <u>voiced</u> (or <u>sonant</u>) when the voice is
         used during its production. Because the voice is used in producing

vowels, some students have difficulty distinguishing the voiced consonants
from the voiceless. Try pronouncing pairs, such as: big-pig; die-tie;
goo-koo; zoo-soo; etc. In Greek the following consonants are voiced:
β [b], γ [g], δ [d], ζ [z] or [dz], λ [l], μ [m], ν [n], ρ [r], ϝ[w], ͺ[y].

§12.22   A consonant is described as <u>surd</u> (or <u>unvoiced</u>, or <u>silent</u>) when
          the voice is not used in its production. In Greek the following
consonants are surd: θ [tʻ] > [θ], κ [k], ξ [ks], π [p], σ [s], τ [t],
φ [pʻ] > [f], χ [kʻ] > [x], ψ [ps].

§12.3   A consonant is described as either a <u>stop</u> or a <u>fricative</u>.
          Certain intermediate sounds, or phonetic developments, are
known as <u>affricates</u> or <u>aspirates</u>.

§12.31   A consonant is described as a <u>stop</u> (or <u>plosive</u>) when the passage
          of air from the lungs is stopped in some part of the throat or
mouth in producing the sound. In Greek, the following consonants are
stops: β [b], γ [g], δ [d], κ [k], π [p], τ [t].

§12.32   A consonant is classified as a <u>fricative</u> (or <u>spirant</u> or con-
          <u>tinuant</u>) when the passage of air is not stopped. It is possible
to continue the sound of a fricative as long as desired; it is not possible
to continue the sound of a stop. The following consonants are fricatives:
θ [θ], λ [l], μ [m], ν [n], ρ [r], σ [s], φ [f], χ [x], ϝ[w], ͺ[y].

§12.321   A consonant is described as an <u>affricate</u> when it is composed of
          a stop followed by a fricative. The Greek consonants ζ [dz],
ξ [ks], and ψ [ps] are affricates. For practical purposes they can be
considered as <u>double consonants</u>.

§12.3211 If the affricate is composed of a stop followed by a sibilant,
          it is sometimes called an <u>assibilate</u>. The Greek affricates,
it will be noted, are all assibilates.

§12.322   A consonant is described as an <u>aspirate</u> when it is composed of a
          stop followed by aspiration [h]. Originally the following Greek

consonants were aspirates: θ [t‛] or [tʰ], φ [p‛] or [pʰ], and χ [k‛] or
[kʰ].

§12.3221 It is reasonably certain that in New Testament times, and for
          some centuries thereafter, θ, φ, and χ were pronounced as
aspirates, in other words, <u>th</u> as in cour<u>th</u>ouse, <u>ph</u> as in u<u>ph</u>olster, and
<u>kh</u> as in tac<u>kh</u>ammer.

§12.323 The development of a stop or an aspirate into a fricative
         is called <u>spirantization</u>. The Greek consonants θ, φ, and χ
spirantized to [θ], [f], and [x] (or [ḫ]), respectively.

§12.4   A consonant is classified according to the part of the body
         used in production, starting from the lips: <u>labial</u>, <u>dental</u>
(<u>alveolar</u>), <u>palatal</u>, <u>velar</u>, <u>uvular</u>, and <u>glottal</u> (or <u>laryngeal</u>). A
few are difficult to describe, but may for convenience be called <u>lingual</u>.

§12.41   A consonant is classified as a <u>labial</u> if it is produced by using
         the lips; if both lips are used, the sound is a <u>bilabial</u>; if
lower lip and upper teeth are used, the sound is a <u>labio-dental</u>; if the
sound passes through the nasal system while the lips are closed, it can
be called a <u>labio-nasal</u>. In Greek, the following consonants are <u>labials</u>:
β [b], π [p], φ [f], and the ancient <u>digamma</u> ϝ [w].

§12.411 μ [m] could be classified as a <u>labio-nasal</u>, but is generally
         called a <u>nasal</u> or <u>sonant</u> or <u>liquid</u>.

§12.412 φ was originally a <u>labial aspirate</u> (cf. §12.322), then spir-
         antized into a <u>labio-dental fricative</u> [f].

§12.413 ψ is a <u>labial affricate</u> (cf. §12.321), but is generally
         considered as a double consonant, a <u>labial</u> [p] + a <u>sibilant</u> [s].

§12.42   A consonant is classified as a <u>dental</u> if teeth are used in the
         production of the sound. Generally the term <u>dental</u> is limited

to the combination of tongue and teeth. Some scholars prefer the term
alveolar as more accurate, since the tongue is usually placed against the
alveolar ridge rather than against the teeth. In Greek, the dentals are
δ [d], τ [t], θ [θ], and at least in part ζ [dz].

§12.421   θ was originally a dental aspirate (cf. §12.322), which
           spirantized into a dental fricative [θ].

§12.422   ζ was at first possibly a dental affricate (§12.321), generally
           considered as a double consonant; it was both dental and sibilant.
Later it simplified to the voiced sibilant [z].

§12.43   A consonant is classified as a velar (or palatal) when the soft
           palate (i.e., the back of the roof of the mouth) is used in pro-
ducing the sound. The tongue is brought up against the roof of the mouth
(velar stop) or near it (velar fricative). In Greek, the following
consonants are velars: γ [g], κ [k], χ [x], and in a sense ξ [ks].

§12.431   χ was originally a velar aspirate (§12.322), later developing
           into a velar fricative [x].

§12.432   ξ [ks] is generally considered as a double consonant. It is
           both velar and sibilant.

§12.44   A consonant is classified as a guttural when it is produced in the
           throat. The only guttural in Greek is the sound indicated by the
mark of rough breathing (‘), indicated phonetically as [h]. Historically
this has developed, sometimes from a sibilant, sometimes from a guttural or
uvular fricative [h]. In some ancient inscriptions, the H (ēta) represented
the original uvular fricative.

§12.45   A number of consonants are difficult to describe physically. Since
           all of them are made by using the tongue in some way to modify the
passage of breath, I have chosen to group them under the name lingual. This
must be further subdivided.

§12.451   If a consonant is produced by placing the tip of the tongue against
             the teeth or roof of the mouth, allowing the sound to pass around
the side of the tongue, it is called a lateral. In Greek, λ (l) is a lateral.

§12.452   If the tip of the tongue is trilled against the roof of the mouth
             or touched briefly to the alveolar ridge (or, as in many American
dialects, rolled back) and the sound allowed to pass around it, the sound is
indicated as [r] (sometimes [R] is used for the back r). Greek ρ [r] is
such a consonant.

§12.453   If the tip of the tongue is placed against the aveolar ridge or
             roof of the mouth, and the sound is allowed to pass through the
nasal cavity, the sound is a nasal, indicated as [n]. Such is Greek ν.

§12.454   If the back of the tongue is pressed against the velum (soft
             palate), and the sound allowed to pass through the nasal cavity,
the sound is a nasalized velar, indicated as [ŋ] as ng in sing. Greek γ
before γ, κ, or χ, is nasalized to this sound.

§12.455   The consonants λ, ν, and ρ are often called liquids. The
             consonants μ, ν, and nasalized γ are often called nasals.
Occasionally μ is included in the liquids. All are sometimes (improperly)
called sonants.

§12.456   If the tip of the tongue is brought near the teeth or the roof of
             the mouth, and the sound is allowed to pass over it, the sound is
called a sibilant. The pure sibilants, voiced [z] and surd [s], are produced near the teeth or alveolar ridge. The lateral sibilants [ž] and [š]
are produced in the roof of the mouth. In Greek, the pure sibilant σ [s],
and the compound sibilants ζ [dz], ξ [ks], and ψ [ps] are found.

§12.46   In Greek there are no uvular consonants. It is possible that
             the koppa was either a back-velar (ḳ) or uvular [q] stop, and the
(ḥ)eta originally was probably a uvular fricative (cf. §12.44).

§12.47   The rough-breathing [h] is a <u>surd glottal fricative</u>.

§12.5   It is customary to refer to certain sounds as <u>semiconsonants</u> or
         <u>semivowels</u>, since they serve in both capacities (e.g. <u>w</u> as in
cow--won, <u>y</u> as in <u>day</u>--<u>yes</u>). These are sometimes represented by the symbols
[u̯] as in <u>persuade</u> and [i̯] as in <u>onion</u>.

§12.51   Greek <u>iota</u> often serves as a consonant [j] or [i̯], particularly
          at the beginning of a word. It is <u>voiced velar fricative</u> or
<u>lateral</u>, and its similarity both to [l] and to [γ] can be seen in numerous
sound-shifts.

§12.52   <u>Digamma</u> was also a semiconsonant [w] or [u̯], the effects of
          which will be seen in numerous sound-shifts.

§13.   In all languages, the proximity of certain sounds causes <u>sound</u>
         <u>shifts</u>, principally assimilation and dissimilation (total or
partial), lengthening and shortening of sounds, metathesis, loss of sounds,
etc. This phonetic change varies from language to language, and from
language group to group, but it is reasonably regular within any particular
language. The description is called "phonetic law"--but law in a descriptive
sense only.

§13.1   <u>Assimilation</u> is the total or partial conformation of one sound to
         another. If the assimilation is toward the front of the word, it
is called <u>progressive</u>; if toward the end of the word, it is called
<u>regressive</u>.

§13.11   A <u>dental stop</u> (δ, τ, θ) influences a preceding stop, resulting in
          <u>regressive, partial or total assimilation</u>. The term <u>stop</u> is used
to include the aspirates φ, θ, and χ, for this and the following rules.

§13.111   When a <u>labial stop</u> (β, π, φ) stands before a <u>dental stop</u>, the labial
           partially assimilates, becoming voiced, surd, or aspirate, depending
on the nature of the dental: β/π/φ + δ > βδ, β/π/φ + τ > ππ, β/π/φ + θ > φθ.
Hence we find the resulting combinations βδ, ππ, and φθ, and no others: ἕβδομος, ἑπτάκις, ὤφθην.

§13.112   Likewise, when a <u>velar stop</u> (γ, κ, χ) stands before a <u>dental stop</u>,
           the velar partially assimilates, becoming voiced, surd, or aspirate,
to agree with the nature of the dental: γ/κ/χ + δ > γδ, γ/κ/χ + τ > κτ, γ/κ/χ
+ θ > χθ. Hence we find the resulting combinations γδ, κτ, and χθ, and no
others: ὄγδοος, ὀκτώ, συναχθῆναι.

§13.1121   The preposition ἐκ in compounds does not undergo assimilation:
           ἐκδύω, ἔκτος, ἔκθετος.

§13.113   When a <u>dental stop</u> (δ, τ, θ) stands before another <u>dental stop</u>, it
           dissimilates to a sibilant. Hence we find the resulting combina-
tions, σδ, στ, and σθ: οἶσθα, πέπεισθαι, ἐπείσθην.

§13.12   The <u>labio-nasal</u> μ influences a preceding <u>labial</u> or <u>velar stop</u>.

§13.121   When a <u>labial stop</u> (β, π, φ) stands before μ, it totally
           assimilates, becoming μμ: φμ > γέγραμμαι, πμ > λέλειμμαι, βμ >
           τέτριμμαι.

§13.1211   However, when this would result in a triple cluster (μμμ), one
           <u>mu</u> is dropped. μπμ > πέπεμμαι.

§13.122   When a <u>dental stop</u> (δ, τ, θ) stands before μ, it often appears
           to become σ: δμ > πέφρασμαι, τμ > ἤνυσμαι, θμ > πέπεισμαι.

§13.1221   Since dental stops appear before μ in other words, the -σμαι
           ending may be analogic.

§13.123   When the <u>surd velar stop</u> (κ) or <u>fricative</u> (χ) stands before μ it
           becomes the voiced velar stop γ: κ/χ + μ > γμ, cf. πέπλεγμαι and
τέτευγμαι.

§13.1231   However, when the combination κμ has developed from an anterior
           phonetic shift, it may remain, cf. κέκμηκα developing from καμ-.

§13.1232 Both κ and χ can stand before μ in the formation of nouns.

§13.1233 Compounds formed with ἐκ violate this rule.

§13.1234 If a triple cluster would result (γμμ), one μ is dropped: γχμ > ἐλήλεγμαι.

§13.13   The nasal lingual ν readily undergoes progressive, partial or total assimilation.

§13.131   Before a labial (β, π, φ, μ, ψ) ν assimilates to become the labio-nasal μ: συμβαίνω, συμπαθής, συμφέρω, συμμορφίζω, συμψηφίζω.

§13.1311 Most verbs in -νω have σ for ν before -μαι in the perf. mid. The ν reappears before τ and θ.

§13.132   Before a velar (γ, κ, ξ, χ) ν partially assimilates to become the velar nasal-γ [ŋ]: ἐλλράφω, ἐγκάθετος, συγξίω, ἐγχρίω.

§13.1321 In many NT MSS this assimilation is not shown.

§13.133   Before the linguals λ and ρ, ν is totally assimilated, resulting in a doubled consonant, λλ, ρρ: συλλέγω, συρρέω.

§13.134   Before the sibilant σ, the nasal ν or a nasal-dental cluster (νδ, ντ, νθ) drops and the preceding vowel is lengthened by compensation (cf. §15.21) *ἐνς > εἷς, *παντς > πᾶς.

§13.1341 In dative plural forms ν drops before σ often without compensatory lengthening: μείζοσιν, ἀφηθέσιν. Participial forms, however, always have compensatory lengthening: -εισι, -ουσι.

§13.1342 The ν of the preposition σύν in compounds with forms with initial σ assimilates and gemination remains, σύσσημον. However, if the uncompounded word had an initial cluster (e.g. στρέφω), simplification also occurs, συν + στρέφω > συστρέφω.

§13.1343 The preposition ἐν in compounds beginning with the liquid or
          the sibilant σ does not change.

§13.135   Since ζ is a double consonant (§12.422), the ν of συν- when compound-
          ed with words beginning with ζ both assimilates and then simplifies,
συν + ζητέω > συζητέω.

§13.14   The presence of a <u>sibilant</u> in a word has certain effects. This is
          of particular importance in future and first aorist forms.

§13.141   Any <u>labial stop</u> (β, π, φ) before σ forms the affricate ψ [ps]:
          φλέψ, λαῖλαψ, γράψω.

§13.142   A <u>dental stop</u> (δ, τ, θ) before σ is assimilated to σσ, then
          simplified to σ: δσ > ἐλπίς, τσ > χάρις, θσ > ὄρνις.

§13.143   A <u>velar stop</u> (γ, κ, χ) before σ forms the affricate, ξ [ks]:
          ἔλεξα, ἐδίωξα, ἦρξα.

§13.1431 The velar stop drops before -σκ in Class 6 verbs: *διδαχσκω
          > διδάσκω.

§13.15   A <u>surd labial, dental</u>, or <u>velar stop</u> (π, τ, κ) before rough
          breathing [h], becomes <u>aspirate</u> of the same category (φ, θ,
and χ, respectively): ἐφίστημι, καθίημι.

§13.16   The presence of <u>consonantal iota</u> [i̯ or j] after a consonant and
          before a vowel causes certain sound shifts. This is of particular
significance in Class 4 verbs.

§13.161   The <u>surd dental stops</u> τ and θ sometimes become σσ before an
          original consonantal <u>iota</u>. It is possible that this resulted
from the shift [tj] > [sj] or [š] (cf. our -tion suffix): μέλισσα.

§13.1611 Usually the resulting σσ simplified to σ: *παντι̯α > πᾶσα
          *μεθι̯ος > μέσος.

§13.1612 If the shift developed to ττ (pronounced [č]?) in Attic, σσ
          remains in Koinē: μέλισσα.

§13.1613   In the fem. of participles and adjectives ντ before consonantal
           ι became νσ; following §13.134 the ν drops with compensatory
lengthening (cf. §15.21): λυσαντι̯α > λυσᾱσα.

§13.1614   After a vowel δ before consonantal ι̯ becomes ζ (pronounced
           [ž]?). This may possibly be explained as [dj] > [ǧ] or [ž].
           *ελπιδι̯ω > ἐλπίζω.

§13.162   <u>Velar stops</u> (γ, κ, χ) before consonantal <u>iota</u> became σσ (pro-
           nounced [š]?). Possibly this was prepalatalization, [kj] >
[č] > [š]: κράσσω, κηρύσσω, ταράσσω.

§13.1621   After a vowel γ and γγ sometimes became ζ before consonantal
           <u>iota</u>: σφάζω, κλάζω.

§13.1622   After a consonant, γ before consonantal <u>iota</u> became δ.

§13.163   Before a consonantal ι̯ λ became λλ (pronounced [lj]?): ἀγγέλλω.

§13.1631   In the m.s.a. of *μεγαλ, the λ dropped: μέγαν.

§13.164   After αν, αρ, or ορ, consonantal <u>iota</u> undergoes metathesis,
           φαίνω, χαίρω, μοῖρα.

§13.1641   After εν, ερ, ιν, ιρ, υν, or υρ, the consonantal ι disappears
           and the preceding ε, ι, or υ undergoes compensatory lengthening
(§15.12).

§13.2   <u>Dissimilation</u> is the process by which two proximate sounds of
           similar phonetic nature become dissimilar. The dissimilation
is <u>progressive</u> or <u>regressive</u>, depending on the direction of the action
(cf. §13.1).

§13.21   When a <u>dental stop</u> stands before another <u>dental stop</u>, it dissimilates
           to a sibilant, with the resulting combinations: σδ, στ, and σθ.
θαυμαδ > ἐθαυμάσθην, θαυμαστός.

§13.22   When a <u>voiced velar stop</u> (γ) stands before another <u>velar stop</u>
            (γ, κ, χ) it dissimilates to the velar nasal [η]: γγ [η]; γκ
[ηk], and γχ [ηx] (or [ηḫ]). This is not apparent in orthography but can
be seen in Greek loan-words in Latin (ἄγγελος = angelus, ἄγκυρα = ancora,
σφίγξ = sphinx).

§13.23   When the <u>sibilant</u> σ stands at the beginning of successive syllables
            through reduplication, the former dissimilates to rough breathing
[h]: *σιστημι > ἵστημι.

§13.24   When aspirates occur at the beginning of successive syllables,
            The first of the two dissimilates to the corresponding surd stop,
e.g. *θριχ- > τρίχος, *θρεφ- τρεφω, *θιθημι > τιθημι. The first aspirate
remains, however, whenever aspiration is lost from the second through subsequent phonetic change, e.g. *θριχ- > θρίξ, *θρεφ- > θρεψω, *θαφ- > θάπτω
but ἐτάφην.

§13.241   The ending -θι of the 1st Aor. pass. impv., however, becomes -τι
            after the θη of the tense stem, i.e. *λυθηθι > λυθητι cf. 2 Aor.
φανηθι.

§13.242   In certain verbs, the aspirate of the stem dissimilates before the
            aspirate of the aorist passive endings: ἐτέθην.

§13.243   The rough breathing may dissimilate before an aspirate, becoming
            a simple vowel (smooth breathing): ἔχω (> *ἕχω, fut. ἕξω).

§13.244   When aspirates are involved in reduplication (§25.41), the first
            always dissimilates to the surd stop, producing the combinations,
π-φ, τ-θ, and κ-χ, e.g. πέφευγα, τίθημι, κέχυμαι.

§13.245   A few roots which originally had two aspirates in the stem have
            dissimilated the <u>first</u> (hence, the lexicon form does not show
two aspirates). The aspirate returns, however, whenever aspiration is lost
from the second through subsequent phonetic change. Sometimes the <u>second</u>
of the aspirates dissimilates. *θριχ > θρίξ, τρίχος; *θρεφ > τρέφω, θρέψω.

§13.3   Consonants also <u>lengthen</u> or <u>reduce</u>. A <u>lengthened</u> consonant is
            called <u>geminate</u>, and the lengthening of consonants is <u>gemination</u>.
In English, we do not distinguish lengthened consonants within a word, but
we do between words (note the difference between <u>from many</u> and <u>from any</u>--
even if no glottal stop is used in the second case). <u>Reduction</u> of consonants
can be <u>partial</u> (geminate to single) or <u>total</u> (consonant drops away).

§13.31   A <u>voiced labial</u>, <u>dental</u>, or <u>velar stop</u> (ββ, δδ, γγ) is never
          doubled in Attic Greek.

§13.311   When the <u>voiced velar stop</u> γ [g] is geminate, the first dis-
          similates to the <u>nasal velar</u> [η]. It is written, however, γγ.

§13.32   Geminate <u>surd stops</u> (π, τ, κ), <u>linguals</u> (λ, ρ), and <u>nasals</u>
          (μ, ν) (§12.45) arise from assimilation, either progressive or
regressive (§13.1).

§13.33   In Classical Greek, an <u>aspirate</u> is never doubled, the first
          becoming the <u>surd</u> of the same category (πφ, τθ, κχ). This
rule is violated in many NT MSS.

§13.34   Initial ρ is doubled when a compound or an inflectional
          morpheme is placed before it. This rule is often violated
in NT MSS. περι(ρ)ρήνυμι (A&G,656), but περιρήξαντες (Acts 16:22).

§13.35   Under certain conditions, certain consonants are <u>dropped</u>.

§13.351   All consonants standing <u>at the end of a word</u> are dropped,
          except: ν, ρ, σ, ξ, and ψ   (cf. 13.54).

§13.3511 The particles ἐκ and οὐκ are often listed as exceptions to this
          rule. They are not, however, exceptions. The basic form of ἐκ
is ἐξ (cf. Lat. <u>ex</u>), which ends in [s]; the [s] drops between consonants,
but is preserved when a vowel follows. The basic form   is οὐκ, but
the original κ falls away except when preserved by a following vowel. In
both cases, the words are proclitics, which means that they are treated
as part of the following word, and not as independent words.

§13.352   A <u>dental stop</u> is dropped before σ (see §13.142).

§13.353   ν before σ is generally dropped (§13.134), and the preceding
          vowel has compensatory lengthening (§15.21). But cf. §13.363

§13.3531 Before -σι of the dative plural ν is dropped without compensatory lengthening.

§13.354 The combinations νδ, ντ, νθ, when they occur before σ in inflection, are always dropped (§13.134).

§13.355 The combinations λσ and ρσ, however, may retain the liquid and drop the sigma.

§13.356 In some verbs whose stems end in ν, the ν is dropped before the κ of the first perfect active stem, before the endings in the perfect mid./pass. stem, and before the θ of the first passive stem, e.g. κρίνω: κέ-κρικα, κέκριμαι, ἐκρίθην, κριθήσομαι; κλίνω: κέκλικα, ἐκλίθην.

§13.36 The sibilant σ has dropped out under certain conditions.

§13.361 Between vowels, σ apparently became the gutteral fricative [h], and then dropped out entirely. This is particularly significant in 3d declension stems ending in σ, in the future of "liquid" verbs, and in certain 2s verb endings.

§13.3611 Single σ which has resulted from reduction of σσ does not fall away.

§13.3612 In certain inflections (e.g. the future, first aorist, and μι-verb forms) σ between vowels is retained.

§13.362 Between consonants, arising through inflection, σ is often dropped.

§13.3621 The σ is retained, however, when it is the initial letter of the second element of a compound word.

§13.3622 The [s] of the preposition ἐξ drops out before a consonant, either in compound forms or when proclitic, and the preposition becomes ἐκ.

§13.363 After the liquids (λ, ν, ρ) the sibilant σ is generally dropped in sigmatic aorist tenses and future tenses (these are the "liquid" or Class-4e verbs), ἀπαγγέλλω. ἀπήγγειλαν. See also §13.353

§13.364 At the beginning of a word, original σ before a vowel has undergone a shift to [h] (rough breathing): *σεπτα > ἕπτα

§13.3641 This rule applies to reduplicated forms of verbs with initial σ
          (cf. §13.23).

§13.3642 Where initial σ is retained before a vowel, it has resulted from
          a phonetic change: σύν < ξυν.

§13.365   Initial σ before μ sometimes has dropped completely and can only
          be reconstructed by comparative study.

§13.366   The sibilant σ usually drops out before μ or ν (except the
          sufformatives beginning with μ) and the preceding vowel is
lengthened in compensation.

§13.367   In the middle 2s endings -σαι and -σο the σ often drops, with
          resulting contraction.

§13.368   Geminate σσ which has resulted from inflection usually reduces
          to σ. That formed by §13.162 does not reduce.

§13.37   The dropping of an original digamma ϝ [w] explains certain
          phenomena.

§13.371   The loss of original digamma from the 2 aor. of certain verbs
          resulted in the diphthongization of the augment with the
following vowel: *εϝιδον > εἶδον.

§13.372   Class 2 verbs with stem ending in -εϝ (§24.232) have lost the
          digamma before vowels, and diphthongized it with the epsilon
before consonants (See Paradigm V-2b): *πλεϝω > πλέω, πλεύσομαι.

§13.3721 These verbs should not contract in present tense stem; however
          they often contract by analogy to vowel-stem verbs.

§13.373   Certain nouns of the 3d declension with stems ending in digamma
          vocalized the [w] to [u] before consonantal sufformatives or

§13.374   In some words, initial σϝ [sw] have both dropped: *σϝος > ὅς, Lat. suus.

§13.4   Metathesis is the transposition of sounds within a word. Often a velar stop is one of the metathesizing sounds, cf. §12.43.

§13.41   According to Goodwin and Gulick (Greek Grammar, §107), the term should not be used in the many cases where a vocalic (sonant) λ, μ, ν, or ρ is represented by the consonant and a vowel written sometimes before, sometimes after it (cf. §10.441).

§13.5   Epenthesis is the insertion of a sound in a word. Epenthetic consonants, when they occur, are generally found in clusters containing labials or dentals and liquids or sibilants.

§13.51   When, as a result of metathesis or syncope (§15.6), μ stands before λ or ρ, an epenthetic β is inserted after the μ. If this alteration has occurred at the beginning of a word, the μ is dropped, and the β remains: *μεμλωκα > μέμβλωκα; *μεσημ(ε)ρια > μεσεμβρία.

§13.52   If metathesis or syncope results in ν standing before ρ, an epenthetic δ is inserted after the ν: *αν(ε)ρος > ἀνδρός.

§13.53   An epenthetic μ sometimes occurs before a labial stop which is followed by λ or σ. *πιπλημι > πίμπλημι; *ληψομαι > λήμψομαι.

§13.54   An epenthetic ν is added to the stem in addition to the present tense stem morpheme αν in Class 5-b verbs: *μαθ > μανθάνω.

§13.541   This epenthetic ν is in turn subject to phonetic change: λαμβάνω, τυγχάνω.

§13.55   Verbs retaining a short final vowel in the stem, and some others, insert σ before θη in the first passive system, and many of these

verbs also insert σ before the endings in the perfect middle/passive system.
(Cf. Smyth §489.)

§14.   The <u>vowel</u> is the fundamental element of speech. It is the sound;
          consonants are merely interruptions or alterations of the sound.

§14.1   The nature of a vowel can be modified by the angle of the jaw,
          the position and tension of the tongue, the shape of the mouth,
etc. It can also be modified by the relative duration between consonants.

§14.11   There is no fully satisfactory system for describing the nature
          of vowels. The vowel [a] is sometimes described as an <u>open</u> vowel,
and the vowels [u] and [i] as <u>closed</u> vowels. Since [i] is made by raising
the front of the tongue toward the hard palate, it is sometimes called a
<u>front</u> vowel. On the other hand, [u] is made by raising the back of the
tongue toward the soft palate; it is therefore called a <u>back</u> vowel. Various
degrees of modification lie within these ranges.

§14.12   The <u>vowel triangle</u> seems to include these characteristics as
          well as any single description. When we pass from [i] to [a]
to [u] we include the simple vowels: [i]-[e]-[ε]-[α]-[a]-[o]-[u]. Umlaut
vowels are modifications on the [i]-[a] side of the triangle made by
rounding the lips (i.e., the introduction of the dominant feature of the
[a]-[o] side of the triangle). See Table D, the Vowel Triangle.

§14.13   The <u>length</u> of a vowel is an observable characteristic, but a
          relative one. Some "long" vowels are actually shorter in
times duration than some "short" vowels. Nevertheless, it is accurate
to speak of <u>long</u> and <u>short</u> vowels.

§14.2   In Greek there are <u>five vowels</u>, each in <u>long</u> and <u>short</u>
          quantities. Not all are differentiated on the orthography.

§14.21   In Greek, the long vowels are: α, η, ι, υ, ω.

§14.22   The short vowels are: α, ε, ι, ο, υ.

§14.23   It will be noted that α, ι, and υ serve to represent both the
          long and short vowel in the corresponding category. In some
grammars, the long vowels are marked ᾱ, ῑ, ῡ, but this is an editorial,
pedagogical technique.

§14.24   All vowels with circumflex accents (§17.12) are long.

§14.3   Pronunciation of the vowels differed from place to place and from
          period to period. It is reasonably certain that α, ε, ι, and ω
were pronounced [a], [ε], [i], and [o], respectively. The o was probably
(ɔ). It is generally held that η was once pronounced [e], but there is some
evidence indicating that it was more like [ä] or [ae], and in the early
Christian era it had already become [i] as in Modern Greek. The υ was
probably an umlauted sound [y] or [ü], but in the early Christian period
it also had become [i].

§14.4   A diphthong is formed by combining two heterogeneous vowels into
          a single syllable. In Greek the only diphthongs are those formed
by combining an open and a closed vowel or a back and a front vowel. See
Table D, Vowel Triangle.

§14.41   If the first vowel is long, the diphthong is sometimes called a
          long diphthong. This includes: ᾳ, ῃ, ῳ, ηυ.

§14.411   Actually, ᾳ, ῃ, and ῳ were no longer diphthongs by New Testament
          times, but had monophthongized (§14.51). Later, ηυ was pronounced
[εf] or [if].

§14.42   If the first vowel is short, the diphthong is sometimes described
          as a "short" diphthong. This includes: αι, ει, οι, υι, αυ, ευ, ου.

§14.421   The term "short" is misleading; a study of accents will show that
          all diphthongs (except final αι and οι) are treated as long,
          cf. §17.1132.

§14.4211 Even a study of accents (added very late) is misleading. What
          we need is a thorough inductive study of the meter of Greek
poetry to determine how Greek authors considered length of diphthongs.

§14.422   All -ι diphthongs monophthongized, almost certainly by 100 B.C.,
          and all -υ diphthongs developed into consonantal syllables
[-f] or [-v] except ου which monophthongized to [u] as in youth.

§14.43   Note that the second vowel in the diphthong is always ι or υ.

§14.44   Some scholars refer to diphthongs with iota subscript (§14.41)
          as improper diphthongs. A difference is also made in some
grammars between genuine and spurious diphthongs, referring to ει and
ου; these are "spurious" when they develop from contraction (§15.513, .514).
The terms are not well chosen.

§14.5   Pronunciation of the diphthongs likewise varied according to
          place and period. From the way scribes confused certain
diphthongs with simple vowels it is clear that monophthongization had
in some instances occurred. Likewise, the omission of the iota in manuscripts indicates that the "improper" diphthongs (§14.44) had also
monophthongized. See Table E, Pronunciation of Diphthongs.

§14.51   When two heterogeneous vowels are blended into a single syllable,
          it is called diphthongization. When the diphthong is reduced to
a single vowel sound, either through the loss of the second element or
through the modification of the combination to form a single vowel sound,
it is called monophthongization.

§14.511   In inscriptions KE often is written for KAI 'and,'
          indicating that monophthongization and reduction had already
taken place.

§15.   Vowels may lengthen or reduce (quantitative vowel gradation),
          undergo phonetic change (qualitative vowel gradation), appear or

disappear (prosthesis, epenthesis, syncope, aphaeresis, etc.), combine
(diphthongization, contraction), etc. An understanding of these phenomena
will help us work our way through some of the "irregularities" of noun
declension and verb conjugation.

§15.1   Under certain conditions (not always definable) a short vowel
           may <u>lengthen</u>. When this lengthening occurs to compensate
for the loss of a consonant, it is called compensatory lengthening (§15.21).
Otherwise it is simply referred to as lengthening.

§15.11   Except in compensatory lengthening, vowels lengthen as follows:
           α lengthens to η (but to ᾱ after ε, ι, or ρ)
           ε lengthens to η
           ι lengthens to ῑ
           ο lengthens to ω
           υ lengthens to ῡ

§15.12   Regular lengthening may be observed in some noun declensions;

§15.121   A number of first declension nouns lengthen the stem vowel except
           in nominative. See Paradigm N-1.

§15.122   Second declension nouns lengthen the stem vowel in dative singular.
           See Paradigm N-2.

§15.123   Third declension masculine and feminine stems ending in ν, ρ, and
           σ, drop the -ς of the nominative singular and lengthen the pre-
ceding vowel if short: *δαιμονς > δαίμων; *λιμενς > λίμην.

§15.13   Regular lengthening may be observed in some verb conjugation.

§15.131   Many Class-1 verbs having a long vowel in the present tense-stem
           show quantitative gradation in other tenses. Where the vowel is
ι or υ this is not readily apparent. See Paradigm V-1.

§15.132   Class 1-b verbs (Contract verbs) lengthen the stem vowel before
           the tense sufformative in all but the present tense-stem. See
Paradigm V-1b.

§15.133   Many verbs retain the short vowel in some or all tense-stems.
           These are generally verbs with stems originally ending in σ or ϝ
but others are analogic formations. See Paradigm V-2b.

§15.134   Verbs which add ε or ο to the stem and verbs which receive a
           final short vowel by metathesis lengthen this vowel in most
cases before adding the tense-stem sufformative.

§15.135   A number of Class-5 verbs lengthen the stem vowel in all tense-
           stems except the present and the second aorist. See Paradigm V-5.

§15.136   A number of Class-6 verbs lengthen the stem vowel in all (or
           nearly all) tense-stems. See Paradigm V-6.

§15.137   Class-7 verbs (μι -verbs) lengthen the stem vowel in most tense-
           stems. See Paradigm V-7.

§15.138   If a verb has an initial vowel it is lengthened to form the
           temporal augment (§24.3135), or the augment in lieu of
reduplication (§24.3145).

§15.1381   The initial vowel of such a verb may be lengthened following the
           prefixing of a reduplicative syllable ("Attic" reduplication,
cf. §24.3147).

§15.14   Adjectives in -ος lengthen ο to ω when forming the comparative,
           unless the preceding syllable is long (i.e. with a long vowel or
followed by two consonants): νέος, νεώτερος; λέπτος, λεπτότερος.

§15.15   The initial short vowel of a word forming the second part of a
           compound is often lengthened.

§15.16   A short vowel is often lengthened when it has undergone metathesis.

§15.17   Some vowels are lengthened by analogy to other forms or stems
           (analogic lengthening).

§15.2   When a consonant or consonantal cluster has dropped, the preceding
           vowel may undergo <u>compensatory lengthening</u>. This may be thought
of as a means of maintaining a long syllable by substituting a long vowel
to compensate for the loss of a consonant or consonants.

§15.21   Compensatory lengthening takes the same form as that described
           in §15.11 except for the following:
           ε lengthens to ει in compensation.
           o lengthens to ου in compensation.

§15.22   Third declension stems in ντ drop the ντ when adding σ in the
           dative plural; the preceding vowel if short is lengthened in
compensation.

§15.23   In the 3 pl. primary active (the ω-endings), o has regularly
           lengthened by compensation: -οντι > -ουσι.

§15.24   Class 4 stems in -εν, -ερ, -ιν, -ιρ, -υν, -υρ when forming
           the present tense stem, lose the consonantal iota and lengthen
the vowel before the liquid (-ενιω > -είνω, -εριω > -είρω).

§15.25   When σ has disappeared before μ or ν, there usually is no
           compensatory lengthening.

§15.3   Under certain conditions a long vowel may reduce.

§15.31   A long vowel may reduce before another long vowel.

§15.32   A long vowel before ι, υ, a nasal or a liquid plus a following
           consonant, may reduce.

§15.4   Ablaut, or <u>qualitative vowel gradation</u>, in Greek as in other
           Indo-European languages, is the alteration of internal vowels

of a stem to effect change in meaning (cf. ride, rode, ridden; sink
sank, sunk, etc.).

§15.41   There is no predictable regularity in ablaut. Usually there is
          a "strong" and a "weak" form, and often there is also a "zero"
form where the vowel has fallen away completely. The terms "strong" and
"weak" are of no descriptive value.

§15.411   The following patterns of vowel gradation are found in Greek
          as well as others less common:

"strong" grades		"weak" grades
ε	ο	α
ει	οι	ι
ευ	ου	υ
ᾱ	ω	α
η	ω	ε/α
ω		ο

§15.412   The following illustrations of qualitative vowel gradation may
          help understand the problem.

	↓strong	↓strong	↓weak
γεν-	ε-γεν-ομην	γε-γον-α	γι-γν-ομαι
πειθ-	πειθ-ω	πε-ποιθ-α	πιθ-ανος
λευθ-	ε-λευ(θ)-σομαι	ελη-λουθ-α	η-λυθ-ον
θε-	τι-θη-μι	θω-μος	θε-τος
Fρηγ-	ῥηγ-νυμι	ερ-ρωγ-α	ερ-ραγ-η

§15.413   In some cases, the reduction to zero-grade vowel has been ob-
          scured by the orthography where we probably should find a vocalic
consonant. *εστλ̣κα > εσταλκα; *ετν̣θην > εταθην.

§15.5   A _succession of two vowel sounds_ not forming a diphthong was
          generally avoided. The resulting phenomena are called contraction,
crasis, elision, aphaeresis, and the addition of a movable consonant.

§15.51   When two vowels or a vowel and a diphthong come together within a
                word, they either diphthongize or contract to form a long vowel.
See Table F, Contraction of Vowels.

§15.511   Two vowels which can unite to form a diphthong simply do so.

§15.512   An α before any o-sound (o, ω, ου, οι) contracts to ω. An α
                before any other vowel or diphthong contracts to ᾱ. If there
was an iota in the uncontracted form (ει, ῃ, οι), there will be iota
subscript in the contracted form.

§15.513   An ε contracts with ε to form ει. It contracts with o to form ου.
                Before any other vowel or diphthong, ε simply drops out.

§15.5131   Loss of ε before another vowel is called hyphaeresis.

§15.5132   In contract nouns of the first declension εα contracts to η
                (or to ᾱ after ε, ι, or ρ).

§15.514   An o before the long vowels, η and ω, contracts to ω; before
                any vowel or diphthong containing iota (including subscript),
o contracts to οι. In all other cases it contracts to ου.

§15.515   In contracts of the 1st and 2d declensions, every short vowel
                before α or before a long vowel or a diphthong vanishes.

§15.516   A long vowel absorbs the following vowel or diphthong. If
                there was an iota in the following diphthong, it is usually
preserved as iota subscript in the contracted form.

§15.5161   The contraction of a long vowel with a short vowel sometimes
                resists contraction by analogy.

§15.517   Vowels that have been juxtaposed through the loss of σ often are
                not   contracted in disyllabic forms: *θε(σ)ος > θεός.

§15.518 Through inflection, a sequence of contractions may occur; in
         such cases, the contraction toward the end of the word usually
takes place first, and the resulting sound contracts with the vowel
preceding it.

§15.52   <u>Crasis</u> is the contraction of a vowel or diphthong at the end
         of a word with the initial vowel or diphthong of the next word
to form a new word. The coronis (§11.552) is placed over the resulting
syllable. καί + ἐκεῖθεν > κἀκεῖθεν.

§15.521 Crasis is rare in the New Testament, being found chiefly in
         combinations with καί and a few examples with the article.

§15.53   <u>Elision</u> is the dropping of the final short vowel when the next
         word begins with a vowel. An <u>apostrophe</u> (ʼ) marks the elision.

§15.531 Elision is particularly common with prepositions except περί
         and πρό.

§15.5311 In the NT, only the prepositions ἀπό, διά, ἐπί, παρά, μετά,
         and the conjunction ἀλλά regularly elide. The preposition
ἀντί elides only before ὧν.

§15.532 If as a result of elision, a surd stop precedes a rough
         breathing, aspiration occurs, in accordance with §13.15.

§15.5321 Aspiration occurs in the New Testament sometimes when the vowel
         of a preposition is elided before a vowel with smooth breathing.
This is probably due to analogic formation.

§15.533 Elision is less frequent in the New Testament than in classical
         Greek. It occurs regularly before pronouns and particles, and
in certain stereotyped prepositional phrases.

§15.534   Elision does <u>not</u> occur with the following:
          the prepositions περί and πρό;
          the conjunction ὅτι;
          monosyllables except those ending in ε;
          dative singular in ι of 3d decl., or dat.pl. in σι;
          words ending in υ.

§15.535   When a compound word is formed by adding a preposition that ends
          in a vowel to a word that begins with a vowel, the vowel of the
preposition is elided in accordance with §15.53, but no apostrophe is used.
If §15.532 is applicable, aspiration also occurs.

§15.54   <u>Apocope</u> is the cutting off of the final short vowel of a word
          before an initial consonant of the following word for euphony or
poetic structure. No apostrophe is used.

§15.55   Movable <u>nu</u> originally was a ν added to the end of a word when
          the following word began with a vowel, to avoid hiatus. It is
added to words ending in -σι, -ξι, or -ψι, to all 3d pers. verb forms
ending in -ε, and to ἐστί 'is.'

§15.551   In the NT, movable nu is used most of the time, whether the
          following word begins with a vowel or not. It is especially
used before pause.

§15.552   Contracted imperfect forms ending in ει do <u>not</u> take movable-nu.

§15.553   <u>Movable sigma</u> is found in a few words, such as οὕτως, ἄχρις, and
          μέχρις.

§15.5531 In the NT, οὕτως is found almost exclusively, while ἄχρι and
          μέχρι rarely have ς, (BDF §21).

§15.5532 The -[s] of ἐξ is not to be considered as movable-<u>sigma</u>, nor is
          the -[k] of οὐκ to be considered as movable-<u>kappa</u>. (See §13.3511).

§15.6   Syncope is the dropping of a short vowel between two single
           consonants.

§15.61   When as a result of syncope, μ or ν would immediately precede
           certain liquids, epenthesis may occur (see §13.5ff.).

§15.62   Original ι and υ diphthongs often vanish before another vowel.
           It is assumed that these were consonantal in such cases.

§15.7   A vowel (usually α) is generally written before or after λ, ν,
           or ρ when the liquid would otherwise occur between consonants.
(In such cases, we are probably dealing with vocalic or sonant λ, ν̥, ρ̥,
see §10.441.)

§15.71   In some cases this is described as metathesis of the vowel and
           the lingual.

§15.8   Prosthesis is the placing of a short vowel before an originally
           initial consonantal cluster. Such a vowel is called "prosthetic"
(or "prothetic"): χθές > ἐχθές.

§15.81   Prosthetic α, ε, or o are sometimes prefixed to words beginning
           with λ, μ, ν, or ρ.

§15.9   A vowel may be assimilated to a vowel in the following syllable.
           This is called vowel harmony.

§16.   The syllable may be defined as the sounds producing a summit of
           sonority. The number of syllables in a word, then, will be
equal to the summits of sonority. Although scholars have difficulty in
defining the idea of a syllable, there seems to be no problem in counting
the syllables in a word, cf. §10.44.

§16.1   The last syllable of a word is called the ultima. The next-to-
           last is called the penult. The syllable before the penult is
called the antepenult.

§16.2   A Greek word has as many syllables as it has separate vowels or diphthongs: ἔ-ως, ἑ-αυ-του.

§16.21   A syllable may begin with either a consonant or a vowel. It may end with either a consonant or a vowel. It may have no consonant at all, but it must have a vowel: α-γα-θος, λε-γω, προ-ϊ-μος.

§16.22   In dividing words according to syllables, certain rules have been observed since ancient times.

§16.221   A single consonant is connected with the following vowel, unless that consonant is part of a prefix. μνη-μα, συν-ηλ-θον.

§16.222   Geminate consonants are generally divided: εκ-χυν-νο-με-νον, θαρ-ρου-μεν.

§16.223   Consonantal clusters (i.e., combinations of two or three consonants) which are found at the beginning of words can also be placed at the beginning of syllables: τε-κμη-ρι-οις, ἱ-στη-μι, ε-κτη-σα-το, πρε-σβυ-τε-ρος.

§16.2231   We must be careful not to let our ideas of initial clusters, derived from English, influence our recognition of Greek clusters. We are not familiar, for example, with such initial clusters as kt-, mn-, km-, gn-, and the like, and some (such as ps-, phth-, chth-) we recognize only because of loan words.

§16.224   Words compounded of two words, or a preposition and a word, are generally syllabified according to the component parts: φιλ-α-δελ-φος, συν-ε-σταλ-μεν-ος.

§16.2241   However, when a vowel has been elided in forming such a compound, the syllabification is as though the compound were a word in its own right: κα-θε-δρας, πα-ρε-δω-καν, κα-ταρ-γει-ται.

§16.3   A syllable is <u>long</u> if it contains a long vowel or a diphthong
         (long "by nature"), or if it contains a short vowel followed by
two consonants or a geminate consonant (long "by position").

§16.31   However, if a short vowel is followed by a combination of a stop
         and a liquid (§12.455), it may be a short syllable.

§17.   <u>Accent</u> may be defined as the imparting of relatively more <u>stress</u>
         to certain syllables and certain words. Accent may also pertain
to <u>pitch</u>. In Greek, the accents were originally indicative of pitch, but
today we use them principally as indicators of stress.

§17.1   Three diacritical marks are used in Greek to indicate accent:
         the <u>acute</u> (´), the <u>grave</u> (`), and the circumflex (^ or ˜).

§17.11   The <u>acute</u> accent, originally indicating rising tone, can stand
         on any of the last three syllables of a word: ἄν-θρω-πος,
λό-γος, ἐ-γώ.

§17.111 If the acute accent stands on the <u>ultima</u>, the word is called
         <u>oxytone</u>: θε-ός.

§17.112 If the acute accent stands on the <u>penult</u>, the word is called
         <u>paroxytone</u>: ἀν-θρώ-που.

§17.113 If the acute accent stands on the <u>antepenult</u>, the word is called
         <u>proparoxytone</u>: θέ-λη-σις.

§17.1131 A word with a <u>long ultima</u> cannot be proparoxytone: ἀν-θρώ-πῳ.

§17.1132 For purposes of defining the rules of accent, a <u>long syllable</u>
         means a syllable containing a long vowel or a diphthong.

§17.1133 A syllable that is long because of double consonants is, for
         purposes of accent, considered short.

§17.1134 The diphthongs αι and οι, when standing at the end of the word
          (i.e., without any consonant following them) are, for purposes
of accent, considered short: ἄν-θρω-ποι.

§17.1135 In certain noun forms, the ω in the endings -εως and -εων is
          considered short: πό-λε-ως.

§17.114   These terms are used in modern linguistics to indicate stress or
          pitch accent on the same respective syllables, hence the student
should become familiar with them.

§17.12   The circumflex accent, originally indicating a rising-and-falling
          tone, can stand only on either of the last two syllables of a
word.   (It has sometimes been pointed out that, since the circumflex was
approximately equivalent to acute plus grave, it was therefore in effect two
syllables.   Hence it could not stand on the antepenult.)

§17.121   A word with a circumflex accent on the ultima is called perispomenon:
          πα-θεῖν.

§17.1211 The circumflex accent, however, can never stand on a short
          syllable (i.e., a syllable containing a short vowel; cf. §17.1132).

§17.122   A word with a circumflex accent on the penult is called
          properispomenon (see §17.1211): ζῶν-τα.

§17.13   The grave accent, originally a falling tone, can only stand
          on the ultima, and then only when closely followed by the next
word: τὸν θεόν.

§17.131   Some editors place a grave accent on the indefinite pronoun
          τις τι.

§17.14   The rules of accent may be summarized as follows:

Accent on	If ultima is long	If ultima is short
ultima	may be ´, `, or ^	may be ´ or `
short penult	must be ´	must be ´
long penult	must be ´	must be ^
antepenult	no accent possible	must be ´

§17.2   An oxytone (cf. §17.111) changes the acute to grave when
          it is followed in the same sentence by another accented word.
ἑαυτὸν ζῶντα (Ac. 1:3).

§17.21   The acute accent remains before an enclitic (cf. §17.82).
          ὁ πατήρ σου.

§17.22   The interrogative particles τίς and τί never alter the acute
          accent: τί θέλει.

§17.23   The acute accent is not altered at the end of a sentence, or
          at the end of a major division in a sentence: Ac. 1:6,7.

§17.3   A word which throws its accent back as far as the rules of
          accent will allow is said to have recessive accent. In general,
verbs have recessive accent (cf. §17.7).

§17.31   The rule of noun accent, briefly stated, is that the accent
          can never be thrown back further than where it stands in the
nominative singular form.

§17.32   The expression, "thrown back," is used with reference to the
          end of the word; in other words, the more the accent moves
toward the beginning of the word, the more it moves back from the end of
the word.

§17.33   A word which has no accent on its last syllable is called
          barytone.

§17.4   A contracted syllable (cf. §15.31) is accented if either of the original syllables had an accent.

§17.41   A contracted penult or antepenult is accented regularly. In other words, it will take acute on the antepenult, circumflex on the penult only if the ultima is short: καλούμενον, κατοικοῦντες, but λαλούντων

§17.42   A contracted ultima will take circumflex unless the original word was oxytone; in that case, it takes the acute: λαβεῖν, ὑψωθείς

§17.43   If neither of the contracting syllables was accented, then the usual rules of accent apply.

§17.5   In elision (cf. §15.53), oxytone prepositions and conjunctions lose their accent when they lose the elided vowel: κατά > καθ'ὑμῶν.

§17.6   The accent of the nominative singular of a <u>noun</u>, and the nominative singular masculine of an <u>adjective</u>, must be learned by observation. All other forms will accent the same syllable if the <u>ultima</u> permits.

§17.61   The last syllable of the genitive and dative of oxytones of the first and second declensions is accented with circumflex. See Paradigms N-1 and N-2.

§17.62   In the first declension, the plural genitive -ῶν (for -έων) has the circumflex. The feminine plural genitive of adjectives and participles in -ος, however, is accented like the masculine and neuter forms.

§17.63   Most monosyllables of the third declension are oxytone in the genitive and dative of singular and plural (-ῶν and -οῖν, however, are perispomenon). See Paradigm N-3.

§17.64   The interrogative particle τίς always accents the first syllable in inflected forms; so do all forms deriving from monosyllabic participles.

§17.7   In general, <u>verbs</u> have <u>recessive</u> accent, i.e. the accent moves as far toward the front of the word as the nature of the syllables will allow.

§17.71   This rule is violated, however, by many infinitival forms.

§17.72   The 2 aor. active participle and all participles of the 3d declension in -ς except the 1 aor. act. also violate the rule; all are oxytone.

§17.73   2 aor. act. imperative forms of certain verbs are oxytone. Their compounds, however, are regular.

§17.74   Compound verbs have recessive accent like simple verbs, except that the accent cannot go further back than the augment or the reduplicated element. In a few verbs, where the compound nature appears to have become lost, this rule is violated.

§17.75   Participles in the inflected forms are accented as adjectives and not as verbs.

§17.76   Verbal adjectives in -τός are oxytone; those in -τέος are paroxytone.

§17.8   Certain words have given up their accent and are known as <u>proclitics</u> and <u>enclitics</u>.

§17.81   Some monosyllables have no accent and are closely joined to the <u>following</u> word; they are called <u>proclitics</u> (they "lean <u>forward</u>" to the next word).

§17.811   The <u>proclitics</u> are: the def. art. in masc. and fem., sing. and plur. nominative forms; the prepositions εἰς, ἐξ (ἐκ), and ἐν; the conjunctions εἰ and ὡς; and the negative particle οὐκ (οὐ, οὐχ).

§17.812   Under certain conditions a proclitic may take an accent, as follows.

§17.8121   When a proclitic stands before an enclitic it is accented: ἔν τε Ἰε-ρουσαλήμ (Ac. 1:8), ὅ τε Πέτρος (Ac. 1:13).

§17.8122   Occasionally a proclitic stands alone or at the end of a clause, and is then accented. This is particularly true of the negative particle οὐ: ὁ δέ φησιν, οὔ (Mt. 13:29), τὸ ναὶ ναὶ καὶ τὸ οὔ οὔ (Jas. 5:12).

§17.82   Some monosyllables and disyllables normally have no accent and are
         treated as part of the <u>preceding</u> word. They are called <u>enclitics</u>
(they "lean upon" the word just spoken).

§17.821   The <u>enclitics</u> are: the personal pronouns μου, μοι, με, σου, σοι, σε;
         the indefinite pronoun τις τι in all inflected forms; the present in-
dicative of ειμι and φημι (except 2d sing.); the particles γε, τε, τοι, περ;
the indefinite adverbs που, ποτε, πω, πως.

§17.8211 Some editors regularly accent the disyllablic forms τινὸς etc.

§17.8212 The interrogative pronouns are to be distinguished from the indefinite
         pronouns by the fact that they are never enclitic.

§17.822   The enclitic generally loses its original accent, but since it prac-
         tically becomes a part of the preceding word, it introduces new fac-
tors for the accenting of that word, as follows.

§17.8221 An oxytone (§17.111) does not change its acute to grave: ἡ σάρξ μου
         (Ac. 2:26).

§17.8222 A perispomenon (§17.121) keeps its accent: ποιεῖν τε (Ac. 1:1).

§17.8223 A paroxytone (§17.112), even though the rules of accent might require
         such by the addition of an enclitic with a long vowel or diphthong
(§17.14), does not add an additional accent: ἡ καρδία μου (Ac. 2:26; an acute
accent now stands on the new antepenult even though the ultima is long), τοὺς
δούλους μου (Ac. 2:18). If the enclitic is disyllabic, it retains its own accent: περὶ ἑτέρου τινός (Ac. 8:34). Cf. Smyth §§183d, 184.

§17.8224 A properispomenon (§17.122) or proparoxytone (§17.113) takes an ad-
         ditional accent (acute) on the ultima: ἡ γλῶσσά μου (Ac. 2:26), τοῦ
πνεύματός μου (Ac. 2:18).

§17.823   If two or more enclitics occur in succession, each receives an accent
         from the following, and the last is unaccented: εἴ τίς τί σοί φησιν
(cf. Smyth §185).

§17.824   ἐστίν is accented ἔστιν when it expresses existence (πιστεῦσαι ...
         ὅτι ἔστιν, Heb. 11:6; τὸ μνῆμα αὐτοῦ ἔστιν ἐν ὑμῖν, Ac. 2:29), or when
it follows οὐκ, μή, εἰ, ὡς, καί, ἀλλά or τοῦτο: τοῦτ᾽ ἔστιν, Ac. 1:19, but cf.

τοῦτό ἐστιν in 2:16), or when it stands first in the clause (ἔστιν γὰρ ὥρα τρίτη, Ac. 2:15).

§17.825   When certain enclitics are written together with the preceding word as single words (e.g. ᾧτινι, οἴδε, μήτε, etc.), the compound is accented as if the enclitic were a separate word.

§17.9   John 9:40-41 contains all marks of punctuation, all breathings, illustrations of all kinds of accent, examples of proclitics and enclitics.

§§18. and 19. are arbitrarily omitted.

Division 2--Morphology

§20.   Morphology is the study of changes in form of the words in a
        language. It is often used as equivalent to inflection, which
is the change in form made to express the relationship of the inflected
word to other words.

§20.1   The inflection of nouns, adjectives, pronouns, and the like,
         is called declension. We decline nouns, adjectives, etc.

§20.11   We also compare adjectives and adverbs, but even the comparative
          and superlative forms can be declined.

§20.2   The inflection of verbs is called conjugation. We conjugate verbs.

§20.3   The uninflected part, or fundamental part, of a word is called
         its stem. The inflected part is called the ending. More properly,
the inflectional elements should be designated as morphemes, since they
are not always at the end of the word. A morpheme is a meaningful unit
of form.

§20.31   Several words of common origin may have the same or similar stems.
          The common origin of such stems is usually called the root.

§20.32   It is possible for the vocalic or diphthongal part of a stem
          to vary from form to form (cf. §§15.4ff.).

§20.33   It is also possible for the consonantal elements of a stem to
          change, but only within the regular sound-shifts of the language
as described in various subdivisions of §13.

§20.34   The last letter or letters of a stem give the stem characteristic.
          If it ends in a vowel, it is called a vowel-stem or a "pure stem."
If it ends in a consonant, it is called an "impure stem." (These terms are

rather meaningless.) Usually the <u>consonantal stems</u> are more closely subdivided, into "mutes" (i.e., labial, dental, or palatal stops), "liquids,"
etc.

§20.4   To <u>parse</u> a word is to describe its form fully, and to explain
         what the construction indicates (or why this form is used in
this place).

§20.41   There is a generally-accepted <u>order of the elements</u> in parsing,
         and the student should learn to use this order.

§20.411 The <u>noun</u> or substantive is parsed according to (1) gender,
         (2) number, and (3) case, together with the nominative singular (or
dictionary form) of the word, and the reason for the use of this form.
Memorize the order: "GNC".

§20.412 The <u>verb</u> is parsed according to (1) tense, (2) voice, (3) mood,
         (4) person, (5) number, together with the basic (dictionary) form
of the verb, and the reason for use of this form. Memorize the order:
"TVMPN".

§20.413 The <u>participle,</u> which is both verb and substantive, is parsed
         first as verb and then as substantive ("TVMGNC").

§20.414 Not every word will have all forms. Omit the items which do
         not apply.

§21.   A <u>noun</u> is a word standing for a person, place or thing. In Greek,
         the noun is inflected to indicate its relationship to other words
in the sentence (cf. §04.21, §20.).

§21.1   A noun is inflected to indicate <u>gender</u>, <u>number</u>, and <u>case</u>.

§21.11   Three <u>genders</u> are indicated in Greek: <u>masculine</u>, <u>feminine</u>, and
         <u>neuter</u>. These are, however, not indicators of sex or personality.

Many impersonal nouns are masculine or feminine. The gender of each noun must be learned when the noun is learned. (Hint: memorize the definite article with the basic form of the word.)

§21.12   Three <u>numbers</u> were indicated in classical Greek: <u>singular</u> (one),
           <u>dual</u> (two), and <u>plural</u> (more than two). The dual is not commonly
found in the New Testament.

§21.13   Five <u>cases</u> are indicated in Greek: <u>nominative</u>, <u>genitive</u>, <u>dative</u>,
           <u>accusative,</u> and <u>vocative</u>.

§21.131   Some grammarians, on the basis of Sanskrit, argue that there are
           eight cases in Greek. This is logical but not descriptive
grammar. The Greek of the classical and post classical periods made use
of at most these five inflected forms to indicate case. Syntax of the
cases will be discussed in Part III.

§21.14   Not all nouns are inflected in the same manner. Those which are
           alike or nearly alike in inflection are grouped together in
<u>declensions</u>. Older grammarians listed ten or more; in the past three
centuries, <u>three declensions</u> have been distinguished (cf. §20.1).

§21.2   Stems originally ending in α are grouped in the <u>First Declension</u>,
           also called the α-declension. Because of contraction, the
influence of proximate consonants or vowels, etc., the original ending often
does not appear. Most nouns of the first declension are feminine. See
Paradigm N-1.

§21.21   The <u>inflectional endings</u> of the first declension noun (fem.)
           are as follows:

Singular (§21.221ff.)		Plural	
nom. ——α – > α/η	(§21.211)	——α ι > αι	(§21.214)
gen. ——α ς > ας/ης		——α έων > ῶν	(§21.215)
dat. ——α ι > ᾳ/ῃ	(§21.212)	——α ισι > αις	(§21.216)
acc. ——α ν > αν/ην		——α νς > ᾱς	(§21.217)
voc. ——α – > α/η	(§21.213)	none	

§21.211   The fem. sing. nominative has no ending.

§21.212   The fem. sing. dative ending is -ι which regularly mono-
          phthongizes and is written as <u>iota</u> subscript (cf. §14.4ff.).

§21.213   The fem. sing. vocative is always like the nominative in this
          declension.

§21.214   The fem.pl. nominative ending is -ι, which is regularly
          retained as a short diphthong (cf. §17.1134). The plural
nominative form regularly serves for a vocative.

§21.215   The fem.pl. genitive ending is -ῶν, resulting from contraction
          of an original -έων or -άων.

§21.216   The fem.pl. dative ending is -ις, possibly arising from *-ισι;
          it regularly forms a diphthong with the stem vowel.

§21.217   The fem.pl. accusative ending is -ς, arising from an original
          *-νς.

§21.22   These endings are added <u>to the stem</u>, i.e., to the stem ending
          in -α, or to the stem modified by ablaut, shortening, or
contraction. Study Paradigm N-1 and note these features.

§21.221   The majority of feminine nouns in the first declension lengthen
          the α (> η) in all singular forms (§15.11).

§21.222   If the stem vowel is preceded by ι or ρ (and in some cases by ε),
          the α does not become η. However, in the NT this rule often does
not apply.

§21.223   If the stem vowel is preceded by a sibilant (σ, ζ, ξ, ψ) or a
          geminate consonant, α > η in gen. and dat. singular only; other
forms retain ᾰ (or reduce ᾱ > ᾰ).

§21.224   Certain stems of the first declension are known as <u>contracts</u>.
These originally ended in two vowels which have contracted
(cf. §15.51 and Table F), and this resultant vowel further contracts with
the vowel of the ending, if any. All plural forms, however, conform to the
basic pattern, probably by analogy (see Paradigm N-1).

§21.2241   Nouns that do not contract probably had stems ending in ϝ.

§21.23   Accent in all forms follows the noun rule (§17.31). However
this is obscured in some forms.

§21.231   Words ending in short-α, undergo compensatory lengthening in
plural accusative as a result of elision (§§13.134; 15.21).

§21.232   Contract stems, since they are long by contraction (§15.51),
always have circumflex on the stem vowel; accordingly they will
be perispomena in all cases (§17.121).

§21.233   Since the plural genitive ending has resulted from contraction,
all first declension words in this case are perispomena (§17.121).

§21.24   There are a few <u>masculine</u> nouns in the <u>first declension</u>. The
stem vowel, in general, follows the rules that apply for
feminine nouns (§21.212ff.). The declension is as follows:

	Singular				Plural		
nom.	——α ς	>	ας/ης	(§21.241)	——α ι	>	αι
gen.	——α ο	:	ου*	(§21.243)	——α έων	>	ῶν
dat.	——α ι	>	ᾳ/ῃ		——α ισι	>	αις
acc.	——α ν	>	αν/ην		——α νς	>	ᾱς
voc.	——α	>	α/η	(§21.242)	none		

*Probably by analogy to 2d decl.

§21.241   The masc.sing. nominative ending is -ς.

§21.242   The masc.sing. vocative ending is -α, in some cases short-ᾰ.

§21.243   In all other forms, the masc. nouns are like the fem. nouns of
          the first declension.

§21.3   Stems ending in o are grouped in the <u>Second Declension</u>, or
          o-declension. Most nouns of the second declension are masculine
or neuter. Since this is the most common declension, it should be learned
thoroughly. See Paradigm N-2.

§21.31   The <u>second declension masculine</u> endings are as follows:

Singular				Plural			
nom.	——o ς > oς	(§21.311)		——o ι > οι	(§21.315)
gen.	——o o > ου	(§21.312)		——o ων > ων	(§21.316)
dat.	——o ι > ῳ	(§21.313)		——o ισι > οις	(§21.317)
acc.	——o ν > ον			——o νς > ους	(§21.318)
voc.	——o ε : ε	(§21.314)		none

§21.311   The masc.sing. nominative ending is -ς, like the masculine of
          1st decl.

§21.312   The masc.sing.genitive ending is -o, which regularly contracts
          with the stem vowel to become -ου (§15.514).

§21.313   The masc.sing.dative ending is -ι, which has monophthongized
          with the stem vowel and lengthened, the ending being preserved
only as <u>iota</u> subscript (§14.51).

§21.314   The masc.sing. vocative ending -ε has normally replaced the
          stem vowel.

§21.315   The masc.plur. nominative ending has united with the stem
          vowel to form a short diphthong (§17.1132).

§21.316   The masc.pl. genitive ending was originally -ων, and not
          like the 1st decl. (cf. §21.215).

§21.317   The masc.pl. dative ending unites with the stem vowel to form
a diphthong (§15.51).

§21.318   The masc.pl. accusative ending was originally *-νς, which elides
the ν with compensatory lengthening to become -ους (§15.21).

§21.32   The <u>second declension neuter</u> endings are as follows:

	Singular			Plural			
nom.	——ο ν	>	ον (§21.321)	——ο α	:	α	(§21.323)
gen.	——ο ο	>	ου	——ο ων	>	ων	
dat.	——ο ι	>	ῳ	——ο ισι	>	οις	
acc.	——ο ν	>	ον (§21.321)	——ο α	:	α	(§21.323)
voc.	——ο ν	>	ον (§21.322)				

§21.321   The nominative endings of all neuters are like the accusative
endings.   (Does this reflect a stage of thinking, that neuter
objects could not be subjects of a verb?)

§21.322   The vocative endings of neuter nouns are the same as the
accusative endings.

§21.323   The neut.pl. accusative ending is short-α, which has replaced
the stem vowel, and the nominative is the same. Possibly this
was an old fem. collective ending (Smyth §229b).

§21.324   In all other forms, the neuter agrees with the masculine.

§21.33   A number of stems end in εο or οο. These contract, according
to §15.51ff., to give nominative forms in -ους (m.) and -ουν (n.).

§21.331   The accent of these contracts is irregular (from the point of
view of the uncontracted form) in that it is based on the
contracted forms.

§21.332   In plural nominative and accusative of neuter contracts, the
          stem -ε contracts with -α to form long -α (instead of η).

§21.34   The "Attic declension" (cf. Smyth §237), i.e. substantives ending
          in -εως, is practically nonexistent in the NT. For discussion,
see Robertson p.260.

§21.341   In accordance with the rules for contraction, the ω dominates all
          sufformative vowels (§15.515).

§21.35   <u>Feminine nouns of the 2d decl.</u> are in all respects like masc.
          nouns of the 2d decl.

§21.4   The <u>third declension</u>, sometimes called the consonant declension,
          includes all regular nouns not of the 1st or 2d declensions. It
is generally described as very irregular, but once the phonetic principles
are understood the declension is seen to be fairly regular. See Paradigm N-3.

§21.41   The inflectional endings of the <u>3d declension</u> noun, <u>masculine</u> and
          <u>feminine</u>, are as follows:

Singular				Plural			
nom.	—c* ς/-	>	† (§21.411ff.)	—c ες	>	ες	(§21.416)
gen.	—c ος	>	ος (§21.412)	—c ων	>	ων	(§21.417)
dat.	—c ι	>	ι (§21.413)	—c* σι	>	†	(§21.418)
acc.	—c α/ν	>	α/† (§21.414ff.)	—c ας/ες	>	ας/ες	(§21.419)
voc.	—c* ς/-	>	† (§21.415ff.)	none			

c = consonant; * consonantal alteration rules apply when adding consonantal
sufformative; † resultant of consonantal alteration. See §§21.5ff.

§21.411   The masc./fem. sing. nom. ending is -ς, with the exception noted
          below. The addition of -ς to a consonantal stem must follow
phonetic rules (cf. §13.14ff.). NOTE: FAILURE TO LEARN PHONETIC RULES
MAKES THE LEARNING OF 3d DECLENSION EXTREMELY DIFFICULT!

§21.4111   If the stem ends in ν, ρ, or σ, the last vowel of the stem is
lengthened and no ending is added to form the sing. nom.

§21.4112   A few stems ending in -ν drop the ν and add -ς, with compensatory
lengthening of the preceding vowel (§15.21).

§21.4113   If the stem ends in -οντ, the τ is dropped, when followed by ς, the
o lengthens to ω and no ending is added to form sing. nom.
(cf. §13.351).

§21.4114   The word πούς, stem ποδ-, is irregular; we would expect m.s.n. *πως.

§21.412   The sing. gen. ending is -ος, added to the stem.

§21.413   The sing. dat. ending is -ι, added to the stem.

§21.414   The m./f. sing. acc. ending is usually -α; in some nouns,
however, it is -ν, with resulting phonetic changes.

§21.4141   Most consonantal stems add -α to form the accusative.

§21.4142   Stems ending in the semiconsonants -ι and -υ add ν to form the acc.

§21.4143   Barytones (cf. §17.33) in -ις/-υς from dental stems drop the dental
and add -ν to form the acc. Oxytones of the same category keep
the dental and add -α.

§21.415   The singular vocative is either the same as the nominative, or the
stem without inflection.

§21.4151   In stems ending in a stop (§12.31), and in oxytones (§17.111) with
stems ending in a liquid or nasal, the vocative is the same as the
nominative.

§21.4152   Barytone (§17.33) stems ending in a liquid or nasal, stems in -ιδ,
barytone stems in -ντ other than participles, and some other stems
do not inflect the stem for the vocative.

§21.416   The m./f. plur. nom. ending is -ες.

§21.417   The plural gen. ending is -ων.

§21.418   The plural dat. ending is -σι, which, when added to the consonant-
            al stem, follows the rules for phonetic shift (§§13.14ff.).

§21.419   The m./f. plur. acc. ending was originally -νς, which usually
            becomes -ας (possibly vocalic [n̥], cf. §10.441). In some nouns
the nom. ending -ες or a lengthened or contracted form is found (Smyth §263a).

§21.42   The inflectional endings of the <u>3d declension neuter</u> are as follows:
          Singular | Plural
nom.   ——c* ς/— > †   (§21.421f.) | ——c   α   > α   (§21.422)
gen.   ——c ος > ος²   (§21.412) | ——c   ων > ων (§21.417)
dat.   ——c ι   > ι   (§21.413) | ——c* σι > †   (§21.418)
acc.   ——c* ς/— > †   (§21.421f.) | ——c   α   > α   (§21.422)
voc.   ——c* ς/— > †   (§21.421) |

c = consonant; *consonantal alteration rules apply when adding consonantal
sufformative; † with resultant consonantal alteration; ²σ-stems drop intervocalic σ and contract juxtaposed vowels.

§21.421   The neut. sing. nom. is the same as the acc., as is the neut.
            sing. voc. In most neuter nouns this is the same as the stem
with loss of final consonants in accordance with §13.351.

§21.4211 Some neuter stems in -ατ have nom./acc./voc. in -αρ.

§21.422   The neut. plur. nom./acc. ending is -α.

§21.43   Most 3d decl. monosyllables accent the last syllable in sing.
            and plur. gen. and dat. forms (cf. §17.63).

§21.44   The stem of most 3d decl. nouns must be determined by dropping
            the ending of the sing. gen. (usually -ος), which facilitates the
study of the 3d declension (see §§21.5ff.).

§21.5   It is helpful to subdivide the third declension according to
           stem characteristics.

§21.51   Stems ending in labial, dental, or velar stops (generally called
           "mutes") can be grouped together. See Paradigm N-3.

§21.511   <u>Labial stems</u>, i.e., those ending in a labial stop, (β, π, φ,
           Table C), in accordance with §13.141 assimilate with the σ of
the sufformatives of sing. nom. and voc. and pl. dat. to form ψ. See
Paradigm N-3, labial stems.

§21.512   <u>Dental stems</u>, i.e., those endings in a dental stop (δ, τ, θ,
           Table C), drop the dental before σ-sufformatives (§13.142), and
in the uninflected neuter forms (sing. nom./acc.voc.) where the dental
would be final (§13.351). Paradigm N-3, dental stems.

§21.5121   Stems ending in a cluster of nasal and dental (νδ/ντ) form a
           special class (cf. §13.354). In the sing. nom. the entire
cluster may drop before -ς, with compensatory lengthening of o to ου
(cf. §15.21), or the final dental may drop (§13.351) leaving a final ν with
lengthening of o to ω (cf. §15.11). In the pl. dat. the cluster always
drops, leaving the ending -σι (with compensatory lengthening of o to ου).

§21.5122   Masculine stems in -οντ (including ptcp.) drop τ and lengthen
           o > ω (cf. §13.331).

§21.5123   Many neut. nouns have stems ending in -τ. In sg. nom./acc./voc.
           the τ drops (without any lengthening of o), and the ending is either
-ς or no morpheme. In a few nouns, -ρ occurs in these forms (cf. §21.4211).
In all such nouns the stem τ drops before the pl. dat. endings.

§21.513   <u>Velar stems</u>, i.e. those ending in a velar stop (γ, κ, χ,
           Table C), assimilate to σ-sufformatives in accordance with
§13.143, to form ξ. See Paradigm N-3, velar stems.

§21.5131 In a few instances, the stem ends in a velar + dental cluster,
specifically κτ. The τ drops before σ-endings, and fusing
of κ and σ follows the rule. In the case of γάλα, gen. γάλακτος, the
cluster drops completely (cf. §13.351).

§21.5132 Nasalized velars (§12.454) are also affected by this rule,
resulting in forms ending in -γξ and -γξι.

§21.5133 The noun γυνή, gen. γυναικός, voc. γυναί, appears to have
dropped the final consonant without adding a sufformative in
nom./voc. (cf. §13.351). In the nom. the stem diphthong has monophthongized
§14.51).

§21.5134 The noun θρίξ, acc. τρίχαν, root *θριχ, is subject to the
rule forbidding two aspirates in adjacent syllables (§13.244).

§21.5135 When the nominative ends in -ξ, the preceding vowel may lengthen.

§21.52 Stems ending in <u>linguals</u> (§12.45), called nasals and liquids,
may be treated as a category.

§21.521 <u>Stems ending in -λ</u> are very rare. The common 3d decl. endings
are added to the stem.

§21.522 <u>Stems ending in -ν</u> usually lengthen the stem vowel in sing. nom.
and do not add a sufformative (cf. §21.4111). Otherwise they are
regular.

§21.5221 A few stems ending in -ν, drop the ν and add ς, with lengthening
(§15.123), in sing. nom. (cf. §21.4112).

§21.523 <u>Stems ending in -ρ</u> usually lengthen the stem vowel in sing. nom.
and do not add a sufformative (cf. §21.4111).

§21.5231 The noun μαρτυρ- drops ρ before ς > μάρτυς.

§21.5232　Some stems ending in -ρ are syncopated (§15.6) in the sing. gen.
　　　　　and dat. and the pl. dat. In such forms, the accent is shifted
to the final syllable.

§21.5233　The noun ἀνήρ, gen. ἀνδρός, is syncopated, and an epenthetic δ
　　　　　(cf. §13.52) is added in the syncopated forms.

§21.5234　It is possible that a vocalic [ṛ] is found in such words, or
　　　　　that vowel grades -ηρ, -ερ, -ρ are involved (cf. §15.411).

§21.53　　Stems ending in σ occasion somewhat more difficulty, due to the
　　　　　nature of the sibilant.

§21.531　The σ of the stem is found only where there is no case ending
　　　　　added (e.g. sing. nom.), since it can stand in final position
(§13.351).

§21.5311　When a vocalic sufformative is added, the intervocalic σ drops
　　　　　out (§13.361) and contraction of the vowels usually occurs
(§15.51).

§21.5312　When the pl. dat. sufformative is added, the resulting σσ is
　　　　　simplified to σ (§13.1611).

§21.532　Stems ending in -εσ are mostly neuter. They undergo vocalic
　　　　　ablaut (§15.4) ending in -ος in sing. nom./acc./voc.

§21.5321　In sing. gen., the ε of the stem contracts with -ος of the
　　　　　ending, to become -ους (Table F).

§21.5322　In sing. dat., the stem ε contracts with sufformative-ι to
　　　　　produce -ει (Table F).

§21.5323　In pl. nom./acc. stem ε contracts with sufformative-α to
　　　　　produce the unusual neuter plural ending -η (Table F).

§21.5324 In pl. dat. the resultant -εσσι simplifies to -εσι (§13.1611).

§21.5325 A few proper names (masc.) with stems in -ες lengthen to -ης
in sing. nom. (Smyth §263b).

§21.533 Stems ending in -ας are all neuter. The sing. nom./acc./voc.
forms end in -ας.

§21.5331 The sing. gen. ends in -ως, resulting from contraction of stem α
and sufformative-ος.

§21.5332 The sing. dat. form ends in -αι, resulting from contraction.
This is sometimes written α by analogy to the 1st declension.

§21.534 Stems ending in -ος are rare. The vowel lengthens in sing. nom./
voc. to -ω, and contracts in sing. acc. to -ω.

§21.54 <u>Stems ending in -ι or -υ</u> may have been originally consonantal
[i̯] and [u̯] respectively. Treated as such they follow a
reasonably regular pattern.

§21.541 Except for the sing. nom., acc., and voc. forms, most nouns
ending in -ι and some ending in -υ drop the -ι or -υ and add ε
to the stem before the sufformatives. The sing. gen. ending is -ως.

§21.542 Accent in words of this type is on the first syllable of disyllabic
stems, yielding proparoxytone forms (§17.113) even in sing. and pl.
gen. where the endings are -ως and -ων.

§21.543 Stems ending in -ι add ς to form m./f. sing. nom. and -ν to form
m./f. sing. acc. The stem form is used for voc. All other cases
are formed in accordance with §21.541.

§21.5431 The ε of the modified stem contracts with the vowels of the
sufformatives in sing. dat. and pl. nom. and acc. according
to §15.51ff.

§21.5432   In m./f. pl. acc. the ending is -ειϛ contracted apparently from an original *-εεϛ, in other words the plur. nom. ending (cf. Smyth §263a).

§21.544   Some stems ending in -υ, as described in §21.541, add -ϛ to form m./f. sing. nom. and -ν to form m./f. sing. acc. The stem is used for voc. In all other cases the words of this category are like those with stems ending in -ι.

§21.5441   Neuter nouns of this category use the stem form for sing. nom./ acc./voc. In the pl. nom./acc. the modified stem vowel ε contracts with the ending -α to produce the unusual neut. pl. nom./acc. ending -η.

§21.545   Most nouns with stems ending in -υ retain the υ throughout, the regular 3d decl. endings being added to the unmodified stem.

§21.5451   The sing. gen. ending is the regular -οϛ. The sing. dat. ending is -ϊ, with diaeresis (§11.551). The pl. acc. ending (except for neuter nouns) is either contracted -ϋϛ or uncontracted -υαϛ.

§21.55   Some 3d declension nouns have stems ending in diphthongs. It is almost certain that these originally ended in the semi-consonants <u>digamma</u> and <u>iota</u>.

§21.551   A few stems in -οι drop the ι, forming feminine nouns with sing. nom. in -ώ. In all other cases (except pl. dat.) the ο of the stem contracts with the vowel of the sufformative. The voc. preserves the original stem form.

§21.552   Stems ending in -ευ (originally -εϜ), drop the υ before vocalic sufformatives. In some cases, contraction follows; in other cases, the vowels remain in hiatus. Before consonantal sufformatives, the <u>digamma</u> vocalized to υ, forming the ευ diphthong.

§21.553   Stems ending in -αυ (originally -αϝ), likewise drop the υ
          before vocalic sufformatives and preserve it before consonantal
sufformatives.   Evidence indicates that contraction did not follow.

§21.5531 This rule is based on the words ναῦς and γραῦς. In the case
          of ναῦς, there seems to be some confusion of an ε-vowel and
an α-vowel. The dialects help us, however, for in Doric the form has α
regularly, while in Homer and Herodotus it has ε and η regularly.

§21.5532 The pl. acc. forms (masc. and fem.) appear to have contracted
          *-αυας to -αῦς.

§21.554   A few 3d declension nouns have stems ending in -ου (originally
          -οϝ). Before vocalic sufformatives the <u>digamma</u> was lost, and
before consonantal sufformatives it vocalized to υ. Evidence indicates
that contraction did not follow.

§21.5541 The forms βοῦς, βοῦν, βοῦ, and βουσί, are not the result of
          contraction but of vocalization of the <u>digamma</u> to υ. Pl. acc.
βόας appears to be the result of syncopation of the <u>digamma</u>; the alternate
form, βοῦς, however, may be syncopation followed by contraction of ο with
an -ες ending.

§21.555   The word οἶς does not properly belong in this category, although
          usually included here. It came from an original *οϝις, as
the Latin <u>ovis</u> indicates, and the Greek stem was almost certainly οϝι-.
With the syncopation of the <u>digamma</u>, the diphthong resulted, found in all
the inflected forms, with the endings added to it.

§21.6   The <u>endings of the three declensions</u> may be summarized as follows:

	1st declension		2d declension		3d declension	
singular	masc.	fem.	m./f.	neut.	m./f.	neut.
nom.	–ς	–	–ς	–ν	–ς/–	–ς/–
gen.	–ου	–ς	–ο	–ο	–ος	–ος
dat.	–ι	–ι > ᾳ	–ι	–ι > ῳ	–ι	–ι
acc.	–ν	–ν	–ν	–ν	–α/ν	–ς/–
voc.	–α	–	–ε	–ν	–ς/–	–ς/–
plural						
nom.	–ι	–ι	–ι	–α	–ες	–α
gen.	–ῶν	–ῶν	–ων	–ων	–ων	–ων
dat.	–ις	–ις	–ις	–ις	–σι	–σι
acc.	–ς	–ς	–νς > –ους	–α	–ας/ες	–α

§21.7 Some nouns are <u>irregular</u>. These cannot be placed in any single declension.

§21.71 Some nouns are declined in part according to one declension, in part according to another. These are called <u>mixed</u> or <u>heteroclitic</u> nouns.

§21.72 <u>Heterogeneous nouns</u> are nouns of one gender in the singular, and of another gender in the plural.

§21.73 <u>Metaplastic nouns</u> are nouns that have different <u>stems</u> in oblique cases from that of the nominative.

§21.74 <u>Defective nouns</u> are nouns that occur only in certain cases or only in one number.

§21.75 <u>Indeclinable nouns</u> are nouns which have the same form for all cases.

§22. An <u>adjective</u> is a word that modifies a noun or other substantive. In Greek, as in many other languages, adjectives are much more regular than nouns. Like nouns, adjectives are inflected to show gender, number, and case. However, since an adjective must usually be capable of modifying a substantive of any gender, each adjective normally is inflected in all three genders.

§22.1   By far the largest class of adjectives has the masculine singular nominative ending in -ος, and the masculine and neuter forms are of the second declension, while the feminine forms are of the first. They are usually called <u>adjectives of the first and second declension</u>, although "adjectives of the 2d—1st—2d declensions" would be more descriptive. All <u>middle participles</u> and all <u>passive participles</u> except aorist are declined in this manner.

§22.11   Masculine adjectives ending in -ος are regular. See §21.31 and Paradigm N-2.

§22.12   Feminine adjectives of this category, if the stem ends in a noncontracting vowel or ρ, take 1st declension sufformatives with α; otherwise, with η. See §21.21 and Paradigm N-1.

§22.121 Adjectives in -οος have feminine in -η.

§22.122 The fem. plur. nom. and gen. forms are accented like the corresponding masculine form.

§22.13   Neuter adjectives of this category follow the declension of neuter nouns of the second declension. See §21.31 and Paradigm N-2.

§22.14   Many adjectives of this category have stems ending in -ε or -ο, which contract with the initial vowels of the sufformatives (cf. §§15.513, .514).

§22.141 All contract forms of these adjectives are perispomena (cf. §17.121).

§22.142   A few adjectives are uncontracted, presumably because the stem
          originally ended in a semiconsonant (§12.5): νέος < *νεϝος,
cf. Lat. novus.

§22.15   A few adjectives are classified as irregular. Except for the
          masculine and neuter nominative and accusative forms, they
are otherwise adjectives of the 2d--1st--2d declensions.

§22.151   μέγας seems to come from an original *μεγαλ, with loss of λ
          before ς or ν and when final (§§13.351, 13.1631). The
anomalous forms are 3d declension.

§22.152   πολύς is regularly 2d--1st--2d in Homer and Herodotus. The
          anomalous forms may come from another stem ending in -ϝ, which
was declined according to the 3d declension.

§22.16   Some adjectives have the same forms for masculine and feminine
          and are therefore adjectives of 2d--2d--2d declension.

§22.161   A few adjectives are of the "Attic" 2d declension, with nominative
          endings in -ως, -ως, -ων (cf. §21.34). For the purpose of accent,
the ω is treated as a short vowel.

§22.2   A number of adjectives are declined in all genders in the third
          declension, hence are called adjectives of the third declension.
Masculine and feminine forms are alike in this category of adjectives.

§22.21   Some of these adjectives have the nominative in -ης, -ης, -ες,
          and are derived from stems originally ending in -εσ (cf. §21.5311).

§22.211   Contraction is irregular: εα contracts to ᾱ after ε, and to
          ᾱ or η after ι or υ. See §§21.41., .411, .4111, and Paradigm N-3.

§22.212   Many barytone compounds in this category have recessive accent
          (cf. §§17.3, .33).

§22.22   Other adjectives have the nominative in -ων, -ων, -ον, and are
          derived from stems originally ending in -ον (cf. §21.522).

§22.221   The neuter forms have recessive accent (cf. §17.3).

§22.222   The plur. acc. ἀληθεῖς is like the plur. nom.

§22.3   Some adjectives are third declension in the masculine and neuter
          and first declension in the feminine, and are commonly designated
as <u>adjectives of the first and third declensions</u>, or more descriptively as
adjectives of the 3d--1st--3d declensions.

§22.31   Feminine adjectives of this category always have ă in singular
          nominative and accusative; in genitive and dative ā follows a
vowel or diphthong, otherwise η. See Paradigm N-3.

§22.311   The fem. plur. gen. always has circumflex accent (§17.62).

§22.32   A number of adjectives of this category have stems ending in -υ,
          and sing. nom. forms in -υς, -εια, -υ.

§22.321   The masculine and neuter forms are declined like nouns of this
          category, except the sing. gen. which ends in -ος (cf. §21.541),
and the neut. plur. nom./acc. which ends in -α (cf. §21.5441).

§22.322   The feminine forms seem to be derived from a stem ending in -εϝ,
          to which has been added -ια endings, with loss of intervocalic ϝ.

§22.323   The <u>perfect active participle</u> in -ως, -υια, -ος (from *-οτς,
          §13.142) is possibly to be related to this development from an
original <u>digamma</u>. Except in sing. nom. and voc., where τ is dropped and o
lengthens to ω, o is found throughout masc. and neut. See Paradigm N-3.

§22.33   Many participles and some adjectives have stems ending in -αντ,
          -εντ, or -οντ. These are declined as adjectives of 3d--1st--3d
declensions (cf. §22.3ff.).

§22.331   The <u>first aorist active participle</u> in -ας, -ασα, -αν, and
          adjectives declined similarly, develop from an original *-αντς
-αντσα -αντ, in accordance with §13.354. See Paradigm N-3.

§22.3311 The feminine forms develop by the addition of -ια to the stem,
          plus the 1st decl. endings (cf. §13.1613).

§22.332   The <u>first</u> and <u>second aorist passive participles</u> in -εις, -εισα,
          -εν, and adjectives declined similarly, develop from an original
*-ντς -ντσα -ντ, in accordance with §13.354, 15.2. See Paradigm N-3.

§22.333   The <u>present active participle</u> in -ων, -ουσα, -ον, and adjectives
          declined similarly, develop from an original *-οντς, in accordance
with §13.354, 15.2. See Paradigm N-3.

§22.3331 The second active participle is declined similarly, adding
          the endings to the simple stem.

§22.3332 The <u>future active participle</u> is declined similarly, adding the
          endings to the future stem (§24.32f.).

§22.334   The present and second aorist participles of -μι verbs form
          the masc. sing. nom. form with -ς instead of -ν.

§22.335   Verbs with stems ending in short vowels contract regularly when
          adding the participle endings (cf. §15.515).

§22.34   Some adjectives have stems in -ν, and nominatives in -ας, -αινα,
          -αν, or -ης, -εινα, -εν. See Paradigm N-3.

§22.341   The feminine forms of these adjectives add -ια, which
          metathesizes in accordance with §13.164.

§22.4   The <u>comparative degree of adjectives</u> in -τερος, -τερα, -τερον,
          follows the declension in §22.1.

§22.41   The <u>superlative degree of adjectives</u> in -τατος, -τατα, -τατον,
         likewise follows the declension in §22.1.

§22.42   Stems in -ο with a short penult lengthen ο to ω before -τερος
         and -τατος. (§15.14).

§22.43   The comparative degree of adjectives in -ιων, -ιων, -ιον,
         follows the declension in §22.22, adding the endings to the
stem and not to the adjective.

§22.44   Some adjectives form the superlative degree ending in -ιστος,
         declined according to §22.1.

§22.45   A number of adjectives form the comparative and superlative
         degrees from different roots. μέγας-μείζων, αγαθός-κρείσσων.

§22.5   Many <u>adverbs</u> are regularly formed from adjectives (including
         adjective pronouns, §23.4). Their form, including the accent,
may be found by changing -ν of the masc. pl. gen. to -ς. They are
occasionally formed in the same manner from participles. δικαίων-δικαίως.

§22.51   The neuter accusative of an adjective (sing. or pl.) may be
         used as an adverb: πέραν, τὰ πολλά.

§22.52   The comparative degree of an adverb may be formed from the
         neuter <u>singular</u> accusative form of the comparative form of
the corresponding adjective: ἐγγύς--ἐγγύτερον.

§22.53   The superlative degree of an adverb may be formed by using the
         neuter <u>plural</u> accusative form of the superlative form of the
corresponding adjective: ἡδέως-ἥδιστα.

§22.54   A number of adverbs are actually nouns or pronouns with fossilized
         case-endings, particularly those indicating place where, place from
which, and place to which: αὐτοῦ, κύκλῳ, τετράκις, ἄνωθεν, ἐκεῖσε, etc.

§22.55   The negative adverbs οὐκ and μή, can be compounded with other
         elements to form words with meanings such as "nowhere" "not yet,"
"by no means," "never," etc. These are best learned as they are encountered.

§22.6   The numerals are adjectives (sometimes used substantivally,
         sometimes adverbially), highly irregular in the cardinal form,
adjectives of 2d--1st--2d decl. in the ordinal (§§22.1ff.).

§22.61   The cardinal 'one' is εἷς, μία, ἕν; an adjective of 3d--1st--3d
         decl. (§22.3) with masc. and neut. from a stem *ἑν- (from *ἐμ- <
*σεμ-, cf. Lat. semel) with loss of -ν and compensatory lengthening in
masc. (§13.134). The fem. form is from the weakened stem *σμ- (§15.411--
.413 and 13.366).

§22.611   The ordinal 'first' is found as πρότερος, literally 'former,
         first of two,' and as πρῶτος, literally 'first (of all)' (cf.
§15.14). The former is an adjective in comparative degreee; the latter
an adjective in superlative degree. In the New Testament, the difference
is not clearly observed.

§22.612   The adverb 'once' is ἅπαξ, which is indeclinable (§21.75).

§22.613   The negative compounds, οὐδείς and μηδείς, are declined like
         εἷς (§22.61).

§22.62   The cardinal 'two' is δύο, indeclinable except for dat. pl.
         δύσιν (§21.74).

§22.621   The ordinal 'second' is δεύτερος, which is an adjective in
         comparative degree, possibly from δεύομαι, 'to be wanting,
inferior to' (cf. Robertson, p. 283). In many languages, the words for
'first' and 'second' are not built from the numbers, but from words for
'head, leader,' etc., and 'follower, repeater,' etc.

§22.622   The adverb 'twice' is δίς. All numeral adverbs have the -ίς or
         -άκις ending.

§22.63   The cardinal 'three' is τρεῖς, τρεῖς, τρία, declined (in plural
         only!) according to 3d decl. (§21.74).

§22.631   The ordinals for numbers from 'three' up except ἕβδομος '7th'
         and ὄγδοος '8th,' are adjectives of superlative degree built from
the cardinal (§22.41).

§22.64   The cardinal 'four' is τέσσαρες, τέσσαρες, τέσσαρα, declined
         (in plural only) according to the 3d decl. (§22.21).

§22.65   Cardinal numbers from 5 to 100, and 105 to 199 are indeclinable
         (§21.75). From 200 up, the cardinals are adjectives of the
2d--1st--2d declension (in plural only) (§22.1ff.).

§22.66   The letters of the Greek alphabet were used for numbers, the
         units being represented by alpha to iota (with accent after
the letter to indicate a number), the tens by iota (10), kappa (20),
etc., to qoppa (90), the hundreds by rho (100) to omega (800), with the
addition of sampi for 900. For 1,000 alpha is used with an accent at
lower left, and so on up to rho for 100,000.

§23.   A pronoun is a word used instead of a noun. It designates a
         person, place, or thing, without naming it. There are four
kinds of pronouns: (1) personal, including intensive and reflexive;
(2) adjective, including demonstrative, indefinite, and adjective personal
pronouns; (3) relative; and (4) interrogative.

§23.1   There are in Koinē Greek four personal pronouns (1st sing.,
         2d sing., 1st pl., 2d pl.) and an intensive pronoun which has
replaced the old 3d pers. pronouns. It is a mistake to think of the
plural forms as related to the singulars--they come from entirely different
words, throughout Indo-European. It is also a mistake to think of the
nominative form of the 1st sing. as related to the oblique forms; they too
come from different words.

§23.11   The 1st pers. pron. sing. is: nom. ἐγώ , gen. ἐμοῦ or μοῦ,
          dat. ἐμοί or μοί, acc. ἐμέ or μέ.

§23.111   The nom. form persists in familiar I.-E. languages: Lat. ego,
          Dut. ik; with prepalatalization and with varying accent:
Ger. ich, Fr. je [žᵉ]; with complete prepalatalization of [g] to [ǧ]
to [ž] to [j] (or [i̯]), Ital. io, Swed. je [i̯ε], etc.

§23.12   The 1st pers. pron. pl. is nom. ἡμεῖς, gen. ἡμῶν, dat.
          ἡμῖν, acc. ἡμᾶς.

§23.121   The rough breathing was originally a sigma (§13.364). The
          original stem was something like *sma-, and does not seem to
be cognate with the 1st pers. pron. pl. in the familiar I.-E. languages
(Lat. noster, Fr. nous, etc.).

§23.13   The 2d pers. pron. sing. is: nom. σύ, gen. σοῦ, dat. σοί,
          acc. σέ.

§23.131   The 2d sing. pronoun developed from *τϝε - (Epic τυνη, Doric
          τυ), cognate with Lat. tu, te, Fr. tu, etc.

§23.14   The 2d pers. pron. plur. is: nom. ὑμεῖς, gen. ὑμῶν, dat.
          ὑμῖν, acc. ὑμᾶς.

§23.141   The original stem probably had digamma, *ϝυμ- or *ϝυσμ-, and is
          cognate with Lat. vester, Fr. vous, and probably Eng. you.
Because of the great use of personal pronouns, they are unusually irregular.

§23.15   The old 3d pers. pronoun gave way to the intensive pronoun αὐτός,
          αὐτή, αὐτό, 'self, same,' which is declined as an adj. of 2d--1st--
2d declension (§22.1). In addition to its use as a personal pronoun, this
word retains its intensive significance when used as a demonstrative before a
noun, and sometimes when used independently.

§23.151   The original 3d pers. pronoun occurs in classical Greek, sing.
gen. οὗ, dat. οἷ, acc. ἕ, developed from *ϝ- (cf. he, she);
plur. nom. σφεῖς, gen. σφῶν, dat. σφίσι, acc. σφᾶς, from *σφ-.

§23.2   The <u>reflexive pronouns</u> are actually compound personal pronouns.
In the sing. they are compounded from the pers. pron. and αὐτοῦ.
In the pl., the 1st and 3d or 2d and 3d are declined separately. The nom.
is lacking throughout.

§23.21   The masc. sing. gen. forms are: ἐμαυτοῦ "of myself," σεαυτοῦ
"of thyself," ἑαυτοῦ "of himself." These pronouns are declined
as adjectives of 2d--1st--2d decl. (§22.1)

§23.212   The neuter is found only in the 3d person.

§23.22   The <u>reciprocal pronoun</u> occurs only in oblique (i.e. not nominative)
plural forms, declined according to 2d--1st--2d declension; (§22.1);
gen. pl. ἀλλήλων "of one another."

§23.3   <u>Adjective pronouns</u> include the possessive pronouns, the definite
article, the demonstrative pronouns, and the indefinite pronouns.

§23.31   The <u>possessive pronouns</u> ἐμός "my," σός "thy," ἡμέτερος "our,"
ὑμέτερος "your," and ἴδιος "one's own," are used infrequently,
possibly with a bit more emphasis than the customary gen. form of the pers.
pron. They are declined as adjs. of 2d--1st--2d decl. (§22.1).

§23.32   The <u>definite article</u> is, strictly speaking, a form of demonstrative
pronoun. In general, it is declined as an adjective of the 2d--1st--
2d declension (§22.1). Note the absence of initial <u>tau</u> (replaced by rough
breathing) in masc. and fem. sing. and pl. of nom.

§23.33   The <u>demonstrative pronouns</u> are οὗτος, αὕτη, τοῦτο, 'this' and
ἐκεῖνος, ἐκείνη, ἐκεῖνο, 'that.' The declension is according to
2d--1st--2d decl. adjs. (§22.1). Note the absence of initial <u>tau</u> in
paralleling the def. art.

§23.331   The demon. pron. ὅδε, ἥδε, τόδε, 'this (here)' is declined exactly like the def. art. with the enclitic δε added (see §17.826).

§23.34   The most common <u>indefinite pronoun</u> is τις, τις, τι, 'someone,
something.' The gen. form is τινός, and the pronoun is declined
according to 3d declension. Except for accent, this word is exactly like
the interrogative pronoun (§23.5).

§23.4   The <u>relative pronouns</u> are ὅς, ἥ, ὅ, 'who, what,' and ὅστις ἥτις
ὅ τι, 'whoever, whatever.' The definite relative pronoun (ὅς) is
declined according to 2d––1st––2d decl. (except the less usual neut. nom.
acc. sing. form). The indefinite relative pronoun (ὅστις) is compounded of
the relative pronoun (ὅς) and the indefinite pronoun (τις), both elements
being inflected in declining the word (§17.826). Note that in nom./-acc.
sing. of the neuter, the two words are written separately.

§23.5   The <u>interrogative pronoun</u> is τίς, τίς, τί, 'who? what?' It
is declined as though from an original stem τιν- (§21.5221), and
follows the pattern of the 3d declension. It always maintains the acute
accent on the <u>iota</u> of the stem.

§23.6   While the pattern is not complete, still there seems to be
sufficient similarity in the structure of the following to
make it useful to the student.

Interrogative	Indefinite	Demonstrative	Relative
πόσος	ποσός	τοσος > τοσοῦτος	ὅσος
how much/many?	some	so much/many	as much/many as
ποῖος	ποῖος	τοιος > τοιοῦτος	οἷος
of what kind?	some kind	such	such as
πότερος	ποτερός	ἕτερος	ὁπότερος
which (of 2)?	(either)	the other	whichever
πηλίκος		τηλίκος > τηλικοῦτος	ἡλίκος
how old/large?		so old/large	as old/large as
τίς τίνος	τις τινός	οὗτος τοῦτο	ὅστις ὅ τι
who?/what?	someone/thing	this one	who/which

πόθεν		ἐντεῦθεν, hence	ὅθεν
whence?		ἐκεῖθεν, thence	whence
πῶς	πώ(ς)	οὕτως	ὡς
how?	somehow	thus so	as, about
ποῦ	πού	αὐτοῦ	οὗ
where?	somewhere	here	where
πότε	ποτέ	τότε	ὅτε
when?	at some time	then	when

§24.   The <u>verb</u> (when used; see §33.5 for predicate adjective) is the principal element in the predicate (§30.12). It asserts or predicates the action or state with reference to the subject, and gives certain other information about that action or state. The Greek verb, by its form, conveys <u>tense</u>, <u>voice</u>, <u>mood</u>, <u>person</u>, and <u>number</u>, each of which is more fully discussed in the following sections.

§24.01   Verbal forms that are defined in person and number, as well as the other features mentioned in §24, are called <u>finite</u> verbal forms. Those which are not so defined, such as the infinitive and participle, are called <u>nonfinite</u> verbal forms.

§24.1   Tense, voice, mood, person, and number are indicated by combining a distinctive verbal <u>stem</u> with a distinctive verbal <u>ending</u>. <u>Tense</u> and <u>voice</u> are indicated partly by changes in the basic stem, in some cases with prefixed elements, and partly by the addition of different sets of endings. <u>Mood</u> is indicated by modifications in the endings or by a different set of endings. <u>Person</u> and <u>number</u> are indicated by the inflectional endings.

§24.11   The <u>basic verbal stem</u> is a hypothetical stem from which the tense-voice stems can be derived. Although it has no independent existence in the language, it often can be related to noun stems or other elements of the language having the same basic meaning. Hypothetical forms as a rule are indicated with an asterisk prefixed (e.g. *λαβ-).

§24.111   Since the modified stem can indicate both tense and voice, it is better to refer to it as the <u>tense-voice stem</u>. Nine different tense-voice systems, each with its own stem, can be identified, but each verb usually has at most six of these.

Tense-voice stem	Used to form
Present (§24.2)	present active tense (§24.4111f.)
	present middle/passive tense (§24.4151f.)
	imperfect active tense (§24.4121f.)
	imperfect middle/passive tense (§24.4161)
Future active/middle (§24.32)	future active tense (§24.4113ff.)
	future middle tense (§24.4153)
1 Aorist act./mid. (§24.33)	1 aorist active tense (§24.4131ff.)
	1 aorist middle tense (§24.4163f.)
2 Aorist act./mid. (§24.34)	2 aorist active tense (§24.4123)
	2 aorist middle tense (§24.4162)
1 Perfect active (§24.35)	1 perfect active tense (§24.4134)
	1 pluperfect active tense (24.414)
2 Perfect active (§24.36)	2 perfect active tense (§24.4135)
	2 pluperfect active tense (§24.4141)
Perfect mid./pass. (§24.37)	perfect middle/passive tense (§24.4156)
	pluperfect middle/passive tense (§24.4165)
	future perfect middle/passive tense
First Passive (§24.38)	1 aorist passive tense (§24.4171)
	1 future passive tense (§24.4154)
Second Passive (§24.39)	2 aorist passive tense (§24.4172)
	2 future passive tense (§24.4155)

§24.112   The <u>tense-voice stem</u> is formed from the basic stem in one or more of the following ways:

the basic stem unaltered (§24.11);

the addition of a thematic vowel (§24.221, .311);

the addition of a consonantal stem indicator (§24.24, .25, .26, .312);

the addition of a syllabic stem indicator (§24.26, .27, .28, .312);

epenthesis (§24.262);

the prefixing of a vowel (syllabic augment) (§24.313ff.);

the alteration of the initial vowel/diphthong (temporal augment) (§24.313ff.);

the prefixing of a syllable (reduplication) (§24.314ff.);

vocalic gradation (Ablaut) of the basic stem vowel (§24.231, .315).

The rules for consonantal alteration (assimilation, dissimilation, metathesis, etc.) and for vowel contraction may cause additional alteration
of the basic stem when any of the modifications are made.

§24.113   The inflectional endings, signifying mood, person, and number,
           consist of one or more of the following elements:

a connecting (or thematic) vowel or diphthong; (§24.221, .311);

lengthening of the thematic vowel;

diphthongization of the thematic vowel;

the appropriate person-number sufformative (§24.4).

Rules for consonantal alteration and vowel contraction may cause
additional alteration.

§24.114   The principal parts of a Greek verb are the indicative first-
           person singular form of each of the following tenses:

present active; (§24.411)

future active (if lacking, use future middle); (§24.4113, .4153)

first (or second) aorist active; (§24.4131, .4123)

first (or second) perfect active; (§24.4134; .4135)

first (or second) perfect middle/passive; (§24.4146)

first (or second) aorist passive, (§24.4171, .4172).

§24.115   Some verbs have no active voice but are used in the middle or
           passive with active meaning. Such verbs are called deponents,
and their principal parts consist of the indicative first-person singular
form of each of the following tenses: present, future, perfect, aorist.

§24.116   No known verb is used in all its tenses. Paradigm verbs in
           grammars always have some hypothetical forms to complete the
paradigm, based on actual forms of other verbs.

§24.117   Finite verbal forms of the future perfect tense do not occur
           in the NT. The participle occurs but rarely and in periphrastic
constructions.

§24.12   Tense, in Greek, refers to the type of action as well as, or even
           more than, the time of action (see §31.5). There are seven tenses:
present, imperfect, future, aorist, perfect, pluperfect, and future perfect.

§24.121   These can be divided into the unaugmented (or primary) tenses
           (present, future, perfect, future perfect), and the augmented
(or secondary) tenses (imperfect, aorist, pluperfect). The terms "primary"
or "principal" and "secondary" or "historical" do not seem to have any
particular merit.

§24.13   Voice indicates how the action or state of the verb is related
           to the subject (see §31.4). In Greek, three voices are dis-
tinguished: active, middle, and passive.

§24.131   Voice is sometimes indicated by different forms of stems
           (see §24.111), but more often it is indicated by two different
sets of endings, one for the active voice, the other for the middle/passive
voice.

§24.132   The middle and passive voices are not morphologically distin-
           guished from each other except in the future and aorist tenses.

§24.14   Mood indicates the relationship of the verb to reality (see
           §31.3). Four moods are distinguished: indicative, imperative,
subjunctive, and optative. The subjunctive and optative moods are indicated
morphologically by modification of the thematic vowel and the use of
distinctive sets of endings. The imperative is distinguished by distinctive
endings. The augmented forms (§24.121) occur only in the indicative.

§24.141   The nonfinite forms, infinitive and participle, are often included
           as moods. These really are not moods and will not be considered

as such in this Handbook, except that in parsing (§24.192) the terms
"infinitive" and "participle" will occupy the position where mood is indicated.

§24.142   The subjunctive, optative, and imperative moods are called
          "dependent" moods, as opposed to the indicative. The infinitive
and sometimes the participle are also classed as dependent moods. It would
be better to reserve the term "dependent" for the clauses in which they are
found. The imperative, as well as the subjunctive or the infinitive used
as an imperative, can hardly be called "dependent."

§24.143   Only the indicative mood is found in all tenses.

§24.1431 The subjunctive is found only in the present, aorist, and perfect
          tenses. The perfect middle/passive subjunctive is formed peri-
phrastically, using the perfect participle plus the subjunctive of the
verb to be.

§24.1432 The optative is found in all tenses except the imperfect and
          pluperfect.

§24.1433 The imperative is found only in the present, aorist, and perfect
          tenses. The perfect active imperative does not occur in the NT,
but is replaced (as often in classical Greek) with the perfect participle
plus the imperative of the verb to be. The perfect passive imperative is
very rare.

§24.1434 It may be noted that the imperfect and pluperfect tenses are
          found in the indicative only, and the future tense is found
in the indicative and optative only.

§24.15   Person refers to any one of the three relationships underlying
          discourse: the one speaking is the first person, the one
spoken to is the second person, and the person or thing spoken about is
the third person. Person is indicated by the inflectional endings.

§24.151   All three persons are indicated in all moods except the imperative,
          which (since it makes no sense to issue commands to yourself)
indicates only second and third persons.

§24.16   In Koinē Greek only two <u>numbers</u> are indicated: <u>singular</u> and
          <u>plural</u>. In classical Greek, the dual number is also found.
Number is indicated by the inflectional ending.

§24.17   The <u>inflectional endings</u> (cf. §24.113) therefore in any given
          tense, voice, and mood, have six forms, one each for first,
second, and third person singular, and one each for first, second, and
third person plural.

§24.171   There are several sets of inflectional endings, differing ac-
          cording to the tense, according to the voice, and according to
the mood. Many grammars distinguish only four sets of endings: primary
(nonaugmented) active, primary passive, secondary (augmented) active, and
secondary passive. There are, however, several exceptions to this pattern.

§24.18   The nonfinite verbal forms likewise are inflected to show tense
          and voice, and in the case of the participle, to show gender,
number and case.

§24.181   The <u>infinitive</u> is a verbal noun (cf. §30.381). As a verb, it
          is altered morphologically to indicate tense and voice, according
to the tense-voice system described above (§24.112), plus characteristic
infinitive endings.

§24.1811 The infinitive does not indicate mood, person, or number, nor
          does it (as a noun) indicate gender, number, and case. It is
indeclinable (§21.75).

§24.1812 The infinitive is found in all tenses except the imperfect and
          pluperfect. It is found in all three voices.

§24.1813 All the infinitive forms of classical Greek are found in the NT.
         However, the future active and middle infinitives are found only
in Acts and Hebrews, and then but rarely. The future perfect infinitive
is very rare and occurs only in certain set phrases.

§24.182   The participle is a verbal adjective (cf. §30.382). As a verb
         it is morphologically capable of indicating tense and voice, as
described above (§24.112). As an adjective, the participle is inflected
to show gender, number and case.

§24.1821 The participle does not indicate mood, person, or number.

§24.1822 The participle is found in all tenses except the imperfect and
         pluperfect. It is found in all three voices.

§24.1823 All the participial forms of classical Greek occur in the NT.
         However, the future active and middle participles are virtually
limited to Luke-Acts and Hebrews. The future perfect participle occurs
very rarely and only in periphrastic constructions.

§24.19   In addition to terminology used in the preceding sections, other
         terms are used in referring to verb forms.

§24.191   To conjugate a verb is to give all the forms of the verb, in its
         tenses, voices, moods, persons, and numbers, in their proper order.

§24.192   To parse a verb is to identify a particular form according to its
         tense, voice, mood, person, and number--in this order--, to give
the basic (lexicon) form of the verb (and meaning), and to tell why this form
is used in its context. (Hint: memorize the order "TVMPN.")

§24.193   A verb paradigm is the complete conjugation of a pattern verb,
         including hypothetical forms where necessary, to aid in identi-
fying or constructing forms of similarly conjugated verbs.

§24.194   A verb <u>synopsis</u> is a representative selection of a verb conjugation
           (usually the first singular of all pertinent tense-voice-mood forms).

§24.2   The formation of the <u>present stem</u>, the most complex of all the
           tense-voice stems, requires careful study. We have seen that a
tense can be considered as a tense-voice stem (§24.112), developed from a
basic stem (§24.111), plus inflectinal endings (§24.113). We shall consider
first only the development of the present stem; the endings will be discussed
later (§24.4ff.).

§24.21   The development of the present stem is conditioned in part by the
           characteristics of the basic stem. Grammarians have distinguished
varying numbers of <u>classes;</u> in this Handbook we distinguish seven, with subdivisions of some of these. While most verbs in the present active indicative first singular end in -ω, a number end in -μι. Grammarians therefore
often distinguish the <u>ω-verbs</u> and the <u>μι-verbs</u> as two "conjugations." In
this Handbook, the μι-verbs are considered as Class 7. Mixed verbs (verbs
using entirely different root-words in their various tenses) might be considered as Class 8 verbs.

§24.22   <u>Class 1 Verbs</u> form the present stem from the basic stem by adding
           a thematic vowel. The inflectional endings are added to this
present stem to form the present tense. If the basic stem ends in a consonant, ι, υ, or a diphthong, the development will be uncomplicated (Class
1a). If the basic stem ends in ᾰ, ε, or ο, there will be contraction of the
stem vowel with the thematic vowel (Class 1b or "Contract Verbs").

§24.221   The <u>thematic vowel</u> (or connecting vowel) is ο before a nasal
           (μ or ν) and ε elsewhere. Hence the thematic vowel is usually
designated as ο/ε. The ο form occurs in 1 sing., 1 pl., and 3 pl.

§24.222   <u>Class-1a verbs</u> are often considered as "regular" verbs. With
           consonantal stems there are no alterations, since the thematic
vowel separates the stem consonant from the consonant of an inflectional

ending. With stems ending in ι, υ, or diphthongs, we may assume an
original final *-ι̯ or *-ϝ. See Paradigm V-la, Class-la verbs.

§24.2221 It is necessary to remember that this statement applies only
           where connecting vowels immediately follow the stem, i.e., in
all forms of the present, imperfect, and second aorist. In any form of
the verb where the stem consonant is brought into contact with another
consonant, whether infixed or sufformative, the rules for consonantal
alteration will apply.

§24.2222 Some verbs reduplicate (cf. §24.314) to form the present stem.
           Note that the vowel of the reduplicated present is ι.

§24.2223 Quantitative (§15.1) and qualitative (§15.4) vowel gradation are
           found in many present stems. In such verbs, the lengthened
vowel (quantitative) or the strong vowel (qualitative) will be found in the
present stem.

§24.223   Class-1b verbs, commonly known as Contract Verbs, follow the
           rules for contraction (Table F). Accordingly, the form of the
present stem will vary, depending on whether the thematic vowel is o or
ε. See Paradigm V-1b, Class-1b verbs.

§24.2231 Contraction will occur in any verb form where the stem vowel
           is brought immediately before another vowel or diphthong, i.e.
in all forms of the present, imperfect, and the second aorist.

§24.2232 It is essential to bear in mind the principle set forth in
           §15.518, according to which the contraction of the thematic
vowel with the vowel of the inflectional ending takes place first, and
then the stem vowel contracts with the vowel or diphthong that has
resulted from the first contraction.

§24.23   Class-2 verbs are developed from verbal stems ending in labial,
           dental, or velar stops (Part III, Table C), often called "mutes,"

which have vowel gradation (§§15.4; 24.315). The basic stem, found in
the 2d aorist, has the normal form of the vowel.

§24.231   The present stem of Class-2 verbs is formed by adding the
          thematic vowel to the "strong" form of the stem, i.e., a
form in which a diphthong or "strong" vowel has replaced the short
vowel of the basic stem (see §15.411).

§24.2311 The strong stem is also used to form the future active/middle,
          the 1st aorist active/middle (if any), the perfect middle/passive,
and the passive stems, and sometimes also the perfect active stem. A
second form is often used to form the perfect active stem. The basic stem,
or weak form, generally occurs in the 2d aorist active/middle and the 2d
passive stems only. Study carefully Paradigm V-2a, Class-2a verbs, and note
the vocalic changes.

§24.2312 Again we must keep in mind the consonantal shifts that will occur
          when stems of this nature (ending in a labial, dental, or velar
stop) are joined immediately to a consonant, whether an infix or an inflectional ending. The present stem is not affected, since the thematic vowel
separates the stem consonant from the following affix.

§24.232   Sometimes included in this category are Class-2b verbs, which
          are formed from stems ending originally in -εϝ, which have vowel
gradation with strong forms in those tense-systems where ϝ has become υ
(before a consonant), and weak forms in those tense-systems where ϝ has
dropped out (before a vowel). See Paradigm V-2b, Class-2b verbs.

§24.2321 A notable feature of Class-2b verbs is the absence of contraction
          where the ϝ has dropped. Accordingly these verbs do not belong
in Class 1b ("Contract Verbs").

§24.2322 A number of contracted forms are found, probably resulting from
          analogy.

§24.24   Class-3 verbs develop from stems ending in a labial stop to which
             τ is added, before affixing the thematic vowel, to form the
present stem.   See Paradigm V-3, Class-3 verbs.   Note that the lexicon form
(the pres. act. ind. 1s.) includes this τ, hence distorts the basic stem.

§24.241   The τ does not occur in any other tense-voice system than the
             present.

§24.2411 Since in all tense-voice systems except the 2d aorist, a consonant
             is regularly added to the verb stem, consonantal alteration will
occur. The basic stem of Class-3 verbs, therefore, will be disguised in all
tense-voice systems. Study Paradigm V-3, Class-3 verbs, carefully.

§24.25   Class-4 verbs, probably the most difficult to comprehend, developed
             the present stem by adding consonantal iota to the basic stem,
and then adding the thematic vowel and the inflectional ending. However,
the addition of consonantal iota caused various kinds of consonantal alteration, depending on the characteristics of the basic stem. It is therefore
necessary to subdivide this class into at least five subdivisions.

§24.251   Class-4a verbs include those with stems ending in a voiced dental
             (δ), velar (γ), or nasovelar (γγ) stop, which undergoes alteration
before ι̣ (see §§13.1614,.1621), so that the present stem regularly ends in
ζ plus the thematic vowel. See Paradigm V-4a, Class-4a verbs.

§24.2511 The future and 1st aorist stems of these verbs will differ, -δσ- >
             -σ, while -γσ- or -γγσ- > -ξ-.

§24.2512 Some verbs appear to have stems ending both in δ and in γ, with
             future stem in ξ (< γσ) and 1 aorist stem in σ (< δσ).

§24.2513 Likewise, the other tense-voice stems will develop differently,
             according to the rules governing the consonants involved.

§24.2514 Very many verbs in -άζω/-ίζω are not dental or velar
            stems, but are denominals (§§25.2, .24) formed by analogy to
this class.

§24.252   Class-4b verbs include those with stems ending in surd velar
            stops (κ, χ), which undergo alteration before ι̥ (see §13.162),
so that the present stem regularly ends in σσ plus the thematic vowel.
See Paradigm V-4b, Class-4b verbs.

§24.2521 A number of stems ending in γ develop as Class-4b verbs, rather
            than 4a, probably due to the analogic effect of the future and
aorist stems.

§24.2522 The future and 1st aorist active/middle stems have ξ (§13.143);
            the perfect middle/passive stem undergoes the consonantal shift
required by the initial consonant of the sufformative; and the (aorist/
future) passive stem has χ before θ (§13.112). The student must therefore
be alert to see the consonantal alterations in this class of verb.

§24.2523 Some grammarians include stems ending in surd dental stops
            (τ, θ) in this class. Clear-cut illustrations, however, are
lacking.

§24.253   Class-4c verbs develop from stems originally ending in -αϝ or
            -υϝ, to which was added consonantal ι̥ and the thematic vowel
to form the present stem. Between vowels, the digamma dropped out and
a diphthong resulted. Before a consonant, the digamma developed into υ.
See Paradigm V-4c, Class-4c verbs.

§24.2531 Note that stems originally ending in -εϝ are Class 2b, and stems
            originally ending in -οϝ are Class 1. Compare the following verbs:

*κλαϝ-	(4c)	pres. κλαίω	fut. κλαύσω	aor.	ἔκλαυσα
*οπυϝ-	(4c)	pres. ὀπυίω	fut. ὀπύσω	aor.	---
*πλεϝ-	(2b)	pres. πλέω	fut. πλεύσομαι	aor.	ἔπλευσα
*ακοϝ-	(1a)	pres. ἀκούω	fut. ἀκούσω	aor.	ἤκουσα

§24.254   <u>Class-4d verbs</u> develop from stems originally ending in -σ, the sigma dropping out and the iota diphthongizing, in the present stem. In other stems, the sigma is preserved (the iota, of course, belongs to the development of the present stem). See Paradigm V-4d, Class-4d verbs.

§24.255   <u>Class-4e verbs</u>, commonly called "liquid verbs," develop from stems ending in -λ, -ν, or -ρ. The influence of ι is not uniform. See Paradigm V-4e, Class-4e verbs.

§24.2551   Stems ending in -λ, develop the present stem in -λλ (cf. §13.163).

§24.2552   Stems ending in -αν or -αρ metathesize the ι and the liquid, the ι diphthongizing with the stem vowel (§13.164).

§24.2553   Stems ending in -εν, -ερ, -ιν, -ιρ, -υν, or -υρ drop the ι and lengthen the stem vowel (ε to ει, cf. §13.1641).

§24.2554   The verb ὀφείλω (stem *οφελ-) develops like stems in -εν.

§24.2555   To form the future stem, liquid verbs add -εσο/ε to the basic stem. The sigma drops out (§13.361), and the vowels contract according to §15.51ff.

§24.2556   To form the 1st aorist active/middle stem, liquid verbs drop the σ (§13.363), and the stem vowel undergoes compensatory lengthening (see §15.21). Some verbs of this category have a 2d aorist built from the basic stem.

§24.2557   A few verbs with liquid stems do not develop as liquid verbs.

§24.26   <u>Class-5 verbs</u> add ν or αν, or νε, να, or υυ to the stem, before adding to the thematic vowel to form the present stem. This class therefore needs to be futher subdivided.

§24.261   Class-5a verbs add -ν to vocalic stems or -αν to consonantal
                stems, before adding the thematic vowel. See Paradigm V-5a,
Class-5a verbs.

§24.262   Class-5b verbs, which have a short vowel in the last (or only)
                syllable of the basic stem, add an epenthetic ν (§13.5ff.) just
before the final consonant of the basic stem, in addition to adding -αν and
the thematic vowel, in order to form the present stem. This epenthetic ν
assimilates to μ before a labial (§13.131) and to nasal-γ before a velar
(§13.132). See Paradigm V-5b, Class-5b verbs.

§24.263   Class-5c verbs add νε, να, or νυ (after a vowel νυ) to the
                basic stem, before adding the thematic vowel, in order to form
the present stem. See Paradigm V-5c, Class-5c verbs.

§24.2631   Most of the verbs that add -νυ develop as μι-verbs (Class 7b,
                §24.282ff.); a few, however, develop as Class-5c verbs.

§24.2632   To form the future and the 1st aorist active/middle tense stems,
                verbs of this class that have a short stem vowel, lengthen the
vowel; verbs with a consonantal stem add a vowel (generally η) before
adding the future/aorist sigma. Class-5b verbs usually have 2d aorist
instead of 1st aorist forms.

§24.2633   Verbs that add η before σ to form the future and 1 aorist
                active/middle stems, often add this η to form other tense-voice
stems.

§24.2634   The verb βαίνω (stem *βα-) properly belongs to Class 5a, although
                its present stem is developed like a liquid (Class-4e) verb.

§24.27   Class-6 verbs add -ισκ (to consonantal stems) or -σκ (to vocalic
                stems) before adding the thematic vowel to form the present tense

stem. In addition, a number of these verbs have reduplication, consisting
of the initial consonant and ι (§24.3141), in the present stem. See
Paradigm V-6, Class-6 verbs.

§24.271   Three verbs drop the final velar stop before adding -σκ:
            διδάσκω (stem *διδαχ -), ἁλύσκω (stem *αλυκ -), and λασκω
(stem *λακ -).

§24.272   Stems ending in -ο or -ᾰ may lengthen the stem vowel, ο > ω
            or ᾰ > ᾱ/η before adding the -σκ element.

§24.273   Stems ending in a consonant and containing a short vowel, may
            reduce that vowel to zero and add η or ω before adding -σκ.

§24.274   Both categories (§24.272 and .273) usually retain the long
            vowel in forming other tense stems.

§24.275   The verb ἀραρίσκω (stem *αρ-) has "Attic" reduplication
            (cf. §24.3147).

§24.276   The verbs μιμνήσκω (stem *μνα -) and θνῄσκω (stem *θαν or
            *θνη -) add -ισκ to a stem ending in a vowel, as indicated
by iota subscript.

§24.277   This class of verbs is often called "inchoative" or "inceptive,"
            although few of the verbs convey such an idea. It is more
accurate to look upon them as denoting action or state taking place in
successive steps.

§24.28   Class-7 verbs (the μι-verbs) are those verbs which develop with-
            out any thematic vowel (§24.221) in the present and 2 aorist
tense-stems. Their first principle part ends in -μι (active) or -μαι
(mid./pass. or deponents). Usually these are set over against the ω-verbs
as two major categories or "conjugations"; however, (a) the ω-verbs far
outnumber the μι-verbs, (b) the differences affect only the present (and if
any, the 2d aorist and 2d perfect) tense stems, and (c) there are a number
of ω-verbs that develop in the same way as μι-verbs in the 2 aor., i.e.

they lack the theme vowel, cf. ἀναβαίνω (ἀνέβην), γιγώσκω (ἔγνων). These are therefore considered as one of the seven basic ways which the present stem develops. Two kinds of μι-verbs are found.

§24.281   Class-7a verbs form the present active indicative by adding the μι- (§24.471) or μαι- (§24.415) endings without any thematic vowel. Usually there is reduplication (with ι, cf. §24.3141), and if the stem ends in a short vowel, it is lengthened in the active voice in the singular (but not in the plural) forms. See Paradigm V-7a, Class-7a verbs.

§24.2811   Dissimilation of the reduplicated consonant follows the rules in §§13.21ff. and 13.22 *θιθημι > τίθημι, *σιστημι > ἵστημι.

§24.2812   Reduplication, if found in the present, is found in all moods, as well as in the infinitive, and the participle.

§24.2813   Lengthening of the stem vowel is found throughout the 2d aorist active indicative (not merely in the singular forms) and the short stem vowel is found throughout the middle/passive indicative and throughout the imperative.

§24.2814   In some verbs, the 2d aorist active indicative forms take the 1st perfect endings (κα, etc.). The plural forms are regular 2d aorist in classical but "kappa" aorist in Koinē.

§24.2815   If the 2d perfect occurs in μι-verbs, it is found only in the plural, the singular being formed according to the 1 perfect.

§24.2816   The thematic vowel (ω/η) does occur in the subjunctive mood of these (and all) verbs.

§24.282   Class-7b verbs form the present stem by adding -νυ (to a consonantal stem) or -ννυ (to a vocalic stem), to which are added the μι-endings. The present and the imperfect tenses are formed from this tense-voice stem. See Paradigm V-7b, Class-7b verbs.

§24.2821 Reduplication is not found in the present stem of Class-7b verbs.

§24.2822 The thematic vowel (ω/η) or diphthong (οι) are added to the -νυ-
infix before the inflectional endings to form the subjunctive and
optative moods, respectively.

§24.2823 Other tense-voice stems are formed in the regular manner, and
anomalies such as lengthened vowels or 1 perfect endings in
the 2 aorist are not found in Class-7b verbs.

§24.2824 Some -νυ- verbs develop as Class-5c verbs (§24.263). In Koinē
this is a marked trend.

§24.283 A number of fairly common verbs may be classified as irregular
μι-verbs: εἰμί 'be,' εἶμι 'go,' ἵημι 'send,' φήμι, 'say,
affirm,' ἧμαι, 'sit' (only in compounds), and κεῖμαι, 'lie.' The forms
of these verbs should be learned as they are encountered in reading.

§24.284 The entire category of Class-7 verbs is in transition in Koinē.
For discussion, cf. BDF §§92-100.

§24.29 Some grammarians include an additional class of verbs (which we
might designate Class-8 verbs) called "irregular" or "mixed,"
composed of verbs that form various tense-voice stems from basic verb stems
that are essentially different (cf. Eng. be, is, were; go, went; etc.).
These various stems will actually be listed as principal parts, and be found
in lexicons under the form of the first principal part. The following are
typical: pres. ὁράω (*ὁρα -), fut. ὄψομαι (*οπ -), 2 aor. εἶδον (*ϝιδ -),
'see'; pres. φέρω (*φερ -), fut. οἴσω (*οι -), 1 aor. ἤνεγκα (*ενεκ -), 'bear.'

§24.291 Except for the fact that teachers require recall of principal
parts, plus the fact that lexicons list such forms in ways that
would never be tolerated in an English dictionary, it would be far better
to learn each basic stem and its derivative stems as independent words.

§24.3   The formation of <u>the other tense-voice stems</u> is less complicated
         than that of the present stem. However, the significant details
should not be overlooked.

§24.31   Terminology that recurs in discussing tense-voice stems needs
         to be clearly understood.

§24.311 <u>Thematic</u> and <u>connecting vowels</u> are found in a number of tense-
         voice stems. The thematic vowels ο/ε have been discussed
(§24.221). Other connecting vowels are:

    ω/η used in all subjunctive forms

    α   used in 1 aor. act./mid. ind. and impv. stems
          and in 1 and 2 perf. act. ind. stems.

    ει used in 1 plpf. act. ind. tense

    οι used in all opt. tenses except 1 aor.

    αι used in 1 aor. act. and mid. opt. tenses

The latter two are usually called "mood suffixes."

§24.312 Certain <u>infixes</u> are used as tense-voice stem indicators:

    σ   used in fut. act./mid. and 1 aor. act./mid. stems and
          in future perfect middle tense.

    κ   used in 1 perf. act. stem and in the aor. of certain μι-verbs

  θε > θη used in 1 aor. pass. tense.

   ε > η   used in 2 aor. pass. tense.

   θης used in 1 fut. pass. tense.

    ης used in 2 fut. pass. tense.

§24.313 An <u>augment</u> is prefixed to the stem in forming the "secondary"
         tenses (§24.121), in the indicative mood only. The significance
of the augment is apparently related to the temporal element, since the
augment is not found in nonindicative moods and nonfinite forms. The
form of the augment is determined by the characteristics of the stem.

§24.3131 When the augment is prefixed to the tense-voice stem, it is
          known as a <u>syllabic augment</u> (since it adds a syllable). When
a vowel or diphthong is lengthened or modified it is known as a <u>temporal
augment</u> (since, at least in theory, the sound is thereby lengthened).

§24.3132 Verbs beginning with a consonant prefix ε- as a syllabic
          augment. The verb θέλω, however, prefixes an η-, and ἄγω
reduplicates: λέγω--ἔλεξα, θέλω--ἤθελεν, ἄγω--ἤγαγον.

§24.3133 Verbs beginning with ρ double the ρ when adding the syllabic
          augment. ῥώννυμι -- ἔρρωσθε.

§24.3134 Sometimes a syllabic augment is found before an initial vowel;
          we may assume that an initial ϝ or σ has dropped out. εἶδον <
          *εϝιδον, εἶχον < *εσεχον.

§24.3135 Verbs beginning with a vowel lengthen the vowel in accordance
          with §15.11 as a temporal augment. ἄρχομαι -- ἤρξατο, ἐρωτάω--
ἠρώτησα, *οπτομαι--ὤφθην, ἱκανόω--ἱκάνωσεν, ὑστερέω--ὑστερήσατε.

§24.3136 Verbs beginning with a diphthong generally lengthen the first
          vowel of the diphthong as temporal augment (αυ > ηυ, ευ > ηυ,
αι > η, ει > η, οι > ω). This rule, however, is often violated in Koinē:
εὗρον, εὐηγγελιζόμην, εἴξαμεν, ἐνείλησεν, οἰκοδόμησεν and ᾠκοδόμησεν,
and note εὐκαίρουν (Mk. 6:31) and ηὐκαίρουν (Ac. 17:21).

§24.3137 Compound verbs consisting of one or more prefixed prepositions
          and the stem, usually are augmented after the prefix and before
the stem: ὑποβάλλω--ὑπέβαλον. In some verbs, where the prepositional
nature of the prefix has been lost, the augment is placed before the prefix.
In a few cases, the augment is placed both before the preposition and before
the verb stem. Whenever an augment interposes between a preposition and a
stem, changes which had occurred (such as elision, assimilation, etc.) are
reversed: καθίστημι--κατέστησεν, ἐξέβαλον--ἐκβάλλω.

§24.3138 In some doubly compounded verbs, double augmentation is found:
          ἀντικαθίστημι -- ἀντεκατέστητε, ἀποκαθιστημι--ἀπεκατέστη.

§24.3139 The word ἀνοίγω is augmented in any of three ways: ἠνοίχθη
          (Ac. 12:10), ἀνεῴχθη (Lk. 1:64), and ἠνεῴχθη (Rev. 20:12).

§24.314   <u>Reduplication</u>, or the syllabic doubling of the initial sound of
             the verb stem, characterizes the perfect, pluperfect, and future
perfect, and occasionally is found in other tenses. Reduplication is found
<u>in all moods</u> of the finite verb and in the nonfinite forms. The significance
of reduplication seems to be related to the completed aspect of the pertinent
tenses. The form of reduplication is determined by characteristics of the
stem.

§24.3141 If the verb stem begins with a single consonant (except ρ), that
             consonant is repeated, followed by a vowel, to form a prefixed
syllable. For the perfect, pluperfect, and future perfect (and an
occasional aorist), the vowel is ε; for the present tense, the vowel is ι:
λείπω--λέλειμμαι, δίδωμι--δώσω.

§24.3142 Verbs with an initial aspirate (§12.322) dissimilate the
             reduplicative consonant in accordance with §13.24:   χρηματίζω--
κεχρημάτισμαι, φιμόω--πεφίμωσο, θεραπεύω--τεθεραπευμένος.

§24.3143 If the verb stem begins with a cluster (two consonants, including
             ζ, ξ, and ψ, but excluding any cluster composed of a stop and a
liquid), or ρ, a syllabic augment (§24.3131) takes the place of reduplication.
Such an augment is found in all moods of the finite verb and in the
infinitives and participles, and not merely in the indicative (cf. §24.313).
κτίζω--ἔκτισμαι, ζωγρέω--ἐζωγρημένος, ξηραίνω--ἐξήραμμαι, ψωριάω--ἐψωριακώς,
ῥίπτω--ἐῤῥιμένος, but ῥαντίζω--ῥεραντισμένος.

§24.3144 Sometimes initial λ is augmented in lieu of reduplication:
             λαμβάνω--εἴληφα.

§24.3145 Verbs beginning with a cluster of a stop and a liquid generally
             reduplicate the initial stop. However the combinations βλ and γλ
sometimes take the augment, and γν always does, in lieu of reduplication.
γράφω--γέγραφα, κλίνω--κέκλικα, but γι(γ)νώσκω--ἔγνωκα.

§24.3146 Verbs beginning with a short vowel lengthen the vowel, and
             verbs beginning with a diphthong may lengthen the first vowel
of the diphthong (cf. temporal augment, §24.3135) in lieu of reduplication.

§24.3147   Verbs beginning with a σ may dissimilate the reduplicated σ to rough breathing (§13.23): *σιστημι > ἵστημι, but σπείρω—ἔσπαρμαι and σῴζω—σέσωκα. Verbs which originally began with σ or ϝ, reduplicated in the normal way; subsequently, with the loss of σ or ϝ, the ε of reduplication that remained contracted with the vowel of the first syllable of the stem, or in some cases remained uncontracted: *ϝεϝωρακα > ἑώρακα, *ϝεϝ(ο)ιδα > οἶδα.

§24.3148   Some verbs, beginning with α, ε, or ο, followed by a single consonant, reduplicate by repeating both vowel and consonant lengthening the vowel in the syllable following the reduplication. This is often called "Attic reduplication": ἐγείρω—ἐγήγερμαι.

§24.3149   In compound verbs, reduplication follows the prepositional prefix, except for indirect compounds, compounds with δυσ-, and compounds that have come to be considered as single words (cf. §24.3137): ἐνεργέω—ἐνήργηκα, ἐπιπίπτω—ἐπιπέπτωκα, συμβάλλω—συμβέβληκα.

§24.315   <u>Vowel gradation</u>, or vocalic alteration, is a common feature in verb stems. It is of two kinds: <u>qualitative vowel gradation</u> (or Ablaut, §§15.4ff.), found in some stems in which the vowel or diphthong changes its basic quality from tense to tense (cf. English <u>ride</u>, <u>rode</u>, <u>ridden</u>; <u>sink</u>, <u>sank</u>, <u>sunk</u>, etc.); and <u>quantitative vowel gradation</u> ("strong" and "weak" forms, §§15.1ff.), found in some stems in which the vowel is found in lengthened (strong), normal (weak), and reduced (zero grade) forms, in various tenses (cf. Eng. <u>hide</u>, <u>hid</u>, <u>hidden</u>; <u>meet</u>, <u>met</u>, etc.).

§24.316   <u>Consonantal shifts</u>, assimilation, dissimilation, simplification, loss of consonant, etc., are common features in verbal forms. The student who has not paid attention to the sections listed under §12. and §13. of this Handbook will have unnecessary difficulty. Conversely, a basic familiarity with the elements of phonetics will help the student see that the verb is after all quite regular.

§24.317   The <u>inflectional endings</u> will be considered separately, in
           detail, in §24.4.

§24.32   The <u>future active/middle stem</u>, from which are derived the
           future active and future middle tenses, is formed by adding σ
and the thematic vowel ο/ε to stems ending in a vowel or a stop consonant.
λυ + σ + ο + μεν > λύσομεν.

§24.321   A short stem vowel is lengthened, ᾰ (except after ε, ι, or ρ)
           > η, ε > η, and ο > ω: φιλέω > φιλήσετε.

§24.322   Verbs with vowel gradation (strong and weak forms) have the
           strong form in the future stem.

§24.323   Stems ending in -λ, -μ, -ν, or -ρ add εσ and the thematic vowel;
           the σ drops out (§13.361), and the ε contracts with the thematic
vowel (cf. §24.223). *αγγελ + έσ + ω > *αγγελέω > ἀγγελῶ.

§24.324   The "Attic" future, in which the σ drops out and the juxtaposed
           vowels contract (καλέσω > καλῶ) is generally not found in NT
Greek. It is found in LXX and in NT quotations from LXX: μετοικιῶ
(Ac. 7:43), παροργιῶ (Rom. 10:19), and in a few other verbs: καθαριεῖ
(Hb. 9:14), φωτιεῖ and φωτίσει, etc.

§24.325   Similarly, the "Doric" future, which forms the future stem by
           adding -σε + ο/ε, with contraction but without syncopating the
σ, is generally not found in NT Greek.

§24.326   Stems in -ευ which drop υ in the present (Class-2b verbs §24.232),
           usually retain the υ in forming the future stem: ῥέω-ῥεύσω.

§24.327   Three verbs have no morphological indication of the future: χέω
           (pres. and fut.), ἔδομαι (pres. ἐσθίω), and πίομαι (pres. πίνω).
cf. Smyth §541. For the fut. χεῶ in LXX and NT, cf. Robertson p.354.

§24.33   The <u>first aorist active/middle stem</u>, from which are derived the
              1 aorist active and 1 aorist middle tenses, is formed by adding σ
to stems ending in a vowel or a stop consonant. For the indicative mood,
an augment (§24.313ff.) is generally prefixed. (Grammars generally indicate
that the aorist infix is σα. It is better, however, to look upon the α as
part of the ending, in view of the 3 sing. form). ε + λυ + σ + α + μεν > ἐλύσαμεν.

§24.331   A short vowel in the stem is generally lengthened as in §24.321:
              ποιέω-εποίησα.

§24.332   Verbs with vowel gradation (§24.315) have the strong form in the
              1 aorist: πείθω, 1 aor. ἔπεισα, 2 aor. ἔπιθον.

§24.333   Stems ending in -λ, -μ, -ν, or -ρ drop σ and lengthen their
              last vowel in the stem (α to η, except after ε, ι, or ρ; ε to η;
o to ω): στέλλω-ἔστειλα, εὐφραίνω-ηὔφρανα.

§24.334   Three μι-verbs (Class 7a, §24.281) have "kappa" aorists, i.e.,
              forms like the 1 perfect, in the 1 aor. act. ind. These are
ἔδωκα, ἧκα, and ἔθεκα. The 2 aorist forms occur elsewhere.

§24.3341   In Koinē, the κ is found in plural forms also; in classical it
              is confined to the singular (BDF §95(1)).

§24.34   The <u>second aorist active/middle stem</u>, from which are derived the
              2 aorist active and 2 aorist middle tenses, is formed from the basic
verb stem (§24.11) and the thematic vowel o/ε. In the indicative mood, an
augment (§24.313) is generally prefixed. ε + λιπ + o + μεν > ἐλίπομεν.

§24.341   Verbs with vowel gradation almost without exception have the
              weak form in the 2 aorist. φεύγω-ἔφυγον.

§24.3411   In a number of forms, the stem vowel reduces to zero (§24.315).
              *εσεχον > ἔσχον.

§24.342   Almost all verbs with thematic vowel in the 2 aorist formations
          are derived from consonantal stems. A notable exception is ἔπιον
(pres. πίνω, stem *πι -).

§24.3421 A number of ω-verbs form the 2 aorist without a thematic vowel.
          These are all vowel stems (i.e., stems ending in a vowel).
          βαίνω-ἔβην γινώσκω-ἔγυων.

§24.343   The μι-verbs (§24.281) regularly form the 2 aorist without a
          thematic vowel. In addition, the stem vowel is sometimes
lengthened. ἵστημι-ἔστην.

§24.3431 In the subjunctive and the optative of μι-verbs, the stem
          vowel contracts with the thematic vowel or mood infix.

§24.35   The <u>first perfect active stem</u>, from which are derived the 1
          perfect active and 1 pluperfect active and future perfect
active tenses, is formed by adding κ to the reduplicated (§24.314) stem.
In the indicative mood, an augment may be prefixed to the reduplicated
stem when forming the 1 pluperfect active tense. The infixes are
usually given as κα for the 1 perfect and κει for the 1 pluperfect. Since
different sets of endings are used, it is better to consider the vowels
as part of the endings. λε + λυ + κ + α + μεν > λελύκαμεν, ε + δε +
δω + κ + ειν > ἐδεδώκειν

§24.351   In general, 1 perfect stems are formed from vowel stems (with
          lenghtening of short vowels, ποιέω-πεποίηκα). Some consonantal
stems add a vowel (α/ε > η) to the basic stem (εἴρω-εἴρηκα).

§24.352   In stems with vowel gradation (§24.315), the strong form is
          usually found in the 1 perfect active stem. πείθω, 1 perf.
πέπεικα, 2 perf. πέποιθα.

§24.353   Many liquid stems have no perfect, or use a 2 perfect.

§24.3531 A few nasal stems drop -ν before adding κ: κρίνω-κέκρικα.

§24.3532 Monosyllabic liquid stems usually change the stem vowel to α:
          *στελ > ἔσταλκα, *τελ > τέταλκα.

§24.3533 Some liquid stems either reduce the stem vowel to zero grade
          and add a vowel to the stem or metathesize the stem vowel before
adding the κ. In some grammars these are described as developing from an
original disyllabic root. *βαλ-/*βαλε- > *βλη-: βέβληκα.

§24.354   Dental stems drop the δ, τ, or θ before adding κ: *θαυμαδ- >
          τεθαύμακα.

§24.355   The future perfect probably does not occur in the NT. The form
          ἐκέκραξα (Ac. 24:20) seems to be a secondary development of a
present κέκραγα (Jn. 1:15), originally a perfect of κράζω (A-G p. 448,
BDF §101).

§24.36   The <u>second perfect active stem</u>, from which are derived the 2
          perfect active and 2 pluperfect active tenses, is formed by
reduplicating (§24.314) the stem, which is almost without exception a
consonantal stem. In forming the 2 pluperfect active indicative, an
augment (§24.313) may be prefixed to the reduplicated stem. The connecting vowel (α in 2 perf., ει in 2 plpf.) may better be considered as part
of the ending. πε + ποιθ + α + μεν > πεποίθαμεν, ε + πε + ποιθ + ει + ν >
ἐπέποιθειν.

§24.361   In Classical Greek, the connecting vowel does not occur between
          the 2 perfect stem and the ending in μι-verbs and a number of
ω-verbs. This rule seems to be inoperative in NT Greek.

§24.362   Stems with qualitative vowel gradation (Ablaut, §24.315) often
          have the stem form with ο in the 2 perfect active stem.
          τρέφω-τέτροφα, *γεν- > γέγονα.

§24.363   Stems with quantitative vowel gradation (strong and weak forms,
           §24.315) generally have strong forms in the 2 perfect active
stem. λείπω-λέλοιπα, πείθω-πέποιθα.

§24.364   Stems ending in labial stops usually undergo consonantal change
           to the aspirated labial (φ), and stems ending in velar stops
usually undergo change to the aspirated velar (χ). λέγω-εἴλοχα,
κόπτω-κέκοφα.

§24.37   The <u>perfect middle stem</u>, from which are derived the perfect
           middle (and passive), the pluperfect middle (and passive), and
the future perfect middle tenses, is formed by reduplicating the stem
(§24.314). In forming the pluperfect middle indicative, an augment
(§24.313) may be prefixed to the reduplicated stem. There is no connecting vowel between the stem and the inflectional endings. λε + λυ + μαι >
λέλυμαι, γε + γραφ + μαι > γέγραμμαι.

§24.371   Finite forms of the future perfect (which is also derived from
           the perfect middle stem) do not occur in the NT, and participial
forms occur but rarely. We note merely that the σ and the thematic ο/ε
of the future stem are added to the reduplicated stem to form the future
perfect.

§24.3711   The form κεκράξομαι (< κε + κραγ + σ + ο + μαι) is fut. perf. in
           form, but is probably a secondary future formed from a secondary
present κέκραγα (cf. §24.355).

§24.38   The <u>first passive stem</u>, from which are derived the 1 future
           passive and 1 aorist passive tenses, is formed by adding the
infix (or tense-voice stem indicator) θε to the normal or modified verbal
stem. In general, the form of the verbal stem will be like that of the
perfect middle stem (§24.37), with lengthened final vowel (if a vowel
stem), or the weak grade (if a stem with vowel gradation), or the zero
grade with long vowel added to the stem.

§24.381   The presence of θ in juxtaposition with the stem will cause
consonantal alteration in line with §§13.112, .113, .15, and .21.

§24.382   The <u>1 future passive tense</u> stem is formed by lengthening θε to θη
(in ind., impv., inf.), and adding σ. For the indicative, the
thematic vowel o/ε is added to this stem, for optative οι, for infinitive ε,
and for participle o, plus the appropriate endings. λυ + θη + σ + ο + μεθα >
λυθησόμεθα.

§24.383   The <u>1 aorist passive indicative tense</u> stem is formed by lengthening θε to θη (in ind., impv., inf.), and prefixing the augment
(§24.313). In other moods except the imperative and in the participle θε
does not lengthen except through contraction with a vowel of the sufformative.
ε + λυ + θη + μεν > ἐλύθημεν.

§24.39   The <u>second passive stem</u>, from which are derived the 2 future
passive and 2 aorist passive tenses, is formed by adding ε to
the verb stem. Stems with qualitative vowel gradation (§24.315) usually
have α in this tense-voice stem.

§24.391   The <u>2 future passive</u> stem lengthens ε to η, adds σ, and then
follows the pattern of the 1 future passive described above
(§24.382). αλλαγ + η + σ + ο + μαι > ἀλλαγήσομαι.

§24.392   The <u>2 aorist passive</u> stem develops exactly like the 1 aorist
passive stem (§24.383) except that θ is omitted in the second
passive stem.

§24.4   A detailed study of the <u>inflectional endings</u> is necessary.

§24.41   The <u>indicative</u> inflectional endings (except for the μι-verb,
which is treated separately in §24.47) are usually divided in
"primary" and "secondary," with active and middle/passive forms in each
catetory. This division is not fully satisfactory, hence we have added to it.

§24.411　　The <u>primary active indicative</u> (ω-endings) are:

1s	--	1p	-μεν
2s	-ες	2p	-τε
3s	-ε	3p	-νσι

In 3p note that ν assimilates to σ, then simplifies, with compensatory lengthening (§13.134).

§24.4111　To form the <u>present active indicative</u> tense, the ω-endings
　　　　　(§24.411) are added to the present stem (§24.2ff.) with the
thematic vowel ο/ε serving as a connecting vowel, as follows:

1s --- + ο + - > -ω		1p --- + ο + μεν > -ομεν	
2s --- + ε + ες > -εις		2p --- + ε + τε > -ετε	
3s --- + ε + ε > -ει		3p --- + ο + νσι > -ουσι	

In 1s the vowel lengthens normally (ο > ω). In 3p the vowel undergoes compensatory lengthening (ο > ου).

§24.4112　　If there is a stem vowel (§20.34), it contracts with the con-
　　　　　tracted (resultant) endings given in §24.4111, as follows:

with α		with ε		with ο	
1s ---α + ω > -ῶ		---ε + ω > -ῶ		---ο + ω > -ῶ	
2s ---α + εις > -ᾶς		---ε + εις > -εῖς		---ο + εις > -οῖς	
3s ---α + ει > -ᾷ		---ε + ει > -εῖ		---ο + ει > -οῖ	
1p ---α + ομεν > -ῶμεν		---ε + ομεν > -οῦμεν		---ο + ομεν > -οῦμεν	
2p ---α + ετε > -ᾶτε		---ε + ετε > -εῖτε		---ο + ετε > -οῦτε	
3p ---α + ουσι > -ῶσι		---ε + ουσι > -οῦσι		---ο + ουσι > -οῦσι	

§24.4113　　To form the <u>future active indicative</u> tense, the ω-endings
　　　　　(§24.411) are added to the future active/middle stem (§24.32)
with contraction of the connecting vowel as in 24.4111, as follows:

1s	-σω	1p	-σομεν
2s	-σεις	2p	-σετε
3s	-σει	3p	-σουσι

§24.4114　When the σ elides, as in Class-4e (liquid) verbs (§24.2555), the
　　　　　resulting contraction is the same as with ε in §24.4112.

§24.4115 Stems that end in any consonant that unites with σ to form a
          double consonant (ξ, ψ, cf. §§13.141, .143) will alter the form
of the endings in §24.4113 accordingly. λεγ + σω > λέξω, γραφ + σω > γράψω.

§24.412   The <u>secondary active indicative</u> endings (ν-endings) are:

1s	-ν	1p	-μεν
2s	-ς	2p	-τε
3s	--	3p	-ν /-σαν

§24.4121 To form the <u>imperfect active indicative</u> tense, the ν-endings are
          added to the present stem (§24.2ff.), with augment (§24.313),
and with the thematic (connecting) vowel, as follows:

1s --- + o + ν > -ον	1p --- + o + μεν > -ομεν
2s --- + ε + ς > -ες	2p --- + ε + τε > -ετε
3s --- + ε + - > -ε	3p --- + o + ν > -ον

§24.4122 If the stem of the verb ends in a vowel, contraction will take
          place as follows:

with α			with ε			with o		
1s —α + ον > -ων			—ε + ον > -ουν			—o + ον > -ουν		
2s —α + ες > -ας			—ε + ες > -εις			—o + ες > -ους		
3s —α + ε > -α			—ε + ε > -ει			—o + ε > -ου		
1p —α + ομεν > -ῶμεν			—ε + ομεν > -οῦμεν			—o + ομεν > -οῦμεν		
2p —α + ετε > -ᾶτε			—ε + ετε > -εῖτε			—o + ετε > -οῦτε		
3p —α + ον > -ων			—ε + ον > -ουν			—o + ον > -ουν		

§24.4123 To form the <u>2 aorist active indicative</u> tense, the ν-endings
          (§24.412) are added to the basic verbal stem (§24.11), with
the augment (§24.313) and the thematic vowel. The forms will be like
the imperfect (§24.4121).

§24.413   To form certain "secondary" tenses, the secondary active endings
          (§24.412) undergo modification at three places. It therefore
seems preferable to regard these as a separate category, which we designate

α-endings, as follows (the α can be viewed as a connecting vowel):

1s	-α	1p	-αμεν
2s	-ας	2p	-ατε
3s	-ε	3p	-αν / -ασι

§24.4131 To form the <u>1 aorist active indicative</u> tense, the α-endings are
        added to the 1 aorist active/middle stem (§24.33), as follows:

1s	- σα	1p	-σαμεν
2s	- σας	2p	-σατε
3s	- σε	3p	-σαν

§24.4132 Liquid stems (Class 4e, §§24.255ff.) elide σ, but otherwise
        retain the 1 aor. act. ind. endings.

§24.4133 If the verb stem ends in a labial, dental, or velar stop, the
        rules of consonantal shift (§§13.131, .142, .143) apply. See
Paradigms: V-1, V-3, V-4.

§24.4134 To form the <u>1 perfect active indicative</u> tense, the α-endings
        (§24.413) are added to the 1 perfect active stem (§24.35),
as follows:

1s	-κα	1p	-καμεν
2s	-κας	2p	-κατε
3s	-κε	3p	-καν / -κασι

§24.4135 To form the <u>2 perfect active indicative</u> tense, the α-endings
        (§24.413) are added to the 2 perfect active stem (§24.36). The
forms are like the 1 perf. act. ind:, with κ omitted.

§24.414   Likewise the secondary active endings when added to the 1 perfect
        active stem (§24.35) to form the <u>1 pluperfect active indicative</u>
tense take somewhat different forms. Hence it is better to learn these
endings separately (the ειν-endings), which are:

1s	-κειν	1p	-κειμεν
2s	-κεις	2p	-κειτε
3s	-κει	3p	-κεισαν

§24.4141   To form the <u>2 pluperfect active indicative</u>, the same endings are
used as for the 1 pluperfect active indicative, except that the κ
is omitted.

§24.415   The primary middle/passive indicative endings (μαι-endings) are:

1s	-μαι	1p	-μεθα
2s	-σαι	2p	-σθε
3s	-ται	3p	-νται

§24.4151   To form the <u>present middle/passive indicative</u> tense, the μαι-endings
are added to the present stem (§24.2ff.) with the thematic vowel
(ο/ε) serving as a connecting vowel, as follows:

1s —— + ο + μαι > -ομαι   1p —— + ο + μεθα > -όμεθα

2s —— + ε + σαι > -ῃ   2p —— + ε + σθε > -εσθε

3s —— + ε + ται > -εται   3p —— + ο + νται   -ονται

In 2s σ elides (§13.161) and ε+αι contracts to ῃ.

§24.4152   In verbs with stems ending in a short vowel, contraction of the
stem vowel with the connecting vowel produces the following forms:

	with α	with ε	with ο
1s	—α + ομαι > -ῶμαι	—ε + ομαι > -οῦμαι	—ο + ομαι > -οῦμαι
2s	—α + ῃ > -ᾷ	—ε + ῃ > -ῇ/-εῖ	—ο + ῃ -οῖ
3s	—α + εται > -ᾶται	—ε + εται > -εῖται	—ο + εται > -οῦται
1p	—α + όμεθα > -ώμεθα	—ε + όμεθα > -ούμεθα	—ο + όμεθα > -ούμεθα
2p	—α + εσθε > -ᾶσθε	—ε + εσθε > -εῖσθε	—ο + εσθε > -οῦσθε
3p	—α + ονται > -ῶνται	—ε + ονται > -οῦνται	—ο + ονται > -οῦνται

§24.4153   To form the <u>future middle indicative</u>, the μαι-endings are added to
the future active/middle stem (§24.32). The inflectional endings
will be like those in §24.4151, with σ before the connecting vowel. Liquid
stems (Class 4e, §24.255) and other forms that drop σ will contract, resulting
in forms like those with ε in §24.4152. λυ + σ + ε + ται > λύσεται.

§24.4154   To form the <u>1 future passive indicative</u> tense, the μαι-endings
are added to the 1 future passive stem (§24.382). The inflectional

endings will be like those in §24.4151, preceded by the 1 passive infix θη
and the future infix σ. λυ + θη + σ + ο + μαι > λυθήσομαι.

§24.4155 To form the 2 future passive indicative tense, the μαι-endings are
            added to the 2 future passive stem (§24.391). The inflectional
endings will be like those of §24.4151, preceded by the 2 passive infix η and
the future infix σ. γραφ + η + σ + ο + μαι > γραφήσομαι.

§24.4156 To form the perfect middle/passive indicative tense, the μαι-
            endings §24.415 are added to the perfect middle stem (§24.37)
without connecting vowel. The endings are like the endings in §24.415 unless
the stem consonant causes a consonantal shift (notably in 2s where labial
and velar stops develop ψ/ξ [§13.141, .143] and in 2p where they become
φ/χ and σ drops out).   γε + γραφ + μαι > γέγραμμαι.
τέταξαι. τέταχθε.

§24.416   The secondary middle/passive indicative endings (μην-endings) are:
                        1s -μην   1p -μεθα
                        2s -σο   2p -σθε
                        3s -το   3p -ντο

§24.4161 To form the imperfect middle/passive indicative tense, the μην-
            endings (§24.416) are added to the present stem (§§24.2ff.),
with the augment (§24.313) and the ο/ε connecting vowel, as follows:
        1s —— + ο + μην > -ομνη   1p —— + ο + μεθα > -όμεθα
        2s —— + ε + σο > -ου   2p —— + ε + σθε > -εσθε
        3s —— + ε + το > -ετο   3p —— + ο + ντο > -οντο
In 2s intervocalic σ falls out and ε+ο contracts to ου.

§24.4162 To form the 2 aorist middle indicative tense, the μην-endings
            (§24.416) are added to the basic verbal stem (§24.11), with
augment and thematic vowel. The forms will look like those of the impf.
mid./pass. ind. (§24.4161). ε + λιπ + ε + σθε > ἐλίπεσθε.

§24.4163 To form the <u>1 aorist middle indicative</u> tense, the μην-endings
           (§24.416) are added to the 1 aorist active/middle stem (§24.33),
with augment and α-connecting vowel, as follows:

1s —— + σα + μην > -σαμην	1p —— + σα + μεθα > -σάμεθα
2s —— + σα + σο > -σω	2p —— + σα + σθε > -σασθε
3s —— + σα + το > -σατο	3p —— + σα + ντο > -σαντο

In 2s the intervocalic σ drops out (§13.161) and α+o > ω.

§24.4164 In verbs with vowel stems, or liquid stems in the 1 aorist, or
           any other form where σ drops out, or for any other reason the
stem vowel is brought into contact with the connecting vowel, contraction
will normally take place (§15.316). ε + φην + σα + σο > ἐφήνω,
ε + φην + σα + σθε > ἐφήνασθε.

§24.4165 To form the <u>pluperfect middle/passive indicative</u> tense, the μην-
           endings (§24.416) are added to the perfect middle stem (§24.37)
without connecting vowel. The endings are like the secondary middle
endings given in §24.416. The presence of labial or velar stops in the
stem has the same effect as described in §24.4154. ε + λε + λυ + μην >
ἐλελύμην.

§24.417   The <u>passive stem</u>, it should be noted, adds the secondary <u>active</u>
           indicative endings (§24.412) to form the <u>aorist passive indicative</u>
tenses.

§24.4171 To form the <u>1 aorist passive indicative</u> tense, the ν-endings
           (§24.412) are added to the 1 aorist passive stem (§24.38), as
follows:

1s —— + θη + ν > -θην	1p —— + θη + μεν > -θημεν
2s —— + θη + ς > -θης	2p —— + θη + τε > -θητε
3s —— + θη + - > -θη	3p —— + θη + σαν > -θησαν

Note the 3p form. It should also be observed that θ influences the final
consonants of consonantal stems in accordance with phonetic rules (see
§§13.111, .112, .113). (ε) + αγ + θη + ν > ἤχθην.

§24.4172 To form the <u>2 aorist passive indicative</u> tense the ν-endings are
           added to the 2 aorist passive stem (§24.392). The forms are like
those of the 1 aor. pass. ind. (§24.4171), except that θ is absent in 2 aor.
pass. ε + λιπ + η + ν > ἐλίπην.

§24.42   In the <u>subjunctive mood</u>, there is no differentiation between primary
           and secondary tenses. All active endings are of "primary" active
type, and all middle endings are of "primary" middle type. The aorist passive
regularly takes active endings in all moods.

§24.421   The inflectional endings for <u>all active subjunctive tenses</u>, and for
           the <u>aorist passive subjunctive</u> tense, are lengthened endings of the
pres. act. ind. (§24.4111). Usually these are described as being formed from
the primary active endings (§24.411) plus the thematic vowel ω/η. However,
this fails to account for the iota subscript in 2s and 3s.

1s	-ω	1p	-ωμεν
2s	-ῃς	2p	-ητε
3s	-ῃ	3p	-ωσι

§24.422   The inflectional endings for <u>all middle/passive subjunctive</u> tenses
           (except the aor. pass. sbjtv. which takes the aor. pass. infin. and
active endings) are the μαι-endings (§24.415) added to the thematic ω/η vowel.

1s	-ωμαι	1p	-ώμεθα
2s	-ῃ	2p	-ησθε
3s	-ηται	3p	-ωνται

§24.43   The <u>optative</u> endings do not distinguish primary and secondary
           tenses. They do distinguish active and middle voices.

§24.431   The sufformatives of the all <u>active optative</u> tenses are:

singular		plural	
1s	-μι	1p	-μεν
2s	-ς	2p	-τε
3s	--	3p	-εν

The connecting vowel (diphthong) for present, future, 2 aorist, 1 and 2 perfect is οι. The connecting diphthong for 1 aorist is αι. λυ + οι + μι > λύοιμι, λυ + σ + αι + μι > λύσαιμι.

§24.432   The sufformatives of all middle/passive optative tenses (except aor. pass. opt.) are the μην–endings (§24.416). In 2s inter-vocalic σ drops out. The connecting diphthongs are οι in all tenses except 1 aorist, and αι in 1 aor. λυ + οι + μην > λυοίμην, λυ + σ + αι + μην > λυσαίμην.

§24.433   The 1 aorist passive optative endings are the same as those of 2 aor. pass. ind. (ν-endings added to η, §24.412), and the connecting diphthong is ει added to the θ of the 1 aor. pass. stem. λυ + θ + ει + η + ν > λυθείην.

§24.44   The endings of the imperative mood are in some ways the most difficult to reduce to a system. One presentation of the basic forms is as follows:

	active singular		active plural
1s	None	1p	None
2s	–θι	2p	–τε
3s	–τω	3p	–ντων/–τωσαν

	middle/passive singular		middle/passive plural
1s	None	1p	None
2s	–σο	2p	–σθε
3s	–σθω	3p	–σθων/–σθωσαν

§24.441   In the present and 2 aorist active imperative, the sufformatives are added to the thematic vowel ο/ε, as follows:

	singular		plural
2s	–ε	2p	–ετε
3s	–ετω	3p	–οντων/–ετωσαν

Note that in 2s no ending is used, and the thematic vowel is left as a final vowel.

§24.442   In the <u>1 aorist active imperative</u>, the endings are added to σ and
            the connecting vowel α:

singular	plural
2s -σον	2p -σατε
3s -σατω	3p -σαντων/-σατωσαν

Note the very irregular 2s form.

§24.443   In the <u>present middle/passive</u> and <u>2 aorist middle imperative</u> the
            endings added to the thematic vowel are:

singular	plural
2s ε + σο > -ου	2p -εσθε
3s -έσθω	3p -έσθων/-έσθωσαν

In 2s intervocalic σ drops out, and ε + o contract to ου.

§24.444   In the <u>1 aorist middle imperative</u> the endings are added to σ and
            the connecting vowel α:

singular	plural
2s -σαι	2p -σασθε
3s -σασθω	3p -σασθων/-σασθωσαν

Note the irregular 2s form.

§24.445   The <u>aorist passive imperative</u> endings are the active forms. The
            following endings are used:

1 aorist passive imperative		2 aorist passive imperative	
singular	plural	singular	plural
2s -θητι	2p -θητε	2s -ηθι	2p -ητε
3s -θητω	3p -θεντων/-θητωσαν	3s -ητω	3p -εντων/-ητωσαν

Note the application of §13.212 in 2s form.

§24.45   The <u>active infinitive</u> endings are:

present--	pres. stem	+ o/ε + εν	> -ειν
future--	fut. stem	+ σ + o/ε + εν	> - σειν
2 aorist--	basic stem	+ o/ε + εν	> - ειν
1 aorist--	1 aor.stem + σ + α	+ ι	> - σαι
1 perfect--	1 pf.stem + κ + ε	+ ναι	> - κεναι
μι-verbs	tense-stem	+ ναι	

The <u>aorist passive infinitive</u> takes active ending:

1 aor. pass.	1 pass. stem + θη + ναι > -θηναι
2 aor. pass.	2 pass. stem + η + ναι > -ηναι

§24.451   The middle/passive infinitive endings (except aorist passive) are:

present--	pres. stem	+ ε + σθαι > -εσθαι
future--	fut. stem	+ σ + ε + σθαι > -σεσθαι
2 aorist--	basic stem	+ ε + σθαι > -εσθαι
1 aorist--	1 aor. mid. stem	+ σ + α + σθαι > -σασθαι
perfect--	perf. mid. stem	+ σθαι > -σθαι
future perf. pass.--	perf. mid. stem	+ σ + ε + σθαο > -σεσθαι
future pass.--	1 pass stem	+ θη + σ + ε + σθαι > -θησεσθαι
μι-verbs	tense-stem	+ σθαι

§24.46   The <u>participle</u> endings have been discussed under adjective morphology
(§§22.32ff.), which should be studied carefully (see also §21.512ff.).
In order to bring them into one place, we merely tabularize them here.

§24.461   The <u>active participle</u> endings are as follows:

present act.	pres. stem	+ ο + ντ >	-ων	-ουσα -ον
pres. μι-verb	pres. stem	+ ντ >	-ς[1]	-σα[1] -ν[1]
future act.	fut. stem	+ σ + ο + ντ >	-σων	-σουσα -σον
1 aorist act.	1 aor. stem	+ σ + α + ντ >	-σας	-σασα -σαν
2 aorist act.	2 aorist stem	+ ο[2] + ντ >	-ών[2]	-οῦσα[2] -όν[2]
1 perfect act.	1 perf. stem	+·κ + Ϝο + τς >	-κώς	-κυῖα -κός
2 perfect act.	2 perf. stem	+ Ϝο + τς >	-ώς	-υῖα -ός

[1]Note absence of connecting vowel. As a result we find three types of vocal-
ization: διδούς-διδοῦσα-διδόν, ἱστάς-ἱστᾶσα-ἱστάν, and τιθείς-τιθεῖσα-
τιθέν. [2]μι-verbs omit connecting vowel with results as in note 1.

§24.462   The <u>middle</u> and <u>passive participle</u> endings are as follows:

			m(2)	f(1)	n(2)
pres. m./p.	pres. stem	+ ο[1] + μεν[2] >	-όμενος	-ομένη	-όμενον
fut. mid.	fut. stem	+ σ + ο + μεν[2] >	-σόμενος	-σομένη	-σόμενον
1 aor. mid.	1 aor. stem	+ σ + α + μεν[2] >	-σάμενος	-σαμένη	-σάμενον

			m(3)	f(1)	n(3)
2 aor. mid.	2 aor. stem	+ o[1] + μεν[2]> -όμενος	-ομένη	-όμενον	
perf. m./p.	2 perf. stem	+ μεν[2]> -μένος	-μένη	-μένον	
fut. pass.	passive stem + θησ + ο + μεν[2]> -θησόμενος	-θησομένη	-θησόμενον		

	m(3)	f(1)	n(3)

1 aor. pass.	1 pass. stem + θε + - + ντς > -θείς	-θεῖσα	-θέν	
2 aor. pass.	2 pass. stem + ε + - + ντς -είς	-εῖσα	-έν	

[1]With the μι-verbs the connecting vowel is not used.

[2]With adjective endings -ος, -η, -ον.

§24.47   The inflectional endings of the μι-verb (Class-7 verbs,
          §24.28) need to be learned only where they differ from the
ω-verb, namely in the present, imperfect, and 2 aorist tenses, and in
the absence of the thematic or connecting vowel in several other forms.

§24.471   The "primary" (nonaugmented) active μι-endings are as follows
           (cf. §24.411):

          singular   plural
          1s -μι   1p -μεν
          2s -ς   2p -τε
          3s -σι (< -τι)   3p -ασι (< -αντι)

§24.4711 These endings are added directly to a vowel-stem (i.e., a
          stem ending in α, ε, or o), usually with lengthening of
the stem vowel to form the <u>present active indicative</u> tense: δι + δο + μι
> δίδωμι, τι + θε + ασι > τιθέασι   (cf. §24.281).

§24.4712 With stems ending in a consonant, ι, υ, and some ending in
          α, ε, or o, the syllable -νυ (or -ννυ after a vowel) is
added to the stem before adding the ending (Class-7-b verbs, cf. §24.282):
δεικ + νυ + μι > δείκνυμι, σβε + ννυ + μι > σβέννυμι.

§24.4713 Irregular μι-verbs, such as εἰμί, εἶμι, etc., must be learned
          as they appear.

§24.472   The "secondary" (augmented) active endings of the μι-verbs
are as follows (cf. §24.412):

singular		plural	
1s	–ν	1p	–μεν
2s	–ς	2p	–τε
3s	––	3s	–σαν (Note!)

§24.4721   These endings are generally added directly to the present stem
(§24.2, .28) to form the <u>imperfect active indicative</u> tense, and
to the basic stem (§24.11) to form the <u>2 aorist active indicative</u> tense.
Augments are used according to the rules given (§24.313). ε + τι + θε + ν >
ἐτίθην, ε + δι + δο + ε > ἐδίδουν (the thematic vowel appears in some
impf. forms); ε + στα + ν > ἔστην.

§24.4722   Some aorists, listed as "2 aorist," infix κ and use the α-endings
(§24.413): ε + δο + κ + α > ἔδωκα (cf. §24.334). We refer to
these as "kappa aorists" rather than "second aorists," since they use the
1 aor. endings.

§24.473   The "primary" (nonaugmented) middle/passive endings are the same
as given for the ω-verb (§24.415). However, in the 2 sing. form,
intervocalic σ does not drop: τι + θε + σαι > τίθεσαι.

§24.474   The "secondary" (augmented) middle/passive endings are the same
as given for the ω-verb (§24.416). However, in the 2 sing. form,
intervocalic σ does not drop: ε + δι + δο + σο > ἐδίδοσο.

§24.475   The imperative endings of the μι-verbs are basically the same
as those given in §24.44, without any connecting vowel.

§24.4751 The pres.act.impv. endings of μι-verbs are those given in §24.44,
         except in 2 sg., which often substitutes -ε (cf. the ω-verb pres.
act.impv. 2 sg., §24.441) for -θι, cf. δι·δο·ε > δίδου, τι·θε·ε > τίθει,
ι·στη·ε (for *σι·στη·ε) > ἵστη.

§24.4752 The pres. mid./pass. impv. endings are those given in §24.44,
         without any connecting vowel.

§24.4753 The 2 aor.act.impv. endings of μι-verbs are those given in §24.44,
         except in 2 sg., where -ς often occurs instead of -θι (cf. the
ω-verb, §24.412), cf. δο·ς > δός, θε·ς > θές, but στη·θι > στῆθι.

§24.4754 The 2 aor.mid.impv. endings are those given in §24.44, without
         any connecting vowel; hence δο·σο > δο·ο (§13.361) > δοῦ, θε·σο >
θε·ο > θοῦ.

§24.4755 The 2 aor.pass.impv. endings are the active endings given in
         §24.44 (cf. §24.417), without connecting vowel, and with the
application of §13.241; hence δο·θε·θι > δόθητι.

§24.48   The inflectional endings, omitting the nonfinite forms, may be
         tabularized as follows. Note that memorizing of this table with-
out understanding all the preceding explanations will be quite insufficient
for recognizing many forms.

	Primary			Secondary			Imperative		Sbjtv.	Opt.
	Active		Middle	Active		Middle	Active	Middle		
	§24.411	§24.471	§24.415	§24.412	§24.413	§24.416	§24.44	§24.44	§24.421	§24.431
1s	-ω	-μι	-μαι	-ν	-α	-μην			-ω	-μι
2s	-ες[1]	-ς	-σαι	-ς	-ας	-σο[3]	-θι[4]	-σο[3]	-ης	-ς
3s	-ε[1]	-σι	-ται	—	-ε	-το	-τω	-σθω	-η	–
1p	-μεν[1]	-μεν	-μεθα	-μεν	-αμεν	-μεθα			-ωμεν	-μεν
2p	-τε[1]	-τε	-σθε	-τε	-ατε	-σθε	-τε	-σθε	-ντε	-τε
3p	-νσι[2]	-ασι	-νται	{ -ν / -σαν }	{ -αν / -ασι }	-ντο	{ -ντων / -τωσαν }	{ -σθων / -σθωσαν }	-ωσι	-τε

[1] Normally with ο/ε connecting vowel; contraction where applicable.

[2] After connecting vowel > ουσι.

[3] Intervocalic σ usually drops and contraction occurs.

[4] Impv. 2s develops very irregularly.

§25.   Word formation is a highly complex subject, and we intend here to give but a few points that may be of help to the beginner. Advanced students should consult the numerous specialized works. In many cases it is well to keep in mind that there is much baseless theory, and in older works this is often fanciful. It seems reasonable to suppose that the concrete came before the abstract, and that elementary nouns and verbs preceded other developments in language.

§25.1   Greek words can usually be traced to a stem, and sometimes this can be traced to a root to which other stems, verbal and nominal, can also be traced. Some developments of the stem we have already seen in verb classification (cf. §24.11ff.). Thus γίνομαι (< *γιγενομαι) is from the stem *γεν which is related to a root *γ-ν, with Ablaut, as the following cognate words indicate: γενέα generation, γένεσις origin, birth, γονεύς parent, γένος race, kind, γεννάω beget, γενετή birth, γενέσια birthday, γέννεμα fruit, γνήσιος true-born, genuine, ἀλλογενής stranger, συγγενής relative, kindred, μονογενής one of a kind, only, γενεαλογία genealogy, παλινγενεσία regeneration, παραγίνομαι come, arrive, etc. (For a useful list, see B.M. Metzger, Lexical Aids for Students of New Testament Greek, pp. 53-94.)

§25.11   A <u>primitive</u> word is formed directly from a root or stem; a
            <u>derived</u> word is formed from another (usually more simple) word.
It is of course possible to derive a word from a derived word. Thus
γράφω 'I write' is formed directly from a root *γραφ, whereas γράμμα
(< *γραφ + ματ) is derived from the verb.

§25.12   A word derived from a noun is called <u>denominal</u>; a word de-
            rived from a verb is called <u>deverbal</u>. The word "denominative"
is often used where I have used "denominal." Thus γράμμα (§25.11) is
deverbal, whereas ἀριθμῶ (< ἀριθμέω) is derived from ἀριθμός 'number,'
hence is denominal.

§25.13   A word derived from a single root or stem is called a <u>simple</u>
            word; a word derived from two or more stems is a <u>compound</u>
word. The illustrations given in §§25.11f. are simple words. The words
ἀλλογενής, παλινγενεσία, γενεαλογία, etc., given in §25.1, are compound
words. It is possible that many "simple" words that are formed of a
stem and a "suffix" are in truth compound words, but the "suffix" is no
longer identifiable as a word.

§25.2   Many <u>verbs</u> are <u>denominal</u>. This is reasonable, since the con-
            crete (the person, place, or thing) is considered to be more
primitive than the abstract. We must use this logic with caution, for
some actions may be considered to be more primitive, and the thing produced by the action may be more abstract.

§25.21   Verbs ending in -αω and -εω (§24.223) are often denominal.
            The -αω verbs are often derived from feminine nouns of the
1st declension, while the -εω verbs are usually from 2d declension
nouns, but sometimes can be traced to adjectives ending in -ης, -ης,
-ες: τιμή 'honor,' τιμάω 'I honor'; φίλος 'friend,' φιλέω 'I love';
ἀπειθής 'disobedient,' ἀπειθέω 'I disobey.'

§25.22   Denominal verbs in -οω are factitive, causative, or forensic.
They sometimes supplant verbs in -ευω or -ιζω (§24.223):
κενός 'empty,' κενόω 'I empty'; δοῦλος 'slave,' δουλόω 'I make a
slave of, count as a slave'; χάρις 'grace,' χαριτόω 'I endue with
grace, look with favor on.'

§25.23   Denominal verbs in -ευω are quite numerous. Like nouns ending in -ευς, they generally have to do with the performing of
an occupation, profession, etc.: ἐπίτροπος 'procurator,' ἐπιτροπεύω
'I govern'; κύριος 'lord, master,' κυριεύω 'I rule over.'

§25.24   Denominal verbs ending in -αζω, -ιζω, or -υζω are often factitive or causative: λίθος 'stone,' λιθάζω 'I stone'; σκάνδαλον 'stumbling-block,' σκανδαλίζω 'I cause to stumble'; *γογγ- possibly the sound of a gong > γογγύζω 'I murmur, grumble.'

§25.241   Denominal verbs from neuter nouns ending in -μα(τ), the verb
taking the ending -ίζω, are often forensic ("to declare to be")
or imitative ("to act like"). ἀναθεματίζω 'I declare to be accursed,'
δογματίζω 'I follow a decree.'

§25.242   Some verbs in -άζω and -ίζω are developed from stems ending in
a velar or dental stop (§§24.251, .252). ἁρπαγή 'forcible
seizure' > ἁρπάζω 'I seize,' *ελπιδς > ἐλπίς 'hope' > ἐλπίζω 'I hope.'
These verbs are not clearly denominal.

§25.25   Denominal verbs ending in -αίνω are often causative. φρήν
'heart,' εὔφρων 'glad,' εὐφραίνω 'I cheer, gladden,' ποίμην
'shepherd,' ποιμαίνω 'I tend, govern.'

§25.26   Verbs ending in -σκω are sometimes inchoative or progressive
(§24.27, .277?). διδαχή 'teaching,' διδάσκω 'I teach';
γνῶσις 'knowledge,' γιγνώσκω > γινώσκω 'I know'; γῆρας 'old age,' γηράσκω
'I grow old.' It is not clear that these are denominal verbs.

§25.3   <u>Compound verbs</u> are formed by prefixing one or two prepositions
        to the uncompounded verb. A verb with three prepositions is
found in the papyri, but only those with one and two are found in the NT.
Each compound should be studied carefully with the aid of a large lexicon.
For the augmented forms, cf. §24.3137f. For reduplicated forms, cf.
§24.3149. ἵστημι 'I put, place, stand,' καθίστημι 'I appoint, ordain,'
κατεφίστημι 'I rise up against.'

§25.31   Some verbs are compounded with adverbs or adverbial elements.
        With such verbs, augment and reduplication is quite irregular
and unpredictable. εὐαγγελίζομαι 'I proclaim good tidings,' δυσφημέω
'I slander.'

§25.311 When adding prefixes to form compound verbs, the rules of eli-
        sion (§15.53, .5311), aspiration (§13.15), assimilation (§13.1,
.3ff.), etc., generally apply.

§25.32   Some verbs are formed from two words, usually a noun and a verb.
        In such compounds, the first element is objective, and stands in
about the same relationship to the verb as it would if placed in an
oblique (i.e., not nominative) case. Such verbs, when augmented or reduplicated, have the element at the beginning of the compounded form.
πληροφορέω 'I bring to the full, convince,' ἑτεροδιδασκαλέω 'I teach
another doctrine.'

§25.4   A number of nouns are <u>primitive</u> or <u>simple nouns,</u> i.e., they are
        of such nature as to suggest that they were used in the earliest
period of the language. Note that the term "primitive" as used here is
not the same as that used in some grammars.

§25.41   A simple noun consists of a root or stem (§20.3, .31), plus the
        case endings. *ποδ > πούς 'foot,' *σαλ > ἅλς 'salt,' *θριχ >
τρίξ 'hair,' *ορνιθ > ορνις 'bird.' Many will be from monosyllabic stems,
but some will have more than one syllable. Most will be concrete, rather
than abstract nouns.

§25.5   Derived nouns are nouns derived from other words, some from
               primitive nouns (denominal nouns), and some from verbs (deverbal
nouns). It is not possible to determine with certainty, in many cases,
which form is derived from which. My personal choice is always to move
from the more concrete to the more abstract, but the ability of primitive
man to deal with abstract ideas is at times amazing.

§25.51   The simplest derived nouns are those with suffixed elements
               added to stems or primitive words. Grammars are filled with
efforts to list these according to categories, and it seems that there is
little to be gained by reproducing these tables in this Handbook. A few
of them will make vocabulary recognition a bit easier.

§25.511 The idea of agent, or doer of the action suggested by the stem,
               may be found in the following suffixes:
-ευ: -ευς γραμματεύς 'scribe,' ἱερεύς 'priest'
-τηρ: -τηρ, -τειρα (cf. Eng. -ter) σωτήρ 'savior'
-τορ: -τωρ, -τρια (cf. Eng. -tor) μαθήτρια 'disciple (f.),' ῥήτωρ 'orator'
-τα: -της μιμητής 'imitator,' λῃστής 'robber'

§25.512 The idea of action, or the doing of the act suggested by the
               stem, seems to be found in the following suffixes:
-τι: -τις πίστις 'faith'
-σι: -σις γνῶσις 'knowledge,' κρίσις 'judgment'
-σια: -σια θυσία 'sacrifice,' κλισία 'a group eating together'
-μο: -μος ἄνεμος 'wind,' κάλαμος 'reed'

§25.513 The result of the action seems to be suggested by the following
               elements:
-μα: -μα βάπτισμα 'baptism'
-εσ: -ος σκότος 'darkness,' ἔλεος 'pity, mercy'
In some cases, -εσ seems rather to denote quality: βάθος 'depth,' βάρος
'weight.'

§25.52   Many nouns are derived from verbs (deverbal nouns), by the ad-
               dition of elements such as the following:

-μος (action): ἁγιασμός 'sanctification,' βαπτισμός 'baptizing'
-μα (result): ἀγνόημα 'unwitting sin,' αἰτίωμα 'accusation'
-σις (abstract): θέλησις 'will,' βίωσις 'manner of life'
-εια (abstract): ἀρεσκεία 'pleasing,' ἱερατεία 'priesthood'
-μονή (abstract): πεισμονή 'obedience,' ἐπιλησμονή 'forgetfulness'

§25.53   A number of abstract nouns are formed from adjectives by the
          addition of the following elements:
-οτης: ἁγιότης 'sanctity, holiness,' μεγαλειότης 'magnificence'
-συνη: ἐλεημοσύνη 'act of mercy,' δικαιοσύνη 'righteousness'
-ια: ἐλαφρία 'levity,' παραφρονία 'madness'
-εια: ἀλήθεια 'truth,' ὠφέλεια 'advantage, benefit'

§25.54   Nouns are derived from other nouns (denominals) by the addition
          of prefixes, suffixes, or by compounding nouns with other words.

§25.541   Nouns are formed by the addition of suffixes such as the follow-
          ing to other nouns:
-ισσα: βασίλισσα 'queen,' Φοινίκισσα 'Phoenician woman'
-ιτης: Ἰσραηλίτης 'Israelite,' Αἰλαμῖται 'Elamites'
-ιον: ἰχθύδιον 'little fish,' παιδίον 'young child'
-ις: Ἑλληνίς 'Greek,' Ἑβραΐς 'Hebrew'
-ισκ: παιδίσκη 'maiden,' νεανίσκος 'youth'

§25.542   Nouns are formed by adding prefixes, prepositions or adverbs,
          to other nouns, as in the case of verb-formation. ὑπεράνω
'above,' περίπικρος 'very bitter,' ἔκπαλαι 'from of old,' συστασιαστής
'fellow-rioter,' διαπαρατριβή 'wrangling'; δυσβάστακτος 'difficult to
carry,' δυσνόητος 'hard to understand,' εὐάρεστος 'well-pleasing,'
εὐπρόσδεκτος 'acceptable,' εὐμετάδοτος 'ready to impart.'

§25.543   The negative of a word is sometimes formed by adding the prefix
          αν- before vowels, α- before consonants, somewhat wrongly called
alpha privative. ἀναρίθμητος 'without number,' ἄνομος 'without law, lawless.'

§25.544   A word may be formed using a noun, adjective, or verb as the
          first part, and a noun or adjective as the last part.

§25.5441 Compounds with verbs are chiefly poetic words.

§25.5442 Compounds in which the principal idea is carried by the second
          part of the word, the first part being a qualifier (called
"synthesis" by the Greeks), are described either as <u>determinative</u> (the
first part, usually an adjective, qualifies the second part) or as
<u>attributive</u> (the first part qualifies the second, and the whole compound
denotes a quality or attribute). ἀγαθοποιός 'acting rightly,' φρενατάτης
'deceiver (of his own mind),' ἑτεροδιδάσκαλος 'teacher of another doctrine.'

§25.5443 In some compounds, the two parts are more-or-less independent
          elements (called "parathesis"), combining to form a new word.
δώδεκα 'twelve,' πεντηκοστή 'Pentecost,' νυχθήμερον '24-hour period.'

§25.5444 New words (nouns or adjectives) could be built by adding suf-
          fixes, as given above to a compound noun. (The Greeks, who
never ran out of words for things, called this "parasynthesis.") ἐπιθανά-
τιος 'condemned to death,' ὑπολήνιον 'vessel under a wine-press,'
ὑπαπόδιον 'footstool.'

§25.6   It seems reasonable to suppose that there were <u>primitive adjec-
          tives</u>. (The very young child soon learns to express such ideas
as "big," "nice.") Some of these may have been the elements from which
stative verbs were built.

§25.61   <u>Verbal adjectives</u> are formed by the addition of -τος to a
          verb stem. γραπτός 'written,' δυνατός 'able.'

§25.62   Adjectives are formed from stems by the addition of suffixed
          elements:

-ο/-α: -ος, -α, -ον ἀγαθός 'good,' μόνος 'only'
-υ/- :   -υς, -εια,-υ ὀξύς 'sharp,' πολύς 'many'
-εσ: -ης, -ης, -ες πλήρης 'full,' ἀληθής 'true'

§25.63 Adjectives are formed from substantives by the suffixing of the
following elements:

-ινος 'having the nature, composed of' (Eng. -ine) ἀληθινός 'true,'
πύρινος 'fiery'

-ικος 'pertaining to, resembling; (Eng. -ic) ἐθνικός 'gentile,
national; εἰρηνικός 'peaceful'

-τικος 'fit for, capable of' (Eng. -tical) αἱρετικός 'capable of
choosing,' διδάκτικος 'apt at teaching'

-εος > -ους 'composed of' (Eng. -ous) χρυσοῦς 'golden,' ἀργυροῦς
'of silver'

§25.64 The formation of verbal adjectives (participles) we have seen
(§24.461, .462).

§25.65 A few adjectives are formed from adverbs by the addition of
-τερος or -τερικος. δεύτερος 'second.'

§25.66 The <u>comparative</u> and <u>superlative</u> of adjectives are formed from
nouns by the addition of -τερος and -τατος, respectively.
Primitive comparatives and superlatives are formed by the addition of -ιων
and -ιστος, respectively. σοφώτερος 'more wise.'

§25.7 Many <u>adverbs</u> are formed by adding -ως to the stem from which
related adjectives have been formed. καλῶς 'well,' δικαίως
'justly,' ἀληθῶς 'truly.'

§25.71 Some adverbs are formed from the accusative neuter (sing. or pl.)
of adjectives. μόνον 'only,' πολύ 'much,' ἀκμήν 'even now.'

§25.711 The comparative of an adverb is formed by using the neuter
singular accusative of the corresponding adjective.

§25.712 The superlative of an adverb is formed by using the neuter
plural accusative of the superlative of the corresponding
adjective.

§25.72   Adverbs of place, time, and manner are sometimes formed with
          the following endings (cf. §23.6).

§25.721   Adverbs of place where -ου: ποῦ 'where?' οὗ 'where';
          adverbs of place whence (from where) -θεν: πόθεν 'whence?'
ἄνωθεν 'from above,' οὐρανόθεν 'from heaven'; adverbs of place to which
-δε/-σε: ἐνθάδε 'here, hither,' ἐκεῖσε 'there, thither.'

§25.722   Adverbs of time, with the ending -τε: πότε 'when?' τότε
          'then,' ὅτε 'when.'

§25.723   Adverbs of manner with the ending -ως: πῶς 'how?' ὅπως 'thus,'
          ὡς 'as,' ἀληθῶς 'truly' (cf. §25.7).

Division III--Syntax

§30.　　Syntax, as the word indicates, is the joining together of words
　　　　　　to convey meaning.　In grammar, syntax is the study of such
arrangement, and the synthesizing of rules defining the various elements
of syntax for any given language.　The native speaker learns by constant
trial and error how to express his meaning and how to understand what
another is saying to him.　For the foreigner, it is necessary to analyze
many sentences and formulate the rules.　Until he does, he can neither
express himself nor understand what is said.　Syntax, therefore, is the
most important part of language study.

§30.1　　The simplest communication of a complete idea is the sentence,
　　　　　　which is a word or group of words containing a subject and a
predicate.　"Fire (subj.) burns (pred.)."

§30.11　　The subject is that about which something is stated.　It is
　　　　　　the person, place, or thing that is, or acts, or is acted upon.
It is that which the sentence is about--hence the name subject.

§30.111　　The simple subject is a noun (§30.311) or pronoun (§30.312).
　　　　　　"God loves."　"He loves."

§30.112　　The complete subject is composed of the simple subject and the
　　　　　　words that explain or complete its meaning (§30.21).　"The God
and Father of our Lord Jesus Christ loves us."

§30.12　　The predicate is that which is stated about the subject, or
　　　　　　that which is predicated.　"God loves."　"God is light."

§30.121　　The simple predicate of a sentence is a verb (§30.33) or
　　　　　　verb-phrase (§30.311).　"God loves." "Christ has risen."

B-127

§30.122   The <u>complete predicate</u> is composed of the simple predicate
          and the words that explain or complete the meaning (§§30.22, .23).
"Christ <u>has risen from the grave</u>."

§30.13   A sentence may be <u>declaratory</u> (declares a fact), <u>interrogative</u>
          (asks a question), <u>imperative</u> (expresses a command or request),
or <u>exclamatory</u> (expresses surprise, grief, or some other emotion as an
exclamation). "Christ died for you." "Do you believe this?" "Repent
and be baptized." "Hallelujah!"

§30.14   The omission of a word that would be necessary for grammatical
          completeness of a sentence or clause is called <u>ellipsis</u>, and
such a clause is elliptical.

§30.141   If there is no possibility of confusion, the subject may be
          omitted, as in imperative sentences spoken directly to the
subject, or in replies to questions.

§30.142   If there is no ambiguity, even the predicate may be omitted. For
          example, the reply "Blue." perfectly communicates the idea in
reply to the question, "Did you use a red pencil or a blue one?" even though
both subject and predicate are lacking. Much more common is the use of
"Yes." or "No." as a complete sentence in reply to a question.

§30.2   Most statements are not simple, therefore other elements are
          present in the sentence. Some are used to modify either the
subject or the predicate, hence are known as <u>modifiers</u> (§30.21, .23).
Some are used to complete the predicate, hence are known as <u>complements</u>
(§30.22). And some are outside the main thread of subject and predicate,
and are therefore <u>independent elements</u> (§30.25).

§30.21   The <u>modifier of the subject</u> may be one or more of the following:

the definite article, "<u>the</u> book," §35.2ff.

a possessive pronoun, "<u>his</u> book," §35.511, §35.52

an interrogative pronoun, "<u>which</u> book?" §35.55

an indefinite pronoun, "<u>any</u> book," §35.56

a demonstrative pronoun, "<u>this</u> book," §35.54

an attributive adjective, "<u>big</u> book," §35.1ff.

an adjectival participle, "<u>inviting</u> book," §35.7ff.

an adjectival infinitive, "book <u>to be read</u>," §35.8

an adjectival phrase, "book <u>on the table</u>," §35.4ff.

an adjectival clause, "book <u>which speaks to us</u>," §35.57

A substantive or phrase used appositively (§30.251) is a type of modifier which approaches the category of an independent element, cf. §35.6ff.

§30.22   The <u>complement of the verb</u> may be one or more of the following:

a direct object, "he hit <u>John</u>," §33.1f.

a predicate nominative, "this is <u>John</u>," §33.4ff.

a predicate adjective, "John is <u>tall</u>," §33.5ff.

an infinitive or infinitival clause, "John wants <u>to sing</u>," §33.6ff.

a cognate accusative, "he ran <u>a race</u>," §33.2ff.

a predicate objective, "they crowned him <u>king</u>," §33.3ff.

a predicate genitive, "the book was <u>John's</u>," §33.7ff.

a predicate dative, "he gave command <u>to the disciples</u>," §33.8ff.

a supplementary participle, "he came <u>running</u>," §33.9ff.

a direct quotation, "he said, '<u>Go!</u>'" §33.13, §37.81ff.

an indirect quotation, "he said <u>he would go</u>," §37.82ff.

§30.221   The complement of the verb when a substantive (§30.31) may in turn be modified by any of the kinds of modifiers listed in §30.21; see also the discussion in §35.ff.

§30.23   The <u>modifier of the predicate</u> may be one or more of the following:

the indirect object, "he gave it <u>to him</u>," §34.11

an adverb, "he ran <u>quickly</u>," §34.2ff.

an adverbial phrase, "he fell <u>through the window</u>," §34.3ff.

an adverbial clause, "he talked <u>while he was working</u>," §34.4ff.

the genitive absolute, "<u>night having come</u>, we departed," §34.5ff.

an adverbial accusative, "I have waited <u>hours</u>," §34.6ff.

§30.24   Modifiers can be used to modify other modifiers (§36.). For ex-
          ample, the <u>adverb</u> often modifies an <u>adjective</u>. "He is <u>very</u> tall."

§30.25   <u>Independent elements</u> include <u>interjections</u>, <u>vocatives</u> (or
          nominatives of direct address), <u>parenthetical statements</u>, etc.

§30.251   <u>Apposition</u> is the setting of a word, phrase, or clause along-
          side another without a connective, usually to define or limit
the latter. A noun or pronoun so used is an <u>appositive</u>, and a phrase or
clause so used is <u>appositional</u>.

§30.3   The <u>words</u> in a sentence have rather well-defined duties in the
          expression of the thought. We classify them according to their
use in the sentence as <u>parts of speech</u>: nouns, pronouns, adjectives,
verbs, adverbs, prepositions, conjunctions, and interjections.

§30.31   <u>Nouns</u> and <u>pronouns</u> are called <u>substantives</u>.

§30.311   A <u>noun</u> is the name of a person, place or thing. It can serve as:
                defined subject (§32.1)
                direct object (§33.1)
                cognate accusative (§33.2)
                predicate nominative (§33.4)
                predicate genitive (§33.7)
                indirect object (§33.8)
                object of a preposition (§34.3ff.)
                adverbial accusative (§34.6)
                a modifier of a noun (§35.3ff.)
                object of a participle (§30.382)
                "subject" of a participle in the genitive absolute (§34.5ff.)
                object of an infinitive (§32.63)
                subject accusative of an infinitive (§32.51)

§30.312   A <u>pronoun</u> is a word which stands for a noun. It designates
          a person, place, or thing (or the plurals), without naming it.
A pronoun can serve in any of the ways a noun does (see §30.311).

§30.313   The substantive to which a pronoun refers is called its
          antecedent.

§30.32   An adjective is a word which describes or defines (limits) a
          substantive. An adjective can serve as a substantive (cf. §30.
311), but as an adjective it serves either as a predicate adjective (§33.5)
or as an attributive adjective (§35.1ff.).

§30.321   An adjective describes a substantive by stating a characteristic
          that sets the substantive apart from other substantives of the
same name. Such adjectives are descriptive adjectives. "A small house."
"A wooden box."

§30.322   An adjective defines or limits a substantive when it designates
          or points out one specific member of the class to which the
substantive refers. Such adjectives are definitive adjectives. "The book."
"That verse." "A chapter." "What verse?"

§30.323   The definite article and the demonstrative pronouns are specific
          kinds of definitive adjectives.

§30.33   A verb is a word which can assert something--usually an action--
          concerning a person, place, or thing. Since some verbs express
state or condition, it is an error to define a verb as an "action word."
For use of the verb see §31.ff. "He runs." "It stands there." "They
were hit." "Wait!"

§30.331   A group of words used as a verb is a verb-phrase. A verb-phrase
          consists of a verb and its auxiliaries. In Greek and other
inflected languages, the periphrastic is the only verb phrase (§30.411).
"I had been running."

§30.34   An adverb is a word which modifies a verb, an adjective, or
          another adverb. Most adverbs answer the question "How?" "When?"

"Where?" or "By how much?" For the adverb as a verb modifier see §30.2ff.,
as an adjective or adverb modifier see §36.1. "They grow tall." "He was
here yesterday." "I went home." "It is very far."

§30.35   A preposition is a word placed before a substantive to indicate
          the relation of that substantive to some other word in the
sentence. The substantive is called the object of the preposition, and
the preposition is said to govern its object. "I got it from him."
"I gave it to Harry." The preposition and substantive may be used as an
adverbial phrase (§34.3ff.) or as an adjectival phrase (§35.4ff.).
Adverbial: "I gave it to Harry" (modifies the verb). Adjectival: "The
man from Mars called" (modifies the noun).

§30.351   According to usage, the object of a preposition will be in a
          particular case. Cf. §§34.311, .312, .313. The expression is
often found that a certain preposition "governs the genitive/dative/accusa-
tive case." This, however, is improper usage of the word "governs."
The preposition governs the noun which is in that case.

§30.352   A preposition is sometimes used before other words than sub-
          stantives (e.g. adjectives, infinitives, etc.). In such usage
the word governed can be considered as performing in part a substantival
use. For the use of the preposition with the infinitive, cf. §§34.42ff.

§30.353   A preposition sometimes governs more than one object.

§30.36   A conjunction is a word used to connect words or groups of
          words. Unlike the preposition, it has no object, and the
connection indicated is much less definite than that indicated by a
preposition.

§30.361   Coördinating conjunctions join words or statements that are
          equal in rank, or coördinate. They may be copulative (and)
or adversative (but). "I gave it to Harry and John." "Harry liked it
but John was noncommittal."

§30.3611 A number of conjunctions (notably μεν, δε, γε, τε, γαρ) are post-
          positive, i.e. they never stand first in their clause. Usually they
stand second, but sometimes they are found in the third position.

§30.362   Subordinating conjunctions are used to introduce subordinate
          (dependent) clauses, i.e. clauses that are dependent on the
main clause, and are principally temporal, local, causal, final or
result.

§30.3621 The temporal clause (§37.51ff.) modifies the main predication
          by telling when it occurred. "I gave it to him when I was
at home."

§30.3622 The local clause (§37.52ff.), tells where it occurred. "I
          gave it to him where he had the greatest need for it."

§30.3623 The causal clause (§37.53ff.), tells why (as a result of what
          cause) the predication occurred. "I gave it to him because
I thought he could use it."

§30.3624 The final or purpose clause (§37.54ff.) tells why (for what
          purpose or objective) it occurred. "I gave it to him to
encourage him."

§30.3625 The result clause (§37.55ff.) tells the result of the main
          predication. "I gave it to him so that he can now hold down
the job." Sometimes the line between result and purpose is very fine.

§30.363   Correlative conjunctions are generally used in pairs to relate
          two otherwise independent statements (either ... or, not only
... but also, etc.), cf. §37.15f. Ellipse is frequently found in correlative statements. "Either you take it or I will be angry." "You
or I will have to go." "Either one." Obviously, context is important.

§30.37   An interjection is a cry or other exclamatory sound, expres-
          sing some emotion or feeling. It has no grammatical connection
with the word or group of words in which it stands, strictly speaking,
hence its name. "Oh well, I guess I can do it." "He saw, alas, that
I was not pleased." Most of our ordinary interjections are not used in
literary language, and some are unprintable.

§30.38   Infinitives and participles are unique in their ability to
              serve a dual capacity in a sentence, in contrast to other
words which are used as a particular part of speech in any given sentence.
It therefore becomes extremely important for us to study the dual usage
of these two parts of speech.

§30.381   An infinitive is a verb-form which serves as both verb and
              noun.   As a verb, it can perform many of the functions of a
verb, in a main clause (§31.326) or a subordinate clause (§§37.325,
.5328, .5425, .5532, etc.).   As a noun it can serve as subject (§32.5, .6),
as object (§33.611) of a verb or as the object of a preposition (§34.34).
It can serve as an adjective (§37.44) or an adverb (§34.42ff., 35.6).

§30.382   A participle is a verb-form that is both verb and adjective.
              Like the infinitive, it can serve in dual capacity in a sentence.
It can be used in the adjectival usages (§30.32), and as a substantive in
any of the noun uses (§30.311).   It can be used adverbially (§34.41ff.)
and it is often used in the genitive absolute as a verb modifier (§34.5).

§30.39   A word may serve in various ways: it may be a noun in one
              sentence and a verb in another, or a noun and an adjective, or
an adjective and an adverb, or an adjective and a pronoun, etc.

§30.4   A group of connected words in a sentence may serve as a part of
              speech.   If the group does not contain a subject and a predicate,
it is called a phrase.   If it does contain a subject and a predicate, it
is called a clause.

§30.41   A phrase can be used as a noun, an adjective, an adverb, or a
              verb.

§30.411   A phrase used as a noun is a noun-phrase; one used as a verb
              is a verb-phrase.   A phrase used as an adjective is an adjective
phrase, and a phrase used as an adverb is an adverbial phrase.   A verb-
phrase is sometimes called a periphrastic, and the use of a periphrastic
is periphrasis.

§30.4111 The use of the verb <u>to be</u> with a participle is found in Greek.
        In classical Greek, ειναι + the perf. ptcp. is used as peri-
phrasis for the perf., plpf., and fut. perf. act. and pass., regularly,
and was extended beyond these usages. In the NT it is approximately the
same, with some of these falling into the background.

§30.4112 The pres. of ειναι + the pres. ptcp. is used to express the
        present imperfect ("I am doing"); the impf. of ειναι + the pres.
ptcp. is used to put some stress on continued activity or state in past
time ("I was doing"). The use of γινεσθαι with the pres. or perf. ptcp.
denotes the beginning of a state or condition. The use of ειναι + the aor.
ptcp. expresses the pluperf. And the use of μελλειν + the inf. is approximately equal to an imminent future ("he is about to, he is going to").

§30.412 Many adjective and adverbial phrases consist of a preposition
        and its object with or without other words.

§30.42   A <u>clause</u> is a group of words that forms part of a sentence and
        that <u>contains a subject and a predicate</u>.

§30.421 If a sentence consists of two or more clauses, each of which
        is able to stand independently as a simple sentence, the sen-
tence is a <u>compound sentence</u>, and the clauses are called <u>coördinate</u>.
"He is going and I am staying home."

§30.422 If a sentence consists of two or more clauses, one or more of
        which cannot stand independently, the sentence is called <u>com-</u>
<u>plex</u>. The clause which can stand alone, is the <u>main</u> or <u>independent</u>
<u>clause</u>. "If he goes, <u>I shall go with him</u>."

§30.4221 The other clause is the <u>dependent</u> or <u>subordinate clause</u>.

§30.43   A subordinate clause, like a phrase, is used as a part of
        speech. If it is used as a noun, it is a noun (or substantive)

clause; if it modifies a substantive, it is an adjectival clause; if it serves as an adverb it is an adverbial clause.

§30.431   Subordinate clauses are generally introduced by subordinating
             words: relative pronouns (who, to whom, whom, etc.) are used
for adjectival clauses (§23.7), and adverbial conjunctions (§30.36) or relative adverbs (so that, where, while, for, etc.) are used for adverbial clauses).

§30.44   It is possible to build a sentence with an unlimited number
            of dependent and independent clauses. Only the inability of
the hearer/reader to comprehend the meaning of the sentence limits the complexity with which the speaker/writer may construct his sentence.

§30.5   The study of syntax usually begins with the basic elements of
           the sentence. Each part of speech is analyzed in its usage.
In my opinion, this results in a knowledge of the parts, but a cor-
responding loss of the sense of the whole. In this Handbook I propose to consider the verb of the predicate as central, and the other parts of the sentence in their relationship to the main verb.

§30.51   Those who wish to have a summary of all the uses of the noun, the
            participle, etc., may use either the cross references in this Hand-
book or one of the several excellent grammars constructed about the parts of speech. L recommend either of the following grammars, supplemented by Blass-Debrunner-Funk (which lacks the fundamentals it presupposes):

William W. Goodwin, rev. by C. B. Gulick, Greek Grammar (Boston: Ginn and Co., 1930/1958; 472 pp.)

Herbert W. Smyth, Greek Grammar (rev. by G.M. Messing; Cambridge, Mass.: Harvard University Press, 1956; 784 pp.)

It is a tragedy that nothing of the scope and clarity of these two grammars has appeared in English for New Testament Greek.

§30.6   Sentence diagrams. There is nothing that will help us grasp the
           structure and sense of a passage like diagramming the sentence.
In this Handbook I have followed the system commonly taught in elementary
English, except that I have adapted it to the typewriter so that all parts
are typed horizontally. I have further tried to keep it simple, for a
diagram needs to be simple to be clear.

§30.61   The simple sentence (§30.1) is basic to the diagram. With all
           modifiers removed, it forms a simple straight line.

§30.611   The verb in the predicate is the central element (§30.12). Note
           how the other elements are placed with reference to the verb.

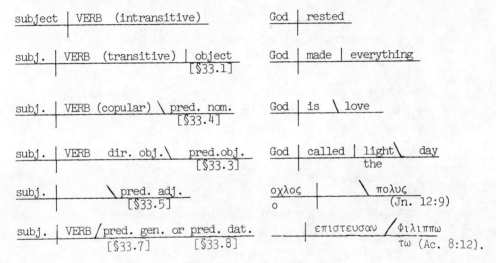

§30.6111 With a compound subject, compound predicate, or even a compound
           verb, the same basic diagram is used.

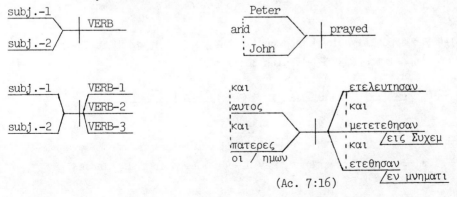

(Ac. 7:16)

§30.6112   There obviously is no limit to the combinations that are theo-
           retically possible, but the method of diagramming is the same.

§30.612   Modifiers of the subject or object, for the purpose of diagram-
           ming, are of four types: (a) the modifier in concord (§35.11);
(b) a substantive in an oblique case (§35.3), or a prepositional phrase
(§35.4); (c) a participle or participial clause (§32.4); (d) an appositive
(§30.251).

§30.6121   Modifiers in concord are placed directly below the word they
           modify.

subj.	VERB	dir. obj.		Father	gives	gift
modifier-1		modifier-1		the		every
modifier-2		modifier-2		loving		good
modifier-3				heavenly		

§30.6122   A substantive in the genitive or dative, or a prepositional
           phrase, is placed after a slant line. If there is more than
a single word, the word group is underlined.

subject	VERB	direct object		Amos	preached	word
/prep.		/obl. case		/from Tekoa		/God's

§30.6123   A participle used adjectivally is placed below the word it
           modifies, connected by a solid vertical line.

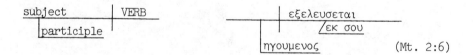

subject	VERB
participle	

εξελευσεται
          /εκ σου
ηγουμενος   (Mt. 2:6)

§30.6124   An appositive is placed beside the word with which it is in
           apposition (§30.251), with the = sign.

appositive = subj. | VERB | obj.   Lord = Christ | saves | us
                   | the

§30.613   The modifiers of the verb (§30.23), for the purpose of diagram-
           ming a simple sentence, may be considered in four classes:

(a) the adverb (§34.2);   (b) the prepositional phrase used adverbially
including the indirect object (§34.3);   (c) the participial phrase/clause
used adverbially (§34.4); and (d) the genitive absolute (§34.5).

§30.6131 The adverb is placed immediately below the verb.

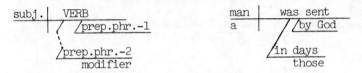

§30.6132 The prepositional phrase is placed below the verb after a slant
line (cf. §30.6122).

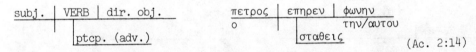

§30.6133 The participial clause is placed below the verb it modifies,
connected with a solid vertical line (cf. §30.6123).

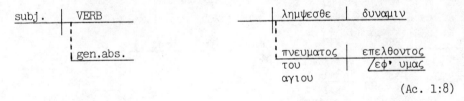

(Ac. 2:14)

§30.6134 The genitive absolute is handled like the adverbial participle
(§30.6133), except that it is connected by a broken vertical
line, as below.

(Ac. 1:8)

§30.614   An infinitive or a noun clause (§32.5), whether subject or object,
is set above the main line on stilts.

infinitive

_____
        /\   VERB \ pred.nom.

to give

_____
        /\   is \ blessed

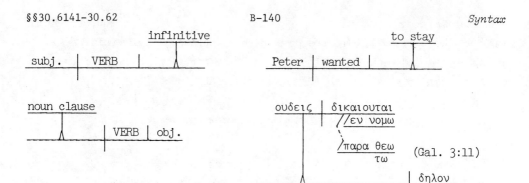

§30.6141 In some diagrams, in order to keep the main predication prominent,
          it is better to put the noun clause below the line for the object.

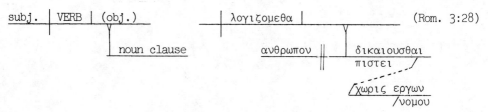

§30.6142 Note how the subject accusative of the infinitive (§32.63)
          is placed before a double line before the infinitive.

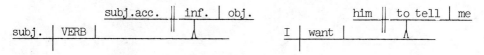

§30.6143 The complementary infinitive (§33.61) is diagrammed like the parti-
          cipial clause (§30.6133).

§30.615   Modifiers of modifiers (§36.) are diagrammed in the same
          way as are modifiers of the subject/object (cf. §30.612).

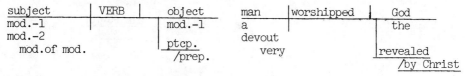

§30.62   The compound sentence (§30.421) is diagrammed as two simple
          sentences joined by a dotted line.

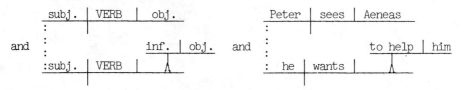

§30.621   I see no reason to use a different diagram for a disjunctive or
          adversative conjunction (§30.361).

§30.63   The complex sentence (§30.422), since it is composed of a main
          (independent) clause and a dependent clause, is diagrammed as
two or more sentences, tied together with diagonal lines. We divide them
into five categories for the purpose of diagramming the sentence: (a) the
correlative clauses (§37.15); (b) the adjectival relative clause
§37.4); (c) the adverbial clause (§37.5); (d) clauses of condition or
concession (§37.6); and (e) clauses of direct or indirect discourse (§37.8).

§30.631   Correlative clauses are diagrammed as two simple sentences
          (cf. §30.61), tied together by a dotted line.

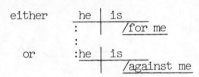

§30.632   The adjectival relative clause is tied to the antecedent of
          the relative pronoun (§35.47) by a broken line. To be con-
sistent, this line should be solid if the relative clause is restrictive
(i.e., cannot be omitted), and broken if it is merely descriptive (i.e. can
be omitted)--but I have not found this device employed in any grammar.

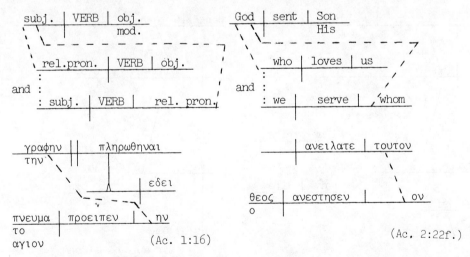

§30.6321 The rel. pron. may be subj. (nom.), dir. obj. (acc.), possessive
        or other gen. modifier, dat. of indirect object, etc., and may
have as its antecedent the subj. or the obj. of the main verb or any of the
modifiers, or it may relate to another relative clause. It is unnecessary
to diagram all the possibilities.

§30.633   The adverbial clause (§37.5), since it defines further the action
        of the verbs (§34.4), is tied to the verb by a solid line. Any
conjunctions or relative adverbs used are placed on (beside) this line.

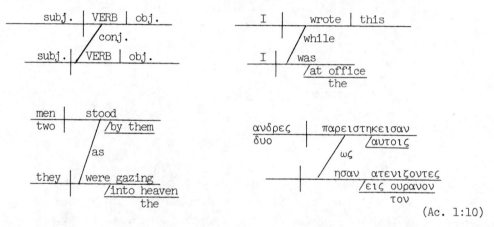

(Ac. 1:10)

§30.6331 An adverbial clause may be further tied to another adverbial
        clause, cf. the following.

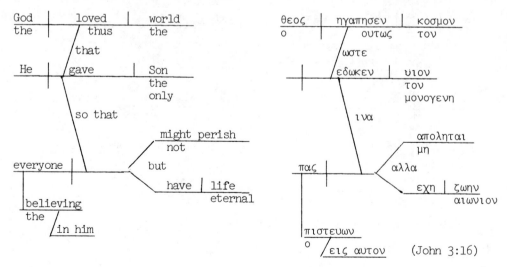

(John 3:16)

§30.6332 The articular infinitive (§37.553) is diagrammed in a manner
          resembling the adverbial prepositional phrase, but with a longer
diagonal line.

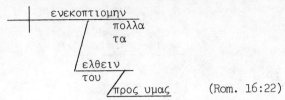

(Rom. 16:22)

§30.6333 If the articular infinitive is used in a noun-clause it is
          placed on stilts:

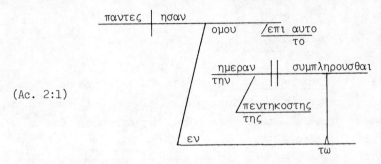

(Ac. 2:1)

§30.634 Clauses of condition or concession (§37.6) are diagrammed in the
         same way as other adverbial clauses. The apodosis (§37.611) is
placed in the position of the main clause, and the conjunction is placed on
the line connecting the two clauses.

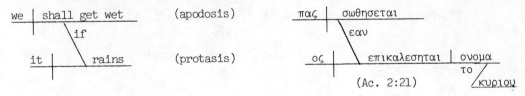

§30.635 Clauses of comparison (§37.7) are diagrammed as adverbial clauses
         with the comparitive conjunction on the line connecting the
clauses. The omitted parts are left blank.

§30.636   Clauses in direct or indirect discourse (§37.8) are treated as
          independent and dependent clauses, respectively.

§30.6361 Direct discourse is diagrammed as a connected, yet independent
          clause.

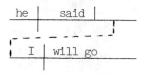

§30.6362 Indirect discourse is diagrammed as a noun clause.

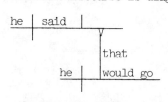

§31.   SYNTAX OF THE VERB. As in all inflected languages (§04.21), the
          verb in Greek can and does serve as both subject and predicate.
It can express a complete sentence. περιεπάτει 'He was walking' (Ac. 3:8).

§31.1   The verb form indicates both person and number of the subject.
          ἤρξατο 'He began' (Ac. 1:1). λήμψεσθε 'You (pl.) shall receive'
(Ac. 1:8).

§31.11   The verb form indicates whether the subject is the person who is
          speaking (1st person), or the person spoken to (2d person), or
the person or thing spoken about (3d person). δώσω 'I will give' (Ac. 2:19).
τί ποιήσωμεν 'What shall we do?' (Ac. 2:37). γέγραπται 'It is written'
(Ac. 2:20). ἐθεάσασθε αὐτὸν 'You have seen him' (Ac. 1:11). μετανοήσατε
'Repent' (Ac. 2:38).

§31.111   When the 1st person form of the verb is used, there is no need
          to add a personal pronoun or other substantive to define the
subject, since it is obvious who the speaker or author is. ἐποιησάμην
'I composed' (Ac. 1:1). If any further definition of the subject is used,

it is for emphasis or contrast. πάντες ἡμεῖς ἐσμεν μάρτυρες 'We all are witnesses' (Ac. 2:32).

§31.112 When the 2d person form is used, there is no need to add any-
        thing to define the subject, since the person being addressed
knows that he is the one spoken to. λήμψεσθε 'You shall receive' (Ac. 1:8).
If any further definition of the subject is used, it is for emphasis or
contrast. αὐτοὶ οἴδατε 'You yourselves know' (Ac. 2:22).

§31.1121 A noun (generally a proper noun) or a pronoun in the vocative
         (or nominative) case may be used in connection with a verb in
the 2d person. This, however, is not the subject of the verb. σὺ κύριε...
ἀνάδειξον... "Thou, O Lord, point out' (Ac. 1:24).

§31.113 When the 3d person form of the verb is used, the subject must be
        further defined (§32.) unless it is clear from the context.
Ἰωάννης ἐβάπτισεν 'John baptized' (Ac. 1:5). εἶπεν 'He [i.e., the Lord,
mentioned in the previous sentence] said' (Ac. 1:7).

§31.114 Some verbs are impersonal, i.e., the subj. is impersonal and
        indefinite. οὐκ ἔβρεξεν 'It did not rain' (Jas. 5:17).

§31.1141 Many verbs are called "impersonal" when they have an infinitive
         or a noun clause for a subject. ἔδει πληρωθῆναι τὴν γραφήν 'It
was necessary (for) the scripture to be fulfilled' (see notes on Ac. 1:16).

§31.115 Sometimes the 3 pl. without a defined subject is used for an
        indefinite "they" (= "one," Fr. on, Ger. sie), and may be
translated by the passive (cf. BDF §130(2)). ·

§31.12 The verb form indicates whether the subject is singular (one
       person or thing, or a collective subject) or plural (more than
one person or thing). ἤρξατο 'He began' (Ac. 1:1). ὑπέστρεψαν 'They
returned' (Ac., 1:12).

§31.121   The verb in the singular may be used when the subject is neuter
           plural referring to things in mass (rather than individually).
παντα ην 'All things were [lit. was]' (Ac. 4:32).

§31.122   If the subject is collective, the sigular form of the verb is
           used of the group as a whole, and the plural form is used if the
group is considered as individuals (cf. "This people is determined" and
"These people are hungry"). ἐγίνετο σημεῖα καὶ τέρατα πολλά 'Many signs
and wonders were happening [sg.]' (Ac. 5:12). προσετίθεντο πιστεύοντες τῷ
κυρίῳ 'Believers were being added (pl.) to the Lord' (Ac. 5:14). Cf.BDF §133.

§31.123   If two or more subjects joined by a conjunction are subjects
           of one verb, the verb is usually in the plural. It may however
agree with the nearer subject. Πέτρος καὶ Ἰωάννης ἀνέβαινον 'Peter and
John went up [pl.] (Ac. 3:1). ἐπίστευσεν αὐτὸς καὶ ἡ οἰκία αὐτοῦ ὅλη
'He and his whole house believed [sg.]' (Jn. 4:53). Cf. BDF §135.

§31.2   It is in predication, however, that the verb principally functions,
          and we must concentrate on the use of the verb in the predicate.

§31.21   A verb which forms a complete statement without any predicate
          complement is known as an intransitive verb; if it describes a
state, instead of an action, it may be called a stative verb. οὗτος ὁ
Ἰησοῦς ἐλεύσεται 'This Jesus shall come' (Ac. 1:11). δεῖ 'It is necessary'
(Ac. 1:21)

§31.22   Many verbs require a predicate complement (§30.22), i.e., some-
          thing to complete the predication.

§31.221   A transitive verb is a verb that requires a direct object to
          complete the predication. ἔδωκαν κλήρους αὐτοῖς 'They gave
lots to them' (Ac. 1:26).

§31.222   Certain verbs (such as to wish, be able, be about to, begin, and
          the like) require another verb, usually in the finitive

(the complementary infinitive, §33.6), to complete the predication.
τί θέλει τοῦτο εἶναι 'What does this want to be?' (Ac. 2:13).

§31.223   Verbs of being, becoming, and the like, take a predicate nomina-
          tive (§33.4). πάντες ἡμεῖς ἐσμεν μάρτυρες 'we all are
witnesses' (Ac. 2:32).

§31.2231   The verb to be, in the sense of to exist, does not require a
          complement, since it is in the nature of a stative verb.
ἦν ὁ λόγος 'The Word was' (Jn. 1:1).

§31.3   Mood, or the attitude in the mind of the speaker concerning
          relationship of the predication to reality (§25.13), is also ex-
pressed by the morphology of the verb. The moods are: indicative (§31.31),
imperative (§31.32), subjunctive (§31.33), and optative (§31.34).

§31.31   The indicative mood is primarily the mood of unqualified as-
          sertion or negation, including questions and exclamations which
pertain to such assertions. There is no doubt or contingency implied.

§31.311   When the statement is expressed affirmatively, it is a declara-
          tory sentence. ἐξέχεεν τοῦτο 'He has poured out this' (Ac. 2:33).

§31.312   Through the use of interrogative adverbs or the tone of the
          voice a questions may be asked, forming an interrogative sentence.
If no doubt or contingency is inferred, the indicative mood is used.
οὐχὶ... οὗτοί εἰσιν...Γαλιλαῖοι; 'Are not these Galileans?' (Ac. 2:7).

§31.313   Through the use of a negative adverb the verb in the predicate
          can be negated. The statement is nevertheless considered to be
declaratory, since it declares something negative about the subject.
οὐ γὰρ οὗτοι μεθύουσιν 'For these are not drunk' (Ac. 2:15).

§31.314   The verb in the indicative may be used in conditional clauses,
          where no doubt or uncertainty is implied. This will be taken
up when we turn to conditional and concessive clauses (§37.6, §37.631).

§31.32   The <u>imperative</u> mood is the mood of commands and prohibitions,
           of exhortations, entreaties, and the like. Since a command
is generally directed to the person or persons spoken to, it is usually
in the 2d person. μετανοήσατε 'Repent' (Ac. 2:38).

§31.321   The subject need not be further defined (§31.112). If it is
           defined, it is for emphasis. δεήθητε ὑμεῖς ὑπὲρ ἐμοῦ 'You pray
for me' (Ac. 8:24).

§31.322   An exhortation or strong wish can be expressed by the 3d person
           of the imperative (sometimes called the <u>jussive</u>). βαπτισθήτω
ἕκαστος ὑμῶν 'Let each one of you be baptized' (Ac. 2:38).

§31.323   An exhortation or strong wish can also be expressed by the
           impersonal 3d person imperative and the indirect object.
τοῦτο ὑμῖν γνωστὸν ἔστω 'Let this be known to you' (Ac. 2:14).

§31.324   The indicative, usually in the future, is sometimes used as an
           imperative (cf. "You shall do it' = "Do it!"). καλέσεις τὸ
ὄνομα αὐτοῦ Ἰωάννην 'You shall call his name John' (Lk. 1:13).

§31.325   The subjunctive, particularly in the negative, may be used as
           an imperative (cf. §31.333).

§31.326   The infinitive may be used as an imperative. However, this is
           rarely found in NT Greek. τῷ αυτῷ στοιχεῖν 'hold true to it'
(Phil. 3:16).

§31.33   The <u>subjunctive</u> mood is the mood of probability or contingency,
           tending to assume unreality rather than reality. As such, its
usage is more common in complex sentences (§37.). It is also used,
however, in simple predicates.

§31.331   The <u>deliberative subjunctive</u> is used to ask a question indi-
           cating great uncertainty or doubt. τί ποιήσωμεν 'What shall
we do?' (Ac. 2:37).

§31.332   The <u>hortatory subjunctive</u> is used in exhortation. κρατῶμεν
τῆς ὁμολογίας 'Let us hold fast the profession' (Heb. 4:14).

§31.333   The subjunctive is sometimes used instead of the imperative in
negative commands. μὴ στήσῃς αὐτοῖς ταύτην τὴν ἁμαρτίαν
'Lay not this sin on them' (Ac. 7:60).

§31.3331   According to Burton, <u>Moods and Tenses</u>, §§163-166, the aor.
sbjtv. forbids the action as an event particularly when it has
not yet begun, and the pres. impv. forbids the continuance of the action.

§31.334   The subjunctive with οὐ μὴ is used for emphatic negation.
οὐ μὴ κριθῆτε 'You will <u>not</u> be judged' (Lk. 6:37).

§31.34   The <u>optative mood</u> basically was used to denote an attainable
wish, and was also used to express future action as dependent
upon circumstances or conditions, hence the potential future. However,
the optative is not commonly found in the NT.

§31.341   The use of the optative without ἄν to express a wish is found
principally in Pauline writings (Burton lists 35 examples).
τὸ ἀργύριόν σου εἴη εἰς ἀπώλειαν 'Thy money be damned' (Ac. 8:20).

§31.3411   The expression μὴ γένοιτο, often translated 'God forbid!',
is the most common optative of wishing, occuring 15x in NT,
14x in Paul.

§31.342   The <u>potential optative</u>, with ἄν, describes a future action or
state contingent on circumstances. This will be discussed
further under complex sentences (§37.646).

§31.35   The participle and infinitive, since they are not properly moods,
are not discussed here. See §30.38, §34.42ff., and §30.382, §34.41.

§31.4   <u>Voice</u>, or the relationship of the subject to the predicate, is
         also indicated by the verb morphology (cf. §24.13). In Greek
there are three voices: active, middle, and passive.

§31.41   The <u>active voice</u> of the verb indicates the action of the subject
         upon the object (transitive), or makes an affirmation about the
subject (intransitive). εἶδεν πᾶς ὁ λαὸς αὐτόν 'All the people saw him'
(Ac. 3:9). τί θαυμάζετε ἐπὶ τούτῳ 'Why do you wonder about this?' (Ac. 3:12).

§31.42   The <u>passive voice</u> indicates the activity of the verb upon the
         subject. Normally, only a transitive verb can be put in the
passive, since only a transitive verb takes an object, and the object of an
active verb becomes the subject of the passive. (Active: "John hit Joe."
Passive: "Joe was hit [by John]."). ἐπήρθη 'He was raised up' (Ac. 1:9).
Cf. τοῦτον τὸν Ἰησοῦν ἀνέστησεν ὁ θεός 'This Jesus God raised up' (Ac. 2:32).

§31.421 Verbs which take two objects (§33.3), when inverted to the
         passive voice, may have a <u>retained object</u> (§33.321, .331).

§31.43   The <u>middle voice</u>, generally the most difficult for us to compre-
         hend, usually indicates that the subject performs the action on
himself, or for his own benefit, or in some way involves himself in the
action beyond being the subject. It is often not distinguishable from the
active, and must often be translated as an active verb. ἤρξαντο λαλεῖν
'They began (mid.) to speak' (Ac.2:4). It is often possible to rationalize
an explanation, but we can never be sure that the verbs developed in the
way we rationalize them. For example, ἀποκρίνομαι 'I answer,' may have
developed from 'I draw a judgment for myself from,' and ἄρχομαι 'I begin'
may have developed from 'I rule myself'--but we would do better to look for
material for inductive study of such matters.

§31.431 The <u>reflexive middle</u> is comparatively rare; more commonly the
         reflexive pronoun is used with the active voice. ἀπήγξατο 'He
hanged himself' (Mt. 27:5).

§31.432   The <u>intensive middle</u> (or "dynamic" or "indirect" middle) puts
stress on the subject as causing the action. ἀπειλησώμεθα
αὐτοῖς μηκέτι λαλεῖν 'Let us charge them no longer to speak' (Ac. 4:17).

§31.433   The <u>permissive middle</u> indicates that the subject permits the
action to affect him, or seeks the action on his own behalf.
ἀνέβη Ἰωσὴφ...ἀπογράψασθαι 'Joseph went up to permit himself to be
enrolled (or to enroll himself)' (Lk. 2:4-5).

§31.44   A verb which has no active form, but which is used in the middle
(or middle and passive) with an active sense, is called a
<u>deponent</u>. The name is poorly <u>chosen</u>. οὓς ἐξελέξατο 'Whom he had <u>chosen</u>'
(Ac. 1:2).

§31.5   <u>Tense</u>, which includes the <u>type of the action</u> as well as (or
perhaps rather than) the <u>time of the action</u> is indicated by the
morphology of the Greek verb also. The student of Greek should discard the
simple idea of "past, present, future" when dealing with Greek tenses, and
concentrate on what is being conveyed by the Greek forms. Some grammarians,
indeed, reject the word "tense" entirely and substitute "aspect"; others
use the German word <u>Aktionsart</u> ('kind of action'). However, in the
indicative, at least, both tense and aspect are denoted.

§31.51   The following chart, found in a number of grammars, may help
clarify the nature of "tense" in the Greek verb.

	Indefinite Action	Continued Action	Completed Action
Present Time		Present γράφω 'I am writing'	Perfect γέγραφα 'I have written'
Past Time	Aorist ἔγραψα 'I wrote'	Imperfect ἔγραφον 'I was writing'	Pluperfect ἐγεγράφειν 'I had written'
Future Time	Future γράψω 'I shall write'		Future Perfect γεγράψεται 'It will have been written'

§31.511   <u>Time of action or state</u>, viewed from the position of the speaker
          is past, present, or future. The indicator of past time generally
is an augment (§14.221). The augment is lacking in all but the indicative
forms, and only the indicative forms carry a time indication. The indicator
of the future is less obvious: it is a combination of the aoristic sigma
(§24.33) (a sign of indefiniteness?) and the primary ending (§24.4131).
The fact that there is no morphological way of expressing an indefinite
present ('I write') or a continued future ('I shall be writing') should give
us pause to rethink the whole matter.

§31.512   <u>Aspect,</u> or kind of action, can be described as either continous
          or completed; a third category is indefinite (the Greek word is
aorist), for an action or state viewed without concern for its aspect.
The morpheme for the aorist is the infixed sigma (except in the 2d aorist)
(§§24.413, .4131). The morpheme for completed action is reduplication
(§24.314).

§31.5121 The basic characteristics of these three aspects is brought out
          most clearly in the infinitives: for example, pres. 'to be doing,'
perf. 'to have done,' aor. 'to do.'

§31.513   The "aoristic present" ('I write') is morphologically lacking,
          possibly because we must think of the nature of present activity
or state as continuing. In English, the indefinite "I write" and the
continuous "I am writing" have different shades of meaning, and differ from
verb to verb as well. "I write," for example, may have not the slightest
implication of present activity. The Greek would use the aorist in some
cases for our aoristic present.

§31.514   The "continuous future" ('I will be writing') is lacking,
          possibly because that which is future is indefinite. The Greek
often uses a future periphrastic if he wants to stress the continuous
nature of future action or state.

§31.52   The <u>present tense</u> conveys the idea of action in progress. It may be used of the past, and it may also be used of the future, but basically it is used of the present. It has been described as "the imperfect of the present." Moule says, "start by seeing whether it can be translated by the English periphrastic present." πῶς ἡμεῖς ἀκούομεν 'How (is it that) we are hearing?' (Ac. 2:8).

§31.521   The <u>historical present</u> is the present indicative used to tell past action in a graphic way. λέγει δὲ αὐτός 'But he himself (i.e. the patriarch David) says' (Ac. 2:34).

§31.522   The <u>futuristic present</u> is the present used to speak vividly of future action or state. ὃ δὲ ἔχω τοῦτό σοι δίδωμι 'What I have this I give (i.e. will give) to you' (Ac. 3:6).

§31.523   The <u>conative present</u> is the use of the present indicative to express action attempted but not completed. διὰ ποῖον αὐτῶν ἔργον ἐμὲ λιθάζετε; 'For which work of these are you stoning (i.e. are you planning to stone) me?' (Jn. 10:32).

§31.524   The <u>gnomic present</u> is the use of the present indicative to express customary actions, general truths, maxims, and the like. πᾶν δένδρον ἀγαθὸν καρποὺς καλοὺς ποιεῖ 'Every good tree produces good fruit' (Matt. 7:17).

§31.525   The present indicative is sometimes used of past action that is still in progress. This is generally translated into English as a perfect ('has been preached'), but sometimes as a present. ὑμεῖς δὲ μαρτυρεῖτε, ὅτι ἀπ᾽ ἀρχῆς μετ᾽ ἐμοῦ ἐστε 'And you bear witness, because from the beginning you have been (lit. are) with me' (Jn. 15:27).

§31.526   The present is used in reported speech ("indirect discourse," §37.82) when the speaker would have used the present. In English we translate this according to the requirements of Eng. syntax, or "sequence of tenses." (Eng., direct: "He said, 'I am going.'"; indirect, "He said he was going.") ἀπυνθάνοντο εἰ Σίμων...ἐνθάδε ξενίζεται 'They asked if Simon was (lit. is) lodging there' (Ac. 10:18).

§31.527   The <u>aoristic present</u> is the use of the present to describe an event that is simultaneous with the telling, when the event is conceived of as a punctiliar idea. ἰᾶταί σε Ἰησοῦς Χριστός 'Jesus Christ has healed (lit. heals) you' (Ac. 9:34).

§31.528   It should be obvious that these distinctions are determined by context alone. There is absolutely no formal difference between a "progressive present" and a "historical present"—and many times even the context is not fully conclusive, as the debate of commentators proves.

§31.53   The <u>imperfect indicative</u> tense conveys the idea of continuous or linear action in past time. It is to be carefully distinguished from the aorist (cf. §31.54) in the kind of action or state described. Many of the statements about the present can be made about the imperfect, and the best initial translation attempt is the Eng. periphrastic past ("I was doing"). The imperfect is found only in the indicative, since it differs from the present only in time, and time is not expressed in the non-indicative tenses. ἐπίπρασκον καὶ διεμέριζον 'They were selling and they were dividing' (Ac. 2:45).

§31.531   The <u>inceptive imperfect</u> is the imperfect used to describe the beginning of a continuing action in past time. ἐξαλλόμενος ἔστη καὶ περιεπάτει 'leaping up, he stood and began to walk' (Ac. 3:8).

§31.532   The <u>iterative imperfect</u> is the imperfect used to describe a customary or repeated action in past time. τις ἀνὴρ... ἐβαστάζετο ὃν ἐτίθουν καθ᾽ ἡμέραν 'A man was carried, whom they placed daily' (Ac. 3:2). (Ac. 4:34).

§31.533   The <u>conative imperfect</u> is the imperfect used to describe action attempted but not completed in past time (cf. §31.523).

συνήλλασσεν αὐτοὺς εἰς εἰρήνην 'He would have reconciled (lit., was reconciling) them unto peace' (Ac. 7:26).

§31.534   The desiderative imperfect is the imperfect used to express a
          wish in an indirect or veiled manner. At times, it is not truly
a wish, but more like the expression, "I could almost do...." (cf. Rom. 9:3,
ηὐχόμην γὰρ ἀνάθεμα εἶναι αὐτός 'For I myself was wishing to be damned'--
certainly not his wish!). ἐβουλόμην καὶ αὐτὸς τοῦ ἀνθρώπου ἀκοῦσαι 'I myself
was also wishing to hear the man' (Ac. 25:22).

§31.535   The use of the imperfect in conditional clauses will be discussed
          under complex sentences (§37.6ff.).

§31.536   Again, we must be warned that only context can determine the
          difference between "inceptive," "iterative," and other imperfects.
We translate 'They began to speak' (Ac. 2:4, §31.531) because they had not
been speaking until that time, and we translate 'He would have reconciled
them' (Ac. 7:26, §31.533) because we know that he failed to reconcile them.
The fact that scholars often engage in long and inconclusive dialogues
over certain statements should be sufficient proof that the differences
are not always clear-cut.

§31.54   The aorist tense conveys the idea of action or state viewed as an
          event. In the indicative mood, it is usually related to past time,
but in other moods and in the infinitive and participle there is no time
reference whatever (αοριστος means 'unlimited, unqualified'). Whereas the
present and imperfect are described as a line (linear), the aorist is
described as a point (punctiliar). It is the most common and most important
of the Greek tenses, and the student of Greek must master its nature. Often
the best English translation is the simple past. ἐγένετο ἄφνω ἐκ τοῦ
οὐρανοῦ ἦχος 'Suddenly there came out of heaven a sound' (Ac. 2:2).

§31.541   The constative aorist is the aorist used to express an action or
          state in its entirety. It may even be used to express activity

over a period of time when that activity is viewed simply as a unitary fact, (e.g. "Mantle batted .343") and no stress on the continuing nature is intended. Ἰωάννης μὲν ἐβάπτισεν ὕδατι 'John baptized with water' (Ac. 1:5). τίνα τῶν προφητῶν οὐκ ἐδίωξαν οἱ πατέρες ὑμῶν; 'Which of the prophets did your fathers not persecute?' (Ac. 7:52).

§31.542   The ingressive (or "inceptive") aorist is the aorist used to indicate the beginning of an action or state. Often it is the meaning of the verb that determines this. "He lived" in the sense of "he came to life" is clearly inceptive, for if we wanted to stress the continuity of life, we would use the imperfect. ἐσίγησεν δὲ πᾶν τὸ πλῆθος καὶ ἤκουον Βαρναβᾶ καὶ Παύλου 'And all the multitude became silent (aor.) and they began to listen to (impf.) Barnabas and Paul' (Ac. 15:12).

§31.543   The culminative (or "resultative") aorist is the aorist used to indicate the culmination of a state or action. Again, the meaning of the verb often determines this. (E.g. "he hit" is culminative, for first he made up his mind, then he swung, and finally he hit). οὐκ ἐψεύσω ἀνθρώποις ἀλλὰ τῷ θεῷ 'You did not lie to men but to God' (Ac. 5:4).

§31.544   The gnomic aorist is the aorist used to express a fact, truth, or the like. In my mind, it can be considered as a culminative aorist. Cf. Dana and Mantey §181(1), Moule, Idiom-Book, p. 12. ἐδικαιώθη ἡ σοφία ἀπὸ πάντων τῶν τέκνων αὐτῆς 'Wisdom is justified by all her children' (Lk. 7:35).

§31.545   The epistolary aorist is the aorist used to describe an action or state at the reader's point of view (cf. the historical present, §31.521). In some ways this is similar to the culminative aorist. Paul writes, "I sent him" (Phil. 2:28). Actually, at the time of writing, Paul is going to send him; when the letter is finished, he sends him; and when the statement is read, the action has culminated. ἔπεμψα πρὸς σέ 'I sent (him) to you' (Ac. 23:30; the letter was accompanying Paul).

§31.546   The <u>dramatic aorist</u> is the aorist used to describe a state of
          mind just reached, or an act expressive of such decision. This is
sometimes called the "tragic aorist." ἔγνων τί ποιήσω 'I have just perceived (lit. I knew, 2 aor.) what I shall do' (Lk. 16:4).

§31.547   Once again let it be stressed that context and the meaning of
          the particular verb are the determining factors. It is false
methodology to "name" the aorist first, and then translate the verb.
Correct methodology works out the clause, and then lets the context determine
the nuance of the aorist that is used. We know from context that the unjust
steward (Lk. 16:4; §31.546) had not known (as an activity over a period
of time), or known (as a maxim) what he was going to do; the context makes
it clear that he has just stumbled on to an idea. It could be called
"culminative" or it could be called "dramatic."

§31.55   The <u>future tense</u> is the nearest approach to pure "tense" of any
          of the Greek tenses. It indicates the time of action more than
the kind of action (in fact, BDF §§314,348 says the future is strictly
time and not kind of action). The close connection (morphologically and
practically) between the fut. ind. and the aor. sbjtv. has led some scholars
to see the future as a late development from the aorist. It is sometimes
maintained that the fut. ind. is aoristic or punctiliar, and not linear,
in its aspect. Translation in Eng. can usually be made by using the Eng.
future tense. δώσω τέρατα ἐν τῷ οὐρανῷ ἄνω 'I will give wonders in heaven
above' (Ac. 2:19).

§31.551   The <u>predictive future</u> is the future used to describe an action
          or state that will occur in the future. Generally the fact,
not the nature, of the action or state is in mind. λήμφεσθε δύναμιν
'You will receive power' (Ac. 1:8).

§31.5511 Since the punctiliar nature is implicit, Burton calls this an
          aoristic predictive future.

§31.5512 When the durative or progressive nature of the action or state
          is implied, Burton calls it a progressive predictive future;
Dana and Mantey call it the progressive future [D&M §178(2)].
ἐν τούτῳ χαίρω· ἀλλὰ καὶ χαρήσομαι 'In this I rejoice, moreover I shall
rejoice' (Phil. 1:18).

§31.5513 Moule, Idiom-Book, p. 10, points out that when the linear or
          progressive sense is clearly intended, the normal expedient
is the use of a periphrastic. He admits, however, that there are some
linear futures in the N.T.

§31.5514 Burton's distinction between "assertive" and "promissory"
          futures (Moods and Tenses, §65), seems to be based more on the
Eng. translation and the use of 'will' or 'shall' than on the Greek text.
After all, our Eng. use of modals is Germanic in origin, and we have no
true future tense, only periphrastic futures.

§31.552 The imperative future is the future used to express a command
          or prohibition. It occurs most frequently in prohibitions
negated by οὐ (§34.221). ἀγαπήσεις τὸν πλησίον σου 'You shall love
your neighbor' (Mt. 5:43, from LXX). οὐ φονεύσεις 'Do not kill'
(Mt. 5:21, also LXX).

§31.553 The deliberative future is the future used for questions, real
          or rhetorical, when some uncertainty is present. Here the fut.
ind. approaches the aor. sbjtv. quite closely. ποῖον οἶκον οἰκοδομήσετέ μοι;
'What kind of house will you build for me?' (Ac. 7:49).

§31.554 The gnomic future is the future used to express an action or state
          which is expected to continue into the future (cf. §§31.524,
31.544). The similarity to the gnomic aorist is apparent. It may in this
case be asked whether it is not a special category of the predicative
future. ἕκαστος γὰρ τὸ ἴδιον φορτίον βαστάσει 'For each one will bear his
own burden' (Gal. 6:5).

§31.555   Again, context is the sole determining factor!

§31.56   The <u>perfect tense</u> in Greek conveys the idea of effect in the
              present as the result of action in the past, or more simply,
completed action. It is not the same as the English perfect (present
perfect), but it approaches it. Translation into English will vary from
verb to verb, but the Eng. perfect is a good starting-point. Possibly the
simple γέγραπται 'It is written' (not 'It was written,' which could mean
that it no longer exists) best illustrates the perfect.

§31.561   The <u>perfect of completed action</u> ("consummative perfect") is the
              perfect used to describe an action as completed and its existing
result. πεπληρώκατε τὴν Ἰερουσαλὴμ τῆς διδαχῆς ὑμῶν 'You have filled
Jerusalem with your teaching (and it is now full)' (Ac. 5:28).

§31.562   The <u>perfect of existing state</u> ("intensive perfect") is the
              perfect used to describe the existing state or condition,
leaving out of view the past action. γέγραπται γὰρ ἐν βίβλῳ 'For it is
written in the Bible' (Ac. 1:20).

§31.5621   Often the meaning of the verb itself requires that it be put
              in one or the other of these categories. It is open to question
whether the categories should be distinguished.

§31.563   Dana and Mantey [§184(3)] distinguish an iterative perfect,
              denoting a process of repeated actions which have brought about
a certain result. It could be called a perfect of repeated action.
θεὸν οὐδεὶς ἑώρακεν πώποτε 'No one has ever seen God' (Jn. 1:18).

§31.564   Burton (§77) distinguishes an intensive perfect (which is not
              the same as Dana and Mantey's "intensive perfect" §31.562 above),
which is in effect an emphatic or intensive present in meaning.
καὶ ἡμεῖς πεπιστεύκαμεν καὶ ἐγνώκαμεν... 'And we believe and know...'
(Jn. 6:69); this could not possibly be translated in past tense!).

§31.565   Burton distinguishes an aoristic perfect which Dana and Mantey
          subsume under the dramatic perfect. It is found frequently in
the N.T. to describe vividly an existing state, hence it is a special
rhetorical usage of the perfect of existing state. οὐκ ἔσχηκα ἄνεσιν
τῷ πνεύματί μου 'I had no peace of mind' (2 Cor. 2:13).

§31.566   These distinctions are fine points on which the experts are
          in a measure of disagreement. The names are less important
than the ideas, and context, as always, plus the meaning of the verb
used, are the determining factors.

§31.57   The pluperfect tense, like the perfect, conveys the idea of
          existing state as a result of completed action. It differs
from the perfect only in this: its point of view is in the past.
The Eng. pluperfect (past perfect) is usually a good starting-point for
translation. καὶ ὧδε εἰς τοῦτο ἐληλύθει 'and he has come here to this
(place)' (Ac. 9:21).

§31.571   Since the pluperfect is only a perfect in past time, the
          same categories can be used to describe it. What Burton calls
the pluperfect of completed action, D&M call "consummative," namely the
plpf. ind. used to convey the idea of an action completed in past time
from the point of view of the speaker or writer. Μαγδαληνή ἀφ' ἧς
δαιμόνια ἑπτὰ ἐξεληλύθει 'Magdalene, from whom seven demons had gone
forth' (Lk. 8:2).

§31.572   Burton's pluperfect of existing state is called by D&M the
          "intensive" pluperfect, the plpf. ind. used to describe a
result existing in past time as the result of a previous action.
ὁ ἄνθρωπος ἐφ' ὃν γεγόνει τὸ σημεῖον τοῦτο 'The man on whom this sign
had happened' (Ac. 4:22).

§31.573   The classification of the plpf. is determined by the meaning
          of the verb and the context.

§32.   THE DEFINED SUBJECT. We have seen that the verb morphology
          is capable of expressing the subject (§§25.14, 25.15, 31.1).
In some cases, for emphasis, clarity, or other reasons, the author or
speaker wishes to define the subject more closely. The subject may be

NOMINATIVE
=subject | VERB |

defined by a noun (§§32.1), a pronoun (§32.2),
an adjective used substantivally (§32.3), a
participle used substantivally (§32.4), an
infinitive (§32.5), or a noun clause (§32.6).
The defined subject may be still more closely
defined by the use of modifiers (§35.).

§32.1   A <u>noun</u> in the nominative case, in concord with the verb in person
          and number (§§31.11ff., 12ff.), may be used to define the sub-
ject. Ἰωάννης ἐβάπτισεν 'John baptized' (Ac. 1:5). γενηθήτω ἡ ἔπαυλις
αὐτοῦ ἔρημος 'Let his residence be deserted' (Ac. 1:20).

§32.11   For details concerning concord of the verb and the defined
          subject, note §§31.121, .122, .123.

§32.2   A <u>pronoun</u> in the nominative case, in concord with the verb in
          person and number (§§31.11ff., .12ff.), may be used to define
the subject in the verb.

§32.21   The <u>personal pronoun</u> (§23.1) may be used under certain condi-
          tions. We must keep in mind that the personal pronoun is
inherent in the verb form.

§32.211   Verbs in 1st or 2d person may have the personal pronoun added
          for contrast or emphasis (§31.111, .112). ἡμεῖς ἐσμεν μάρτυρες
'We are witnesses' (Ac. 2:32). ὃν ὑμεῖς ἐσταυρώσατε 'Whom <u>you</u> crucified'
(Ac. 2:36).

§32.212   The 3d pers. pronoun singular in the nom. is an intensive pronoun
          (see §23.15), and can be used with the verb in any person and
number. καθὼς αὐτοὶ οἴδατε 'As you <u>yourselves</u> know' (Ac. 2:22).

§32.213   The personal pronoun is sometimes used with the verb in what
           appears to be a Hebraism or Semitism (cf. §03., 03.1), see BDF
§277(2).

§32.214   Like the noun, the pronoun is found in unusual concord, cf.
           §31.121, .122, .123.

§32.22   The interrogative pronoun in the nominative (§23.5) may be used
           in an interrogative sentence when the speaker or writer wants
the subject to be more precisely defined. It regularly agrees in number
with the verb. τίς σε κατέστησεν ἄρχοντα καὶ δικαστὴν ἐφ᾽ ἡμῶν; 'Who
appointed you ruler and judge over us?' (Ac. 7:27).

§32.23   The indefinite pronoun in the nominative (§23.34) may be used
           when the subject is indefinite. παραγενόμενος δέ τις ἀπήγγειλεν
αὐτοῖς 'Someone came and told them' (Ac. 5:25).

§32.24   The demonstrative pronoun (§23.33) in the nominative may be used
           to define the subject. In such cases it is used substantivally
and must be translated 'this one,' 'that one,' 'those,' etc. οὐ γὰρ...
οὗτοι μεθύουσιν 'For these (men) are not drunk' (Ac. 2:15).

§32.241   The definite article, as a demonstrative pronoun (§23.32)
           can be used in the nominative to define the subject. It will
have to be translated 'this man,' 'these men,' etc. ὁ δὲ ἔφη 'And that
one (or he) said' (Ac. 7:2).

§32.25   The relative pronoun (§23.4), except when used indefinitely, is
           used in the nominative to define the subject of the verb in
relative clauses (§37.412). We shall consider this under complex sentences
(§37.4).

§32.3   Adjectives may be used substantivally, hence may be used in the
           nominative in any way that a noun can be used (§32.1ff.).
τὴν ἐπισκοπὴν αὐτοῦ λαβέτω ἕτερος 'His episcopacy let another take' (Ac. 1:20).

§32.31   The neuter singular of an adjective with the definite article is
           often used as an abstract noun.

§32.4   <u>Participles</u>, being verbal adjectives, may likewise be used sub-
           stantivally. When they are so used,   usually
with a definite article, they generally have to be translated into Eng.
by a relative clause, although in some cases an equivalent noun may be used.
οἱ μὲν οὖν συνελθόντες ἠρώτων αὐτόν 'So those who had gathered together
asked him' (Ac. 1:6).

§32.41   The neuter participle with the definite article may be used
           as an abstract noun.

§32.5   An <u>infinitive</u>, being a verbal noun, may be used to define the
           subject. It usually takes the neut. sg. nom. of the definite
article in such case. τὸ δὲ ἀνίπτοις χερσὶν φαγεῖν οὐ κοινοῖ τὸν ἄνθρωπον
'But eating (= to eat) with unwashed hands does not defile a man'
(Mt. 15:20).

§32.51   The infinitive in turn, since it is verbal, may have its own
           subject, object, or other modifiers. In such case the infinitive
clause serves as a <u>noun clause</u> defining the subject of the verb.
οὐκ ἦν δυνατὸν κρατεῖσθαι αὐτὸν ὑπ' αὐτοῦ 'It was not possible for him to
be held by it' (lit., 'him to be held by it was not possible') (Ac. 2:24).

§32.511   The subject of an infinitive is in the accusative case.

§32.6   A <u>noun clause</u> (§37.3) may serve to define the subject of a verb.
           Except for participial and infinitival clauses, just considered
above, these will be considered under complex sentences (§37.2ff.).

§33.   The COMPLEMENT OF THE VERB in the predicate. Some verbs have a
           meaning that is complete in itself, perhaps needing only a more
closely defined subject (intransitive or stative verbs). Other verbs are
incomplete and need the addition of a word or group of words (a complement)

```
                ACCUSATIVE
   nom.  |  VERB  | = object
```

in order to complete the meaning.
(Cf. "He sits" and "he said.")

§33.1   The direct object is a substantive or clause serving as a com-
          plement of a transitive verb. It indicates that which receives
the action of or is produced by the main verb of the predicate.

§33.11   A noun or pronoun in the accusative case may serve as the direct
          object of a transitive verb. λήμψεσθε δύναμιν 'You shall
receive power' (Ac. 1:8). ἠρώτων αὐτόν 'They asked him' (Ac. 1:6).

§33.111   An adjective or participle used substantivally may be the
          direct object.

§33.12   A noun clause may be the direct object (§37.32ff.).
          τί θέλει τοῦτο εἶναι; 'This wishes to be what?' (= "What is
this?") (Ac. 2:12).

§33.121   An infinitive or infinitival clause may be the direct object (§33.611).
          See noun clauses, §33.12.

§33.13   Verbs of saying, knowing, thinking, and the like may take a
          direct quotation, often introduced by ὅτι, as direct object.
εἶπεν δὲ Πέτρος ἀργύριον καὶ χρυσίον οὐχ ὑπάρχει μοι 'Peter said, "I
have no silver and gold"' (Ac. 3:6).

§33.131   If an indirect quotation (§37.83) stands after such a verb, it
          is a dependent clause, and will be considered under complex
sentences.

§33.2   The cognate accusative. Any verb whose meaning permits may take
          an accusative of related signification. Thus, many intransitive
verbs, which cannot take a direct object, can take a cognate accusative,
and transitive verbs may serve in an intransitive way with the cognate accusative. (Cf., for example, the difference between "I sail a boat" and
"I sail the seas.") τὸν καλὸν ἀγῶνα ἠγώνισμαι 'I have fought the good
fight' (2 Tim. 4:7).

§33.21   The cognate accusative is not necessarily a cognate word; it may
          be any related idea. τὸ ποτήριον ὃ ἐγὼ πίνω πίεσθε 'The cup
which I drink you shall drink' (Mark 10:39).

§33.22   An extension of the use of the cognate accusative is found with
          verbs of motion, where a noun in the accusative may complete the
predicate by expressing the ground over which the motion occurs. προῆλθον
ῥύμην μίαν 'They went ahead one street' (Ac. 12:10); ἦλθον ἡμέρας ὁδόν
'they went a road (= journey) of a day' (Lk. 2:44).

§33.23   The accusative of effect is used to express a result effected by
          the action of the verb. (Cf. "To break a hole," "to negotiate
a peace.") δαρήσεται πολλάς 'he shall be beaten many (stripes, blows)'
(Lk. 12:47).

§33.3   Certain verbs are capable of taking two objects. This is to be
          distinguished from the compound object (two direct objects), and
is known by several names, such as the "accusative of the person and the
thing," "accusative of object and result," "accusative of object and cognate object," etc., each having its own distinctives. We may call the
various types by the general term objective complement, or predicate
objective.

§33.31   Verbs of naming, choosing, appointing, making, thinking regard-
          ing, and the like may take a predicate objective (or predicate
accusative) in addition to the object accusative. The predicate objective
is sometimes called the complementary object. καὶ κύριον αὐτὸν καὶ
χριστὸν ἐποίησεν ὁ θεός 'God made him both Lord and Christ' (Ac. 2:36 ,
where there are two predicates objective, "Lord" and "Christ").

§33.311   When such a statement is inverted to the passive construction,
          the direct object becomes the subject of the passive verb, and
the predicate objective becomes a predicate nominative (or, if the syntax
requires, a predicate genitive). καλέσεις τὸ ὄνομα αὐτοῦ Ἰωάννην 'You
shall call his name John' (Lk. 1:13), but κληθήσεται Ἰωάννης 'He shall be
called John' (Lk. 1:60).

§33.32   Verbs of asking, demanding, teaching, reminding, concealing,
depriving, clothing or unclothing, taking away, and the like,
can take two objects, the object of the person (direct object) and the
object of the thing. ἀποστασίαν διδάσκεις ἀπὸ Μωϋσέως τοὺς κατὰ τὰ
ἔθνη πάντας Ἰουδαίους 'You are teaching all the Jews who are among the
gentiles apostasy from Moses' (Ac. 21:21).

§33.321   When such a statement is inverted to the passive construction,
the direct object becomes the subject of the passive verb, and
the object of the thing is retained in the <u>accusative</u> case. οὗτος ἦν
κατηχημένος τὴν ὁδὸν τοῦ κυρίου 'This one was catechized (in) the way
of the Lord' (Ac. 18:25).

§33.33   Verbs of making, fashioning, and the like may take two impersonal
objects, the accusative of the object and the accusative of the
result. θῶ τοὺς ἐχθρούς σου ὑποπόδιον τῶν ποδῶν σου 'I will appoint your
enemies the footstool of your feet' (Ac. 2:35).

§33.331   When such a statement is inverted to the passive, the object
becomes the subject of the passive verb, and the result is
retained as object of the result in the accusative.

§33.34   Verbs of swearing, adjuring, and the like, may take two objects,
the accusative of the person to whom the oath is made, and the
accusative of the person or thing by which it is made. It is impossible
to represent this in English translation. ὁρκίζω ὑμᾶς τὸν Ἰησοῦν ὃν Παῦλος
κηρύσσει 'I swear to you by the Jesus whom Paul preaches' (Ac. 19:13).

§33.35   In all cases where the verb may take two objects, an infinitive,
or a noun clause may replace one (or possibly both) of the
objects. ὡς πεποιηκόσιν τοῦ περιπατεῖν αὐτόν 'As causing him to walk'
(= as though we caused...) (Ac. 3:12).

§33.4   The <u>predicate nominative</u>. With verbs of being, becoming, and
the like, the complement of the verb is really a further
definition of the subject. It is therefore in the nominative case.
ἡμεῖς ἐσμεν μάρτυρες 'We are witnesses' (Ac. 2:32).

§33.41   The verb <u>to be</u> is often omitted when a simple copulative use is
          intended. ὅτι μὲν γὰρ γνωστὸν σημεῖον γέγονεν δι' αὐτῶν...φανερόν
'For that a notable sign has happened through them...(is) clear' (Ac. 4:16).

§33.42   The predicate nominative occurs after verbs of naming, calling,
          and the like, in the passive voice (cf. §33.311).

§33.43   The predicate nominative may be a noun clause, an infinitive,
          or an infinitival clause. τί ἐστιν τὸ ἐκ νεκρῶν ἀναστῆναι
'What is the "resurrection from the dead"?' (Mk. 9:10).

§33.5   The <u>predicate adjective</u>. When the complement is an adjective,
          the verb <u>to be</u> is usually omitted, and the predication is made
by use of the predicate adjective. The predicate adjective must be
distinguished from the attributive adjective. (Pred. adj.: "The boy is
tall"; attrib. adj. "The tall boy.") οὐδεὶς ἀγαθός 'No one is good'
(Lk. 18:19).

§33.51   The predicate adjective is almost invariably <u>anarthrous</u>
          (i.e. without the definite article). It may precede or follow
the subject which it is serving to predicate. ὁ εἷς Φαρισαῖος καὶ ὁ ἕτερος
τελώνης 'The one (was) a Pharisee and the other (was) a tax-collector'
(Lk. 18:10). καλὸν οὖν τὸ ἅλας 'Salt then is good' (Lk. 14:34).

§33.511   The <u>position</u> of the adjective relative to the definite article
          is called the "predicate position" in distinction to the
position of the attributive adjective (which is called the "attributive
position"). We shall consider the attributive adjective when we consider
the modifiers of the substantive (§35.).

§33.52   The predicate adjective may be a participle or participial clause
          used adjectivally.

§33.521   The predicate adjective may be followed by a complementary infinitive
          (§33.61). οὗ οὐκ εἰμί ἄξιος τὸ ὑπόδημα τῶν ποδῶν λῦσαι 'of whom I am
not worthy to loose the sandal of the feet' (Ac. 13:25).

§33.6   The <u>predicate_complement</u> may be an <u>infinitive</u> or <u>infinitival</u>
          clause.

§33.61   The <u>complementary infinitive</u> is an infinitive used to complete the
          thought expressed by certain verbs, nouns, or adjectives.

§33.611   Verbs of wishing, commanding, advising, permitting, beginning, at-
          tempting, and the like, usually require another verb to complete the
meaning. The infinitive may be in indirect discourse (§37.8211). It will
usually be anarthrous (without the definite article). ὧν ἤρξατο ὁ Ἰησοῦς ποιεῖν τε καὶ διδάσκειν 'which Jesus began to do and to teach' (Ac. 1:1).

§33.612   In many cases the complementary infinitive is in fact a noun or noun-
          clause serving as the direct object of the verb (cf. "I desire to see
you" = "I desire a sight of you"). In such cases, the def. art. (n.s.a.) may
precede the inf. οὐ παραιτοῦμαι τὸ ἀποθανεῖν 'I am not begging off dying' (Ac.
25:11).

§33.613   The complementary infinitive may follow a noun or adjective, cf.
          §33.521.

§33.7   The <u>predicate_genitive</u>. Certain verbs, or verbs under certain
          conditions, take the complement of the predicate in the
genitive case.

§33.71   Verbs of being, becoming, and other copulative verbs, may take a
          <u>predicate genitive</u>. ὃ ἦν Σίμωνος 'which was Simon's' (Lk. 5:3).

§33.711   The predicate genitive may be any of several of the usages of
          the genitive: possessive, subjective, objective, partitive,
genitive of measure, or genitive of material. ἐγὼ εἰμι Παύλου 'I am of Paul'
(1 Cor. 1:12). οὐκ ἐσμὲν νυκτὸς οὐδὲ σκότους 'We are not of (the) night,
nor of darkness' (1 Th. 5:5).

§33.72   Verbs of naming, etc. (§33.31) may take a predicate genitive in
          place of the predicate accusative. ἐπὶ τῇ στοᾷ τῇ καλουμένῃ
Σαλομῶντος 'on the porch called Solomon's' (Ac. 3:11).

§33.73   Any verb whose action affects the object only in part may take
          a complement in the genitive. μετελάμβανον τροφῆς 'Partaking
(of) food' (Ac. 2:46).

§33.74   Certain verbs, which by nature do not act upon the object in
          the same way that "action" verbs do, such as tasting, smelling,
hearing, perceiving, comprehending, remembering, forgetting, desiring,
caring for, sparing, neglecting, wondering at, admiring, despising, and
the like, may take a genitive of the object.

§33.741   Verbs of hearing, learning, etc., may take an accusative of the
          thing heard or learned, and a genitive of the person from whom
heard or learned. ἣν ἠκούσατέ μου 'Which you heard from me' (Ac. 1:4).

§33.742   Verbs of touching, taking hold, claiming, aiming at, hitting,
          missing, beginning, attaining, making trial of, and the like,
take a genitive of the object. The English translation of many of these
requires a prepositional complement. ἔχιδνα...καθῆψεν τῆς χειρὸς αὐτοῦ
'A viper...fastened on his hand' (Ac. 28:3).

§33.7421 The verb to take hold of may take an object accusative of the
          person and/or an object genitive of the part of the person.
πιάσας αὐτὸν τῆς δεξιᾶς χειρὸς ἤγειρεν αὐτόν 'Taking him by the right
hand he raised him up' (Ac. 3:7).

§33.743   Verbs of fulness and want or lack take the genitive of material.
          ἐπλήσθησαν πάντες πνεύματος ἁγίου 'They all were filled with the
Holy Spirit' (Ac. 2:4).

§33.7431 The verb to fill takes the accusative of the thing filled and
          the genitive of the material. πεπληρώκατε τὴν Ἰερουσαλὴμ τῆς
διδαχῆς ὑμῶν 'You have filled Jerusalem with your teaching' (Ac. 5:28).

§33.7432 The verb to want (lack) may take a cognate accusative (§33.2) of
          the thing as well as a genitive. προσδεόμενός τινος '(as though)
needing anything more' (Ac. 17:25).

§33.7433 The verb δεῖ may take a dative of the person as well as the genitive.

§33.744 Verbs of removing, differing, restraining, releasing, failing, ceasing, giving up, and the like, may be followed by a genitive of separation. Usually the English translation requires the preposition "from." μέλλειν τε καὶ καθαιρεῖσθαι τῆς μεγαλειότητος αὐτῆς 'even about to be deposed from her magnificence' (Ac. 19:27).

§33.7441 Verbs of depriving and taking away may take a genitive in place of the accusative of the thing. ἐκώλυσεν αὐτοὺς τοῦ βουλήματος 'He hindered them from their plan' (Ac. 27:43).

§33.745 Verbs of surpassing, being inferior, and the like, take a genitive of comparison. πολλῶν στρουθίων διαφέρετε ὑμεῖς 'You are worth more than many sparrows' (Mt. 10:31).

§33.746 Verbs of accusing, prosecuting, convicting, acquiting, condemning, and the like, take a genitive denoting the crime and an accusative of the person. καὶ γὰρ κινδυνεύομεν ἐγκαλεῖσθαι στάσεως 'For we are in danger of being charged with rioting' (Ac. 19:40).

§33.7461 These verbs may take a cognate accusative (§33.2) on which the genitive depends.

§33.747 Verbs expressing emotions, such as admiration, wonder, affection, hatred, pity, anger, envy, or revenge, may take a genitive of the cause of the emotion. A number of these verbs have lost this characteristic in the NT. BDF §176. ἐπεμελήθη αὐτοῦ 'He took care of him' (Lk. 10:34).

§33.748 Compound verbs (§25.3), whose meaning would suggest an object accusative, may take an object in the case governed by the preposition in the compound. κατεγέλων αὐτοῦ 'They laughed him to scorn' (Mt. 9:24).

§33.8   The <u>predicate dative</u>. Certain verbs, such as to benefit, serve,
           obey, defend, assist, please, trust, satisfy, advise, exhort, and
their opposites, or verbs expressing friendliness, hostility, blame, abuse,
reproach, envy, anger, threats, and the like, take a dative of the object,
where in Eng. a direct object is found.

§33.81   Certain impersonal verbs take the dative of the person with the
           genitive of the thing (§33.7433).

§33.82   With verbs of being or becoming, the dative may be used to
           indicate possession. The verb may be omitted. ὄνομα αὐτῷ Ἰωάννης
'His name was John' (lit. [the] name to him [was] John') (Jn. 1:6).

§33.83   Many compound verbs, especially those compounded with εν-, συν-,
           or επι-, take a predicate in the dative where the English trans-
lation suggests a transitive verb with a direct object. μὴ παρενοχλεῖν
τοῖς ἀπὸ τῶν ἐθνῶν 'Not to trouble those of the gentiles...' (Ac. 15:19).

§33.84   The dative of indirect object is discussed in §34.1.

§33.9   The <u>supplementary participle</u>. The participle is sometimes added
           to certain verbs to complete the idea expressed by the verb, in
a way similar to the complementary infinitive (§33.61).

§33.91   The addition of the ptcp. of the verb <u>to say</u>, while it falls into
           this category, is usually classed as a Semitism, corresponding to
the Heb. **lē'mōr**. διεμαρτύρατο δέ πού τις λέγων 'Someone testified some-
where saying' (Heb. 2:6).

§33.92   The use of the pres. ptcp. with a verb of <u>being</u> is called the
           periphrastic, and for all intents and purposes forms a verb
phrase (§30.411) that tends to emphasize continuous activity in the time
indicated by the tense of the verb <u>to be</u>. ἦσαν δὲ ἐν Ἰερουσαλὴμ κατοικοῦντες Ἰουδαῖοι 'Now Jews were dwelling in Jerusalem' (Ac. 2:5).

§33.93   The use of the supplementary participle with verbs of a modified
           sense of being or doing (such as ὑπάρχω, τυγχάνω, ἄρχομαι,
παύομαι, etc.) in the NT is confined mainly to Lk-Ac, Paul, and Heb.
(cf. BDF §414).

§34.   MODIFIERS OF THE VERB. The verb in the predicate may be modified
           by various means (cf. §30.2). In general, verb modifiers are
adverbs, or adverbial phrases and clauses. In addition, the indirect object,
the genitive absolute, and the

nominative	VERB	accusative
	DATIVE	
	= modifier	

cognate accusative are sometimes
classified as verb modifiers.

§34.1   The <u>dative</u> case may be looked on principally as the case of
           the verb modifier. (For use of the dative as a noun modifier,
see §§35.32ff.). It may be used to modify the verb by indicating that to
which or for which the predication occurs, that by which or with which it
occurs, or the time when or place where the predication occurs.

§34.11   The <u>indirect object</u>. Certain transitive verbs, such as to give,
           to tell, etc., take a more remote or <u>indirect object</u>, as well as
a nearer or direct object. The indirect object classically was in the dative
case, and some of this usage remains in the NT. There is a tendency, however,
to use a prepositional phrase in NT times. ἔδωκαν κλήρους αὐτοῖς 'They
gave lots to them; (Ac. 1:26). Ἀλέξανδρος...ἤθελεν ἀπολογεῖσθαι τῷ δήμῳ
'Alexander...wished to make a defense to the people' (Ac. 19:33).

§34.12   The dative may modify a passive verb by defining the <u>agent</u> or the
           <u>means</u> of the action (cf. §35.322). ὁ θεὸς τῆς δόξης ὤφθη τῷ
πατρὶ ἡμῶν 'the God of glory was seen by our father (= appeared to ...)'
(Ac. 7:2).

§34.121   BDF says there is only one genuine example of dat. of agent in
           NT, viz. Lk. 23:15. The others are either instrumental or depend
on the similarity of the passive with the deponent meaning. (BDF §191).

§34.13   The dative may modify a verb by stating the <u>means</u> of the predication.
           βοῶντα φωνῇ μεγάλῃ 'crying with a great sound (Ac. 8:7). ἀνεῖλεν δὲ
Ἰάκωβον ... μαχαίρῃ 'he killed James with a sword' (Ac. 12:2).

§34.14　　The <u>dative of time</u>. The dative may modify the verb by defining
　　　　　the time of the action/state (cf. §35.323). περιέτεμεν αὐτὸν
τῇ ἡμέρᾳ τῇ ὀγδόῃ 'He circumcised him on the eighth day' (Ac. 7:8).
τῇ τε ἐπιούσῃ ἡμέρᾳ ὤφθη αὐτοῖς 'On the following day he appeared to
them ....' (Ac. 7:26). ἱκανῷ χρόνῳ 'for some time' (Ac. 8:11). This last
illustration is contrary to classical usage which restricts the temporal
dat. to a point of time (BDF §§200-201).

§34.141　　The dat. of <u>place</u> is rare in the NT. A stereotyped example is
　　　　　τῇ δεξιᾷ αὐτοῦ 'to/at his right hand' (Ac. 5:31).

§34.15　　The <u>dative of advantage</u>. The dative may be used to define the
　　　　　person to whose <u>advantage</u> or <u>disadvantage</u> the predication of the
verb pertains. ἀνεθρέψατο αὐτὸν ἑαυτῷ εἰς υἱόν 'she brought him up for
herself as a son' (Ac. 7:21). ἐκπεπλήρωκεν τοῖς τέκνοις 'he fulfilled to
(their) children' (Ac. 13:32).

§34.16　　The <u>dative of reference</u>. The dative is used to denote the person
　　　　　or thing with reference to which the predication holds true
(cf. §35.3231). τοῦ γενομένου ὁδηγοῦ τοῖς συλλαβοῦσιν Ἰησοῦν 'who became
a guide to those who seized Jesus' (Ac. 1:16). ἀπεθάνομεν τῇ ἁμαρτίᾳ
'We died to sin' (Rom. 6:2).

§34.17　　The <u>dative of cause</u>. The dative may be used to modify the verb
　　　　　by indicating the cause of the action. Ἐὰν μὴ περιτμηθῆτε
τῷ ἔθει τῷ Μωϋσέως 'If you are not circumcised according to the custom of
Moses ...' (Ac. 15:1). τῇ ἀπιστίᾳ ἐξεκλάσθησαν 'They were broken off
because of unbelief' (Rom. 11:20).

§34.2　　The <u>adverb</u> is the simple verb modifier (§30.34) asking the
　　　　　questions, <u>How? When? Where? Why? How long?</u> or <u>By how much?</u>
in interrogative sentences, and answering such questions in declarative
sentences. τί ἑστήκατε '<u>Why</u> are you standing?' (Ac. 1:11). ἐγένετο ἄφνω
ἐκ τοῦ οὐρανοῦ ἦχος 'A sound <u>suddenly</u> came out of heaven' (Ac. 2:2).

§34.21　　Certain nouns or adjectives in the neut. acc. are used as verb
　　　　　modifiers. οὕτως ἐλεύσεται ὃν τρόπον ἐθεάσασθε αὐτὸν πορευόμενον
'He shall thus come <u>in which manner</u> (= as) you saw him going' (Ac. 1:11).

§34.22   The <u>negative adverbs</u> need particular attention. Two forms are
found, οὐ and μή each of which can be compounded with other
particles (such as οὐδείς, μηκέτι, etc.). οὐ is the negative of fact and
statement; μή is the negative of will and thought. οὐ is used with the
indicative and with the particple (but cf. §34.2225); μή is used with the
subjunctive and with the imperative. For optative and infinitive, see
following sections.

§34.221   The negative adverb οὐκ (οὐ, οὐχ) or one of its compounds is used
to negate any word or statement where no uncertainty is implied.

§34.2211 οὐ can be used to negate a word (οὐ-privative). οὐκ ὀλίγοι
'Not a few' (Ac. 12:18).

§34.2212 οὐ is used to negate verbs in the indicative mood. οὐκ ἤθελεν
'He did not wish...' (Mk. 9:30). Cf. 1 Th. 5:6, §33.711.

§34.2213 οὐ is used to negate verbs in the optative mood, except in wishes.

§34.2214 οὐ is used in indirect discourse after ὅτι and ὡς.

§34.222   The negative adverb μή or one of its compounds is used to negate
a clause or sentence in which some uncertainty or doubt is implied.

§34.2221 μή is used to negate verbs in the subjunctive (§31.33). But
cf. 1 Pet. 3:3, Ac. 7:60, §31.333.

§34.2222 μή is used to negate verbs in the imperative (§31.32). Ac. 1:20.

§34.2223 μή is used to negate verbs after ἵνα or ὅπως in the indicative,
subjunctive, or optative in final or object clauses, unless the
clause follows μή 'lest,' in which case the verb is negated by οὐ. §30.6331.

§34.2224 μή is usually used to negate the infinitive in all constructions
except indirect discourse (§37.82). Cf. Ac. 7:19, §34.4223. In
indirect discourse, the negative of the corresponding direct discourse is
generally used.

§34.2225 μή is used to negate the participle when it indicates a condition
or is equivalent to a conditional relative clause.

§34.2226   Verbs containing a negative idea, such as hindering, forbidding,
            denying, and the like, if followed by an infinitive, may add μή
to strengthen the negative idea. This cannot be translated into English.

§34.23   The negative adverb generally stands before the word it negates.

§34.24   The simple negative adverb, followed in the clause by one of
            its compounds, is merely strengthened by the compound.

§34.241   On the other hand, if a simple negative adverb is followed by the
            same adverb in the same clause, each retains its negative force,
and if they belong to the same expression, they cancel each other.
οὐ παρὰ τοῦτο οὐκ ἔστιν ἐκ τοῦ σώματος 'Not because of this is it not of
the body' (= It is still part of the body) (1 Cor. 12:15).

§34.3   <u>Adverbial phrases</u>, i.e. prepositional phrases used adverbially,
            are used to modify the verb. The adverbial character of prep-
ositions can be seen in their use in forming compound verbs. The student
must bear in mind that prepositional phrases can also be used adjectivally
to modify the substantive. It is necessary in each case to ask what the
prepositional phrase is modifying.

§34.31   The <u>prepositional phrase</u> consists of a preposition and the sub-
            stantive (object of the preposition) which it governs, plus any
modifiers of the substantive. The noun will be in the case required by the
preposition.

§34.311   In general, the genitive case after the preposition denotes that
            from which or through which anything proceeds, or about which
anything is. For prepositions requiring the genitive see §35.41.

§34.312   In general, the dative case after the preposition denotes that
            in which, on which, or near which anything takes place, with
(i.e. in company with) which anything is, or upon or concerning which cause,
anything takes place. For prepositions requiring the dative case see §35.42.

§34.3121   ἐν + dat. after verbs of motion sometimes is used with reference
to the rest following the motion, hence it may appear to be used
where we would expect an accusative. Mt. 26:23.

§34.313   In general, the accusative case following a preposition denotes
that toward which, over which, along which, or upon which, motion
takes place; the reason for which or by which, the extent of time during
which, the extent of space in which, or the measure or number to which or
exceeding which anything occurs. For prepositions requiring the accusative
case see §35.43.

§34.32   Abstractions must be handled with great caution. Each preposition
should be studied in a large lexicon. The difference in usage in
an adverbial phrase (i.e. with a verb) from that in an adjectival phrase
should be carefully noted.

§34.33   Certain adverbs have come to be used as prepositions, and are
followed by substantives in the case required. These are known
as improper prepositions (cf. §35.44).

§34.34   An infinitive or infinitival clause may serve as the object of a
preposition. ἕως τοῦ ἐλθεῖν αὐτὸν εἰς καισάρειαν 'Until he came
to Caesarea'.

§34.4   Adverbial_clauses, or clauses used to modify the verb, include
participial clauses (§34.41), infinitival clauses (§34.42), and
clauses that properly will be considered under complex sentences (§37.).
This distinction does not follow in English, since participial and infinitival clauses have to be translated as dependent clauses, hence appear
always to be complex sentences.

§34.41   The participle is often used adverbially, either as a single
word, or in a participial phrase. Since in Greek there is no
finite verb in such a clause, we include it here under the simple sentence.

§34.411   The participle may indicate the time of the action, hence it is
a temporal adverb.

§34.4111 The time indicated by the <u>aorist</u> participle, unless this is part
          of the action of the main verb, is anterior to that of the main
verb. ἀτενίσας δὲ Πέτρος εἰς αὐτὸν...εἶπεν 'Peter having looked intently
on him said' (Ac. 3:4; this may be counted as part of the action of the
main verb, hence "Peter while gazing on him said."). ἰδὼν δὲ ὁ Πέτρος
ἀπεκρίνατο πρὸς τὸν λαόν 'Peter having seen answered the people' (Ac. 3:12);
here the participle is anterior, (= "When Peter saw [what was happening]
he answered").

§34.4112 The time indicated by the <u>present</u> participle is contemporaneous
          with that of the main verb. προφήτης οὖν ὑπάρχων...προϊδὼν
ἐλάλησεν... 'Being therefore [at that time] a prophet, (and) having fore-
seen [prior to the message] he spoke' (Ac. 2:30-31; here we see the difference between the pres. and the aor. ptcp.).

§34.4113 The time indicated by the <u>future</u> participle is subsequent to
          that of the main verb. This usage is rare in the NT.

§34.4114 In all instances it is important to notice that the time of the
          action is determined from the main verb and its context. The
tense of the participle is relevant in approximately the manner indicated--
and there are many exceptions.

§34.412 The participle may indicate the <u>cause</u> of the action. ἰδὼν δὲ
          ὅτι ἀρεστόν ἐστιν τοῖς Ἰουδαίοις προσέθετο συλλαβεῖν καὶ Πέτρον
'and seeing that it was pleasing to the Jews (= because it was...) he
proceeded to seize Peter also' (Ac. 12:3).

§34.413 The participle may indicate the <u>means</u>, manner, manner of employ-
          ment, and similar circumstances of the action. τότε ὁ Παῦλος
ἐκτείνας τὴν χεῖρα ἀπελογεῖτο 'Then Paul, stretching forth his hand, made
his defense' (Ac. 26:1). προσῆλθον αὐτῷ ὄχλοι πολλοὶ ἔχοντες μεθ' ἑαυτῶν
χωλούς, κ.τ.λ. 'Great crowds came to him, having with themselves lame,
etc.' (Mt. 15:30; BDF §419 calls this "pleonastic").

§34.414 The participle, particularly the fut. ptcp. may indicate the
          <u>purpose</u> or intention of the action. ὃς ἐληλύθει προσκυνήσων
εἰς Ἰερουσαλήμ 'Who had come purposing-to-worship to Jerusalem' (Ac. 8:27).

§34.415   The participle may indicate the condition (the protasis, §37.611)
          of an action. Its tense will correspond with the tense in which
the verb would have stood if the indicative, subjunctive, or optative had
been used (pres. ptcp. standing for imperfect). For particulars, see the
discussion of conditional sentences (§37.6ff.).

§34.416   The circumstantial participle is sometimes distinguished from other
          adverbial usages since it simply indicates an attendant circumstance
to the action of the main verb. It is usually translated by a finite verb.
ἀτενίσας δὲ Πέτρος εἰς αὐτὸν ... εἶπεν 'Peter looked at him intently and said'
(Ac. 3:4); ἀναστάς Πέτρε θῦσον καὶ φάγε 'Rise, Peter, slaughter and eat' (Ac.
10:13).

§34.42   The infinitive may be used to modify the verb. As in the case of
          the participle, the English translation is generally in the form
of a clause, giving the appearance of a complex sentence.

§34.421   The infinitive may be used in a temporal capacity, to relate the
          action of the main verb to some other action. In such usage, the
infinitive is constructed with a preposition and the definite article in the
case required by the preposition; it therefore serves as a noun in a prepositional phrase used adverbially.

§34.4211 The time indicated by the use of πρίν (or πρὶν ἤ) + the infinitive
          is subsequent to that of the main verb. πρὶν ἐλθεῖν ἡμέραν κυρίου
τὴν μεγάλην 'before the great day of the Lord comes' (Ac. 2:20).

§34.4212 The time indicated by the use of ἐν τῷ + the infinitive is con-
          temporaneous with that of the main verb. ἐν τῷ πορεύεσθαι
ἐγένετο αὐτὸν ἐγγίζειν τῇ Δαμασκῷ ' As he journeyed it happened that he
drew near to Damascus' (Ac. 9:3).

§34.4213 The time indicated by the use of μετὰ τό + the infinitive is
          anterior to that of the main verb. οἷς καὶ παρέστησεν ἑαυτὸν
ζῶντα μετὰ τὸ παθεῖν αὐτὸν 'To whom also he showed himself living (= alive)
after he suffered' (Ac. 1:3).

§34.422   The infinitive may be used to modify the main verb by indicating
          the purpose or result of the action. The line between purpose
and result is very fine, and in many cases the meaning of the verb is the
sole determining factor. Further distinctions of "actual result," "conceived result," and "intended result" are entirely based upon the meaning
of the context, and "intended result" is clearly purpose. σκεῦος ἐκλογῆς
ἐστίν μοι οὗτος τοῦ βαστάσαι τὸ ὄνομά μου ἐνώπιον ἐθνῶν 'A chosen vessel
is this one to me to carry my name before nations' (Ac. 9:15).

§34.4221 The simple infinitive may be used, in which case it is similar
          to a complementary infinitive (cf. §33.6).

§34.4222 The infinitive with τοῦ may be used, in which form it is a verbal
          noun in the genitive. ὡς ἰδίᾳ δυνάμει ἢ εὐσεβείᾳ πεποιηκόσιν τοῦ
περιπατεῖν αὐτόν 'As if our own power or piety had made him walk' (Ac. 3:12).

§34.4223 The infinitive may be used after εἰς or πρός, in which form it is
          a verbal noun in the accusative (required by the prepositions),
indicating purpose, intention, and the like. οὗτος κατασοφισάμενος τὸ
γένος ἡμῶν ἐκάκωσεν τοὺς πατέρας τοῦ ποιεῖν τὰ βρέφη ἔκθετα αὐτῶν εἰς τὸ μὴ
ζῳογονεῖσθαι 'This one, dealing craftily with our race, mistreated our
fathers [to cause them] to make their infants outcasts that they might not
be preserved alive' (Ac. 7:19; here we can see τοῦ + inf. [§34.4222] and
εἰς τὸ + neg. inf.).

§34.4224 The infinitive may be used after ὥστε or ὡς usually indicating
          the result of the action of the main verb. In this usage the
infinitive more nearly resembles a finite verb in a subordinate clause.
καὶ γνωστὸν ἐγένετο...ὥστε κληθῆναι τὸ χωρίον ἐκεῖνο...Ἀκελδαμάχ 'And it
became well known..so that that field was called...Akeldama' (Ac. 1:19).

§34.423   The infinitive after διὰ may be used to indicate the cause of
          the action. διαπονούμενοι διὰ τὸ διδάσκειν αὐτοὺς τὸν λαὸν
'Annoyed because of their teaching the people' (Ac. 4:2).

§34.424   The subject of the infinitive, if used in such a construction, will be in the accusative case.

§34.5   The <u>genitive absolute</u>. Sometimes the verb is modified by a participle or a participial clause which stands outside the syntax of the clause (i.e., it is neither subject nor object; it is not indirect object, nor is it in apposition with any of these). Such a construction is called "absolute" and in Greek it normally is in the genitive case.

§34.51   The subject of the participial clause of a genitive absolute is in the genitive case and as a rule must be expressed, since it is not related to any substantive in the main clause. λήμψεσθε δύναμιν ἐπελθόντος τοῦ ἁγίου πνεύματος ἐφ᾽ ὑμᾶς 'You shall receive power, the Holy Spirit having come upon you' (Ac. 1:8).

§34.511   In unusual cases, the participle may stand alone when the subject is general (like "men") or when it can readily be inferred from the context. GG §1570a.

§34.512   Sometimes, in order to make the principal clause more prominent, the genitive absolute does pick up one of the substantives in the main clause. λαλούντων δὲ αὐτῶν πρὸς τὸν λαὸν ἐπέστησαν αὐτοῖς οἱ ἱερεῖς 'While they were speaking to the people, the priests came upon them' (Ac. 4:1). Cf. GG §1570b.

§34.52   The participle in a genitive absolute is used circumstantially or adverbially, hence the sections above (§34.41ff.) should be consulted.

§34.53   In classical Greek, participles of impersonal verbs stand in the <u>accusative absolute</u>. The only accusative absolute which has been identified (?) in the NT is Ac. 26:3, and this is not impersonal: μάλιστα γνώστην ὄντα σε πάντων τῶν κατὰ Ἰουδαίους ἐθῶν 'You being especially familiar with the Jewish customs.'

§34.6   The <u>adverbial accusative</u>. Sometimes the verb is modified by
          a noun in the accusative case which is clearly not a direct
object (§33.1), nor is it a cognate accusative (§33.2), for it limits the
action of the verb upon the object by denoting a part, character, quality,
or some other restriction. It is sometimes called the "accusative of
specification," or better, the adverbial accusative.

§34.61   The accusative may limit the verb by a measure of distance or
          time. καὶ ἐκεῖ ἔμειναν οὐ πολλὰς ἡμέρας 'And they stayed
there not many days' (Jn. 2:12).

§34.62   The accusative may limit the verb by defining the manner of the
          action. δωρεὰν ἐλάβετε δωρεὰν δότε 'Freely you received, freely
give' (Mt. 10:8).

§34.63   The accusative may limit the verb by referring it specifically to
          some character or quality; this is often called the "accusative
of reference." (Rom. 15:17).

§34.631   The subject-accusative of an infinitive (§34.424) may be looked upon
          as an accusative of reference (Robertson, <u>Grammar</u>, 489f.).

§34.64   The similarity of the adverbial accusative to the extended usages
          of the cognate accusative (§33.21) will be obvious, and sometimes
the decision in terminology will be highly subjective.

§35.   NOUN MODIFIERS. A noun or other substantive, whether subject,
          direct object, indirect object, or in any other usage, may be
modified in one or more of several ways (see §30.21).

§35.1   The <u>attributive adjective</u>. A substantive may be modified by an
          adjective. (For the predicate adjective, see §33.5ff.; we are
concerned here only with the attributive adjective.).

§35.11   The attributive adjective agrees with its noun in gender, number,
          case, and definiteness. τὴν ὥραν τῆς προσευχῆς τὴν ἐνάτην

'the ninth hour of prayer' (Ac. 3:1). ἐπὶ τῇ ὡραίᾳ πύλῃ 'At the beautiful gate' (Ac. 3:10). βλέπω δὲ ἕτερον νόμον 'But I see another law' (Rom. 7:23).

§35.111　　An attrib. adj. belonging to several nouns generally agrees with the nearest or most prominent one; it is understood with the others. εἰς πᾶσαν πόλιν καὶ τόπον 'to every city and place' (Lk. 10:1).

§35.112　　A collective noun in the singular may be modified by a plural adjective.

§35.113　　When the subject-accusative of an infinitive is omitted because it is the same as the subject of the main verb, adjectives or adjectival forms which would agree with the omitted subject-accusative are attracted into the nominative of the subject of the main verb. ἐλπίζω γὰρ διαπορευόμενος θεάσασθαι ὑμᾶς 'For I hope when passing through to see you' (Rom. 15:24; obviously the ptcp. is modifying the inf. 'to see' and not the verb 'I hope.').

§35.12　　The <u>position of the attributive adjective</u> is important (cf. the position of the predicate adjective, §33.5). The attrib. adj. may stand either before the noun or after it, but if the noun is definite (arthrous), the adjective must be preceded by the definite article.

§35.121　　If the attrib. adj. precedes a definite noun, it will be between the definite article and the noun. τοῦ ἁγίου πνεύματος 'The Holy Spirit' (Ac. 1:8).

§35.122　　If the attrib. adj. follows an arthrous noun, the definite article is repeated before the adjective. τῷ πνεύματι τῷ ἁγίῳ 'the Holy Spirit' (Ac. 7:51).

§35.123　　If there is any difference between these two positions, it is quite subtle. BDF §270 says that in the first position (the adj. preceding the noun) the emphasis is rather on the adjective, in the second

(the noun preceding the adjective) the emphasis is more on the noun.
GG §962 says that the first is the most common and the most simple and
natural, the second is rather formal. My own study of the variant forms of
'the Holy Spirit' has not yielded any clear-cut distinction.

§35.124   The adjectives πᾶς 'all' and ὅλος 'whole' are an exception
          to this rule.

§35.1241 πᾶς ὁ or ὅλος ὁ, in the so-called predicate position (§33.51),
          means 'all.' πάσης τῆς Ἀσίας 'All Asia' (Ac. 19:26).

§35.1242 ὁ πᾶς or ὁ ὅλος, in the attributive position (§35.12), means
          'the whole of.' ἦσαν οἱ πάντες ἄνδρες ὡσεὶ δώδεκα 'They were,
the whole group of men, about twelve' (Ac. 19:7).

§35.1243 πᾶς before an anarthrous substantive (without the article) means
          'any' (= 'every'). πᾶν δένδρον (Mt. 3:10) is 'any tree' not
'every tree' in the sense of all trees.

§35.13   An adjective or participle, usually with the definite article,
          may be used substantivally (§32.3, .4).

§35.2   The <u>definite article</u> is the most common modifier of the noun.
          A noun or other substantive with the definite article is called
"arthrous"; without the definite article it is "anarthrous." The def. art.
agrees with the noun in gender, number, and case.

§35.21   Originally the definite article was a demonstrative pronoun (the
          def. art. seems to have developed late, if at all, in the
several Indo-European and Semitic languages [I can't speak for the others]),
and this nature can still be seen. It would be a mistake, however, to
suppose that the def. art. is only deictic. Actually, it serves in three
general roles.

§35.211   The def. art. can serve to make a noun or substantive <u>particular</u>.
          Out of all the men in the genus, I am speaking about a particular

man, "the man." In this sense, the Greek def. art. is translated by the
Eng. def. art.

§35.2111 The anaphoric use of the def. art., which may be the earliest,
            is a limited particularizing use. <u>Anaphora</u> (the Greeks had a
name for nearly everything!) is the reference back to what is known or
assumed to be known. I mention a house, possibly I describe it, and then
I refer to it as "the house," i.e., the house I have referred to.
Any noun, once it has been defined, can be considered particular.
εἶδεν δύο πλοῖα ... ἐμβὰς δὲ εἰς ἓν τῶν πλοίων 'He saw two boats ... getting
into one of the boats' (Lk. 5:2-3).

§35.2112 A second particularizing use of the def. art. is <u>elative</u> (or
            <u>idealizing</u>). "The prophet" is a particular prophet in his office,
but not necessarily a particular prophet in historical identification.
ἡ ἀγάπη is "Christian Love" or the idealized love presented in the gospel
and exemplified in Christ.

§35.2113 Perhaps in this category we can include the use of the def. art.
            where we would use the possessive pronoun in English. Παῦλος
ἐκτείνας τὴν χεῖρα 'Paul, stretching forth his hand....' (Ac. 26:1).

§35.2114 The definite article, in general, is used with proper names
            only anaphorically (to indicate that it is the person or place
previously mentioned), or with certain well-known persons. Cf. §35.241.

§35.212   The def. art. can serve to make a substantive <u>generic</u>, i.e.
            to make it representative of a class. In English we generally
omit the def. art. in such usage. ὁ ἄνθρωπος, generically, is "man."
In some uses, the generic and the ideal tend to overlap.

§35.2121 Possibly in this category we may include the def. art. with
          distributive force. We are talking about a class, but we mean
the individual members of the class. In English, we would translate
this either by "a" or by "each."

§35.213   The third category of usage of the definite article we may
          call <u>grammatical</u> or syntactical. The def. art. is used to
identify the case of an indeclinable word, or to make a substantive of
another part of speech, or to relate a phrase or clause to some other
part of a sentence. ἐκ τούτων τῶν δύο 'Of these two' (Ac. 1:24).

§35.2131 The definite article is used to indicate that an adjective,
          an adverb, or participle is used substantivally. ἀπὸ Σαμουὴλ
καὶ τῶν καθεξῆς 'beginning with Samuel and those following' (Ac. 3:24).

§35.2132 The definite article is used before a prepositional phrase
          or an adjectival clause, to indicate its relationship to a
substantive. ταῖς δώδεκα φυλαῖς ταῖς ἐν τῇ διασπορᾷ 'To the twelve
tribes which are in the Diaspora' (lit. 'to the twelve in-the-Diaspora
tribes') (James 1:1).

§35.2133 Sometimes this leads to an accumulation of articles.
          τὸ τῆς δόξης καὶ τὸ τοῦ θεοῦ πνεῦμα 'The spirit which is
of glory and of God' (1 Pet. 4:14). τῆς τῶν ἀποστόλων ὑμῶν ἐντολῆς
'(To remember)...the commandment which was from your apostles.'
(2 Pet. 3:2).

§35.2134 The definite article is always used with a noun that is defined
          by a demonstrative pronoun (see §32.23).

§35.2135 Certain nouns, such as γῆ 'earth,' πράγματα 'works, deeds,' υἱός
         'son, descendant,' and others that are obvious from the
context, can be omitted, the def. art. serving as a demon. pron.

§35.214 The original nature of the def. art. (the demon. pron.) can still
         be seen in the use of the def. art. alone <u>as a personal pronoun.</u>
ὁ δὲ ἐπεῖχεν αὐτοῖς 'And he (or that one) was observing them' (Ac. 3:5).

§35.2141 This construction is frequently followed by a participle.
         In some cases the ptcp. can be looked upon as a substantive
with the def. art., but in other cases, the substantival nature is less
clear. οἱ μὲν οὖν διασπαρέντες διῆλθον εὐαγγελιζόμενοι τὸν λόγον
'They then that had been scattered went everywhere preaching the word'
(Ac. 8:4).

§35.22   The definite article agrees with its substantive in gender,
         number and case.

§35.221 The def. art. may be used for two or more substantives in the
         same gender and number. Otherwise, the def. art. is repeated
in concord with the substantives. ἐν πάσῃ τῇ Ἰουδαίᾳ καὶ Σαμαρείᾳ
'In all Judea and Samaria' (Ac. 1:8). οἱ υἱοὶ ὑμῶν καὶ αἱ θυγατέρες ὑμῶν
'Your sons and your daughters' (Ac. 2:17).

§35.23   <u>Position</u>. The definite article is placed immediately before
         the substantive it modifies, with notable exceptions.

§35.231 The postpositive particles are regularly placed after the article
         when an arthrous substantive stands at the beginning of a clause.
τὸν μὲν πρῶτον λόγον ἐποιησάμην 'I wrote the first treatise' (Ac. 1:1).

§35.232   An attributive adjective (§35.1ff.) may stand between the def.
          art. and the substantive. ἐν τῇ ἰδίᾳ ἐξουσίᾳ 'In his own
authority' (Ac. 1:7). If the attributive adjective stands after the
substantive, the def. art. is repeated, see §35.122.

§35.2321 For the adjectives πᾶς and ὅλος, see §35.124.

§35.2322 For the position of the demonstrative pronoun, see §35.54.

§35.2323 The genitive of the pronoun generally cannot stand between
          the def. art. and its substantive. οἱ υἱοὶ ὑμῶν 'Your sons'
(Ac. 2:17). μου ἡ καρδία 'My heart' (Ac. 2:26,Nestle).

§35.233   A genitival substantive or a prepositional phrase may stand
          between the def. art. and its substantive. Usually, however,
they are placed after the substantive, and the def. art. is repeated.

§35.24   The definite article may be omitted under certain conditions.

§35.241   It is generally omitted before proper names unless they have
          been previously mentioned (the anaphoric use), or are well known.
Note Σαῦλος in Ac. 8:1, but ὁ Σαῦλος in 9:1; Κορνήλιος in 10:1, but
ὑπὸ τοῦ Κορνηλίου in 10:17. Likewise, when Peter is first mentioned to
Cornelius, it is Πέτρος, although the def. art. has been used previously
with Peter's name.

§35.242   It is generally omitted before θεός and κύριος when referring
          to God or the Lord, but is used when referring to the God or
the Lord of the Jews or the Christians. There are exceptions to this rule.

§35.243   It is often omitted before a noun standing before a genitive,
          possibly a reflection of the construct state in Hebrew. BDF §259,
however, points out that pure Greek offers parallels. ἐν ἡμέραις Ἡρῴδου
'In the days of Herod' (Mt. 2:1).

§35.244   It is often omitted in prepositional phrases, particularly those
            which have become "fossilized" from the period before the def.
art. developed. ἀπ' ἀγορᾶς 'from the Agora (market)' (Mk. 7:4), ἐπὶ θύραις
'at the doors' (Mt. 24:33), πρὸς ἑσπέραν 'toward (the) evening' (Lk. 24:29),
πεσὼν ἐπὶ πρόσωπον 'falling on his face' (Lk. 5:12).

§35.245   It is sometimes omitted with ordinal numbers, with θάνατος
            'death,' νεκροί 'the dead,' ἔθνη 'the gentiles,' etc.

§35.246   It is sometimes omitted with ἅγιον πνεῦμα. BDF §257(2) suggests
            that with the article the Holy Spirit is "more or less a person,"
and without the article, a divine spirit entering into man.

§35.247   The def. art. is always omitted before the predicate adjective
            (§33.5), except in those predicates which must have the article
for their particular significance.

§§35.25   There is no <u>indefinite article</u> as such in NT Greek. When there
            was need for one, either of two means of supplying the need was
used.   (It is likewise true that there is no true definite article in the
familiar Indo-European languages. Eng. an [> a before consonants], Fr. un,
Ger. ein. etc., are the numeral "one.")

§35.251   The indefinite pronoun τις (§23.34) is sometimes used as an
            indefinite article. It is translated 'a certain' -- which is
more definite than the word implies. τις ἀνήρ 'a man' (i.e. a particular
member of the genus, but not definitely specified) (Ac. 3:2).

§35.252   The numeral one εἷς μία ἕν (§22.61) is sometimes used. προσελθὼν
            εἷς γραμματεὺς εἶπεν 'a scribe coming to (him) said' (Mt. 8:19).
ἤκουσα ἑνὸς ἀετοῦ 'I heard an eagle' (Rev. 8:13).

§35.3   The <u>adjectival substantive</u>. A noun may be modified by another
            substantive in an oblique case (i.e. gen., dat., or acc.).
In Eng. translation it becomes necessary to use a prepositional phrase
or other construction.

§35.31   The <u>adjectival genitive</u>. The genitive is used frequently in
Greek, and the adjectival use is probably the most common use
of the genitive.   Basically, it represents either source or origin

nominative	VERB	accusative
GENITIVE	dative	GENITIVE
= modifier		= modifier

(the true genitive), or separation
(the ablatival genitive), but
each of these categories is subdivided.

§35.311   The <u>attributive genitive</u> is the genitive used in a manner
similar to an attributive adjective, to define a noun.   In a
sense all adjectival genitives are such, but some are clearly in this
category. ἐν βίβλῳ ψαλμῶν 'In the book of Psalms' (= the Psalm-book)
(Ac. 1:20). βάπτισμα μετανοίας 'a baptism of repentance' (Mk. 1:4).

§35.3111   The <u>genitive of reference</u> is quite similar to the attributive
genitive, and the choice of terminology is rather subjective.
καρδία πονηρὰ ἀπιστίας 'an evil heart of unbelief' (Heb. 3:12).

§35.3112   The <u>genitive of apposition</u> is closely related to the attributive
genitive. ἀπὸ ὄρους τοῦ καλουμένου [ὄρους]'Ελαιῶνος 'from the
mount called [mount] of Olives' (Ac. 1:12); τὸ σημεῖον'Ιωνᾶ 'The sign
of Jonah' (Lk. 11:29); πόλεις Σοδόμων καὶ Γομόρρας 'The cities of Sodom
and Gomorrah' (2 Pet. 2:6).

§35.3113   The use of the genitive in Semitic fashion is found in the NT
as in LXX, in constructions such as the following. ἐπὶ θρόνου
δόξης αὐτοῦ 'Upon the throne of his glory' (= his glorious throne)
(Mt. 19:28); ἐκ τοῦ σώματος τοῦ θανάτου.τούτου 'From the body of this
death' (= this dead body) (Rom. 7:24); ἐν ἀνθρώποις εὐδοκίας 'To men of
[his] good pleasure' (Lk. 2:14); ἐκ τοῦ μαμωνᾶ τῆς ἀδικίας 'From the
mammon of unrighteousness; (Lk. 16:9).   Some of these could be classified
as attributive genitive (§35.311) or in one of the other categories,
except that they are so clearly in Hebrew idiom.   In some cases the absence
of the definite article from the genitive (precisely as in Hebrew) is
further indication.

§35.3114 The word order used in the attributive genitive was usually
          like that of the attributive adjective (§35.12), i.e. either
between the def. art. and its noun, or following the noun with the def.
art. repeated. But in NT the former is rarely found and the second is
falling into disuse. ὁ ἄρτος ὁ τοῦ θεοῦ 'The bread which is from God'
(Jn. 6:33ℵ); ἐὰν μὴ περιτμηθῆτε τῷ ἔθει τῷ Μωϋσέως 'If you are not
circumcised by the custom of Moses...' (Ac. 15:1). In place of the
classical form is found more commonly the substantive followed by the
modifier in the genitive. τῇ διακονίᾳ τοῦ λόγου 'to the ministry of
the word' (Ac. 6:4).

§35.312 The possessive genitive is the genitive used to show possession,
         defining whose substantive is intended. In Eng. we often use
--'s to show the possessive genitive. The most common use is with the gen.
of the pronouns. οἱ υἱοὶ ὑμῶν 'your sons' (Ac. 2:17). Ἰάκωβος Ἀλφαίου
'James [the son] of Alphaeus (Ac. 1:13).

§35.3121 The genitive of close relationship is quite similar to the
          possessive genitive. In fact, expressions with 'the son of,'
etc., could be placed in either category. Δαυὶδ τὸν τοῦ Ἰεσσαί 'David
the [son] of Jesse' (Ac. 13:22).

§35.313 The subjective genitive is the gen. used, particularly with
         words of action or feeling, to indicate the subject of that
action or feeling. The subjective genitive may be identified by asking
whether the action proceeded from the substantive in the genitive.
γογγυσμὸς τῶν Ἑλληνιστῶν 'The murmuring of the Hellenists' (i.e. it
proceeded from them) (Ac. 6:1); ἀπὸ τοῦ βαπτίσματος Ἰωάννου 'the baptism
of John' (i.e., that which John administered, not that which John
received) (Ac. 1:22).

§35.314 The objective genitive is the gen. used to indicate the
         object of the feeling or action (cf. §35.313). ἡ τοῦ πνεύματος
βλασφημία 'the blasphemy of (= against) the Spirit' (Mt. 12:31);
ζῆλον θεοῦ ἔχουσιν 'they have a zeal of (= for) God' (Rom. 10:2;

in context it could not be "God's zeal" or zeal proceeding from God).
In many instances, the decision is almost impossible. What of ἐπὶ πάσῃ τῇ
μνείᾳ ὑμῶν (Phil. 1:3)--is 'every remembrance of you' = whenever you think
of me, (subj. gen.) or = whenever I think of you (obj. gen.)? And is
ἡ ἀγάπη τοῦ θεοῦ (1 Jn. 2:4 and elsewhere) 'the love which comes from God'
(subj. gen.) or 'the love we have for God' (obj. gen.)? Perhaps the Greek
author never asked that question--the distinction is ours. Context tells
us what was in his mind.

§35.315   The genitive of material or contents is the gen. used to modify
           a substantive by telling the material of which it consists or
which it contains.   ἀτμίδα καπνοῦ 'vapor of smoke' (Ac. 2:19).

§35.3151   The genitive of description is quite similar to the gen. of
           material. Χωρίον Αἵματος 'Field of Blood' (Ac. 1:19).

§35.3152   The genitive of comparison has fallen out of use in NT times,
           but a few examples remain. ἦσαν δὲ πλείους τεσσαράκοντα
'There were more than forty' (Ac. 23:13); ὁ δὲ ὀπίσω μου ἐρχόμενος
ἰσχυρότερός μού ἐστιν 'But the one coming after me is stronger than
(lit. of) me' (Matt. 3:11; for accents cf. §17.823).

§35.316   The genitive of measure is the gen. used to define a substantive
           by a measure of space, time, or value. It approaches an adverbial
use, and the student must be very careful to determine whether the genitive
is modifying a substantive or a verb. σαββάτου ἔχον ὁδόν 'having a journey
of a sabbath' = 'a sabbath's journey' (Ac. 1:12).

§35.317   The genitive of cause or origin is the gen. used to define the
           source, origin, or cause of the substantive it modifies.
τὴν ἐπαγγελίαν τοῦ πατρός 'the promise of (= originating from) the Father'
(Ac. 1:4).   διὰ τῆς παρακλήσεως τῶν γραφῶν 'through the comfort of the
scriptures' (= the comfort which the scriptures cause) (Rom. 15:4).
τὰ γὰρ ὀψώνια τῆς ἁμαρτίας θάνατος 'For the wages of sin is death' (Rom. 6:23).

§35.318   The <u>partitive genitive</u> (or genitive of the whole) is the gen.
            used with substantives denoting a part. It may follow any noun,
pronoun, adjective (particularly a superlative), arthrous participle, or
adverb, which denotes a part. τίνα τῶν προφητῶν οὐκ ἐδίωξαν οἱ πατέρες ὑμῶν;
'Which one of the prophets did your fathers not persecute?' (Ac. 7:52).

§35.3181   Generally the two elements of the partitive agree in gender.
            But in some instances the word μέρος 'part' is understood,
and the word modified by the gen. is neut. sg. ἕως ἐσχάτου τῆς γῆς
'unto the last [part] of the earth' (Ac. 1:8). τὸ τρίτον τῆς γῆς
'the third [part] of the earth' (Rev. 8:7).

§35.3182   The <u>geographic genitive</u> is a partitive genitive. Ναζαρὲθ τῆς
            Γαλιλαίας 'Nazareth of (= in) Galilee' (Mk. 1:9); ἐν Ταρσῷ τῆς
Κιλικίας 'in Tarsus of (= in) Cilicia' (Ac. 22:3).

§35.3183   Sometimes the modified substantive is omitted, and only the
            partitive genitive remains. συνῆλθον δὲ καὶ τῶν μαθητῶν ἀπὸ
Καισαρείας σὺν ἡμῖν 'And [some] of the disciples from Caesarea also went
with us' (Ac. 21:16).

§35.319   With nouns or adjectives having the same meaning as verbs listed
            above under predicate genitive (§33.7ff.), adnominal genitives
may be used similarly to the adverbial genitives. In this category generally are found the genitive of purpose, the genitive of separation, the
genitive of comparison, and the like.

§35.3191   With adjectives of fullness or the opposite. πλήρης πνεύματος
            ἁγίου 'full of the Holy Spirit' (Lk. 4:1).

§35.3192   With adjectives of worth or guilt. ἔνοχος θανάτου 'deserving
            of death' (Matt. 26:66). ἀνάξιοί ἐστε κριτηρίων ἐλαχίστων
'Are you not worthy of judgment of smallest things?' (1 Cor. 6:2).

§35.3193 With adjectives of sharing. κοινωνοὶ τῶν οὕτως ἀναστρεφομένων
          γενηθέντες 'partakers with those who were being treated thus'
(Heb. 10:33). προώρισεν συμμόρφους τῆς εἰκόνος τοῦ υἱοῦ αὐτοῦ 'He fore-
ordained [them to be] conformed to the image of his son' (Rom. 8:29).

§35.3194 With adjectives of strangeness. ξένοι τῶν διαθηκῶν τῆς
          ἐπαγγελίας 'Strangers from the covenants of the promise'
(Eph. 2:12).

§35.32   The adjectival dative. The dative case is basically an adverbial
          case, used principally for modifying the verb (§34.1). It is
only rarely used as a modifier of nouns and adjectives of action or feeling,
and then principally with nouns and adjectives which are cognate with verbs
taking the dative (§33.8). The dative can be divided into three principal
categories: the dative proper (that to or for which anything is done),
the instrumental (that by or with which anything is done), and the locative
(the time or place in which anything is done).

§35.321   The dative of indirect object (objective dative, sometimes
          included under dative of reference) is the use of the dative
after a noun or substantive in the way that the indirect object would be
used with a corresponding verb. ἥτις κατεργάζεται δι᾿ ἡμῶν εὐχαριστίαν
τῷ θεῷ 'which through us works thanksgiving to God' (2 Cor. 9:11—obviously
it does not "work to God" but "works thanksgiving to God," hence this is
adjectival). τὸ εὐπάρεδον τῷ κυρίῳ '(your) devotion to the Lord'
(1 Cor. 7:35). (For dat.indir.obj. with verbs, §34.11.)

§35.322   The dative of agent (instrumental dative) is disappearing in
          NT Greek. With passive verbs it is almost entirely replaced by
prepositional phrases. A clear case is found in Ac. 5:34 τίμιος παντὶ
τῷ λαῷ 'honored by all the people.' The participial use is adverbial,
[ὄρει] κεκαυμένῳ πυρί 'to a mountain blazing with fire' (Heb. 12:18 D).

§35.323   The locative dative may be used of place, time, or logical
          sphere. The dative of place and the dative of time,

both of which are not common in the NT, do not seem to be used adjectivally.
The dative of logical sphere is generally subdivided further.

§35.3231 The <u>dative of reference</u> is used to modify a substantive by
            referring or relating it to some other substantive.
μακάριοι οἱ καθαροὶ τῇ καρδίᾳ 'Happy (are) the clean with reference to their
heart' (Mt. 5:8). πᾶσιν τοῖς κατοικοῦσιν Ἰερουσαλὴμ φανερόν '[is] clear
to all the inhabitants of Jerusalem' (Ac. 4:16--this might be classed as
"indirect object," §33.321). Κύπριος τῷ γένει 'a Cypriot by race' (Ac. 4:36).

§35.3232 The <u>dative of likeness</u> can be looked upon as a dative of
            reference. τίνι δὲ ὁμοιώσω τὴν γενεὰν ταύτην; ὁμοία ἐστὶν
παιδίοις καθημένοις ἐν ταῖς ἀγοραῖς... 'To what shall I liken this generation?
It is like children sitting in the markets...' (Mt. 11:16). ἡμεῖς ὁμοιοπαθεῖς
ἐσμεν ὑμῖν ἄνθρωποι 'We are men of like passions to you' (Ac. 14:15).

§35.3233 The <u>dative of advantage</u> is used to modify a substantive by
            indicating the person or thing for whose advantage or disadvantage
it is. ἐδόθη μοι σκόλοψ τῇ σάρκι 'there was given to me a stake in/for
the flesh' (2 Cor. 12:7). εἴτε γὰρ ἐξέστημεν, θεῷ· εἴτε σωφρονοῦμεν, ὑμῖν
'For if we are outside (ourself), (it is) for God; if we are in our right
mind, (it is) for you' (2 Cor. 5:13--as we have translated it, the datives
have become adverbial, but I feel they are adjectival in Gk).

§35.3234 The <u>ethical dative</u>, in my opinion, is an extension of the dative
            of advantage. καὶ ἦν ἀστεῖος τῷ θεῷ 'and he was beautiful
to/for God' (Ac. 7:20). Possibly υἱὸς μονογενὴς τῇ μητρί 'a son, an only
son to his mother' (Lk. 7:12).

§35.33   The <u>adjectival accusative</u>. Basically, the accusative is the
            case of the direct object, the predicate objective, and the like.
It is the case of the verbal complement. It only becomes an adjectival ·
element by extension, with nouns and other substantives that have inherent
verbal characteristics.

§35.331   The <u>accusative of specification</u> is used with a noun or adjective,
          as well as with a verb or even a whole sentence, to denote a
part, character, or quality to which the expression refers. This is sometimes
called the "accusative by synecdoche" and the "limiting accusative." A
common illustration is "blind in the eyes"--but even here we see the adverbial
character showing through, for it defines the adjective blind by the location
or extent of the blindness. πεπληρωμένοι καρπὸν δικαιοσύνης 'filled with
fruit of righteousness' (Phil. 1:11--but this is really a predicate of the
participle). ἀνέπεσαν οὖν οἱ ἄνδρες τὸν ἀριθμὸν ὡς πεντακισχίλιοι
'Therefore the men sat down, the number about 5,000 (Jn. 6:10).

§35.4   The <u>adjectival prepositional phrase</u>. A substantive may be
         modified by a prepositional phrase. In Koinē Greek, the pre-
positional phrase increasingly displaced the simple inflected substantive
without preposition.

§35.41   Prepositions governing a substantive in the <u>genitive case</u> include
         the following:
ἀντί (22x) 'for, in place of, against'; ἀνθ' ὧν 'therefore'
ἀπό (645x) 'from'; for ὑπό causal, παρά + gen., often for ἐξ
διά (386x) 'through (place, time, manner)'
ἐξ/ἐκ (915x) 'out of, from'; = ὑπό causal; 'by, belonging to'
ἐπί (220x) local 'upon, at, by'; metaph. 'over' temp. 'at time of';
          interchangeable with ἐπί + dat. and + acc.
κατά (73x) 'against'; local, 'down from, throughout'
μετά (364x) 'with, among'; more frequent than σύν (exc. Acts)
παρά (79x) 'from the side of'
περί (293x) 'about, concerning'; sometimes = ὑπέρ
πρό (47x) 'before' (mainly temporal)
πρός (1x) 'for'
ὑπέρ (130x) 'for, on behalf of'; some interchange with περί + gen.
ὑπό (167x) 'by' (of agent, mainly after passives)

§35.411 It should be borne in mind that every preposition needs to be
         studied with a large lexicon (like Arndt & Gingrich).

§35.42   Prepositions governing a substantive in the <u>dative case</u>
          include the following.

ἐν (2713x) loc. 'in, into,' (temp.) in, at, during'; (metaph.) 'in';
          (inst.) 'by, with'; (advantage) 'for.'

ἐπί (182x) 'before, upon'; causal, final, consecutive, temporal;
          interchangeable with ἐπί + gen. and + acc.

παρά (52x) 'at the side of, in the house of, among; (fig.) 'with'

πρός (6x) 'by, at' (giving way to πρός + acc.)

σύν (127x) 'with, together with'; synonym of μετά

§35.43   Prepositions governing a substantive in the <u>accusative case</u>
          include the following:

ἀνά (13x) distrib. 'each'; ανα μεσον, ανα μερος 'in turn'

διά (280x) consec. 'on account of'; 'through' (Lk. 17:11).

εἰς (1753x) 'to, into'; distrib. 'up to'; purpose 'to, for';
          causal 'because of'

ἐπί (476x) 'upon, up to, to'; interchangeable with ἐπί + gen./dat.

κατά (398x) 'according to'; distrib. 'each, every'; for poss. or
          subj. gen.; causal

μετά (103x) 'after' (temporal)

παρά (60x) 'to the side of, beside'; metaph. opp. κατά 'contrary to,
          beyond'; 'more than, minus, except, almost, because'

περί (38x) 'around, about' (loc. and temp.); 'concerning'

πρός (688x) 'to, towards'; temp. 'about'; 'in accordance with'

ὑπέρ (19x) 'over, above, beyond, more than' (not locally)

ὑπό (50x) 'under'

§35.44   <u>Improper prepositions</u> (originally adverbs, but which never
          form compounds with verbs) began to increase in use in the
Hellenistic period, and continued to do so in NT, where there are 17
"proper" prepositions, and 42 "improper" prepositions. The more significant are listed below. Except as noted, all are followed by the
genitive case.

ἅμα (3x) + dat. 'together with'   ἔξω (13x) 'out of'

ἄνευ (3x) 'without'   ἐπάνω (3x) 'above'

ἀντικρυς (1x) 'opposite'   ἔσω (6x) 'within'

ἀπέναντι (6x) 'opposite'   ἕως (86x) 'as far as'

ἄχρι(ς) (45x) 'until'   κατέναντι (9x) 'over against, before'

ἐγγύς (11x) 'near' +G/+D   μεταξύ (7x) 'between'

ἐκτός (9x) 'outside'   μέχρι(ς) (18x) 'until'

ἔμπροσθεν (46x) 'before' (space)   ὀπίσω (32x) 'after'

ἔναντι (3x) 'before'   ὄπισθεν (2x) 'behind, after'

ἐναντίον (5x) 'before'   ὀψέ (2x) 'late in'

ἕνεκα ⎫   πέραν (9x) 'over, beyond'

ἕνεκεν ⎭ (22x) 'on account of'   πλήν (5x) 'besides, except'

ἐντός (2x) 'within   χάριν (4x) 'for the sake of'

ἐνώπιον (93x) 'in the sight of'   χωρίς (38x) 'without, apart from'

§35.441   A number of these propositions have been formed by compounding a preposition with an adverb: ἔναντι, ἀπέναντι, κατέναντι, ἐπάνω, ἔμπροσθεν, ὑποκάτω.

§35.45   In imitation of Hebrew idiom, a few <u>nouns</u> are used as <u>preposi-tions</u> in the LXX and NT. For mippᵉnê 'before,' lit. 'from the face of,' ἀπὸ προσώπου + gen. (Ac. 3:20; 5:41; 7:45). For lipnê 'before (to the face of),' πρὸ προσώπου (Ac. 13:24). For bipnê κατὰ προσώπον (Ac. 3:13) and εἰς πρόσωπον (2 Cor. 8:24). For bᵉyaḏ 'by' (lit. 'by the hand of') εἰς χεῖρας (Lk. 23:46) or ἐν (τῇ) χειρί (Ac. 7:35) or διὰ χειρός/χειρῶν (Ac. 2:23, 5:12). For miyyaḏ 'from (the hand of)' ἐκ χειρός (Ac. 12:11).

§35.46   For word order, the prepositional phrase is often treated as an attributive adjective, standing either between the def. art. and the substantive it modifies, or after the substantive with the def. art. repeated. There is an increasing tendency in the NT, however, to omit the def. art. in the latter position (in other words, to use the "predicate position" of the adjectival phrase). ταῖς φυλαῖς ταῖς ἐν τῇ διασπορᾷ 'to the tribes which are in the Diaspora' (Jas. 1:1). τοῖς κατὰ τὴν

Ἀντιόχειαν ... ἀδελφοῖς 'to the brethren at Antioch' (Ac. 15:23).
τὴν ὑμῶν ἀγάπην ἐν πνεύματι 'your love (which is) in (the) spirit' (Col.1:8).
τὸν Ἰσραὴλ κατὰ σάρκα 'Israel according to the flesh' (1 Cor. 10:18).

§35.5   A <u>pronoun</u> (§30.312) may be used to modify a noun or other
          substantive.

§35.51   With substantives whose meanings permit, a <u>personal pronoun</u>
          in an oblique case (gen., dat., acc.) may be used wherever a noun
would have been so used (cf. §35.3ff).

§35.511   The <u>personal pronoun</u> in the genitive case (i.e. used as a possessive
          pronoun), is one of the most common of these modifiers
(cf. §35.311). ἀπὸ τῶν ὀφθαλμῶν αὐτῶν 'from their eyes' (Ac. 1:9).

§35.52   The <u>possessive pronoun</u> (§23.31) is used attributively to
          modify a noun or other substantive. τῆς ἐμῆς καρδίας
'of my heart' (Rom. 10:1).

§35.53   The <u>intensive pronoun</u> αὐτός (§23.15) requires particular
          attention.

§35.531   In the "attributive position" (§35.12), it means 'the same.'
          ὁ γὰρ αὐτὸς κύριος 'the same Lord' (Rom. 10:12).

§35.532   In the "predicate position" (§33.511), it is translated
          'himself, herself, itself, themselves.' αὐτὸ τὸ πνεῦμα
συνμαρτυρεῖ τῷ πνεύματι ἡμῶν 'The Spirit himself witnesses together
with our spirit.' (Rom. 8:16).

§35.5321 When the intensive pronoun is used to modify a personal pronoun,
          the pers. pron. may be omitted, and αὐτός is translated 'I
myself,' 'he himself,' 'you yourselves,' etc., as the sentence requires.
αὐτοὶ γὰρ ἀκηκόαμεν 'For we ourselves have heard' (John 4:42).

§35.533   In the adnominal genitive (modifying a noun), αὐτοῦ/αὐτῆς/αὐτῶν
          serves as a possessive pronoun (§35.511). καὶ τοῖς ἀδελφοῖς αὐτοῦ
'and with his brothers' (Ac. 1:14).

§35.54   The demonstrative pronoun (§23.33) may be used as a noun
          modifier. Note that it takes the "predicate position" (§33.511).
οὗτος ὁ Ἰησοῦς 'this Jesus' (Ac. 1:11). ἐν ταῖς ἡμέραις ἐκείναις
'in those days' (Ac. 2:18).

§35.55   The interrogative pronoun (§23.5) may be used to modify a
          substantive. ποῖον οἶκον οἰκοδομήσετέ μοι 'What kind of house
would you build for me? (Ac. 7:49).

§35.56   The indefinite pronoun (§23.34) may be used as a noun modifier.
          In some instances this approaches the Eng. indefinite article
and may be translated 'a/an.' The translation 'a certain' may make the
modified noun more definite than the construction warrants. τις ἀνήρ
'a man' (i.e., a particular, yet indefinite man) (Ac. 3:2).

§35.57   A relative clause (§30.431) may be used to modify a noun.

§35.571   The rel. pron. agrees with its antecedent in gender and number;
          its case, however, is generally determined by the syntax of its
own clause. τοῖς ἀποστόλοις...οὓς ἐξελέξατο...οἷς καὶ παρέστησεν ἑαυτόν
'to the apostles...whom he had chosen...to whom also he showed himself'
(Ac. 1:2-3). ἔστησαν...Βαρσαββᾶν, ὃς ἐπεκλήθη Ἰοῦστος 'They set forth...
Barnabas, who was called Justus' (Ac. 1:23). τις ἀνήρ...ὃν ἐτίθουν
'a man whom they put...' (Ac. 3:2).

§35.5711 Note the following sentences and the case used in each
          instance:
              The boy who threw the stone is here.
              The boy whose hat was found is here.
              The boy to whom you gave it is here.
              The boy whom you called   is here.

§35.572   If the relative pronoun has two or more antecedents, it will
          be plural. If one of the antecedents is a male person, it will
be masculine; but if the antecedents are things, the rel. pron. will be
neuter. ἀπέστειλαν πρὸς αὐτοὺς Πέτρον καὶ Ἰωάννην, οἵτινες καταβάντες
'They sent to them Peter and John, who went down...' (Ac. 8:14-15).
Πρίσκαν καὶ Ἀκύλαν...οἵτινες 'Prisca and Aquila...who' (Rom. 16:3).
ἐν βρώσει καὶ ἐν πόσει ἢ ἐν μέρει ἑορτῆς ἢ νεομηνίας ἢ σαββάτων, ἅ ἐστιν...
'about food and drink or about a portion in a festival or a new moon or
sabbaths, which things are...' (Col. 2:16-17).

§35.573   In certain constructions, however, the case of the relative
          pronoun is <u>attracted</u> to the case of the antecedent. In general
the NT follows the rules for classical Greek, namely the relative pronoun
must be the object accusative of its clause, the antecedent must be either
genitive or dative, and the clause must not be greatly separated from the
antecedent. The case will be described as "genitive (or dative) by at-
traction." καὶ τῆς διαθήκης ἧς ὁ θεὸς διέθετο 'and of the covenant which
(gen. vice acc.) God appointed' (Ac. 3:25). δυνάμεσι καὶ τέρασι καὶ
σημείοις οἷς ἐποίησεν 'powers and wonders and signs which (dat. vice acc.)
he did' (Ac. 2:22).

§35.5731 If the antecedent as described in §35.573 is omitted, the rel.
          pron. is nevertheless attracted to the case of the antecedent,
and if a preposition would have governed the antecedent, it is used before
the rel. pron. οὐ περὶ τοῦ κόσμου ἐρωτῶ ἀλλὰ περὶ ὧν δέδωκάς μοι 'Not
for the world do I ask, but for [those] whom thou gavest me' (Jn. 17:9).

§35.5732 When the relative pronoun immediately follows, the antecedent
          is sometimes attracted to the case of the relative. τὸν ἄρτον
ὃν κλῶμεν οὐχὶ κοινωνία τοῦ σώματος τοῦ Χριστοῦ ἐστιν; 'The bread which
we break, is it not the communion of the body of Christ?' (1 Cor. 10:16).

§35.5733 There are irregularities in the observance of these rules in the NT.

§35.574   A relative clause may be used to indicate contingency by the use
          of one of the conditional participles in conjunction with the
relative pronoun. Such a relative clause is actually a type of conditional
clause (§37.647). πᾶσα ψυχὴ ἥτις ἐὰν μὴ ἀκούσῃ τοῦ προφήτου ἐκείνου
ἐξολεθρευθήσεται 'Every person, whoever does not hear that prophet, shall
be utterly destroyed' (Ac. 3:23).

§35.6   An <u>appositive</u>, i.e., a substantive denoting the same person,
          place, or thing, in apposition with a substantive, may be used
as a modifier. In a sense, the appositive is parenthetical since it could
be omitted without altering the meaning. Syntactically, it is treated as
a modifier. In our diagrams, we indicate it by the sign = .

§35.61   The appositive will generally be in concord with the substantive
          it modifies. Ἰησοῦν τὸν Ναζωραῖον ἄνδρα ἀποδεδειγμένον ἀπὸ τοῦ
θεοῦ 'Jesus the Nazarene, a man pointed out by God...' (Ac. 2:22).

§35.611 A substantive in apposition with two or more substantives is
          usually plural. πέμψαι...Ἰούδαν...καὶ Σίλαν ἄνδρας... 'to send
Judas and Silas, men...' (Ac. 15:22).

§35.612 The appositive may be in the genitive when the sense implies
          the possessive. τῇ ἐμῇ χειρὶ Παύλου 'by my hand, Paul's'
(1 Cor. 16:21).

§35.613 A noun which might stand in the partitive genitive (§35.316)
          may take the case of the words denoting its parts.

§35.62   The appositive is sometimes used where we might use a
          comparison; we translate by placing "as" before the appositive.

§35.63   A noun may be in apposition with an entire sentence; if it is
          closely related to the subject it is nominative, otherwise it
is accusative.

§35.64   An infinitive may be used as an appositive. This is sometimes
          called the <u>epexegetic</u> infinitive. ἔκρινα δὲ ἐμαυτῷ τοῦτο τὸ μὴ
πάλιν ἐν λύπῃ πρὸς ὑμᾶς ἐλθεῖν 'But I decided for myself this, not to come
to you again in pain' (2 Cor. 2:1).

§35.65   An entire clause may be used as an appositive. τοῦτο γινώσκετε
          ὅτι ἤγγικεν ἡ βασιλεία τοῦ θεοῦ 'Know this, that the kingdom of
God has come near' (Lk. 10:11).

§35.7   A <u>participle</u> may be used to modify a noun or other substantive.
ἄνδρα ἀποδεδειγμένον ἀπὸ τοῦ θεοῦ ... τοῦτον ... ἀνείλατε
'A man appointed by God ... this one you killed' (Ac. 2:22-23). ὁ λίθος
ὁ ἐξουθενηθεὶς ὑφ᾽ ὑμῶν 'the stone which was rejected by you' (Ac. 4:11).

§35.71   The <u>attributive participle</u> is generally translated by a relative
         clause. If the substantive is definite, the participial modifier
is also definite (cf. examples in §35.7).

§35.8   An <u>infinitive</u> may be used to modify a substantive (Cf. §37.44).
         It is generally translated into Eng. by an infinitive. οὗ οὐκ
εἰμὶ ἄξιος τὸ ὑπόδημα τῶν ποδῶν λῦσαι ' The sandals of whose feet I am
not worthy to unloose' (Ac. 13:25).

§35.9   A <u>numeral</u>, cardinal or ordinal, may be used to modify a sub-
         stantive (§22.6). τὸν μὲν πρῶτον λόγον ἐποιησάμην 'I composed
the first treatise' (Ac. 1:1). μετὰ τῶν ἕνδεκα ἀποστόλων 'with the
twelve apostles' (Ac. 1:26).

§36.   MODIFIERS OF MODIFIERS. Any modifier may in turn be modified
         by another modifier. Obviously, this can become quite compli-
cated, and the various possibilities are too numerous to discuss and
illustrate. Representative types will be given below.

§36.1   An <u>adjective</u> (§30.32ff.) or any modifier serving in an adjectival
         capacity (§35.ff.) can be modified by an adverb (§30.34) or any
word or word-group used in an adverbial capacity. ἐχάρησαν χαρὰν μεγάλην
σφόδρα 'they rejoiced (with) <u>exceeding</u> great joy' (Mt. 2:10).

§36.2   An <u>adjectival genitive</u> (§35.31ff.) can be modified by an
         adjective or any word or word-group serving as an adjective.
ὑποπόδιον τῶν ποδῶν σου 'a footstool of <u>your</u> feet' (Ac. 2:35; the genitive
ποδῶν modifying ὑποπόδιον and the genitive σου modifying ποδῶν. It might
be added that the def. art. is also modifying the modifier.).

§36.21   The <u>possessive genitive</u> (§35.312) can indeed be used in a chain
          of modifiers. χωλὸς ἐκ κοιλίας μητρὸς αὐτοῦ 'lame from his
mother's womb' (Ac. 3:2; the participle ὑπάρχων is modified by the prepositional phrase ἐκ κοιλίας, the noun of which is in turn modified by the
genitive μητρός, and this finally is modified by the pronoun in the genitive
αὐτοῦ).

§36.3   An <u>appositive</u> (§35.6ff.) may be modified by an adjective or an
          adjectival phrase/clause. ἄνδρα ἀποδεδειγμένον ἀπὸ τοῦ θεοῦ εἰς
ὑμᾶς 'a man attested by God to you' (Ac. 2:22; ἄνδρα is in apposition with
Ἰησοῦν, and is modified by the ptcp. ἀποδεδειγμένον; the ptcp., we note, is
further modified, adverbially, by two prepositional phrases and by three
nouns in the dative).

§36.4   An <u>adverb</u> (§30.34), or any word or group of words serving in an
          adverbial capacity (cf. §§34.2ff., 34.3ff., 34.4ff.) can be
modified by any of the adverbial modifiers (cf. §34.). If the adverbial
modifier is composed of a noun or other substantive, this in turn may be
modified adjectivally.

§36.41   The adverbial modifier is often a <u>participle</u> which can be further
          modified. ἐξελθὼν ἐκ γῆς Χαλδαίων κατῴκησεν ἐν Χαρράν 'departing
from (the) land of the Chaldeans, he settled in Haran' (Ac. 7:4; the main
verb is modified temporally by the ptcp. ἐξελθών, which in turn is
modified by the prepositional phrase ἐκ γῆς, and this is modified by a
proper noun in the genitive Χαλδαίων).

§36.42   The adverbial modifier is very often a <u>prepositional phrase</u>,
          the substantive of which can be further modified. παρέστησεν
ἑαυτὸν ζῶντα...ἐν πολλοῖς τεκμηρίοις 'he showed himself (to be) living...
by many convincing proofs' (Ac. 1:3; the verb παρέστησεν is modified by
the prepositional phrase ἐν τεκμηρίοις, and the noun in this phrase is
modified by the adjective πολλοῖς). To say that an "adverb" is modified
by an "adjective" is contrary to our rules of grammar--but if we analyze
the parts of speech that are used, we find that there is no violation of
grammatical rules.

§36.421   Again, a chain of modifiers is possible. ἐν ταῖς ἡμέραις ταύταις
            ἀναστὰς Πέτρος ἐν μέσῳ τῶν ἀδελφῶν εἶπεν 'in those days, Peter,
standing in (the) midst of the brethren, said' (Ac. 1:15; the main verb is
modified by an adverbial ptcp. ἀναστάς which is modified adverbially by a
prepositional phrase ἐν μέσῳ; the noun of this phrase is modified by a
noun in the genitive ἀδελφῶν, which is modified by a definite article).

§36.43   The adverbial modifier may be an <u>infinitival clause,</u> and this
            may be modified further by another infinitival clause. οὗτος
...ἐκάκωσεν τοὺς πατέρας τοῦ ποιεῖν τὰ βρέφη ἔκθετα αὐτῶν εἰς τὸ μὴ
ζωογονεῖσθαι 'that one treated the fathers wickedly so as to make them
expose their infants in order that they might not be kept alive' (Ac. 7:19;
the main verb ἐκάκωσεν is modified by the purpose clause [§37.54] introduced by τοῦ ποιεῖν, and this purpose clause is further modified by a
result clause εἰς τὸ μὴ ζωογονεῖσθαι).

§36.5   Obviously, there are many other possibilities that could be
            listed. The student should keep his eyes open and list the
most interesting of those he sees.

§37.   COMPOUND AND COMPLEX SENTENCES. Many sentences are not simple
            (§30.1), but compound (§30.421) or complex (§30.422) or both.
Since the ability to recognize subtle shades of meaning in the relationship
between parts of a compound or complex sentence is basic, the student must
work at complete mastery of this subject.

§37.1   A <u>compound sentence</u> is composed of coördinate clauses, which
            may be conjunctive or disjunctive.

§37.11   Conjunctive clauses in a sentence are generally joined by a
            conjunction such as and, for, moreover, etc. The intention is
to join two or more statements in a single sentence. Each part is an independent sentence. οἱ νεανίσκοι ὑμῶν ὁράσεις ὄψονται καὶ οἱ πρεσβύτεροι
ὑμῶν ἐνυπνίοις ἐνυπνιασθήσονται 'Your young men shall see visions and
your old men shall dream dreams' (Ac. 2:17).

§37.12   Disjunctive clauses are generally joined by a conjunction such
         as but, yet, however, etc. The intention is to contrast two
or more statements in a single sentence. Each part is an independent
sentence. Ἰωάννης μὲν ἐβάπτισεν ὕδατι ὑμεῖς δὲ ἐν πνεύματι βαπτισθήσεσθε
ἁγίῳ 'John baptized with water, but you shall be baptized with the holy
spirit' (Ac. 1:5).

§37.13   <u>Asyndeton</u> is the placing of clauses in juxtaposition without
         a conjunction. This is not considered to be "good Greek."
δέδεσαι γυναικί; μὴ ζήτει λύσιν 'Are you bound to a wife? Don't seek
a divorce' (1 Cor. 7:27).

§37.14   Compound sentences can be broken into their component parts,
         and each part treated as a simple sentence. Often there is
ellipsis in one or more parts (§30.14). The main task is to observe the
type of connection between the parts. ὁ ἥλιος μεταστραφήσεται εἰς σκότος
καὶ ἡ σελήνη εἰς αἷμα 'The sun shall be changed into darkness, and the
moon [shall be changed] into blood' (Ac. 2:20).

§37.15   The <u>correlative sentence</u> is a special type of compound sentence,
         in which the parts are tied together in such way that each part
is dependent on the other for meaning. Correlative conjunctions (§30.363)
are used, καθὼς ἠγάπησέν με ὁ πατήρ κἀγω ὑμᾶς ἠγάπησα 'As the father
loved me, so I have loved you' (Jn. 15:9).

§37.151   Sometimes one of the correlative words is omitted, and if the
         predicates are the same, a predicate may be omitted, resulting
in what appears to be a simple sentence. εἰ δίκαιόν ἐστιν ἐνώπιον τοῦ
θεοῦ ὑμῶν ἀκούειν μᾶλλον ἢ τοῦ θεοῦ 'Whether it is right before God to
listen to you rather than [to listen to] God...' (Ac. 4:19).

§37.2   A <u>complex sentence</u> consists (at least) of a main (or independent)
         clause, and a subordinate (or dependent) clause (§30.422).
It is necessary to identify first the main clause, then determine how it

is related to the subordinate clause. The subordinate clause is, in effect,
a <u>modifier</u>, affecting the meaning of the main clause.

§37.21   A clause, since it can serve as a single part of speech (§30.4),
          can be substantival, adjectival, or adverbial.

§37.3   A <u>substantival clause</u>, often called a noun clause, can serve as
          the subject or the object of the main verb (§32.1), or as an
appositive (§35.6).

§37.31   As <u>subject</u>, the substantival clause may be constructed either
          with a finite verb or with an infinitive (§30.381).

§37.311   The substantival clause introduced by οτι followed by the
          indicative usually adds the element of result to the main
predication. οὐ μέλει σοι ὅτι ἀπολλύμεθα 'It is not a care to you that
we perish?' (Mk. 4:38).

§37.312   The substantival clause introduced by ἵνα followed by sbjtv. adds
          the element of purpose to the main predication. συμφέρει ὑμῖν
ἵνα ἐγὼ ἀπέλθω 'It is profitable for you that I go away' (Jn. 16:7).

§37.313   An <u>infinitive clause</u> may be the subject of the sentence. This
          approaches a simple sentence in construction. καλὸν ἀνθρώπῳ
γυναικὸς μὴ ἅπτεσθαι 'It is good for a man not to touch a woman' (1 Cor. 7:1).

§37.32   A substantival clause may serve as <u>object</u> of the main verb.

§37.321   The object may be a noun clause introduced by ὅτι with the
          indicative. ἐγὼ πεπίστευκα ὅτι σὺ εἶ ὁ Χριστὸς ὁ υἱὸς τοῦ θεοῦ
'I have believed that you are the Christ the son of God' (Jn. 11:27).

§37.3211 After verbs of saying, knowing, thinking, and the like, this is
          considered to be indirect discourse (§37.8ff.).

§37.322   The object may be a noun clause introduced by ἵνα or οπως, with the subjunctive particularly after verbs of saying, asking, wishing, and the like. This, too, might be considered as indirect discourse (§37.82). εἰπὲ τῷ λίθῳ τούτῳ ἵνα γένηται ἄρτος 'Say to this stone that it should become bread' (Lk. 4:3). ἐρωτῶν αὐτὸν ὅπως ἐλθὼν διασώσῃ τὸν δοῦλον αὐτοῦ 'asking him that having come he might heal (= that he might come and heal) his slave' (Lk. 7:3).

§37.323   After verbs of fearing or caution, an object clause is introduced with μὴ followed by the subjunctive (cf. §31.33), and is translated 'lest' or 'that.' βλέπετε μὴ τις ὑμᾶς πλανήσῃ 'See [to it] lest anyone lead you astray' (Mk. 13:5).

§37.3231   The negative of this construction uses μὴ οὐ 'lest not.' μήποτε οὐκ ἀρκέσῃ ἡμῖν καὶ ὑμῖν 'lest by chance there not be enough for us and for you' (Mt. 25:9).

§37.324   The object clause is occasionally introduced without a conjunction (asyndeton, §37.13).

§37.325   The object clause may be an infinitival clause. ἐγὼ γὰρ ἔμαθον ἐν οἷς εἰμι αὐτάρκης εἶναι 'For I have learned to be content in what[ever] things I am' (Phil. 4:11).

§37.33   A substantival clause may be in apposition with a noun in the main clause, as an <u>appositive clause</u>. ὅτι αὕτη ἐστὶν ἡ μαρτυρία τοῦ θεοῦ ὅτι μεμαρτύρηκεν περὶ τοῦ υἱοῦ αὐτοῦ 'Because this is the witness of God, that he has witnessed concerning his son' (1 Jn. 5:9).

§37.331   An appositive clause may be introduced by ὅτι with the indicative. αὕτη δέ ἐστιν ἡ κρίσις ὅτι τὸ φῶς ἐλήλυθεν εἰς τὸν κόσμον 'This is the judgment, that the light has come into the world...' (Jn. 3:19).

§37.332   An appositive clause may be introduced by ἵνα with the subjunctive. καὶ πόθεν μοι τοῦτο ἵνα ἔλθῃ ἡ μήτηρ τοῦ κυρίου μου πρὸς ἐμέ;

'And whence [is] this to me, that the mother of my Lord should come to me?'
(Lk. 1:43).

§37.333   An appositive clause may be an infinitive clause. θρησκεία
          καθαρὰ ... αὕτη ἐστίν·ἐπισκέπτεσθαι ὀρφανοὺς καὶ χήρας 'Pure
religion ... is this: to watch over orphans and widows' (Jas. 1:27).

§37.4   An adjectival_clause may be used to define any substantive,
          whether subject, direct or indirect object, predicate nomina-
tive, appositive, or modifier, in the main clause. ἄχρι οὗ ἀνέστη
βασιλεὺς ἕτερος ὃς οὐκ ᾔδει τὸν Ἰωσήφ 'Until another king came along who
did not know Joseph' (Ac. 7:18). μνημονεύετε τοῦ λόγου οὗ ἐγὼ εἶπον ὑμῖν
'Remember the word which [cf. §35.573] I spoke to you' (Jn. 15:20).

§37.41   The adjectival clause is introduced by a relative pronoun
          (§23.4), relative adverb (§30.34), or adverbial phrase (§30.411).
βασιλεὺς ἕτερος ὃς οὐκ ᾔδει τὸν Ἰωσήφ 'Another king who knew not Joseph'
(Ac. 7:18). ἐν γῇ Μαδιάμ οὗ ἐγέννησεν υἱοὺς δύο 'In the land (of) Midian
where he begat two sons' (Ac. 7:29).   εἰς τὴν γῆν ταύτην εἰς ἣν ὑμεῖς
νῦν κατοικεῖτε 'Into this land in which you now dwell' (Ac. 7:4).

§37.411   The relative pronoun has been discussed, §35.57ff., above.

§37.412   A relative clause introduced by ὅς or one of the other simple
          relatives refers to a particular person or thing. A clause
introduced by ὅστις or another compound relative refers to a person or
thing in general or indicates the class, character, quality, or capacity
of a person or (occasionally) a thing.

§37.4121 The NT writers, particularly Luke, do not observe this
          distinction. (BDF §293.)

§37.4122 The rel. pron. is sometimes omitted, particularly when two or
          more adjectival clauses are connected with a conjunction. The
omission occurs even when the rel. prons. would be in different cases.

§37.413   Relative adverbs of time, place, or manner, are used to introduce
          the corresponding clauses. Cf. Eng. "the day when he said,"
"the house where he lived," and "a man as old as he was." εἰς τὸν οἶκόν
μου ἐπιστρέψω ὅθεν ἐξῆλθον 'I will return to my house whence I came out'
(Mt. 12:44). εὗρεν τὸν τόπον οὗ ἦν γεγραμμένον 'He found the place where
it was written' (Lk. 4:17).

§37.4131 Adverbial phrases can be substituted for relative adverbs (cf.
          Eng. "in which" for "when" and "where" in previous section).
ἐλεύσεται ὃν τρόπον ἐθεάσασθε 'He shall come in the manner in which you
have seen...' (Ac. 1:11).

§37.42   The position of a relative clause is largely a matter of personal
          preference. It may precede the main clause, be incorporated in
the main clause, or follow the main clause. ἃ ὁ θεὸς ἐκαθάρισεν σὺ μὴ κοίνου
'What things God has cleansed (= declared clean), don't you profane
(= declare common)' (Ac. 10:15). οὐ δυνάμεθα γὰρ ἡμεῖς ἃ εἴδαμεν καὶ ἠκούσαμεν
μὴ λαλεῖν 'For we are not able what things we know and have heard not to speak'
(Ac. 4:20). ἐπισκέψασθε δὲ ἀδελφοί ἄνδρας ἐξ ὑμῶν ... οὓς καταστήσομεν ἐπὶ
τῆς χρείας ταύτης 'You, brothers, look for men from your fellowship whom
we shall appoint over these needs' (Ac. 6:3).

§37.43   A participial clause may be used adjectivally. Ἰωσὴφ ὁ ἐπικληθεὶς
          Βαρναβᾶς 'Joseph, who was named Barnabas (lit. 'the having-been-
called Barnabas') (Ac. 4:36).

§37.431   It is important for us to keep in mind that this is indeed a
          "clause," for the ptcp. has verbal power as well as adjectival.
For this reason we must always translate such a ptcp. with a clause.

§37.432   A rel. pron. is generally not used with adjectival participial
          clauses, but is replaced by the def. art.

§37.433   For the temporal significance of the participle, cf. §34.411ff.

§37.434   The participial clause may be used as a <u>predicate adjective</u>
              (§33.5) of the verb <u>to be</u>. This is in effect a periphrastic
construction (§30.411). ἰδοὺ οἱ ἄνδρες...εἰσὶν ἐν τῷ ἱερῷ ἑστῶτες καὶ
διδάσκοντες τὸν λαόν 'Behold, the men...are in the temple standing and
teaching the people' (Ac. 5:25).

§37.44   An <u>infinitive clause</u> may be used adjectivally (cf. §30.32),
              particularly with nouns cognate with verbs that take a comple-
mentary infinitive (§33.61). ἔδωκεν αὐτοῖς ἐξουσίαν τέκνα θεοῦ γενέσθαι
'He gave to them capability to become children of God' (Jn. 1:12).

§37.45   The verb of a relative clause is often omitted when the same
              verb is used in the main clause.

§37.5   An <u>adverbial clause</u> may be used to modify a verb, an adjective,
              or an adverb (§30.34). Adverbial clauses are usually identified
according to one of the adverbial categories, such as temporal, local,
purpose, result, etc.

§37.51   A <u>temporal clause</u> is used to modify the main verb by relating
              it in time to some other action or state which was prior to,
or contemporary with, or after the predication of the main verb.

§37.511   Temporal clauses are generally introduced by conjunctions,
              relative adverbs, or adverbial phrases to indicate the time
relationship.

§37.5111 A clause introduced by πρίν or πρὶν ἤ 'before,' followed by
              the subjunctive, optative, or the articular infinitive in the
accusative (§34.4211) is <u>subsequent</u> to the main verb. ("I came before
you called.") ὁ ἥλιος μεταστραφήσεται εἰς σκότος...πρὶν ἐλθεῖν ἡμέραν κυρίου
'The sun shall be changed into darkness...before the day of the Lord comes'
(Ac. 2:20). This construction is not common in NT.

§37.5112 A clause introduced by ἕως followed by the aor. indic. marks the
              end of a period of time ("until"), and makes the predication

of the temporal clause <u>the terminus of the state or action</u> of the main verb.
ὁ ἀστὴρ...προῆγεν αὐτοὺς ἕως ἐλθὼν ἐστάθη ἐπάνω οὗ ἦν τὸ παιδίον 'The star
...went before them until coming it stood over where the young child was'
(Mt. 2:9). The pres. ind. and perhaps the fut. ind. are also found. If the
subjunctive follows (usually with ἄν), the clause indicates a contingency.
ἴσθι ἐκεῖ ἕως ἄν εἴπω σοι 'Stay there until (whatever time) I tell you
(to leave)' (Mt. 2:13).

§37.5113 A clause introduced by ἕως followed by the pres. indic. (or
          sometimes another tense), indicates <u>contemporary</u> action ("as
long as, while"). Cf. §34.4212. ἡμᾶς δεῖ ἐργάζεσθαι τὰ ἔργα τοῦ πέμψαντός
με ἕως ἡμέρα ἐστίν 'We must work the works of the one who sent me as long
as it is day' (Jn. 9:4). The subjunctive is also found. καθίσατε ὧδε ἕως
προσεύξωμαι 'Sit here while I pray' (Mk. 14:32).

§37.5114 A clause introduced by ὅτε followed by the indicative marks
          <u>contemporary</u> activity or state. If the imperfect tense is used,
the element of duration is indicated ("as long as, while"); if the aorist
is used, the point of time is noted ("when"). ὅτε δὲ ἤμελλεν προαγαγεῖν αὐτόν
'When he was about to bring him out (= while he was in the first stage)'
(Ac. 12:6). ὅτε δὲ ἀνέβησαν ἐκ τοῦ ὕδατος 'But when they came out of the
water (= at the point of time when)' (Ac. 8:39).

§37.5115 A clause introduced by ὡς is quite similar to one introduced by
          ὅτε. Followed by the pres. or impf. ind. it means "while, as
long as." Followed by the aor. ind. it means "when, after." Followed by
the sbjtv. and ἄν or ἐάν, it has an element of contingency ("when, as soon
as"). ὡς ἀτενίζοντες ἦσαν 'While they were gazing' (Ac. 1:10). ὡς δὲ ἤκουσαν
τοὺς λόγους τούτους 'When they heard these words' (Ac. 5:24). τὰ δὲ λοιπὰ
ὡς ἄν ἔλθω διατάξομαι 'The remaining matters when(ever) I come I shall give
instructions' (1 Cor. 11:34).

§37.5116 A clause introduced by ὅταν followed by the pres. sbjtv. has
          <u>contemporary</u> significance ("whenever, as often as"); followed
by the aor. sbjtv., it has a punctiliar aspect ("when"). In any clause,

contingency is indicated by the use of ἄν and the sbjtv. In the NT, the
indicative is sometimes used in pres., impf., aor., or fut. ὅταν δὲ
εἰσφέρωσιν ὑμᾶς ἐπὶ τὰς συναγωγάς 'and as often as they bring you before
the synagogues' (Lk. 12:11). ἐλεύσονται δὲ ἡμέραι καὶ ὅταν ἀπαρθῇ ἀπ'
αὐτῶν ὁ νυμφίος 'The days will come even when the bridegroom will be taken
away from them' (Lk. 5:35).

§37.5117 Other relative adverbs are found, such as ἄχρι (with or without
         οὗ) 'until' (Ac. 7:18) or 'as long as' (Lk. 21:24); μέχρι οὗ
'until' (Mk. 13:30); ἐπειδή 'when, after' (Lk. 7:1, etc.).

§37.5118 Adverbial phrases or clauses are often used instead of
         relative adverbs.

§37.5119 The adverbial participle (34.41ff.) is very often used to
         construct a temporal clause. Review the significance of the
tenses used (§§31.52, .54, .55).

§37.512 A temporal clause is either definite or indefinite.

§37.5121 A temporal clause is definite when the action occurs (or occurred)
         at a definite point in time. The indicative mood is used, and
the negative is οὐ. ἐπειδή ἐπλήρωσεν πάντα τὰ ῥήματα αὐτοῦ εἰς τὰς ἀκοὰς
τοῦ λαοῦ εἰσῆλθεν εἰς Καφαρναούμ 'After he had ended all his sayings in
the hearing of the people he entered Capernaum' (Lk. 7:1).

§37.5122 A definite temporal clause usually refers to action in the
         present or past.

§37.5123 A temporal clause is indefinite when the action occurs in the
         future (indefinite), or when it occurs an unspecified number of
times, or (rarely) when it continues for an indeterminate period. The
subjunctive mood with ἄν is used (also the optative without ἄν and occasionally the indicative). The negative is μή. ὅταν ἄγωσιν ὑμᾶς

'Whenever they may bring you' (Mk. 13:11). ἕως οὗ ἀρνήσῃ με τρίς 'until
you have denied me thrice' (Jn. 13:38).

§37.5124   In such clauses the present is used of action not completed
           and the aorist of action completed or action simply occurring.

§37.513   The temporal conjunctions of duration ("while, so long as") or
          termination ("until, till") may also indicate purpose.

§37.52   A <u>local clause</u> is used to define the main clause by locating
          the place (literally or metaphorically) of the predication
of the main verb. If the local clause modifies a noun or other substantive
of place, it is adjectival (see §37.4ff.). If it modifies a verb, it is
adverbial and is considered here.

§37.521   A local clause is introduced by a relative adverb ("where,
          whither," etc.) or by an adverbial phrase ("in which, to which,
from which," etc.).

§37.5211   The relative adverbs are ancient declined forms whose endings
           indicate 'at,' 'from,' and 'to' (all used in a local sense),
but by usage these have been worn down, and some of the forms have fallen
into disuse.

§37.5212   The rel. adv. ὅπου + ind. indicates place ('where'). It is
           sometimes used in correlative statements in combination with ἐκεῖ
'where ... there.' Followed by ἄν + sbjtv. it is less definite ('wherever')
and sometimes refers to a place in time ('whenever'). ἦλθον εἰς Θεσσαλονίκην
ὅπου ἦν συναγωγὴ τῶν Ἰουδαίων 'They came to Thessalonica where there was a
synagogue of the Jews' (Ac. 17:1). ἀκολουθήσω σοι ὅπου ἐὰν ἀπέρχῃ 'I will
follow you wherever you (may) go' (Lk. 9:57). ὅπου ἐὰν ᾖ τὸ πτῶμα ἐκεῖ
συναχθήσονται οἱ ἀετοί 'Wherever the body is (may be), there will be
gathered together the vultures' (Mt. 24:28).

§37.5213 The rel. adv. οὗ + ind. is similar to ὅπου and can likewise be
          used in correlation with ἐκεῖ (Mt. 18:20). Followed by the sbjtv.
+ ἐάν it has the idea of 'wherever' (1 Cor. 16:6). It may be used metaphorically of the circumstance "where" (Rom. 4:15). Its basic nature (genitive
of the rel. pron.) is shown by the frequency with which it is used to
introduce local clauses modifying nouns of place. ὅτε εἰσῆλθον εἰς τὸ
ὑπερῷον ἀνέβησαν οὗ ἦσαν καταμένοντες... 'When they had entered, they went
up into the upper room where were staying ...' (Ac. 1:13; cf. 2:2; 7:29;
12:12, etc.).

§37.5214 The rel. adv. ὅθεν is used to indicate the place from which the
          action of the main verb proceeds ("from which place, where").
Metaphorically it is used to indicate "from which fact," "for which reason,"
and therefore "hence." This is an ancient form of a rel. pron., and is
used with clauses modifying nouns of place. κἀκεῖθεν ἀπέπλευσαν εἰς
Ἀντιόχειαν ὅθεν ἦσαν παραδεδομένοι τῇ χάριτι τοῦ θεοῦ 'And from there they
sailed to Antioch, where they had been commended to the grace of God'
(Ac. 14:26). Cf. Ac. 26:19.

§37.5215 Several other adverbs are used with local clauses. Some of
          these have been given in §23.7, which should be reviewed here.

§37.5216 Adverbial phrases are used to introduce local clauses. These
          are obviously the result of the preposition displacing the
earlier case-endings.

§37.522 The verb in a local clause will be indicative if the place is
          definite, or if the action was prior to the time of making the
statement even if the place is indefinite. The verb will be subjunctive
if the place is indefinite and the time of the predication is future.
See the illustrations in §37.5212.

§37.53 A <u>causal clause</u> sets forth the reason for the predication of
          the main clause (it answers the question "Why?"). It may be
coördinate or subordinate.

§37.531   The coördinate causal clause is commonly an independent clause
             introduced by γάρ 'for,' giving the reason for the preceding
statement or statements. διότι τὸ γνωστὸν τοῦ θεοῦ φανερόν ἐστιν ἐν
αὐτοῖς· ὁ θεὸς γὰρ αὐτοῖς ἐφανέρωσεν 'For that which is known of God is
clear to them; for God revealed (it) to them' (Rom. 1:19).

§37.532   The subordinate causal clause is introduced by a subordinating
             conjunction, a relative adverb, or an adverbial phrase.

§37.5321   A causal clause may be introduced by ὅτι 'because, since,'
             (literally 'that,' but developing from διὰ τοῦτο ... ὅτι 'for
this reason ... that'), followed by the indicative. ὁ δὲ εἶπεν Λεγιών
ὅτι εἰσῆλθεν δαιμόνια πολλὰ εἰς αὐτόν 'He said, "Legion," because many
demons had entered into him' (Lk. 8:30). Cf. διὰ τοῦτο ὑμεῖς οὐκ ἀκούετε
ὅτι ἐκ τοῦ θεοῦ οὐκ ἐστέ 'On account of this you are not hearing: because
you are not from God' (Jn. 8:47).

§37.5322   Quite similar is the conjunction διοτι + ind. 'because, for.'
             This conj. develops into an inferential "therefore."
διότι οὐκ ἦν αὐτοῖς τόπος ἐν τῷ καταλύματι 'Because there was no place
for them in the inn' (Lk. 2:7). διότι καὶ ἐν ἑτέρῳ λέγει 'Therefore also
in another (Psalm) he says...' (Ac. 13:35).

§37.5323   The causal clause may be introduced by καθότι + ind. 'in view of
             the fact that, because,' or by καθότι ἄν + ind. 'to the degree
that, as.' καθότι οὐκ ἦν δυνατὸν κρατεῖσθαι αὐτὸν ὑπ' αὐτοῦ 'Because he
could not be held by it' (Ac. 2:24). καὶ διεμέριζον αὐτὰ πᾶσιν καθότι ἄν
τις χρείαν εἶχεν 'And they were dividing them to all, as (= to the degree
that) anyone had need' (Ac. 2:45).

§37.5324   The causal clause may be introduced by διόπερ + ind. 'therefore,
             for this reason.' This conj. may be used (e.g. with the impv.)
in a way similar to γάρ (§37.531), in a coördinate causal (or inferential)
sentence. διόπερ εἰ βρῶμα σκανδαλίζει τὸν ἀδελφόν μου οὐ μὴ φάγω κρέα εἰς

τὸν αἰῶνα 'Therefore if food causes my brother to stumble, I will never
eat meat...' (1 Cor. 8:13).   διόπερ ἀγαπητοί μου φεύγετε ἀπὸ τῆς εἰδωλολατρίας
'Therefore my beloved, flee from idolatry' (1 Cor. 10:14).

§37.5325   The causal clause may be introduced by ἐπεί or ἐπειδή + ind.
            'because, since.'   τὸν δὲ Παῦλον Ἑρμῆν ἐπειδὴ αὐτὸς ἦν ὁ
ἡγούμενος τοῦ λόγου 'And (they called) Paul "Hermes," because he was
the leader of the word' (Ac. 14:12).

§37.5326   The conj. ὡς may be used with the ptcp. in concord, or in the
            gen. abs. (§34.5), to form a causal clause. Literally it means
"as one who..." and develops to mean "the reason for acting so," or
"because." The construction implies that the action of the ptcp. is the
supposed cause of the action of the principal verb. The negative is οὐ.
οὐχ ὡς τοῦ ἔθνους μου ἔχων τι κατηγορεῖν '...not because I had anything
to charge against my nation' (lit. 'not as having...') (Ac. 28:19).

§37.5327   The ptcp. without a conj. may be used in a causal clause. If
            the subj. of the causal clause is the same as the subj. of the
main clause, the ptcp. agrees in GNC. If it is a different subj., the
ptcp. will be in gen. abs. (§34.5). The negative is μή. Ἰωσὴφ δὲ ὁ ἀνὴρ
αὐτῆς δίκαιος ὤν... 'But Joseph her husband, being a righteous man
(= because he was a righteous man)' (Mt. 1:19). μὴ ἔχοντος δὲ αὐτοῦ
ἀποδοῦναι ἐκέλευσεν αὐτὸν ὁ κύριος πραθῆναι 'And he not having anything
for paying (= because he was not able to pay), the master ordered him
to be sold' (Mt. 18:25).

§37.5328   An articular infinitive (§33.611) in the accusative after διά
            may be used to express a causal clause. The negative is μή.
ἀνέβη δὲ καὶ Ἰωσὴφ ... διὰ τὸ εἶναι αὐτὸν ἐξ οἴκου καὶ πατριᾶς Δαυίδ
'And Joseph also went up ... because of his being from the house and
clan of David' (Lk. 2:4).

§37.5329   A relative pronoun may introduce a causal clause. οἵτινες
            ἀπεθάνομεν τῇ ἁμαρτίᾳ πῶς ἔτι ζήσομεν ἐν αὐτῇ; 'We who have
died to sin, how shall we yet live in it?' (Rom. 6:2).

§37.533   The finite verb in a causal clause is in the indicative mood,
          since there can be no contingency or uncertainty in mind when
something is set forth as the cause of another.

§37.54   The purpose clause sets forth the purpose or aim or goal of
         the action of the main verb. It answers the question "Why?
For what purpose?" and explains "in order that." Purpose clauses are
sometimes called final clauses and are divided into "pure final clauses"
(distinct purpose conceived as aim of action) and "semi-final clauses"
(direction of the action toward a given result). The line between the
two is very indefinite.

§37.541   The subjunctive mood is regularly used (the negative with μή),
          since the goal is only purposed and not achieved. In some
passages, the future indicative appears (which may be erroneously used
for the aor. sbjtv.). The pres. ind. is found only in passages that are
textually disputed. The optative does not appear in purpose clauses in
the NT.

§37.542   Purpose clauses with finite verbs are introduced by ἵνα or
          another conjunction.

§37.5421 ἵνα + sbjtv. 'that, in order that' is used after verbs in the
          ind. or impv. in almost every tense, to declare purpose. ἵνα
μαρτυρήσῃ περὶ τοῦ φωτός 'that he might witness concerning the light'
(Jn. 1:7). The negative is ἵνα μή. ἵνα μὴ σαλευθῶ 'in order that I
might not be shaken' (Ac. 2:25). Note the use of fut. ind.: ἵνα
ξυρήσονται τὴν κεφαλήν 'so that they would shave their head' (Ac. 21:24).

§37.5422 ὅπως + sbjtv. 'in order that' may be used, usually without ἄν.
          ὅπως ἀναβλέψῃς καὶ πλησθῇς πνεύματος ἁγίου 'that you might
receive your sight and be filled with the Holy Spirit' (Ac. 9:17).
With αν: ὅπως ἂν ἔλθωσιν καιροὶ ἀναψύξεως 'that there might come times of
refreshing' (Ac. 3:20). The negative is ὅπως μή.

§37.5423 The difference between ἵνα and ὅπως is not marked. However, in
          Lk. 16:27f. and 2 Th. 1:11f. both conjunctions are used, the one

setting forth the immediate purpose of the action, and the other setting forth
the ultimate purpose. ἐρωτῶ σε οὖν πάτερ ἵνα πέμψῃς αὐτὸν εἰς τὸν οἶκον
τοῦ πατρός μου ἔχω γὰρ πέντε ἀδελφούς ὅπως διαμαρτύρηται αὐτοῖς ἵνα μὴ
καὶ αὐτοὶ ἔλθωσιν εἰς τὸν τόπον τοῦτον τῆς βασάνου 'So I ask you, Father,
that you send him to my father's house, for I have five brothers, so that
he might warn them, so that they too might not come into this place of
torment' (Lk. 16:27f.).

§37.5424 ὡς + sbjtv. 'in order that' may introduce a purpose clause.
         ὡς τελειώσω τὸν δρόμον μου 'so that I might complete my course'
(Ac. 20:24). The same particle may introduce a purpose clause with an
infinitive (Ac. 20:24 var. τελειωσαι).

§37.5425 The <u>infinitive</u> without the article, or with the article in the
          genitive, can be used to express purpose (cf. §34.422).
εἰς οὓς ἐγὼ ἀποστέλλω σε ἀνοῖξαι ὀφθαλμοὺς αὐτῶν 'To whom I am sending you,
in order to open their eyes' (Ac. 26:17f.). The preposition εἰς or πρός
+ the artic. inf. (§33.611) in the accusative may also be used.
μετανοήσατε οὖν καὶ ἐπιστρέψατε εἰς τὸ ἐξαλειφθῆναι ὑμῶν τὰς ἁμαρτίας
'Repent therefore and turn again in order that your sins might be blotted
out' (lit. 'unto being-blotted-out your sins') (Ac. 3:19). The conjunctions
ὡς and ὥστε with the anarthrous inf. can be used in a similar way (cf.
Mt. 27:1, Lk. 9:52).

§37.5426 The <u>adverbial participle</u> (usually future) may be used as
          a purpose clause (cf. §34.414).

§37.5427 A relative pronoun + fut. ind. or aor. sbjtv. may be used to
          indicate purpose. οὓς καταστήσομεν ἐπὶ τῆς χρείας ταύτης
'Whom we shall appoint over this need' (= 'so that we may appoint...')
(Ac. 6:3).

§37.55   The <u>result clause</u> sets forth the result of the action
         predicated by the main clause. It answers the question
"So what happened?" Result clauses are sometimes called <u>consecutive clauses</u>.

§37.551   By its nature, the result clause will be in the indicative
          mood if constructed with a finite verb. The negative is οὐ.
(Many result clauses, however, are constructed with the infinitive.
The negative then is μή.).

§37.552   Result clauses are usually introduced by ὥστε, but sometimes
          by other particles.

§37.5521 ὥστε + ind. 'so that,' or + inf. (§37.5531) 'so as to' may be
          used to introduce a result clause. The principal clause may
contain ουτως 'thus,' τοιουτος 'such a kind,' or τοσουτος 'so large, so
great.' ὥστε καὶ Βαρναβᾶς συναπήχθη αὐτῶν τῇ ὑποκρίσει 'so that even
Barnabas was carried along with them in the hypocrisy' (Ga. 2:13).

§37.5522 ἵνα + sbjtv. 'so that' may introduce a result clause. The
          result is probable rather than actual. In some passages it is
the result that follows from God's purpose. Here the line between purpose
and result becomes indistinct. καὶ ἦν παρακεκαλυμμένον ἀπ᾽ αὐτῶν ἵνα μὴ
αἴσθωνται αὐτό 'and it was concealed from them, so that they might not
understand it' (Lk. 9:45).

§37.553   The infinitive is commonly used in result clauses.

§37.5531 ὥστε + inf. 'so as to, so that' may be used in a result clause.
          ὥστε κληθῆναι τὸ χωρίον ἐκεῖνο...Ἀκελδαμάχ 'so that that field
was called Akeldama' (lit. 'so as to be called...') (Ac. 1:19). The
distinction sometimes made between ὥστε + articular infinitive and ὥστε +
anarthrous inf. does not stand up before the texts.

§37.5532 The articular infinitive in the genitive, without prep. or
          conj. may be used for a result clause (cf. §34.4222). The
article may be omitted, and an anarthrous inf. used in the same way.
διὰ τί ἐπλήρωσεν ὁ Σατανᾶς τὴν καρδίαν σου ψεύσασθαί σε τὸ πνεῦμα τὸ ἅγιον
'Why has Satan filled your heart, so that you lied to the Holy Spirit?'
(lit. 'to lie...') (Ac. 5:3).

§37.554   In theory, the use of the infinitive should indicate the potential
          result, while the use of the indicative should give the actual
result. Moule (<u>Idiom-Book</u>, p. 141) says, "But, as a fact, the Indicative
is rare and the Infinitive serves for both potential and actual consequences.

§37.6   <u>Clauses of condition or concession</u> belong to a special
          category of adverbial clauses that need special treatment.

§37.61   In conditional and concessive sentences, the main clause is
          closely related to (we might say "dependent" on) the secondary
clause, or conditioned by it. Even the terminology must be altered.

§37.611   The subordinate clause is called the <u>protasis</u> ('stretching
          forward'): it expresses an assumed condition or concession.
The main clause is called the <u>apodosis</u> ('giving back'): it declares
what will be the resultant action or state under the assumed condition.
Protasis: "If it rains" -- apodosis: "we shall get wet."

§37.6111   The main clause (apodosis) may be declaratory, interrogative,
          imperative, or exclamatory (cf. §30.13).

§37.6112   The protasis ("if-clause") may stand before, after, or be
          included within, the main clause. "If I were you, I'd go."
"Stay there, if you want to." "We shall indeed, if we carry out this
plan, be very well satisfied."

§37.6113   It is possible to have two or more protases with one apodosis,
          and they may be conjunctive ("if ... and if ...") or
disjunctive ("if ... or if ..."). It is possible to refer to different
times (and use different tenses) in a sequence of protases or apodoses.
"If you were here yesterday, and are here again today, and will be
tomorrow, why don't you pay rent or bring food?"

§37.6114   Instead of the protasis with εἰ 'if,' any of the following may
          be used: a participle (often in genitive absolute), an adverb,
a prepositional phrase, a relative clause, or some other single word

or phrase. The protasis may be entirely omitted when it is clearly implied
by the context. "What happens if I say No?" "You'll go anyway"
(add, "if you say No").

§37.612   The difference between a conditional sentence and a concessive
            sentence is simply this: in the conditional sentence the
apodosis becomes reality on the condition that ("if") the protasis is
realized; in the concessive sentence the apodosis becomes reality in
spite of ("even if, although") the protasis. Conditional: "If it rains,
I shall stay home." Concessive: "Even if it rains, I shall go."

§37.6121   The protasis of a conditional sentence is generally introduced
            by εἰ (or ἐάν for εἰ + ἄν) 'if.'

§37.6122 The protasis of a concessive sentence is introduced by καὶ εἰ
            or καὶ ἐάν 'even if' or by εἰ καί or ἐὰν καί 'although.'
The negative is οὐδ'εἰ or μηδ'εἰ (ἐάν) 'not even if.' With the ptcp. καίπερ
'although' is also found.

§37.62   There are a number of variables in the construction of a
            conditional or concessive sentence. Each of the possibilities
must be noted.

§37.621   Variables of time: the sentence may be expressed in past,
            present, or future.

§37.6211 Some conditions are expressed in either past or present, but in
            reality have no time significance. They are simple statements
of cause and effect. These are called simple conditions. "If you study,
you learn." "If the moon was full, the house was visible."

§37.622   Variables of degree of reality or doubt expressed: the sentence
            may be contrary to fact (or "unreal"), it may be noncommittal
("general"), or it may be more or less probable ("more vivid" or "less
vivid").

§37.6221 <u>Present conditions</u> can only be noncommittal or general. "If

         you are hungry, eat"--I have not committed an opinion concerning
your hunger. Present conditions can be <u>simple</u> ("If you do this, I'll pay
you") or <u>general</u> ("If you work well, I'll praise you" = whenever you
work well...).

§37.6222 In English the present condition (subjunctive) can also be

         contrary to fact ("If this were Tuesday, I'd be in class" =
this is not Tuesday, hence I am not in class). In Greek such construction
is expressed by the imperfect.

§37.6223 <u>Past conditions</u> can be noncommittal or contrary to fact.

         <u>Noncommittal</u>: "If I was there, I paid my way"--I have not
stated whether I was there. <u>Contrary-to-fact</u>: "If I had been there
I would have paid for you" = I was not there, hence did not pay for you.
There can be no doubt about the outcome, for it is a fact; there can only
be lack of knowledge about it. Past conditions can be <u>simple</u> (a single
act) or <u>general</u> (a repeated action or a general truth), cf. §37.6221.

§37.6224 <u>Future conditions</u> can only be <u>probable</u>. But the degree of

         probability in the speaker's mind is variable. There is a
<u>more probable</u> (or "more vivid") future condition ("If you [will] take me,
I shall go"), and a <u>less probable</u> (or "less vivid") future condition
("If you would take me, I would go"). Because the degree of probability
exists only in the speaker's mind, many grammarians prefer the terms "more
vivid" and "less vivid," and avoid reference to probability.

§37.6225 Sometimes a special category of the more vivid future condition

         is indicated, when the speaker has strong feelings concerning the
outcome. Smyth calls this the "emotional future condition" (<u>Grammar</u> §2328).

§37.63   The <u>moods</u> used in protasis and apodosis express the reality,

         unreality, or probability of a condition. In some categories,
the use of ἄν is required.

§37.631   The <u>indicative</u> in general indicates reality or unreality.

     The <u>subjunctive</u> in the protasis indicates a greater degree of probability. The <u>optative</u> in protasis and apodosis indicates a lesser degree of probability.

§37.632   The <u>negative</u>, whether in protasis, or apodosis, or both, is that which is required by the mood: οὐ for the indicative, otherwise μή.

§37.64   Combining the elements we have set down, we can make the following analysis.

§37.641   The <u>simple condition</u> is expressed by using εἰ 'if' + any indicative tense in the protasis, and any tense or mood in the apodosis. εἰ οὖν τὸ φῶς τὸ ἐν σοὶ σκότος ἐστίν·τὸ σκότος πόσον 'If therefore the light that is in you is darkness, how great (is) that darkness!' (Mt. 6:23).

§37.6411   The <u>past simple condition</u> is expressed in the same way, using a past tense in the protasis. εἰ οὖν τὴν ἴσην δωρεὰν ἔδωκεν αὐτοῖς ὁ θεός...ἐγὼ τίς ἤμην δυνατὸς κωλῦσαι τὸν θεόν; 'If therefore God gave them the same gift...who was I, able to hinder God?' (Ac. 11:17).

§37.6412   Note the variations in tense used. εἰ κεκοίμηται σωθήσεται 'If he has fallen asleep he will be saved (= get well)' (Jn. 11:12). εἰ γὰρ νεκροὶ οὐκ ἐγείρονται οὐδὲ χριστὸς ἐγήγερται 'For if (the) dead are not raised, neither has Christ been raised' (1 Cor. 15:16). εἰ δὲ πνεύματι ἄγεσθε οὐκ ἐστὲ ὑπὸ νόμου 'But if you are led by (the) spirit, you are not under law' (Gal. 5:18).

§37.6413   The negative in the protasis is usually μή. Where οὐ is used, it probably negates a word in the protasis and not the entire protasis.

§37.642   The <u>contrary-to-fact</u> (or <u>unreal</u>) <u>condition</u> is expressed by using εἰ 'if' + an augmented (secondary) tense in the protasis, and ἄν + an augmented tense in the apodosis. The ἄν may be omitted. οὗτος εἰ ἦν προφήτης ἐγίνωσκεν ἄν τίς καὶ ποταπὴ ἡ γυνὴ 'This one, if he were a prophet, would have known who and what sort (is) the woman' (Lk. 7:39). εἰ ὁ θεὸς πατὴρ ὑμῶν ἦν ἠγαπᾶτε ἄν ἐμέ 'If God were your father, you

would have loved me' (Jn. 8:42). εἰ ἦς ὧδε οὐκ ἄν μου ἀπέθανεν ὁ ἀδελφός
'If you had been here my brother would not have died' (Jn. 11:32).

§37.6421 The negative in the protasis is μή, even though it is indicative.
          εἰ μὴ ἦν οὗτος παρὰ θεοῦ οὐκ ἠδύνατο ποιεῖν οὐδέν 'If this one
were not from God, he would not be able to do anything' (Jn. 9:33).

§37.6422 The ἄν is regularly omitted with verbs implying possibility,
          necessity, obligation, and the like.

§37.643   The present general condition is expressed by using ἐάν + a
          verb in the subjunctive in the protasis, and the (present)
indicative or imperative in the apodosis. κἂν εἴπω ὅτι οὐκ οἶδα αὐτόν
ἔσομαι...ψεύστης 'If I said that I don't know him, I would be a liar'
(Jn. 8:55). ἐάν τις περιπατῇ ἐν τῇ ἡμέρᾳ οὐ προσκόπτει 'If anyone
walks in the day(light) he does not stumble' (Jn. 11:9). ἐὰν ἔλθῃ πρὸς
ὑμᾶς δέξασθε αὐτόν 'If he comes to you, receive him' (Col. 4:10).

§37.6431 It is evident that some of these are close to, if not identical
          with the simple condition (§637.641), except for the use of
ἐάν + sbjtv. Moule, Idiom-Book, p. 149, speaks of the difficulty of
classifying conditional sentences which "belong by meaning in one class,
but by form in another."

§37.644   The more vivid future condition is expressed by using ἐάν in the
          protasis, generally with the subjunctive, and a future indica-
tive or equivalent in the apodosis. There is considerable variation in
the protasis of this type of condition. ἐὰν ἀγαπᾶτέ με τὰς ἐντολὰς τὰς ἐμὰς
τηρήσετε 'If you love me, you will keep my commandments' (Jn. 14:15).
καὶ τοῦτο ποιήσομεν [ABCDΨ ποιήσωμεν] ἐὰν ἐπιτρέπῃ ὁ θεός 'And this we
will do if God permit' (Heb. 6:3). ἐὰν ἐμοί τις διακονῇ τιμήσει αὐτὸν
ὁ πατήρ 'If anyone serve me, him the father will honor' (Jn. 12:26).

§37.6441 With εἰ + sbjtv.: Lk. 9:13; 1 Cor. 14:5.

§37.6442 With εἰ or ἐάν + fut. ind.: Ac. 8:31; 2 Tim. 2:12.

§37.6443 With εἰ + pres. ind.: Matt. 8:31; 1 Cor. 10:27.

§37.645   The <u>less vivid future condition</u>, which is rare or nonexistent
in the NT, is expressed by using εἰ + the optative in the
protasis, and ἄν + opt. in the apodosis. Burton (p. 107) points out that
protases occur in 1 Cor. and 1 Pet., but never with a regular apodosis,
and apodoses occur in Lk. and Ac., but never with a regular protasis.
ἔσπευδεν γὰρ εἰ δυνατὸν εἴη αὐτῷ τὴν ἡμέραν τῆς πεντηκοστῆς γενέσθαι
εἰς Ἱεροσόλυμα 'For he was hurrying, if possible that he might be in
Jerusalem on the day of Pentecost' (Ac. 20:16). Cf. Ac. 24:19.

§37.646   The conditional sentence may be tabularized as follows:

Protasis	Apodosis	Category	
εἰ + indicative	indicative or equivalent	simple	§37.641
εἰ + past indicative	(ἄν) + past indicative	unreal	§37.642
ἐάν + subjunctive	present indicative	general	§37.643
ἐάν + sbjtv./other	future indicative	more vivid	§37.644
εἰ + optative	ἄν + optative	less vivid	§37.645

§37.647   In Greek, as in English, even good speakers and writers often
violate the grammatical rules for sequence of tenses, use of
subjunctives, and combinations of protasis and apodosis. Many exceptions
will be found to the rules as given above. We offer them here simply as
starting-points for study of the conditional sentence. For exegesis,
consult good grammars and commentaries on the passage.

§37.65   Much of what has been said about conditional sentences
applies also to <u>concessive sentences</u>. Several points in
addition should be noted.

§37.651   The apodosis of a concessive sentence has an adversative
meaning: it expresses what the speaker considers to be so in
spite of what is presented in the protasis. ("Even if he slays me, I
will trust him.")

§37.652   If the speaker does not concede that the condition exists, but
wishes to say that <u>even if (for the sake of argument) it</u>

should exist, nevertheless ... (followed by the apodosis), he introduces
the protasis with καὶ εἰ or καὶ ἐάν 'even if.' ἀλλὰ καὶ ἐὰν ἡμεῖς ἢ
ἄγγελος ἐξ οὐρανοῦ ὑμῖν εὐαγγελίζηται παρ' ὃ εὐαγγελισάμεθα ὑμῖν ἀνάθεμα
ἔστω 'But even if we or an angel from heaven were to preach to you a
gospel other than we have preached to you, let him be damned' (Gal. 1:8).

§37.6521 Sometimes the καί is simply conjunctive, and the clause that
         follows is conditional, not concessive. καὶ εἰ ἀγαπᾶτε τοὺς
ἀγαπῶντας ὑμᾶς ποία ὑμῖν χάρις ἐστίν; 'And if you love those who love
you, what kind of grace do you have?' (Lk. 6:32).

§37.6522 To express a negative protasis ("not even if") one of the
         following is used, as required by the sentence: οὐδ'εἰ,
οὐδ'ἐάν, μηδ'εἰ, μηδ'ἐάν.

§37.653 If the speaker concedes that the condition exists, and wishes
        to say that <u>although it does, this is not an obstacle</u> to the
fact predicated by the apodosis, he introduces the protasis with εἰ καὶ
or ἐὰν καί 'although.' εἰ καὶ οὐ δώσει αὐτῷ ἀναστὰς διὰ τὸ εἶναι φίλον
διά γε τὴν ἀναίδειαν αὐτοῦ ἐγερθεὶς δώσει... 'Although he will not get
up and give to him through being a friend, yet because of his persistence
he will rise and give...' (Lk. 11:8).

§37.6531 The distinction between καὶ εἰ (§37.652) and εἰ καὶ (§37.653)
         does not always obtain. The primary importance of context
must not be disregarded!

§37.654 A participle, alone or introduced by καίπερ or καὶ ταῦτα may
        be used in a concessive clause. The negative is οὐ. καίπερ
ὢν υἱὸς ἔμαθεν ὑπακοήν 'Although he was a son he learned obedience'
(Heb. 5:8).

§37.66 There is great variety in the ways of expressing condition and
       concession, and we cannot record here all the combinations that
can be found in the NT. The protasis is sometimes omitted. The apodosis

is sometimes omitted. The two parts, as we have seen (§37.645), are not always of the same kind. One of the factors that lend beauty and force to a language is variety. Our task is to observe each method of expression that we meet, to seek to discover just what shade of meaning the author intended, and to try to reproduce that shade of meaning in our own language. This is a continuing task in Biblical study.

§37.67   εἰ is sometimes merely a conjunction introducing <u>direct</u> or
         <u>indirect discourse</u> (§37.8). "I don't know if he will come"--
the "if" is not conditional here. We are not saying that if he comes
I will thereby lose knowledge. We are saying "I don't know whether he
will come," or "I don't know the answer to 'Will he come?'"

§37.7   <u>Clauses of comparison</u> serve to describe or define the predication
         of the main clause by comparing it (in quality or quantity) with
some other predication.

§37.71   The comparison may be in <u>quality</u> or <u>manner</u> ("just as"), in
         which case the main clause may have a correlative adverb ("so")
(cf. §30.34).

§37.711   Such a clause may be introduced by ὡς 'as,' ὥσπερ or καθάπερ
         'just as,' or a similar particle. ὑμεῖς ἀεὶ τῷ πνεύματι τῷ ἁγίῳ
ἀντιπίπτετε ὡς οἱ πατέρες ὑμῶν καὶ ὑμεῖς 'You always resist the Holy Spirit,
as your fathers, even you' (Ac. 7:51).

§37.712   The adverbial phrase ὃν τρόπον '(in) which manner/way, just as'
         is used often in LXX and occurs in NT. μὴ ἀνελεῖν με σὺ θέλεις
ὃν τρόπον ἀνεῖλες ἐχθὲς τὸν Αἰγύπτιον; 'Do you want to kill me the way
(= as) you killed the Egyptian yesterday?' (Ac. 7:28).

§37.7121   The <u>correlative adverb</u> (cf. §37.71) may be οὕτως 'thus, so.'
         οὗτος ὁ Ἰησοῦς...οὕτως ἐλεύσεται ὃν τρόπον ἐθεάσασθε αὐτὸν
πορευόμενον... 'This Jesus...shall so come as you saw him going...'
(Ac. 1:11).

§37.713   The <u>comparative particle</u> ἤ 'than' is usually found in comparisons
           of single words, but it also occurs introducing a comparison
clause. εὐκοπώτερόν ἐστιν κάμηλον διὰ τρυπήματος ῥαφίδος διελθεῖν ἢ
πλούσιον εἰσελθεῖν εἰς τὴν βασιλείαν τοῦ θεοῦ 'It is easier (for) a camel
to go through an eye of a needle than (for) a rich man to enter into the
kingdom of God' (Mt. 19:24).

§37.72   The comparison may be of <u>quantity</u> or <u>degree</u> ("in proportion as"),
          in which case the main clause usually has a correlative demon-
strative ("by so much" or "to such a degree" [cf. §23.6]).

§37.721   Such a clause is generally introduced by ὅσῳ or ὅσον 'in
           proportion as.' The <u>correlative demonstrative</u> is τοσούτῳ or
τοσοῦτον 'by so much.' In the NT this is only found in Hebrews. τοσούτῳ
κρείττων γενόμενος τῶν ἀγγέλων ὅσῳ διαφορώτερον παρ᾽ αὐτοὺς κεκληρονόμηκεν
ὄνομα 'In proportion as he has been called by a more excellent name than
them, to such degree has he become better than the angels' (Heb. 1:4).

§37.73   Ellipsis, or the omission of part of one clause (§30.14), is
          quite common. "I can do anything better than you" = "I can do
anything better than you can do the same thing"; but "I can do anything
better than sing" = "I can do anything better than I can sing." Such
comparisons at times become quite tricky.

§37.731   The verb of the comparative clause is commonly omitted if it is
           the same as the verb of the main clause. ἐσμεν εὐηγγελισμένοι
καθάπερ κἀκεῖνοι 'We have been evangelized even as also they (have been
evangelized)' (Heb. 4:2).

§37.732   When the verb is omitted, the subject of the comparative
           clause with ὡς or ὥσπερ is sometimes attracted into the case
of the other member of the comparison (usually the acc.). Cf. English
"I am taller than he (is tall)" often becomes "I am taller than him."

§37.74   The moods used for verbs in comparative clauses generally follow
          the rules for conditional sentences. The indicative is used
unless there is some contingency, and then the subjunctive is used.

§37.8   <u>Indirect discourse</u> and <u>indirect question</u> are to be distinguished
from <u>direct discourse</u> and <u>direct question</u>.

§37.81   <u>Direct discourse</u> (and <u>direct question</u>) is the presentation of
the exact words of another writer or speaker, or of the same
author in another place. Whether the quotation is exact or not--indeed,
whether it is historical or not--is beside the point. An author of fiction
uses direct discourse to present quotations which he knows he is making
up, but he presents them as the exact words of one of his characters.

§37.811   Direct discourse is often introduced by ὅτι (sometimes called
"ὅτι recitative"). This can be translated by "quote," or it
can be omitted in translation. It should <u>not</u> be translated by "that,"
for in Eng. this signifies indirect discourse. (Note well: "He said
that I will go" does <u>not</u> mean the same thing as "He said, 'I will go,'"
or "he said [quote] I will go").

§37.812   In the NT direct discourse is often introduced by λέγων (in
the proper GNC) 'saying.' This is possibly taken over from
Hebrew idiom through LXX. It is better omitted in translation.

§37.813   A direct question may be introduced by εἰ, perhaps a Hebraism.
εἰ ταῦτα οὕτως ἔχει; 'Are these things so?' (Ac. 7:1).
(Cf. §37.67.)

§37.82   <u>Indirect discourse</u> (and <u>indirect question</u>) is a paraphrase of
the quotation, the author not attempting to give the exact
words. It may be a very minor paraphrase (e.g. changing the person and
number of verb forms), or it may be a complete rephrasing of the quotation.

§37.821   After verbs of saying, thinking, etc., <u>indirect discourse</u> is
usually introduced by ὅτι 'that' followed by a verb in the
indicative, infinitive, or (occasionally) participle. ἐπ' ἀληθείας
καταλαμβάνομαι ὅτι οὐκ ἔστιν προσωπολήμπτης ὁ θεός 'In truth I
perceive that God is no respecter of persons' (Ac. 10:34). ὁ μὲν οὖν
Φῆστος ἀπεκρίθη τηρεῖσθαι τὸν Παῦλον εἰς Καισάρειαν 'So Festus replied

(that) Paul was being kept in Caesarea' (Ac. 25:4). ἀκούσας δὲ Ἰακὼβ ὄντα
σιτία εἰς Αἴγυπτον 'And Jacob, hearing (that) there was grain in Egypt...'
(Ac. 7:12).

§37.8211　The infinitive may be used in indirect discourse. (Cf. "He
　　　　　told me to go" = "He said to me, 'Go.'")

§37.8212　Indirect discourse may also be introduced by ὥς, πῶς,
　　　　　or ὡς ὅτι. ὑμεῖς ἐπίστασθε ὡς ἀθέμιτόν ἐστιν 'You know that it
is unlawful....' (Ac. 10:28). ἀπήγγειλεν ἡμῖν πῶς εἶδεν τὸν ἄγγελον
'He reported to us how (= that) he saw the angel....' (Ac. 11:13).
κατὰ ἀτιμίαν λέγω ὡς ὅτι ἡμεῖς ἠσθενήσαμεν 'In dishonor I say that we were
weak' (2 Cor. 11:21).

§37.8213　The participle may be used in direct discourse

§37.822　After verbs of asking, inquiring, wondering, etc., indirect
　　　　　question is usually introduced by τίς or τί. πυνθάνομαι οὖν
τίνι λόγῳ μετεπέμψασθέ με; 'I am therefore asking for what reason you
sent for me' (Ac. 10:29).

§37.823　After verbs of commanding, exhorting, warning, etc.,
　　　　　indirect discourse may be expressed in one of three forms.

§37.8231　A direct command may be presented indirectly by a rhetorical
　　　　　(or deliberative) question (§31.311) using the subjunctive.
ναί λέγω ὑμῖν τοῦτον φοβήθητε 'Yes, I say to you (that) you should fear
him' (Lk. 12:5).

§37.8232　An indirect command may be expressed by using ἵνα or ὅπως followed
　　　　　by the subjunctive. αἰτούμενοι χάριν κατ' αὐτοῦ ὅπως μεταπέμψηται
αὐτὸν εἰς Ἰερουσαλήμ 'asking (as) a favor from him that he would send him
to Jerusalem' (Ac. 25:3).

§37.8233　An indirect command may be expressed by the infinitive. οἵτινες
　　　　　τῷ Παύλῳ ἔλεγον διὰ τοῦ πνεύματος μὴ ἐπιβαίνειν εἰς Ἱεροσόλυμα
'Who were saying to Paul through the Spirit not to go up to Jerusalem'
(Ac. 21:4).

§37.83   The tense and mood of the verb(s) in indirect discourse in
           classical Greek are determined by the verb of the main clause.
In NT Greek, however, the tense and mood of the original quotation are
usually retained in indirect discourse. (Cf. Eng. "He said, 'I will go,'"
becomes "He said that he would go.") εἶδεν ὁ ὄχλος ὅτι Ἰησοῦς οὐκ ἔστιν ἐκεῖ
'The crowd saw that Jesus was (lit. is) not there' (Jn. 6:24).

§37.831   After secondary (augmented) tenses (§24.121) the tense is sometimes
           changed. αὐτὸς γὰρ ἐγίνωσκεν τί ἦν ἐν τῷ ἀνθρώπῳ 'For he himself
knew what was in man' (Jn. 2:25).

§37.832   The mood is sometimes changed to optative, particularly in Luke
           and particularly in indirect question, but there is no consistency
even in Luke. προσδοκῶντος δὲ τοῦ λαοῦ...περὶ τοῦ Ἰωάννου μήποτε αὐτὸς εἴη
ὁ Χριστός 'And the people were looking and wondering in their heart about
John whether this one would be the Christ' (Lk. 3:15).

§37.833   According to Robertson p. 1031, the use of sbjtv. in indirect
           discourse indicates that the sbjtv. was used in the original
quotation. According to Burton's note on Ac. 5:34 (p. 133), the same may
be said for Luke's use of the optative here and perhaps elsewhere. The
question has been asked, however, who would be using the optative in
direct discourse at that period of Greek?

§37.84   The person may be changed in indirect discourse. When repeating
           what the person you are addressing said, in indirect discourse
you change his 1st person form to 2d person. (Direct: "You said, 'I will
do it'." Indirect: "You said that you would do it.") When speaking of
a third person, the 3d person form is used. (Direct: "He said, 'I will
do it'." Indirect: "He said that he would do it.") The first person
obviously remains the same.

Part III
TABLES AND PARADIGMS

Table A. The Alphabet

GREEK	Modern Printed	Early Xn Uncial	Codex Vaticanus	7th-4th Cents. B.C.	Oldest East Greek	Late	Early	PHOENICIAN
Alpha	A α							Aleph
Beta	B β ϐ							Beth
Gamma	Γ γ							Gimel
Delta	Δ δ							Daled
Epsilon	E ε ϵ							Hê
[Digamma]	Ϝ							Waw
Zeta	Z ζ ӡ							Zayin
Eta	H η							Ḥeth
Theta	θ θ ϑ							Ṭeth
Iota	I ι							Yod
Kappa	K κ ϰ							Kaf
Lambda	Λ λ							Lamed
Mu	M μ							Mem
Nu	N ν							Nun
Xi	Ξ ξ							Samek
Omicron	O o							ʿAyin
Pi	Π π ϖ							Pê
[Sam]								Ṣaddê
[Qoppa]	ϙ							Qof
Rho	P ρ							Resh
Sigma	Σ σ ϛς							S(h)in
Tau	T τ							Tau
Upsilon	Y υ							
Phi	Φ φ φ							
Chi	X χ							
Psi	Ψ ψ ψ							
Omega	Ω ω							

Until the official change in 403/2 B.C. there were several local (epichoric) alphabets. There has been some combining of these to make this table. In West Greek, Xi and Chi were represented by the letters Chi and Psi in Eastern orthography, respectively. Greek was originally written, like Phoenician, from right to left, and the letters faced in the opposite direction.

C-1

CODEX SINAITICUS (Acts 1:1-5)

Reproduced full size with the bottom eleven lines cut off. Compare this with Codex Vaticanus. Note the use of abbreviations, division of words, spelling of certain words, etc.

The passage is transcribed in modern type on the facing page, and then written with spaces between words, hyphens to show word-division, writing out of abbreviations, and capitalization of proper names.

Note the complete absence of accents and punctuation. The sign ¨ is used occasionally in Codex Sinaiticus where we would expect rough breathing, but this is not consistent.

Codex Sinaiticus (א) and Codex Vaticanus (B) are fourth-century uncials, and among the earliest extant manuscripts of the New Testament. (See Lesson 58.)

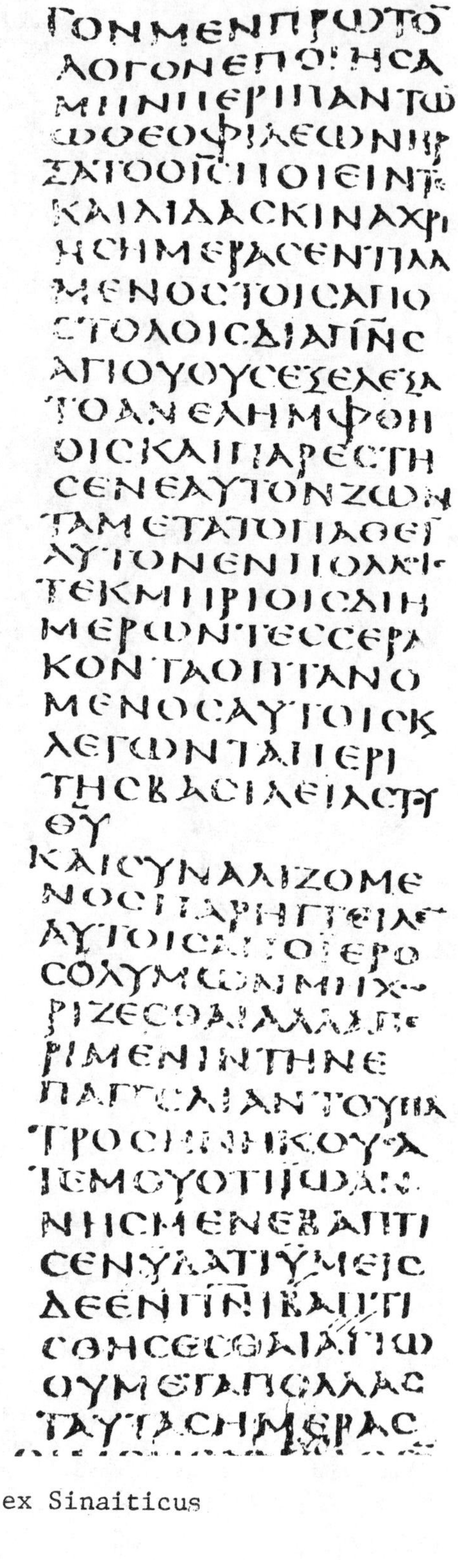
ΤΟΝΜΕΝΠΡΩΤΟ
ΛΟΓΟΝΕΠΟΙΗCΑ
ΜΗΝΠΕΡΙΠΑΝΤΩ
ΩΘΕΟΦΙΛΕΩΝΗΡ
ΞΑΤΟΟΙCΠΟΙΕΙΝΤΕ
ΚΑΙΔΙΔΑCΚΙΝΑΧΡΙ
ΗCΗΜΕΡΑCΕΝΤΙΛΑ
ΜΕΝΟCΤΟΙCΑΠΟ
CΤΟΛΟΙCΔΙΑΠΝC
ΑΓΙΟΥΟΥCΕΞΕΛΕΞΑ
ΤΟΑΝΕΛΗΜΦΘΗ
ΟΙCΚΑΙΠΑΡΕCΤΗ
CΕΝΕΑΥΤΟΝΖΩΝ
ΤΑΜΕΤΑΤΟΠΑΘΕΙ
ΑΥΤΟΝΕΝΠΟΛΛΟΙ
ΤΕΚΜΗΡΙΟΙCΔΙΗ
ΜΕΡΩΝΤΕCCΕΡΑ
ΚΟΝΤΑΟΠΤΑΝΟ
ΜΕΝΟCΑΥΤΟΙCΚ
ΛΕΓΩΝΤΑΠΕΡΙ
ΤΗCΒΑCΙΛΕΙΑCΤΟΥ
ΘΥ
ΚΑΙCΥΝΑΛΙΖΟΜΕ
ΝΟCΠΑΡΗΓΓΕΙΛΕ
ΑΥΤΟΙCΑΠΟΙΕΡΟ
CΟΛΥΜΩΝΜΗΧΩ
ΡΙΖΕCΘΑΙΑΛΛΑΠΕ
ΡΙΜΕΝΙΝΤΗΝΕ
ΠΑΓΓΕΛΙΑΝΤΟΥΠΑ
ΤΡΟCΗΝΗΚΟΥCΑ
ΤΕΜΟΥΟΤΙΙΩΑΝ
ΝΗCΜΕΝΕΒΑΠΤΙ
CΕΝΥΔΑΤΙΥΜΕΙC
ΔΕΕΝΠΝΙΒΑΠΤΙ
CΘΗCΕCΘΑΙΑΓΙΩ
ΟΥΜΕΤΑΠΟΛΛΑC
ΤΑΥΤΑCΗΜΕΡΑC

Figure 2. Codex Sinaiticus

CODEX SINAITICUS (Acts 1:1-5)

ΤΟΝΜΕΝΠΡΩΤΟ̄	1 τον μεν πρωτον
ΛΟΓΟΝΕΠΟΙΗΣΑ	λογον εποιησα-
ΜΗΝΠΕΡΙΠΑΝΤΩ̄	μην περι παντων
ΩΘΕΟΦΙΛΕΩΝΗΡ	ω Θεοφιλε ων ηρ-
ΞΑΤΟΟῙ̄ΣΠΟΙΕΙΝΤΕ	ξατο ο Ιησους ποιειν τε
ΚΑΙΔΙΔΑΣΚΙΝΑΧΡΙ	2 και διδασκιν αχρι
ΗΣΗΜΕΡΑΣΕΝΤΙΛΑ	ης ημερας εντιλα-
ΜΕΝΟΣΤΟΙΣΑΠΟ̄	μενος τοις απο-
ΣΤΟΛΟΙΣΔΙΑΠ̄Ν̄Σ̄	στολοις δια πνευματος
ΑΓΙΟΥΣΕΞΕΛΕΞΑ	αγιου ους εξελεξα-
ΤΟΑΝΕΛΗΜΦΘΗ	το ανελημφθη
ΟΙΣΚΑΙΠΑΡΕΣΤΗ	3 οις και παρεστη-
ΣΕΝΕΑΥΤΟΝΖΩΝ̣	σεν εαυτον ζων-
ΤΑΜΕΤΑΤΟΠΑΘΕῘ	τα μετα το παθειν
ΑΥΤΟΝΕΝΠΟΛΛΟΙΣ	αυτον εν πολλοις
ΤΕΚΜΗΡΙΟΙΣΔΙΗ	τεκμηριοις δι' η-
ΜΕΡΩΝΤΕΣΣΕΡΑ	μερων τεσσερα-
ΚΟΝΤΑΟΠΤΑΝΟ	κοντα οπτανο-
ΜΕΝΟΣΑΥΤΟΙΣΚ̣	μενος αυτοις και
ΛΕΓΩΝΤΑΠΕΡΙ	λεγων τα περι
ΤΗΣΒΑΣΙΛΕΙΑΣΤΟΥ	της βασιλειας του
Θ̄Ῡ	θεου
ΚΑΙΣΥΝΑΛΙΖΟΜΕ	4 και συναλιζομε-
ΝΟΣΠΑΡΗΓΓΕῙΛΕ̄	νος παρηγγειλεν
ΑΥΤΟΙΣΑΠΟῙΕΡΟ	αυτοις απο Ιερο-
ΣΟΛΥΜΩΝΜΗΧΩ	σολυμων μη χω-
ΡΙΖΕΣΘΑΙΑΛΛΑΠΕ	ριζεσθαι αλλα πε-
ΡΙΜΕΝΙΝΤΗΝΕ	ριμενιν την ε-
ΠΑΓΓΕΛΙΑΝΤΟΥΠΑ	παγγελιαν του πα-
ΤΡΟΣΗΝΗΚΟ̤ΥΣΑ	τρος ην ηκουσα-
ΤΕΜΟΥΟΤΙῙΩΑΝ	5 τε μου οτι Ιωαν-
ΝΗΣΜΕΝΕΒΑΠΤΙ	νης μεν εβαπτι-
ΣΕΝΫΔΑΤΙΫΜΕΙΣ	σεν υδατι υμεις
ΔΕΕΝΠ̄Ν̄ΙΒΑΠΤΙ	δε εν πνευματι βαπτι-
ΣΘΗΣΕΣΘΑΙΑΓΙΩ	σθησεσθαι αγιω
ΟΥΜΕΤΑΠΟΛΛΑΣ	ου μετα πολλας
ΤΑΥΤΑΣΗΜΕΡΑΣ	ταυτας ημερας

Reproduced full size, the bottom 16 lines of the column
have been cut off. This passage is transcribed in modern
type and then rewritten with editorial changes on the
opposite page. Study it carefully.

```
Ā  ΤΟΝΜΕΝΠΡѠΤΟΝΛΟΓΟΝ
   ΕΠΟΙΗϹΑΜΗΝΠΕΡΙΠΑΝΤω̄
   ѠΘΕΟΦΙΛΕѠΝΗΡΞΑΤΟ
   ῙϹΠΟΙΕΙΝΤΕΚΑΙΔΙΔΑϹΚ·Γ
   ΑΧΡΙΗϹΗΜΕΡΑϹΕΝΤΕΙΛ
   ΜΕΝΟϹΤΟΙϹΑΠΟϹΤΟΛΟΙϲ
   ΔΙΑΠΝΕΥΜΑΤΟϹΑΓΙΟΥΟΥϲ
   ΕΞΕΛΕΞΑΤΟΑΝΕΛΗΜΦΘΗ·
   ΟΙϹΚΑΙΠΑΡΕϹΤΗϹΕΝΕΥ
   ΤΟΝΖѠΝΤΑΜΕΤΑΤΟΠΛ
   ΘΕΙΝΑΥΤΟΝΕΝΠΟΛΛΟΙϲ
   ΤΕΚΜΗΡΙΟΙϹΔΙΗΜΕΡѠΝ
   ΤΕϹϹΕ̂ΡΑΚΟΝΤΑΟΠΤΑΝο
   ΜΕΝΟϹΑΥΤΟΙϹΚΑΙΛΕΓω̄
   ΤΑΠΕΡΙΤΗϹΒΑϹΙΛΕΙΑϹΤΥθ̄·
   ΚΑΙϹΥΝΑΛΙΖΟΜΕΝΟϹΙΛ
   ΡΗΓΓΕΙΛΕΝΑΥΤΟΙϹΑΠΟ
   ΪΕΡΟϹΟΛΥΜѠΝΜΗΧѠΡΙ
   ΖΕϹΘΑΙΑΛΛΑΠΕΡΙΜΕΝΕΓ̄
   ΤΗΝΕΠΑΓΓΕΛΕΙΑΝΤΟΥ
   ΠΑΤΡΟϹΗΝΗΚΟΥϹΑΤΕϟ
   ΟΤΙΪѠΑΝΗϹΜΕΝΕΒΑΠΤΙ
   ϹΕΝΫΔΑΤΙΫΜΕΙϹΔΕΕΝ
   ΠΝΕΥΜΑΤΙΒΑΠΤΙϹΘΗϹε
   ϹΘΕΑΓΙѠΟΥΜΕΤΑΠΟΛλλϲ
   ΤΑΥΤΑϹΗΜΕΡΑϹ ΟΙΜΕΝ
```

Figure 3. Codex Vaticanus

ΤΟΝΜΕΝΠΡΩΤΟΝΛΟΓΟΝ	1	τον μεν πρωτον λογον
ΕΠΟΙΗΣΑΜΗΝΠΕΡΙΠΑΝΤΩ̄		εποιησαμην περι παντων
ΩΘΕΟΦΙΛΕΩΝΗΡΞΑΤΟ		ω θεοφιλε ων ηρξατο
Ῑ͞ΣΠΟΙΕΙΝΤΕΚΑΙΔΙΔΑΣΚΕῙ		Ιησους ποιειν τε και διδασκειν
ΑΧΡΙΗΣΗΜΕΡΑΣΕΝΤΕΙΛΑ	2	αχρι ης ημερας εντειλα-
ΜΕΝΟΣΤΟΙΣΑΠΟΣΤΟΛΟΙΣ		μενος τοις αποστολοις
ΔΙΑΠΝΕΥΜΑΤΟΣΑΓΙΟΥΟΥΣ		δια πνευματος αγιου ους
ΕΞΕΛΕΞΑΤΟΑΝΕΛΗΜΦΘΗ·		εξελεξατο ανελημφθη·
ΟΙΣΚΑΙΠΑΡΕΣΤΗΣΕΝΕΑΥ	3	οις και παρεστησεν εαυ-
ΤΟΝΖΩΝΤΑΜΕΤΑΤΟΠΑ		τον ζωντα μετα το πα-
ΘΕΙΝΑΥΤΟΝΕΝΠΟΛΛΟΙΣ		θειν αυτον εν πολλοις
ΤΕΚΜΗΡΙΟΙΣΔΙΗΜΕΡΩΝ		τεκμηριοις δι'ημερων
ΤΕΣΣ͡ΕΡΑΚΟΝΤΑΟΠΤΑΝΟ		τεσσαρακοντα οπτανο-
ΜΕΝΟΣΑΥΤΟΙΣΚΑΙΛΕΓΩ̄		μενος αυτοις και λεγων
ΤΑΠΕΡΙΤΗΣΒΑΣΙΛΕΙΑΣΤΟΥΘ̄Ῡ·		τα περι της βασιλειας του θεου·
ΚΑΙΣΥΝΑΛΙΖΟΜΕΝΟΣΠΑ	4	και συναλιζομενος πα-
ΡΗΓΓΕΙΛΕΝΑΥΤΟΙΣΑΠΟ		ρηγγειλεν αυτοις απο
Ϊ̈ΕΡΟΣΟΛΥΜΩΝΜΗΧΩΡΙ		Ιεροσολυμων μη χωρι-
ΖΕΣΘΑΙΑΛΛΑΠΕΡΙΜΕΝΕῙ		ζεσθαι αλλα περιμενειν
ΤΗΝΕΠΑΓΓΕΛΕΙΑΝΤΟΥ		την επαγγελειαν του
ΠΑΤΡΟΣΗΝΗΚΟΥΣΑΤΕΜ͡Ο͟Υ		πατρος ην ηκουσατε μου
ΟΤΙϊΩΑΝΝΗΣΜΕΝΕΒΑΠΤΙ	5	οτι Ιωαννης εβαπτι-
ΣΕΝΫΔΑΤΙϊΜΕΙΣΔΕΕΝ		σεν υδατι υμεις δε εν
ΠΝΕΥΜΑΤΙΒΑΠΤΙΣΘ͡ΗΣΕ		πνευματι βαπτισθησε-
ΣΘΕΑΓΙΩΟΥΜΕΤΑΠΟΛΛΑΣ		σθε αγιω ου μετα πολλας
ΤΑΥΤΑΣΗΜΕΡΑΣ ΟΙΜΕΝ		ταυτας ημερας

α β γ δ ε ε ϝ ζ ζ η η ϑ θ ι κ κ λ μ ν ν

ξ ξ ο π ϖ ρ σ ς τ ϡ υ φ φ χ ψ ω

NOTE: δ ρ ϋ π ν υ ο ο ξ ζ ς π τ γ ν γ χ ϑ φ

ΔΙΟΤΙ ΤΟΣΟΝ ηγαπησεν ο θεος τον ΚΟΣΜΟΝ ωστε εδωκε τον
Υιου αυτου τον μονογενη δια να μη απολεσθη πας ο
πιστευων εις αυτον αλλα να εχη ζωην αιωνιον.

TABLE C. THE CONSONANTS

	LABIAL		DENTAL		VELAR		GLOTTAL
		Labiodental		Alveolar		Uvular	
	Stop	Fricative	Stop	Fricative	Stop	Fricative	
Voiced (V)	β [b] >	> [v]	δ [d] > [δ]	[ɪ]<¹	γ [g]		
Surd (S)	π [p]		τ [t]		κ [k]		
Aspirate(S)	φ [p'] >	> [f]	θ [t'] > [θ]		χ [k'] >	> [x]	' [h]
Assibilate	ψ [ps]		ζ [dz]		ξ [ks]		
Sibilant(S)				σ [s]			
Nasal (V)		μ [m]		ν [n]	γγ²[ŋ]		
Lateral (S)				λ [l]			
Flip (?)(S)				ρ [r]		ρ̇ [R]?	
Semivowel		ϝ [u̯]		ι [i̯]			

¹Prepalatalization   ²Also γκ γχ γξ

TABLE D.   THE VOWEL TRIANGLE

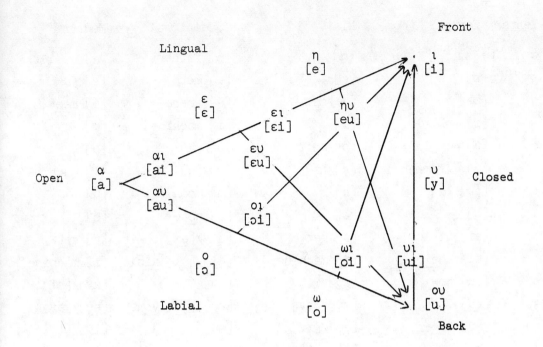

TABLE F.   CONTRACTION OF VOWELS AND DIPHTHONGS

Vowel	before		α	ᾱ	αι	ᾳ	ε	ει¹	ει²	η	ῃ	ι	ο	οι	ου	υ	ω	ῳ
→ α		>	α	ᾱ	αι	ᾱͅ	ᾱ	ᾱͅ	ᾱ	ᾱ	ᾱͅ	αι	ω	ῳ	ω	αυ	ω	ῳ
ᾱ		>	ᾱ									ᾱͅ						
→ ε		>	η/ᾱ		η	η/αι	ει²	ει¹	ει²	η	ῃ	ει¹	ου	οι	ου	ευ	ω	ῳ
η		>			ῃ		η	ῃ	η	η	ῃ	ῃ			ῳ			
ι		>										ῑ						
→ ο		>	ω/ᾱ				ου	οι	ου	ω	οι/ῳ	οι	ου	οι	ου		ω	ῳ
υ		>										ῡ				ῡ		
ω		>	ω									ῳ					ω	

[1]genuine
[2]spurious, arising from contraction or compensatory lengthening.
NT does not always differentiate between genuine and spurious ει.

Cf. Smyth §59

C-7

Letter	Early	NT	Traditional	Modern
α	[α] father [a] ask	[α]	[α] father	[α]
ε	[ε]	[ε]	[ε] met	[ε]
η	[ae] ?	[æ] man	[e] there	[i] meet
ι	[i]	[i]	[i] machine	[i]
ο	[ɔ]	[ɔ] soft	[ɔ]/[a]	[ɔ]
υ	[y] ? French u	[y]/[i]	[y]/[u]	[i] machine
ου	[ɔu]	[u]	[u] moon	[u]
ω	[o]	[o]	[o] note	[o]
αι	[ai] aisle	[ε] get	[ai]/[ei] their	[ε] get
ει	[εi] their	[i] machine	[ei]/[ai] aisle	[i] machine
αυ	[au] now	[au] ?	[au]	[av]/[af][1]
ευ	[εu] ?	[εu]/[εv]	[εu],[iu] youth	[εv]/[εf][1]
ηυ	[eu] ?	[eu]/[iv] ?	[eu]	[iv]/[if][1]
οι	[ɔi]	[ɔi]/[i] ?	[ɔi] oil	[i]
ωι	[oi]	[oi]	[oi] throwing	[oi]
υι	[ui] ?	[wi] week	[wi]	[ii] three-E
ᾳ	[ai] AI	[a] ?	[a] father	[a]
ῃ	[ei] HI	[e]/[ε]	[ei] their	[i]
ῳ	[oi] ΩI	[o]	[o] note	[o]

[1][-v] before vowels and voiced consonants; [-f] before surds.

TABLE G.   THE PREPOSITIONS

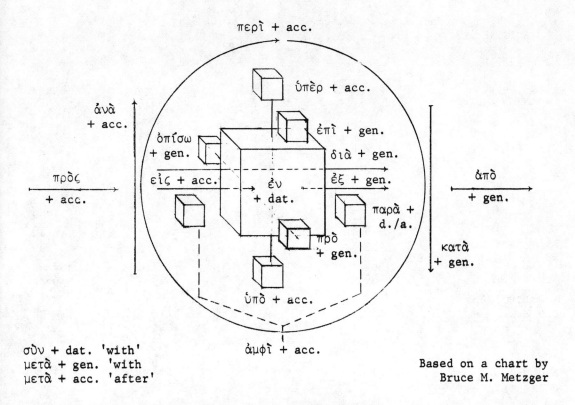

σὺν + dat. 'with'
μετὰ + gen. 'with
μετὰ + acc. 'after'

Based on a chart by
Bruce M. Metzger

THE SYNOPTIC PARADIGMS

The following pages contain synoptic paradigms, i.e. paradigms arranged
in such a way as to show readily the similarities and differences.
Hence they are arranged horizontally, rather than vertically, and a
study of the vertical columns provides comparative analysis.

Nouns, adjectives, pronouns, the definite article, and participles are
combined in the noun paradigms, classified by the three declensions.
Marginal notes and references to the text will make the study more profitable.

The verbs are grouped in eight classes, some of which are subdivided
further. So far as practical, each of the classes has been arranged by
phonetic characteristics of the stems, and two illustrations of each
have been given wherever possible. Hypothetical forms are omitted except
for a very few, and these are marked with asterisk (*). NT forms have
been given wherever I could locate them, then forms from Hellenistic Greek
have been used to fill in the tables. I had planned to mark these with
footnotes, but the resulting tables became too unwieldy. An examination
of any word in Arndt & Gingrich will quickly show the actual NT forms.

FIRST DECLENSION -- SINGULAR

	Nom. Sing.	Gen. Sing.	Dat. Sing.	Acc. Sing.
FEMININE				
Basic ending §21.21	$-$	$-\varsigma$	$-\iota$	$-\nu$
Def.art.	ἡ	τῆς	τῇ	τήν
Rel.pron.	ἥ	ἧς	ᾗ	ἥν
Stem in α>η[1]	$-\eta$	$-\eta\varsigma$	$-\eta$	$-\eta\nu$
	τιμή	τιμῆς	τιμῇ	τιμήν
	νεφέλη	νεφέλης	νεφέλῃ	νεφέλην
ᾰ > α/η[2]	δόξα	δόξης	δόξῃ	δόξαν
ᾱ after ι[3]	οἰκία	οἰκίας	οἰκίᾳ	οἰκίαν
ᾰ after ι[3]	ἀλήθεια	ἀληθείας	ἀληθείᾳ	ἀλήθειαν
ᾱ after ρ[3]	χώρα	χώρας	χώρᾳ	χώραν
άα > ᾶ[4]	μνᾶ	μνᾶς	μνᾷ	μνᾶν
έα > ῆ[4]	γῆ	γῆς	γῇ	γῆν
Demon.pron.	αὕτη	ταύτης	ταύτῃ	ταύτην
Pers.pron.	αὐτή	αὐτῆς	αὐτῇ	αὐτήν
ADJECTIVES				
-ος -α -ον[3]	μικρά	μικρᾶς	μικρᾷ	μικράν
-ος -η -ον[6]	ἀγαθή	ἀγαθῆς	ἀγαθῇ	ἀγαθήν
-ς -σα -ν	πᾶσα	πάσης	πάσῃ	πᾶσαν
-υς -η -υ	πολλή	πολλῆς	πολλῇ	πολλήν
-ας -η -α	μεγάλη	μεγάλης	μεγάλῃ	μεγάλην
PARTICIPLES				
-ς -σα -ν[7]	λύσασα	λυσάσης	λυσάσῃ	λύσασαν
-ων -σα -ον[7]	λύουσα	λυούσης	λυούσῃ	λύουσαν
-ως -υια -ος[7]	λελυκυῖα	λελυκυίας	λελυκυίᾳ	λελυκυῖαν
-εις -εισα -εν[6]	λυθεῖσα	λυθείσης	λυθείσῃ	λυθεῖσαν
MASCULINE[8]				
Basic ending	$-\varsigma$[9]	$-ου$[10]	$-\iota$	$-\nu$
	προφήτης	προφήτου	προφήτῃ	προφήτην
	νεανίας	νεανίου	νεανίᾳ	νεανίαν
	μαθητής	μαθητοῦ	μαθητῇ	μαθητήν

[1] §21.221 [3] §21.222 [5] §22.3 [7] Cf. §24.461 [9] §21.241

[2] §21.223 [4] §21.224 [6] Cf. §24.462 [8] §21.24 [10] Probably analogic

Note how noun rules of accent are observed.
Vocative forms in feminine are like nominative.
Vocative singular in masculine ends in -α (§21.242).

Nom. Pl.	Gen. Pl.	Dat. Pl.	Acc. Pl.	Notes
				FEMININE
-ι[1]	*-εων > -ῶν[12]	*-ισ(ι) > -ις[13]	*-νς > -ς[14]	Basic ending
αἱ	τῶν	ταῖς	τάς	Def.art.
αἵ	ὧν	αἷς	ἅς	Rel.pron.
-αι	-ῶν[15]	-αις	-ᾱς[14]	
τιμαί	τιμῶν	τιμαῖς	τιμάς	
νεφέλαι	νεφελῶν	νεφέλαις	νεφέλας	
δόξαι	δοξῶν	δόξαις	δόξας	
οἰκίαι	οἰκιῶν	οἰκίαις	οἰκίας	
ἀλήθειαι	ἀληθειῶν	ἀληθείαις	ἀληθείας	Note accent[15]
χῶραι	χωρῶν	χώραις	χώρας	
μναῖ	μνῶν	μναῖς	μνᾶς	
συκαῖ	συκῶν	συκαῖς	συκᾶς	
αὗται	τούτων[15]	ταύταις	ταύτας	Demon.pron.
αὐταί	αὐτῶν	αὐταῖς	αὐτάς	Pers.pron.
				ADJECTIVES
μικραί	μικρῶν	μικραῖς	μικράς	
ἀγαθαί	ἀγαθῶν	ἀγαθαῖς	ἀγαθάς	
πᾶσαι	πασῶν	πάσαις	πάσας	
πολλαί	πολλῶν	πολλαῖς	πολλάς	
μεγάλαι	μεγάλων[15]	μεγάλαις	μεγάλας	Note gen.
				PARTICIPLES
λύσασαι	λυσασῶν[15]	λυσάσαις	λυσάσας	1 aor. ptcp.
λύουσαι	λυουσῶν	λυούσαις	λυούσας	pr.act.ptcp.
λελυκυῖαι	λελυκυιῶν	λελυκυίαις	λελυκυίας	pf.act.ptcp.
λυθεῖσαι	λυθεισῶν	λυθείσαις	λυθείσας	aor.ps.ptcp.
				MASCULINE[8]
-ι	-ῶν	-ις	-ς	Basic ending
προφῆται	προφητῶν	προφήταις	προφήτας	
νεανίαι	νεανιῶν	νεανίαις	νεανίας	
μαθηταί	μαθητῶν	μαθηταῖς	μαθητάς	

[11] §21.214   [13] §21.216
[12] §21.215   [14] §21.217 cf. §13.134

[15] Feminine nouns of 1st and 2d declensions have accent on ultima (perispomenon) in gen.pl. Adjectives do not observe this rule. Participles are like nouns in this matter.

In the plural, the vocative is always like the nominative.

SECOND DECLENSION -- SINGULAR

		Nom. Sing.	Gen. Sing.	Dat. Sing.	Acc. Sing.
MASCULINE					
Basic ending[1]		-ς	-ο[2]	-ι[3]	-ν
Stem in -ο[4]		-ος	-οο > -ου	-οι > -ῳ	-ον
λογο-	ὁ	λόγος	λόγου	λόγῳ	λόγον
ἀνθρωπο-	ὁ	ἄνθρωπος	ἀνθρώπου	ἀνθρώπῳ	ἄνθρωπον
ὁδο-	ἡ[5]	ὁδός	ὁδοῦ	ὁδῷ	ὁδόν
νησο-	ἡ	νῆσος	νήσου	νήσῳ	νῆσον
υἱο-	ὁ	υἱός	υἱοῦ	υἱῷ	υἱόν
δουλο-	ὁ	δοῦλος	δούλου	δούλῳ	δοῦλον
Contracts[6]					
*'Ιησοε-(?)	ὁ	'Ιησοῦς	'Ιησοῦ	'Ιησοῦ	'Ιησοῦν
νοο-	ὁ	νοῦς	νοῦ	νῷ	νοῦν
χρυσεο-		χρυσοῦς	χρυσοῦ	χρυσῷ	χρυσοῦν
ἁπλοο-		ἁπλοῦς	ἁπλοῦ	ἁπλῷ	ἁπλοῦν
Def.art.		ὁ	τοῦ	τῷ	τόν
Rel.pron.		ὅς	οὗ	ᾧ	ὅν
Demon.pron.		οὗτος	τούτου	τούτῳ	τοῦτον
ADJECTIVES					
-ος -α/η -ον	ὁ	δίκαιος	δικαίου	δικαίῳ	δίκαιον
-ος -ος -ον	ὁ/ἡ	ἔρημος	ἐρήμου	ἐρήμῳ	ἔρημον
Comparative		μικρότερος	πρεσβυτέρου	ἀσθενεστέρῳ	διπλότερον
Superlative			τιμιωτάτου	τιμιωτάτῳ	
PARTICIPLE		λυόμενος	λυσαμένου	λυομένῳ	καλούμενον
NEUTER[7]					
Basic ending		-ν	-ο	-ι	-ν
Stem in -ο		-ον	-ου	-ῳ	-ον
δωρο-	τό	δῶρον	δώρου	δώρῳ	δῶρον
ὀστεο-	τό	ὀστοῦν	ὀστοῦ	ὀστῷ	ὀστοῦν
Def.art.		τό	τοῦ	τῷ	τό
Demon.pron.		τοῦτο	τούτου	τούτῳ	τοῦτο

[1] §21.31
[2] §21.312
[3] §21.313
[4] §21.314
[5] Except for gender, 2d decl. fem. nouns are like masc.
[6] Vocative like genitive
[7] §21.32
[8] §21.322

C-12

Nom. Pl.	Gen. Pl.	Dat. Pl.	Acc. Pl.	Notes
				MASCULINE
-ι[9]	-ων[10]	*-ισ(ι) > -ις	*-νς[12] > -ς	Basic ending
-οι	-ων	-οις	*-ονς > -ους	Stem in -ο
οἱ λόγοι	λόγων	λόγοις	λόγους	Note gen.pl.
οἱ ἄνθρωποι	ἀνθρώπων	ἀνθρώποις	ἀνθρώπους	
αἱ ὁδοί	ὁδῶν	ὁδοῖς	ὁδούς	Feminine!
αἱ νῆσοι	νήσων	νήσοις	νήσους	Feminine!
οἱ υἱοί	υἱῶν	υἱοῖς	υἱούς	
οἱ δοῦλοι	δούλων	δούλοις	δούλους	
οἱ νοῖ	νῶν	νοῖς	νοῦς	
χρυσοῖ	χρυσῶν	χρυσοῖς	χρυσοῦς	
ἁπλοῖ	ἁπλῶν	ἁπλοῖς	ἁπλοῦς	
οἱ	τῶν	τοῖς	τούς	Def.art.
οἵ	ὧν	οἷς	οὕς	Rel.pron.
οὗτοι	τούτων	τούτοις	τούτους	Demon.pron.
				ADJECTIVES
δίκαιοι	δικαίων	δικαίοις	δικαίους	
ἄλογοι	ἀλόγων	ἀλόγοις	ἀλόγους	
ἰσχυρότεροι		ὑστέροις		
μεμεστώμενοι	εἰσπορευομένων		σωζομένους	PARTICIPLE
				NEUTER[7]
-ᾰ[13]	-ων	-ισ(ι) > -ις	-ᾰ	Basic ending
-α	-ων	-οις	-α[14]	Stem in -ο
τὰ δῶρα	δώρων	δώροις	δῶρα	
τὰ ὀστᾶ	ὀστέων/ὀστῶν	ὀστοῖς	ὀστᾶ	Contract[15]
τά	τῶν	τοῖς	τά	Def.art.
ταῦτα	τούτων	τούτοις	ταῦτα	Note Nom./Acc.

[9]§21.315   [12]§21.318   [14]§21.323
[10]§21.316   [13]§21.321   [15]§21.33ff.
[11]§21.317

THIRD DECLENSION (m. & f.) -- SINGULAR

MASC.& FEM.		Nom. Sing.	Gen. Sing.	Dat. Sing.	Acc. Sing.
Basic ending		-ς[1]	-ος[2]	-ι[3]	-α[4]
or		--			-ν[5]
Labial stems	ἡ	φλέψ	φλεβός	φλεβί	φλέβα[6]
§21.511	ὁ	λίψ			λίβα
β	ὁ	ἄραψ	ἄραβος		
π	ὁ	Αἰθίοψ	Αἰθίοπος		
	ὁ	κώνωψ	κώνωπος		κώνωπα
	ἡ	λαῖλαψ	λαίλαπος		
Dental stems	ἡ	ἐλπίς	ἐλπίδος	ἐλπίδι	ἐλπίδα[7]
δ §21.512	ὁ	παῖς	παιδός		παῖδα
	ἡ	χιλιάς	χιλιάδος		χιλιάδα
§21.4114	ὁ	πούς	ποδός		ποδά
τ	ἡ	χάρις	χάριτος	χάριτι	χάριν/χάριτα
	ὁ	θής	θητός	θητί	θῆτα[6]
§24.461		λελυκώς	λελυκότος	λελυκότι	λελυκότα
θ	ὁ/ἡ	ὄρνις	ὄρνιθος	ὄρνιθι	ὄρνιν[6]
ντ §21.5121	ὁ	ὀδούς	ὀδόντος		ὀδόντα
		λύων	λύοντος	λύοντι	λύοντα
		λύσας	λύσαντος	λύσαντι	λύσαντα
		λυθείς	λυθέντος	λυθέντι	λυθέντα
		ὤν	ὄντος	ὄντι	ὄντα
§21.5122	ὁ	ἄρχων	ἄρχοντος	ἄρχοντι	ἄρχοντα
		πᾶς	παντός	παντί	πάντα
κτ	ἡ	νύξ	νυκτός	νυκτί	νύκτα
Velar stems					
γ §21.513	ἡ	φλόξ	φλογός	φλογί	φλογά
γγ	ὁ	σάλπιγξ	σάλπιγγος	σάλπιγγι	σάλπιγγα[6]
κ	ὁ	φύλαξ	φύλακος	φύλακι	φύλακα[6]
§21.5133	ἡ	γυνή	γυναικός	γυναικί	γυναῖκα
ρκ	ἡ	σάρξ	σαρκός	σαρκί	σάρκα[6]
χ §21.5134	ἡ	θρίξ	τριχός	τριχί	τρίχα[6]
	ὁ/ἡ	ὄρνιξ	ὄρνιχος	ὄρνιχι	ὄρνιχα
Liquid stems					
ν §22.61		εἷς	ἑνός	ἑνί	ἕνα
ν §21.522	ἡ	ῥίς	ῥινός	ῥινί	ῥῖνα
		τις	τινος	τινι	τινα
	ὁ	ποιμήν	ποιμένος	ποιμένι	ποιμένα
	ὁ	αἰών	αἰῶνος	αἰῶνι	αἰῶνα
λ §21.521	ὁ	ἅλς	ἁλός	ἁλί	ἅλα
ρ §21.523	ὁ	σωτήρ	σωτῆρος	σωτῆρι	σωτῆρα[11]
	ὁ	ῥήτωρ	ῥήτορος	ῥήτορι	ῥήτορα[11]
	ὁ	πατήρ	πατρός	πατρί	πατέρα[11]
	ὁ	ἀνήρ	ἀνδρός	ἀνδρί	ἄνδρα[11]

[1]Read carefully §21.411ff.
[2]§21.412   [3]§21.413
[4]§21.4141   [6]§21.4151
[5]§21.414   [7]§21.4152

THIRD DECLENSION (m. & f.) -- PLURAL

Nom. Pl.		Gen. Pl.	Dat. Pl.	Acc. Pl.	
-ες[8]		-ων	-σι[9]	-ας[10]	MASC. & FEM. Basic ending
αἱ	φλέβες	φλεβῶν	φλεψί	φλέβας	βσ > ψ
οἱ	Ἄραβες				
					πσ > ψ
					§13.142
οἱ		παίδων	παισίν	παῖδας	δσ > σ
αἱ	χιλιάδες	χιλιάδων	χιλιάσιν		
οἱ	πόδες	ποδῶν	ποσίν	πόδας	
αἱ	χάριτες	χαρίτων	χάρισιν	χάριτας	τσ > σ
οἱ	θῆτες	θητῶν	θησί	θῆτας	
	λελυκότες	λελυκότων	λελυκόσι	λελυκότας	
οἱ/αἱ	ὄρνιθες	ὀρνίθων	ὄρνισι	ὄρνιθας	θσ > σ
οἱ	ὀδόντες	ὀδόντων		ὀδόντας	
	λύοντες	λυόντων	λύουσι	λύοντας	οντσ > ουσ
	λύσαντες	λυσάντων	λύσασι	λύσαντας	αντσ > ασ
	λυθέντες	λυθέντων	λυθεῖσι	λυθέντας	εντσ > εισ
	ὄντες	ὄντων	οὖσιν	ὄντας	οντσ > ουσ
οἱ	ἄρχοντες	ἀρχόντων	ἄρχουσι	ἄρχοντας	οντσ > ουσ
	πάντες	πάντων	πᾶσιν	πάντας	αντσ > ασ
αἱ		νυκτῶν	νυξί	νύκτας	κτσ > ξ
					§13.143
αἱ	σάλπιγγες		σάλπιγξι	σάλπιγγας	γγσ > γξ
οἱ	φύλακες		φύλαξι	φύλακας	κσ > ξ
αἱ	γυναῖκες	γυναικῶν	γυναιξίν	γυναῖκας	
αἱ		σαρκῶν	σαρξί	σάρκας	ρκσ > ρξ
αἱ	τρίχες	τριχῶν	θριξίν	τρίχας	χσ > ξ
			ὄρνιξι		ὀρνιχέσσι
αἱ	ῥῖνες	ῥινῶν	ῥισί	ῥῖνας	νσ > σ
	τίνες	τίνων	τισιν	τίνας	§13.3531
οἱ	ποιμένες	ποιμένων	ποιμέσι	ποιμένας	
οἱ	αἰῶνες	αἰῶνων	αἰῶσιν	αἰῶνας	
οἱ	ἄλες	ἁλῶν	ἄλσι	ἄλας	
οἱ	σωτῆρες		σωτῆρσι		
οἱ	ῥήτορες		ῥήτορσι		
οἱ	πατέρες	πατέρων	πατράσιν	πατέρας	τερσ > τρασ
οἱ	ἄνδρες	ἀνδρῶν	ἀνδράσιν	ἄνδρας	νερσ > νδρασ[15]

[8]§21.416   [10]§21.419   [15]§13.52

[9]§21.418

THIRD DECLENSION (ctd.) -- SINGULAR

		Nom. Sing.	Gen. Sing.	Dat. Sing.	Acc. Sing.
Stems in *-σ	ἡ	*τριηρες	*τριηρεσος	*τριηρεσι	*τριηρεσα
§21.53ff.		> τριήρης	> τριήρους	> τριήρει	> τριήρα
		ἀληθής	ἀληθοῦς	ἀληθῆ	ἀληθές
-οι > -ο	ἡ	πειθω	πειθοῦς	πειθοῖ	πειθώ
-ι §21.54	ἡ	δύναμις	δυνάμεως	δυνάμει	δύναμιν
	ἡ	πόλις	πόλεως	πόλει	πόλιν[12]
-υ (-F)	ὁ	πῆχυς	πήχεως	πήχει	πήχυν[12]
§21.55	ὁ	βασιλεύς	βασιλέως	βασιλεῖ	βασιλέα[12]
	ὁ	ἰχθύς	ἰχθύος	ἰχθύϊ	ἰχθύν[12]
	ἡ	γραῦς	γραός	γραΐ	γραύν[12]
§21.5541	ὁ	βοῦς	βοός	βοΐ	βοῦν[12]

THIRD DECLENSION (neut.) -- SINGULAR

NEUTER[13]

		Nom. Sing.	Gen. Sing.	Dat. Sing.	Acc. Sing.
Basic ending		-- or -ς	-ος	-ι	-- or -ς
-τ §21.5123	τό	ὄνομα	ὀνόματος	ὀνόματι	ὄνομα[14]
-σ §21.53	τό	γένος	γένους	γένει	γένος
	τό	γέρας	γέρως	γέραι	γέρας
-ης -ης -ες		ἀληθές	ἀληθοῦς	ἀληθεῖ	ἀληθές
-ντ §21.5121		πᾶν	παντός	παντί	πᾶν
		ὄν	ὄντος	ὄντι	ὄν
		λῦον	λύοντος	λύοντι	λῦον
		λῦσαν	λύσαντος	λύσαντι	λῦσαν
§24.462		λυθέν	λυθέντος	λυθέντι	λυθέν
-Fτ		λελυκός	λελυκότος	λελυκότι	λελυκός
-ων -ων -ον		μεῖζον	μείζονος	μείζονι	μεῖζον
§22.61		ἕν	ἑνός	ἑνί	ἕν
§23.34		τι	τινος	τινι	τι

[11]Voc. adds short vowel to stem   [13]§21.32
[12]Voc. drops ς of nom.   [14]§21.322

THIRD DECLENSION (ctd.) --PLURAL

Nom. Pl.		Gen. Pl.	Dat. Pl.	Acc. Pl.	
αἱ	*τριηρεσες	*τριηρεσων	*τριηρεσσι	*τριηρεσες	Acc. in -ες?
	> τριήρεις	> τριήρων	> τριήρεσι	> τριήρεις	
	ἀληθεῖς	ἀληθῶν	ἀληθέσιν	ἀληθεῖς	
οἱ	ἥρωες	ἡρώων	ἥρωσι	ἥρωας	
αἱ	δυνάμεις	δυναμέων	δυνάμεσιν	δυνάμεις	
αἱ	πόλεις	πόλεων	πόλεσιν	πόλεις	Acc. in -ες?
οἱ	πήχεις	πήχεων	πήχεσι	πήχεις	*πηχεϝος
οἱ	βασιλεῖς	βασιλέων	βασιλεῦσι	βασιλέας	*βασιλεϝος
οἱ	ἰχθύες	ἰχθύων	ἰχθύσι	ἰχθῦς	Ion. ιχθυας
αἱ	γραῦς	γραῶν	γραυσί	γραῦς	*γραϝος
οἱ	βόες	βοῶν	βουσί	βοῦς	*βοϝος

THIRD DECLENSION (neut.) -- PLURAL

	-α	-ων	-σι	-α	NEUTER[13] Basic ending
τὰ	ὀνόματα	ὀνομάτων	ὀνόμασιν	ὀνόματα	
τὰ	γένη	γενῶν	γένεσι	γένη	ε(σ)α > εα > η
τὰ	γέρα	γερῶν	γέρασι	γέρα	α(σ)α > ᾱ
τὰ	ἀληθῆ	ἀληθῶν	ἀληθέσιν	ἀληθῆ	
τὰ	πάντα	πάντων	πᾶσιν	πάντα	
τὰ	ὄντα	ὄντων	οὖσιν	ὄντα	Pr.act.ptcp.
	λύοντα	λυόντων	λύουσι	λύοντα	
	λύσαντα	λυσάντων	λύσασιν	λύσαντα	Aor.act.ptcp.
	λυθέντα	λυθέντων	λυθεῖσι	λυθέντα	Aor.pass.ptcp.
	λελυκότα	λελυκότων	λελυκόσι	λελυκότα	Pf.pass.ptcp.
	μείζονα	μειζόνων	μείζοσι	μείζονα	or n./a. μείζω
	τρία	τριῶν	τρισί	τρία	§22.63
	τινα	τινων	τισι	τινα	

PARADIGM V-1a   PRINCIPAL PARTS, Class-1a´ Verbs

Present	Future A/M	Aorist A/M	Perfect Act.	Perfect M/P	Aorist Pass.

Stems in -υ/-ι

Present	Future A/M	Aorist A/M	Perfect Act.	Perfect M/P	Aorist Pass.
λύω	λύσω	ἔλυσα	λέλυκα	λέλυμαι	ἐλύθην
θύω	θύσω	ἔθυσα	τέθυκα[1]	τέθυμαι[1]	ἐτύθην[1]
χρίω	χρίσω	ἔχρισα		κέχρι(σ)μαι[1]	ἐχρίσθην

Stems in -αυ/-ευ/-ου, -αι/-ει/-οι

Present	Future A/M	Aorist A/M	Perfect Act.	Perfect M/P	Aorist Pass.
ἀκούω	ἀκούσω	ἤκουσα	ἀκήκοα[2]		ἠκούσθην
κρούω	κρούσω	ἔκρουσα	κέκρουκα	κέκρουμαι	ἐκρούσθην
παύω	παύσω	ἔπαυσα	πέπαυκα	πέπαυμαι	ἐπαύθην
θραύω	θραύσω	ἔθραυσα		τέθραυμαι[1]	ἐθραύσθην
προφητεύω	προφητεύσω	ἐπροφήτευσα			
παίω	παίσω	ἔπαισα	πέπαικα		
πταίω	πταίσω	ἔπταισα	ἔπταικα		
κλείω	κλείσω	ἔκλεισα	κέκληκα	κέκλειμαι	ἐκλείσθην
σείω	σείσω	ἔσεισα	σέσεικα	σέσεισμαι	ἐσείσθην
οἴομαι	οἰήσομαι			οἶμαι (?)	ᾠήθην

Labial stems (§12.41, §13.141, etc.)

Present	Future A/M	Aorist A/M	Perfect Act.	Perfect M/P	Aorist Pass.
θλίβω	θλίψομαι	ἔθλιψα	τέθλιφα[1]	τέθλιμμαι	ἐθλίφθην
τρίβω	τρίψω	ἔτριψα	τέτριφα	τέτριμμαι	ἐτρίφθην
σέβομαι					
σήπω			σέσηπα		ἐσάπην
τρέπω	τρέψω	ἔτρεψα	τέτροφα[3]	τέτραμμαι	ἐτρέφθην
λάμπω	λάμψω	ἔλαμψα			
πέμπω	πέμψω	ἔπεμψα	πέπομφα[3]	πέπεμμαι	ἐπέμφθην
ἀλείφω	ἀλείψω	ἤλειψα	(ἀλήλιφα)	ἀλήλιμμαι	ἠλείφθην[4]
στρέφω	στρέψω	ἔστρεψα	(ἔστροφα)	ἔστραμμαι	ἐστράφην[4]
γράφω	γράψω	ἔγραψα	γέγραφα	γέγραμμαι	ἐγράφθην

Dental stems (§12.42, §13.142, etc.)

Present	Future A/M	Aorist A/M	Perfect Act.	Perfect M/P	Aorist Pass.
καθεύδω	καθευδήσω				
ἐρείδω		ἤρεισα			
σπεύδω		ἔσπευσα			
φείδομαι	φείσομαι	ἐφησάμην			
ψεύδομαι	ψεύσω	ἔψευσα		ἔψευσμαι	ἐψεύσθην
*πι·πετω					
> πίπτω	πεσοῦμαι	ἔπεσον	πέπτωκα		
πείθω	πείσω	ἔπεισα	πέπεικα	πέπεισμαι	ἐπείσθην

Velar stems (§12.43, §13.143, etc.)

Present	Future A/M	Aorist A/M	Perfect Act.	Perfect M/P	Aorist Pass.
ἄγω	ἄξω	ἤγαγον[2]	ἦχα	ἦγμαι	ἤχθην
ἀνοίγω	ἀνοίξω	ἀνέῳξα / ἤνοιξα	ἀνέῳγα / ἤνοιγα	ἀνέῳγμαι / ἠνοίγμαι	ἀνεῴχθην
λέγω	λέξω	ἔλεξα	εἴλοχα[3]	λέλεγμαι	ἐλέχθην
διώκω	διώξω	ἐδίωξα	δεδίωκα	δεδίωγμαι	ἐδιώχθην
πλέκω	πλέξω	ἔπλεξα		πέπλεγμαι	ἐπλέχθην
*τιτεκω					
> τίκτω	τέξομαι	ἔτεκον	τέτοκα[3]		ἐτέχθην

Present	Future A/M	Aorist A/M	Perfect Act.	Perfect M/P	Aorist Pass.

Velar stems (continued)

ἄρχω	ἄρξω	ἦρξα			
*σεχω	*σεχσω	*εσεχον	*εσεχηκα		
> ἔχω	> ἕξω/σχήσω	>ἔσχον	> ἔσχηκα	ἔσχυμαι	ἐσχέθην
δέχομαι	δέξομαι	ἐδεξάμην		δέδεγμαι	ἐδέχθην
φθέγγομαι		ἐφθεγξάμην			
ἄγχω		ἠγξάμην			
ἐλέγχω	ἐλέγξω	ἤλεγξα		ἐλήλεγμαι	ἠλέγχθην

Lingual stems (§12.45) (most lingual stems develop as Class-4e verbs)

βούλομαι	βουλήσομαι			βεβούλημαι	ἐβουλήθην
ὀφείλω	ὀφειλήσω	ὠφείλησα	ὠφείληκα		ὠφειλήθην
μέλω	μελήσω	ἐμέλησα	μεμέληκα	μεμέλημαι	ἐμελήθην
μέλλω	μελλήσω	ἐμέλλησα			
μένω[5]	μενῶ	ἔμεινα	μεμένηκα		
*γι·γενομαι					
> γίνομαι	γενήσομαι	ἐγενόμην	γέγονα[3]	γεγένημαι	
δέρω[5]	δερῶ	ἔδειρα		δέδαρμαι	ἐδάρην

Sibilant stems

βρίσω	βρίσω	ἔβρισα	βέβρικα		
*αιδεσομαι					
> αἰδέομαι	αἰδέσομαι	ἠδεσάμην		ἤδεσμαι	ἠδέσθην
*σπασω>σπάω σπάω	σπάσω	ἔσπασα	ἔσπακα	ἔσπασμαι	ἐσπάσθην
*ζεσω > ζέω ζέω	ζέσω	ἔζεσα			
*ξεσω > ξέω				ἔξεσμαι	

PARADIGM V-1b, Class-1b Verbs (§24.223), "Contract Verbs"

α	ζάω[6]	ζήσω	ἔζησα	ἔζηκα		
	ἐρωτάω	ἐρωτήσω	ἠρώτησα	ἠρώτηκα	ἠρώτημαι	ἠρωτήθην
	γεννάω	γεννήσω	ἐγέννησα	γεγέννηκα	γεγέννημαι	
ε	ποιέω[6]	ποιήσω	ἐποίησα	πεποίηκα	πεποίημαι	ἐποιήθην
	εὐλογέω	εὐλογήσω	εὐλόγησα	εὐλόγηκα	εὐλόγημαι	εὐλογήθην
	αἰτέω	αἰτήσω	ᾔτησα	ᾔτηκα	ᾔτημαι	ᾐτήθην
	ἀγαπάω	ἀγαπήσω	ἠγάπησα	ἠγάπηκα	ἠγάπημαι	ἠγαπήθην
ο	δηλόω[6]	δηλώσω	ἐδήλωσα	δεδήλωκα	δεδήλωμαι	ἐδηλώθην
	στερεόω		ἐστερέωσα			ἐστερεώθην
	χόω	χώσω	ἔχωσα	κέχωκα[1]	κέχωσμαι[1]	ἐχώσθην

[1] §13.24   [3] Note Ablaut, §15.4   [5] Sometimes Class 4e
[2] Unusual reduplication   [4] Cf. A&G 778   [6] Always contracted

PARADIGM V-2a

Stems that undergo Ablaut (§15.4) in developing tense-stems

Present	Future A/M	Aorist A/M	Perfect Act.	Perfect M/P	Aorist Pass.
λείπω	λείψω	ἔλιπον	λέλοιπα	λέλειμμαι	ἐλείφθην
πείθω	πείσω	⌠ἔπεισα ⌡ἔπιθον	⌠πέποιθα ⌡πέπεικα	πέπεισμαι	ἐπείσθην
φεύγω	φεύξομαι	ἔφυγον	πέφευγα		

PARADIGM V-2b

Stems ending originally in digamma, developing strong forms.

Present	Future A/M	Aorist A/M	Perfect Act.	Perfect M/P	Aorist Pass.
*νεϝω > νέω	νεσοῦμαι	ἔνευσα	νένευκα		
πλέω[1]	πλεύσομαι	ἔπλευσα	πέπλευκα	πέπλευσμαι	ἐπλεύσθην
χέω	χεῶ	ἔχεα		κέχυμαι[2]	ἐχύθην
πνέω		ἔπνευσα			
ῥέω	ῥεύσω				

[1]Class-2b verbs do not normally contract; exceptions are probably analogic.
[2]§13.24

PARADIGM V-3

Labial stems that add τ to form present tense stem (§24.24)

Present	Future A/M	Aorist A/M	Perfect Act.	Perfect M/P	Aorist Pass.
βάπτω	βάψω	ἔβαψα		βέβαμμαι	ἐβάφθην
βλάπτω	βλάψω	ἔβλαψα	βέβλαφα	βέβλαμμαι	ἐβλάφθην
κάμπτω	κάμψω	ἔκαμψα		κέκαμμαι	ἐκάμφθην
κόπτω	κόψω	ἔκοψα	κέκοφα	κέκομμαι	ἐκόπην
κρύπτω	κρύψω	ἔκρυψα	κέκρυφα	κέκρυμμαι	ἐκρύφθην
σκάπτω	σκάψω	ἔσκαψα	ἔσκαφα	ἔσκαμμαι	ἐσκάφην
σκέπτομαι	σκέψομαι	ἐσκεψάμην			
ἅπτω		ἧψα			ἥφθην
ὄπτομαι	ὄψομαι			ὧμμαι	ὤφθην

Stems that add consonantal iota (and undergo resulting phonetic shifts) to form the present tense-stem (§24.25)

PARADIGM V-4a.   Class-4a verbs

Stems ending in δ and some ending in γ (§24.251)

-δ	θαυμάζω	θαυμάσω	ἐθαύμασα	τεθαύμακα[1]		ἐθαυμάσθην
	δοξάζω	δοξάσω	ἐδόξασα	δεδόξακα	δεδόξασμαι	ἐδοξάσθην
	πειράζω	πειράσω	ἐπείρασα	πεπείρακα	πεπείρασμαι	ἐπειράσθην
	ἀγιάζω	ἁγιάσω	ἡγίασα	ἡγίακα	ἡγίασμαι	ἡγιάσθην
	κομίζω	κομίσω/-ιῶ	ἐκόμισα	κεκόμικα	κεκόμισμαι	ἐκομίσθην
	ἐγγίζω	ἐγγίσω/-ιῶ	ἤγγισα	ἤγγικα		
	ἐλπίζω	ἐλπιῶ	ἤλπισα	ἤλπικα		
	βαπτίζω[2]	βαπτίσω	ἐβάπτισα	βεβάπτικα	βεβάπτισμαι	ἐβαπτίσθην
	*σεδ- > ἕζομαι		εἰσάμην			
-γ	σφάζω	σφάξω	ἔσφαξα		ἔσφαγμαι	
	κράζω	κράξω	ἔκραξα	κέκραγα		
-γγ	κλάζω	κλάγξω				
	σαλπίζω	{ σαλπίγξω				
		σαλπίσω	ἐσάλπισα			

[1] §13.24   [2] Secondary development from βάπτω, Class 3, stem *βαπ.

PARADIGM V-4b.   Class-4b verbs

Velar stems (§24.252)

	Present	Future A/M	Aorist A/M	Perfect Act.	Perfect M/P	Aorist Pass.
-γ	πράσσω	πράξω	ἔπραξα	πέπραχα	πέπραγμαι	
	ἀλλάσσω	ἀλλάξω	ἤλλαξα	ἤλλαχα	ἤλλαγμαι	ἠλλάγην
	τάσσω	τάξομαι	ἔταξα	τέταχα	τέταγμαι	ἐτάχθην
	φράσσω	φραγήσομαι	ἔφραξα			
	πλήσσω		ἔπληξα			
	πτύσσω		ἔπτυξα			
-κ	κηρύσσω	κηρύξω	ἐκήρυξα	κεκήρυχα	κεκήρυγμαι	ἐκηρύχθην
	φυλάσσω	φυλάξω	ἐφύλαξα			
	ἑλίσσω	ἑλίξω	εἵλιξα		εἵλιγμαι	εἱλίχθην
-χ	ταράσσω	ταράξω	ἐτάραξα		τετάραγμαι	ἐταράχθην
	ὀρύσσω		ὤρυκα			ὠρύχθην

PARADIGM V-4c.   Class-4c verbs

Stems with original digamma (§24.253)

	Present	Future A/M	Aorist A/M	Perfect Act.	Perfect M/P	Aorist Pass.
*καϝιω >	καίω	καύσω	ἔκαυσα		κέκαυμαι	ἐκαύθην
	κλαίω	κλαύσω	ἔκλαυσα			
	ὀπυίω	ὀπύσω				

Note: Verbs in ευ/ου (εϝ/οϝ) are usually Class 1a or Class 2b.

PARADIGM V-4d. Class-4d verbs

Stems originally ending in sigma (§24.254)

Present	Future A/M	Aorist A/M	Perfect Act.	Perfect M/P	Aorist Pass.
δαίομαι	δάσομαι	ἐδασάμην			

PARADIGM V-4e. Class-4e Verbs

"Liquid verbs": stems ending in λ/ν/ρ (§24.255)

	Present	Future A/M	Aorist A/M	Perfect Act.	Perfect M/P	Aorist Pass.
-λ	ἀγγέλλω	ἀγγελῶ	ἤγγειλα	ἤγγελκα	ἤγγελμαι	ἠγγέλην
	βάλλω	βαλῶ	ἔβαλον	βέβληκα	βέβλημαι	ἐβλήθην
	στέλλω	στελῶ	ἔστειλα	ἔσταλκα	ἔσταλμαι	ἐστάλην
	τέλλω	τελοῦμαι	ἔτειλα	τέταλκα	τέταλμαι	
	ἅλλομαι	ἁλοῦμαι	ἡλάμην			
	ἰάλλω	ἰαλῶ	ἵηλα			
-ν	κρίνω	κρινῶ	ἔκρινα	κέκρικα	κέκριμαι	ἐκρίθην
	κτείνω	κτενῶ	ἔκτεινα	ἔκτονα		
	εὐφραίνω	εὐφρανῶ	ηὔφρανα			ηὐφράνθην
	φαίνω	φανοῦμαι	ἔφανην			
	μιαίνω				μεμίαμμαι	ἐμιάνθην
	μένω see Paradigm V-1a					
-ρ	καθαίρω	καθαρῶ	ἐκάθηρα		κεκάθαρμαι	ἐκαθάρθην
	χαίρω	χαρήσομαι	ἐχάρην			
	ἐχθαίρω	ἐχθαροῦμαι	ἤχθηρα			
	ἐγείρω	ἐγερῶ	ἤγειρα		ἐγήγερμαι	ἠγέρθην
	αἴρω	ἀρῶ	ἦρα	ἦρκα	ἦρμαι	ἤρθην
	*εἴρω[1]	ἐρῶ		εἴρηκα	εἴρημαι	ἐρρέθην

[1]Unused present; the verb is usually listed under λέγω (Class 8).

PARADIGM V-5a.   Class-5a Verbs

Stems that add ν/αν to form the present tense-stem (§24.261)

Present	Future A/M	Aorist A/M	Perfect Act.	Perfect M/P	Aorist Pass.
ἁμαρτάνω	ἁμαρτήσω	ἡμάρτησα	ἡμάρτηκα	ἡμάρτημαι	ἡμαρτήθην
πίνω	πίομαι	ἔπιον	πέπωκα	πέπομαι	ἐπόθην
δύνω		ἔδυσα		δέδυμαι	
ὀπτάνομαι	ὄψομαι	ὠφάμην			
βλαστάνω		ἐβλάστησα			
κάμνω		ἔκαμον			
τέμνω		ἔτεμον		τέτμημαι	ἐτμήθην
φθάνω		ἔφθασα	ἔφθακα		
ἱκνέομαι		ἱκόμην			
βαίνω	βήσομαι	ἔβην	βέβηκα		

PARADIGM V-5b.   Class-5b Verbs

Stems adding epenthetic ν plus -αν to form present tense-stem (§24.262)

Present	Future A/M	Aorist A/M	Perfect Act.	Perfect M/P	Aorist Pass.
μανθάνω[1]	μαθήσομαι	ἔμαθον[1]	μεμάθηκα		
λανθάνω	λήσω	ἔλαθον	λέληθα	λέλησμαι	
λαγχάνω[2]	λήξομαι	ἔλαχον	εἴληχα		
πυνθάνομαι		ἐπυθόμην			
τυγχάνω		ἔτυχον	τέτυχα		
λιμπάνω[3]					ἐλείφην
λαμβάνω	λήμφομαι	ἔλαβον	εἴληφα	εἴλημμαι	ἐλήμφθην
θιγγάνω[4]	θίξομαι	ἔθιγον			

[1]Stem *μαθ; in most cases the stem will be seen in the 2d aorist.
[2]νχ > γχ   [3]νπ > μπ   [4]νγ > γγ

PARADIGM V-5c.   Class-5c Verbs

Stems adding νε/να/νυ to form present tense-stem (§24.263)[1]

Present	Future A/M	Aorist A/M	Perfect Act.	Perfect M/P	Aorist Pass.
βυνέω	βύσω	ἔβυσα	βέβυσμαι		
κυνέω[2]		ἔκυσα			
ἰσχνέομαι	ἰσχνήσομαι	ἐσχόμην			
δαμνάω	δαμάσω/-μάω	ἐδάμασα			
ὀμνύω	ὀμοῦμαι	ὤμοσα	ὀμώμοκα	ὀμώμασμαι	ὠμόσθην

[1]Most νυ verbs develop as -μι verbs (Class 7b).
[2]By NT period this developed as Class 1b.

PARADIGM V-6. Class-6 Verbs

Verbs that add σκ/ισκ to form present tense-stem (§24.27)[1]

Present	Future A/M	Aorist A/M	Perfect Act.	Perfect M/P	Aorist Pass.
γηράσκω	γηράσω	ἐγήρασα	γεγήρακα		
*διδαχσκω					
> διδάσκω	διδάξω	ἐδίδαξα	δεδίδαχα		ἐδιδάχθην
εὑρίσκω	εὑρήσω	ηὗρον/εὗρον	ηὗρηκα	ηὗρημαι	ηὑρέθην
γι(γ)νώσκω	γνώσομαι	ἔγνων	ἔγνωκα	ἔγνωσμαι	ἐγνώσθην
μιμνήσκω	μνήσω	ἔμνησα		μέμνημαι	ἐμνήσθην
πιπράσκω			πέπρακα	πέπραμαι	ἐπράθην
ἀραρίσκω		ἦρσα	ἄραρα		
ἀποθνήσκω	ἀποθανοῦμαι	ἀπέθανον	τέθνηκα[2]		
ἀναλίσκω	ἀναλώσω	ἀνήλωσα			ἀνηλώθην
*παθσκω					
> πάσχω	πείσομαι	ἔπαθον	πέπονθα[3]		

[1]A number of Class-6 verbs reduplicate in the present.
[2]§13.24
[3]Smyth suggests a stem *πυθ.

PARADIGM V-7a.   Class 7-a Verbs

Verbs adding μι endings to stem to form present tense-stem (§24.28)

	Present	Future A/M	Aorist A/M	Perfect Act.	Perfect M/P	Aorist Pass.
-α	ἵστημι[1]	στήσω	ἔστησα	ἕστηκα	ἕσταμαι	ἐστάθην
	ὀνίνημι	ὀνήσω	ὤνησα			ὠνήθην
	πίμπρημι[2]	πρήσω	ἔπρησα		πέπρημαι	ἐπρήσθην
	δύναμαι	δυνήσομαι			δεδύνημαι	ἐδυνήθην
	κρέμαμαι	κρεμήσομαι				
	ἐπίσταμαι	ἐπιστήσομαι				ἠπιστήθην
	φήμι	φήσω	ἔφησα			
-ε	τίθημι[3]	θήσω	ἔθηκα[4]	τέθεικα[3]	τέθειμαι	
-ο	δίδωμι	δώσω	ἔδωκα[4]	δέδωκα	δέδομαι	ἐδόθην
	ἀφίημι	ἀφήσω	ἀφῆκα[4]	ἀφεῖκα	ἀφεῖμαι	ἀφείθην
	εἰμί	ἔσομαι				

[1]From *σι·στημι   [2]Epenthetic ν > μ before labial.
[3]§13.24   [4]Note "kappa aorist."

ADD ABOVE

PARADIGM V-7b.   Class-7b Verbs

Verbs that add νυ/ννυ to stem and μι endings to form present tense-stem

Present	Future Λ/M	Λorist A/M	Perfect Act.	Perfect M/P	Aorist Pass.
δείκνυμι	δείξω	ἔδειξα	δέδειχα	δέδειγμαι	ἐδείχθην
πήγνυμι	πήξω	ἔπηξα			ἐπήχθην
ζεύνυμι	ζεύξω	ἔζευξα		ἔζευγμαι	ἐζεύχθην
μίγνυμι	μίξω	ἔμιξα		μέμιγμαι	ἐμίχθην
*απ·ολνυμι			⌠ἀπολώληκα		
> ἀπόλυμι	ἀπολοῦμαι	ἀπώλεσα	⌡ἀπόλωλα		
κεράννυμι		ἔκρασα		κέκραμαι	ἐκράθην
σβέννυμι	σβέσω	ἔσβεσα	ἔσβηκα		ἐσβήσθην
στρώννυμι	στρώσω	ἔστρωσα		ἔστρωμαι	ἐστρώθην

PARADIGM V-8.　Class-8 Verbs

"Irregular" or mixed verbs; verbs which are commonly formed into paradigms, although they are from different roots.　(§24.29)

Present	Future A/M	Aorist A/M	Perfect Act.	Perfect M/P	Aorist Pass.
αἱρέω[1]	{ αἱρήσω[1] ἑλῶ[2]	{ εἷλον[2]	ᾕρηκα[1]	ᾕρημαι[1]	ᾑρέθην[1]
ἔθω[3]			εἴωθα[3]		
εἴδω[4]	εἰδήσω[4]		οἶδα[4]		
{ ἐσθίω[5] ἔσθω[5]	φάγομαι[6]	ἔφαγον[6]			
λέγω[7]	ἐρῶ[8]	{ εἶπον[9] εἶπα[9]	εἴρηκα[8]	εἴρημαι[8]	{ ἐρρέθην[8] ἐρρήθην[8]
ὁράω[10]	ὄψομαι[12]	εἶδον[13]	{ ἑώρακα[10] ἑόρακα[10]		
τρέχω[14]	δραμοῦμαι[15]	ἔδραμον[15]			
φέρω[16]	οἴσω[17]	{ ἤνεγκα[18] ἤνεγκον[18]	ἐνήνοχα[18]		ἠνέχθην[18]

[1] Stem *αἱρε- (Class 1b).
[2] Stem *ἑλ-, cf. ἑλετός -ή -όν (Class 4e)
[3] Stem *σϝεθ-, cf. ἐθίζω, τὸ ἔθος; used only in perf.
[4] Stem *ϝιδ-, cf. Lat. video; 2 aor. is used for paradigm of ὁράω, and perf. is used as a present 'I know,' perhaps *ϝεϝιδα.
[5] Stem *εδ (θ unexplained), cf. ἐδεστός, τὸ ἐδανόν, and Eng. edible.
[6] Stem *φαγ-/φαγε- cf. τὸ φάγημα, ὁ φάγων; used in pres. only in late Greek.
[7] Stem *λεγ- (Class 1a), cf. fut. λέξω and 1 aor. ἔλεξα, λεκτέος, etc.
[8] Stem *ϝερ-, pres. εἴρω (Class 4e); replaced in NT and Attic in pres. by λέγω and in aor. by εἶπον, otherwise not irregular.
[9] Stem *ϝεπ-, pres. ἔπω is generally replaced by φημί or λέγω and fut. by ἐρῶ.
[10] Stem *ϝορα- (Class 1b), cf. ἡ ὅρασις, τὸ ὅραμα.
[12] Stem *οπ-, cf. ὄπτομαι (Class 3), ἡ ὀπτασία, and Eng. optic.
[13] Stem *ϝιδ-, cf. Note 4 above; 'I have seen' = 'I know.'
[14] Stem *θρεχ- (§13.24), aor. ἔθρεξα is rare; cf. θρεκτός, θρεκτικός
[15] Stem *δραμ(α)-, cf. τὸ δράμημα, not used in pres.
[16] Stem *φερ-, used only in pres. and imperf.
[17] Stem *οι-, cf. οἰστός, οἰσθήσομαι, ἀνοῖσαι/ἀνῷσαι
[18] Stem *ενεγ- (less likely ενεκ-/ενεγκ-).

[This list is obviously shorter that the lists of irregular verbs in such works as Robertson, Short Grammar, 48-56, 241-2441, Moulton, Grammar, 2:224-266, or Dana and Mantey, Manual Grammar, 325-327.　The student who has mastered the basic principles of phonetic shifts will quickly discover that most of the "irregular" verbs are quite regular.　It is better to learn the verbs by classes than in a disorganized mass of words whose only arrangement is alphabetical. Cf. Goodwin and Gulick, Greek Grammar §650, and Smyth, Greek Grammar §§529-531.]

For ἔχω see Paradigm V-1a (velar stems).
For πάσχω see Paradigm V-6.
For πίνω see Paradigm V-5a.
For πίπτω see Paradigm V-1a (dental stems).
For τίκτω see Paradigm V-1a (velar stems).
For γίνομαι see Paradigm V-1a (lingual stems).

Part IV
BASIC VOCABULARY

FREQUENCY VOCABULARY

There are about 137,328 words in the Greek NT, representing a vocabulary of
about 6,436 words. (Word-counts are taken from R. Morgenthaler, *Statistik des
neutestamentlichen Wortschatzes*.) The number of words in Acts is 18,374, representing a vocabulary of 2,038 words. The Gospel of Luke is approximately the
same size as Acts. The following distribution is found:

	NT	Acts	Luke
Substantives	1,878	588	664
Verbs	1,845	775	799
Adjectives	685	186	181
Adverbs	271	113	115
Names	570	260	162
Other	187	116	134
Totals	5,436	2,038	2,055

In the NT and in Acts, the following frequency distribution is found:

Symbol used in HNTG	Frequency indicated	Number of words in this frequency group in NT (group)	(cumulative)	in Acts (group)	(cumulative)
A1	over 200x	81 =	81	81 =	81
A2	100–199x	90 =	171	87 =	168
B1	70–99x	72 =	243	67 =	235
B2	50–69x	75 =	318	72 =	307
C1	40–49x	69 =	387	61 =	368
C2	30–39x	87 =	474	70 =	438
D1	25–29x	79 =	553	54 =	492
D2	20–24x	92 =	645	68 =	560
E1	17–19x	88 =	733	51 =	611
E2	15–16x	81 =	814	44 =	655
F1	13–14x	94 =	908		
F2	12x	64 =	972		
G1	11x	83 =	1,055		
G2	10x	79 =	1,134		
H1	8–9x	217 =	1,351		
H2	6–7x	296 =	1,647		
H3	5x	221 =	1,868		
J1	4x	322 =	2,190		
J2	3x	470 =	2,660		
J3	2x	842 =	3,502		
K	1x	1,934 =	5,436		

The implications of this analysis for vocabulary learning are staggering. Only
about 10% of the words occur 25 times or more, and only 25% occur eight times or
more. These obviously are the words to learn. Fully 35% of the words occur
only once each, and 65% of the words occur four times or less. It is almost a
waste of time to learn these words; very few of them are truly significant. We
therefore stress learning only the most frequent words in the NT. All words
(except proper names) that occur 10 times or more are listed in this Frequency
Vocabulary. The numbering follows *The New Englishman's Greek Concordance* and
Strong's Exhaustive Concordance of the Bible. Thus, by turning to the same
number in NEGC a student can quickly see how the word is used in various con-
texts.

18 A2 ἀγαθός -ή -όν good (9:43 3x)*
21 G1 ἀγαλλιάω (1b) I exult, rejoice, am glad (2:26 2x)
25 A2 ἀγαπάω (1b) I love (0x)
26 A2 ἀγάπη -ης ἡ love (0x)
27 B2 ἀγαπητός -ή -όν beloved (15:25 1x)
32 A2 ἄγγελος -ου ὁ messenger, angel (5:19 21x)
37 D1 ἁγιάζω (4a) I sanctify, consecrate (20:32 2x)
38 G2 ἁγιασμός -οῦ ὁ sanctification, holiness (0x)
40 A1 ἅγιος -α -ον holy, sacred (1:2 53x) [hagiology]
50 D2 ἀγνοέω (1b) I do not know, am ignorant (13:27 2x) [agnostic]
58 G1 ἀγορά -ᾶς ἡ market place, Agora (16:19 2x)

59 C2 ἀγοράζω (4a) I buy, purchase (0x)
68 C2 ἀγρός -οῦ ὁ field (4:36 1x) [agronomy]
71 B2 ἄγω (1a) I lead, bring (5:21 26x) [pedagogy]
79 D1 ἀδελφή -ῆς ἡ sister (23:16 1x)
80 A1 ἀδελφός -οῦ ὁ brother (1:14 57x) [Adelphian]
86 G2 ᾅδης -ου ὁ Hades, the underworld (2:27 2x)
91 D1 ἀδικέω (1b) I act unjustly, do wrong, hurt (7:24 5x)
93 D1 ἀδικία -ας ἡ unrighteousness, wrongdoing (1:18 2x)
94 F2 ἄδικος -ος -ον unjust, dishonest (24:15 1x)
102 G2 ἀδύνατος -ος -ον powerless, impossible (14:8 1x)

114 E2 ἀθετέω (1b) I declare invalid, nullify, reject (0x)
129 B1 αἷμα -ατος τό blood (1:19 11x) A&G 22 [haemoglobin]
139 H1 αἵρεσις -εως ἡ sect, party, heretical sect (5:17 6x) [heresy]
142 A2 αἴρω (4e) I take/lift up, take away (4:24 9x)
154 B1 αἰτέω (1b) I ask, request, demand (3:2 10x)
156 D2 αἰτία -ας ἡ cause, reason, charge, accusation (10:21 8x)
165 A2 αἰών -ῶνος ὁ long time, age, eon, eternity A&G 26 (3:21 2x)
166 B1 αἰώνιος -α -ον eternal, ages ago (13:46 2x)
167 G2 ἀκαθαρσία -ας ἡ impurity, refuse, immorality (0x)
169 C2 ἀκάθαρτος -ος -ον unclean, impure (5:16 5x)

173 F1 ἄκανθαι -ῶν αἱ thorns (0x)
189 D2 ἀκοή -ῆς ἡ hearing, listening, ear (17:20 2x)
190 B1 ἀκολουθέω (1b) I follow (12:8 4x)
191 A1 ἀκούω (1a) I hear (1:4 89x) A&G 31 [acoustic]
199 H1 ἀκριβῶς accurately, carefully (18:25 5x)
203 D2 ἀκροβυστία -ας ἡ foreskin, uncircumcision (11:3 1x)
220 G1 ἀλέκτωρ -ορος ὁ cock, rooster (0x)
225 A2 ἀλήθεια -ας ἡ truthfulness, truth (4:27 3x)
227 D1 ἀληθής -ής -ές truthful, honest, true, real (12:9 1x)
228 D1 ἀληθινός -ή -όν true, dependable, genuine (0x)

230 E1 ἀληθῶς truly, really (12:11 1x)
235 A1 ἀλλά but, yet, rather (1:4 30x) A&G 37
240 A2 ἀλλήλων (pl.gen.) one another (4:15 8x)
243 A2 ἄλλος -η -ο other (2:12 7x) [allopath]
245 F1 ἀλλότριος -α -ον belonging to another, alien (7:6 1x)
254 G1 ἅλυσις -εως ἡ chain (12:6 4x)
260 G2 ἅμα at the same time, simultaneously, together (24:26 2x)
264 C1 ἁμαρτάνω (5a) I sin, do wrong (25:8 1x)
266 A2 ἁμαρτία -ας ἡ sin (2:38 8x) A&G 42 [hamartiology]
268 C1 ἁμαρτωλός -ός -όν sinful, sinner (0x)

*9:43 is first occurrence in Acts; 3x = frequency in Acts. A&G is page reference

in Arndt & Gingrich.

281 A2 ἀμήν verily, truly (0x) [Amen]
290 D2 ἀμπελών -ῶνος vineyard (0x)
297 F1 ἀμφότεροι -αι -α both (8:38 3x)
302 A2 ἄν -soever (often impossible to translate) (3:20 15x) A&G 47ff
303 F1 ἀνά among, between, each, apiece (0x) A&G 49
305 B1 ἀναβαίνω (5a §24.2634) I go up, ascend (1:13 18x)
308 D1 ἀναβλέπω (1a) I look up, see again, gain sight (9:12 5x)
312 F1 ἀναγγέλλω (4e) I report, announce (14:27 5x)
314 C2 ἀναγινώσκω (6) I read, read aloud (8:28 8x)
318 E1 ἀνάγκη -ης ἡ necessity, compulsion, distress (0x)

321 D2 ἀνάγω (1a) I lead/bring up, sail (7:41 17x)
337 D2 ἀναιρέω (8) I take away, destroy (2:23 19x)
345 F1 ἀνάκειμαι (7a) I am/recline at table (0x)
350 E2 ἀνακρίνω (4e) I question, examine, judge (4:9 5x)
353 F1 ἀναλαμβάνω (5b) I take up/along, adopt (1:2 8x)
373 F2 ἀναπαύω (1a) I rest, cause to rest (0x)
377 F2 ἀναπίπτω (1a) I lie down, recline (0x)
386 C1 ἀνάστασις -εως ἡ resurrection, rise (1:22 11x) A&G 59
391 F1 ἀναστροφή -ῆς ἡ conduct, behavior, way of life (0x)
395 G2 ἀνατολή -ῆς ἡ rising, east (0x) [Anatolia]

402 F1 ἀναχωρέω (1b) I withdraw, retire, go along (23:19 2x)
417 C2 ἄνεμος -ου ὁ wind (27:4 4x) [anemometer]
430 E2 ἀνέχομαι (1a) I endure, bear (18:14 1x) A&G 65
435 A1 ἀνήρ ἀνδρός ὁ man, male (1:10 100x) A&G 65 [androgynous]
436 F1 ἀνθίστημι (7a) I withstand, resist (13:8 2x)
444 A1 ἄνθρωπος -ου ὁ man, human being (4:9 46x) A&G 67 [anthropoid]
446 H3 ἀνθύπατος -ου ὁ   proconsul (13:7 5x)
450 A2 ἀνίστημι (7a) I raise, rise, get up (1:15 45x)
455 B1 ἀνοίγω (1a) I open (5:19 17x)
458 F1 ἀνομία -ας ἡ lawlessness (0x)

473 D2 ἀντί + gen. instead of (12:23 1x) [anti-]
509 F1 ἄνωθεν from of old, from above, again (26:5 1x)
514 C1 ἄξιος -α -ον worthy, equal in value (13:25 7x) [axiology]
518 C1 ἀπαγγέλλω (4e) I report, announce (4:23 16x)
520 E2 ἀπάγω (1a) I lead away (12:19 3x)
530 F1 ἅπαξ once (0x)
533 G1 ἀπαρνέομαι (1b) I deny (0x)
537 C1 ἅπας -ασα -αν the whole, all, everybody/-thing (2:7 10x)
544 F1 ἀπειθέω (1b) I disbelieve, disobey (17:5 3x)
565 A2 ἀπέρχομαι (8) I go away, depart (4:15 5x)
568 E1 ἀπέχω (1a) I receive in full, am distant (15:20 2x)

570 G1 ἀπιστία -ας ἡ unfaithfulness, unbelief (0x)
571 D2 ἄπιστος -ος -ον unbelievable, unbelieving (26:8 1x)
575 A1 ἀπό + gen. from (1:4 112x) [apo-]
588 H2 ἀποδέχομαι (1a) I welcome, recognize (2:41 5x)
591 C1 ἀποδίδωμι (7a) I give away/up/out, return, reward (4:33 4x)
599 A2 ἀποθνῄσκω (6) I die (7:4 4x)
601 D1 ἀποκαλύπτω (3) I reveal, disclose (0x) [apocalyptic]
602 E1 ἀποκάλυψις -εως ἡ revelation, disclosure (0x) [apocalypse]
611 A1 ἀποκρίνομαι (4e) I answer, reply (3:12 21x)

615 B1 ἀποκτείνω (4e) I kill (3:15 6x)
622 B1 ἀπόλλυμι (7a) I destroy, ruin, lose, perish (5:37 2x)
626 G2 ἀπολογέομαι (1b) I make my defense (19:33 6x) [apologetic]

629 G2 ἀπολύτρωσις -εως ἡ release, redemption (0x)
630 B2 ἀπολύω (1a) I set free, pardon (3:13 15x)
649 A2 ἀποστέλλω (4e) I send away (3:20 24x)
652 B1 ἀπόστολος -ου ὁ messenger, delegate (1:2 28x) [apostle]
680 C2 ἅπτω (3) I light, (mid.) touch, hold (28:2 1x)
684 E1 ἀπώλεια -ας ἡ destruction, waste (8:20 1x)
686 C1 ἄρα so then, indeed (7:1 5x) A&G 103

694 D2 ἀργύριον -ου τό silver, money (3:6 5x) [argyrol]
700 E2 ἀρέσκω (6) I strive to please, please (6:5 1x)
706 E2 ἀριθμός -ου ὁ number (4:4 5x) [arithmetic]
720 C2 ἀρνέομαι (1b) I deny, refuse, repudiate (3:13 4x)
721 C2 ἀρνίον -ου τό lamb (0x)
726 F1 ἁρπάζω (4a) I seize (8:39 2x)
737 C2 ἄρτι now, just now (0x)
740 A2 ἄρτος -ου ὁ bread, loaf (2:42 5x)
744 G1 ἀρχαῖος -α -ον ancient, old (5:7 3x)
746 B2 ἀρχή -ῆς ἡ beginning, ruler (10:11 4x) A&G 111 [arch-]

749 A2 ἀρχιερεύς -έως ὁ high priest (4:16 22x)
756 B1 ἄρχω (1a) I rule, (mid.) begin (1:1 10x) [-arch]
758 C2 ἄρχων -οντος ὁ ruler, prince, official (3:17 11x) A&G 113
766 G2 ἀσέλγεια -ας ἡ licentiousness, debauchery (0x)
769 D2 ἀσθένεια -ας ἡ sickness, weakness, timidity (28:9 1x) [asthenia]
770 C2 ἀσθενέω (1b) I am sick, weak, in need (9:37 3x) [asthenia]
772 D1 ἀσθενής -ής -ές weak, feeble (4:9 3x)
779 F2 ἀσκός -οῦ ὁ leather bag, wine-skin (0x)
782 B2 ἀσπάζομαι (4a) I greet, welcome (18:22 5x)
783 G2 ἀσπασμός -οῦ ὁ greeting (0x)

792 D2 ἀστήρ -έρος ὁ star (0x) [astronomy]
816 F1 ἀτενίζω (4a) I gaze upon, look intently at (1:10 10x)
833 F2 αὐλή -ῆς ἡ court, courtyard (0x)
837 D2 αὐξάνω (5a) I grow, increase (6:7 4x) [auxanometer]
839 F1 αὔριον on the morrow, soon (4:3 4x)
846 A1 αὐτός -ή -ό self, the same; 3 sg. pron. (exc. nom.) (1:3
        694x); study A&G 122f or a good grammar on this word!
851 G2 ἀφαιρέω (1b) I take away, rob (0x)
859 E1 ἄφεσις -εως ἡ release, pardon (2:38 5x)
863 A2 ἀφίημι (7a irreg.) I let go, send away, remit (5:38 3x) [A&G 125f]
868 F1 ἀφίστημι (7a) I mislead, withdraw, keep away (5:37 6x)

873 G2 ἀφορίζω (4a) I separate, set apart, take away (13:2 2x)
878 G1 ἄφρων -ων -ον foolish, ignorant (0x)
891 C1 ἄχρι + gen. until, as far as (1:2 15x)
B 906 A2 βάλλω (4e) I throw, place, put (16:23 5x) [ballistic]
907 B1 βαπτίζω (4a) I baptize (1:5 21x) A&G 131f [baptize]
908 D2 βάπτισμα -ατος τό baptism (1:22 6x)
910 F2 βαπτιστής -οῦ ὁ Baptist (surname of John) (0x)
928 F2 βασανίζω (4a) I torture, torment (0x)
932 A2 βασιλεία -ας ἡ kingship, kingdom (1:3 8x) [basilica]
935 A2 βασιλεύς -έως ὁ king (4:26 20x)
936 D2 βασιλεύω (1a) I become/am king, rule (0x)

941 D1 βαστάζω (4a) I take up, carry, endure (3:2 4x)
968 F2 βῆμα -ατος τό tribunal, judicial bench (7:5 8x) [bema]
975 C2 βιβλίον -ου τό book, scroll (0x) [bibliography]

976 G2 βίβλος -ου ἡ book (usually sacred) (1:20 3x) [Bible]
987 C2 βλασφημέω (1b) I revile, blaspheme (13:45 4x) [blaspheme]
988 E1 βλασφημία -ας ἡ slander, defamation (0x) [blasphemy]
991 A2 βλέπω (1a) I see, look at (1:9 14x)
994 F2 βοάω (1b) I cry aloud (8:7 3x)
1012 F2 βουλή -ῆς ἡ purpose, decision, counsel (2:33 7x)

1014 C2 βούλομαι (1a) I wish, want, desire (5:28 14x)
1027 F2 βροντή -ῆς ἡ thunder (0x)
1033 E1 βρῶμα -ατος τό food (0x)
1035 G1 βρῶσις -εως ἡ eating, corrosion, food (0x)
Γ 1060 D1 γαμέω (1b) I marry, get married (0x) [bigamy]
1062 E2 γάμος -ου ὁ wedding, marriage (0x)
1063 A1 γάρ (postpositive) for, so (1:20 80x) A&G 151
1065 C2 γε (encl.) yet, at least (2:18 4x) A&G 152
1067 F2 γέεννα -ης ἡ Gehenna (0x)
1073 G1 γέμω (pres. and impf. only) I am full (0x)

1074 C1 γενεά -ᾶς ἡ family, descent, race (2:40 5x) [genealogy]
1080 B1 γεννάω (1b) I beget, bear (2:8 7x)
1085 D2 γένος -ους τό race, descendants, people (4:6 9x) [genocide]
1089 E2 γεύομαι (1a) I taste, come to know (10:10 3x)
1092 E1 γεωργός -οῦ ὁ farmer (0x) [George]
1093 A1 γῆ γῆς ἡ earth, ground, land (1:8 33x) [geometry]
1096 A1 γίνομαι (1a) I come to be, become (1:16 124x) A&G 157ff
1097 A1 γινώσκω (6) I know, comprehend (1:7 16x) A&G 159ff
1100 B2 γλῶσσα -ης ἡ tongue, language (2:3 6x) [isogloss]
1107 D2 γνωρίζω (4a) I make known, know (2:28 2x) [ignore]

1108 D1 γνῶσις -εως ἡ knowledge (0x) [Gnosis]
1110 E2 γνωστός -ή -όν known, remarkable, intelligible (1:19 10x)
1118 D2 γονεῖς -έων οἱ parents (0x) [-gony]
1119 F2 γόνυ -ατος τό knee (7:60 4x)
1121 E2 γράμμα -ατος τό letter, document (26:24 2x) A&G 164 [-gram]
1122 B1 γραμματεύς -έως ὁ secretary, clerk, scribe (4:5 4x)
1124 B2 γραφή -ῆς ἡ scripture (1:16 7x) A&G 165 [-graph]
1125 A2 γράφω (1a) I write, record (1:20 12x)
1127 D2 γρηγορέω (1b) I awake, am alert (20:31 1x)
1131 E2 γυμνός -ή -όν stripped, naked (19:16 1x) [gym-]

1135 A1 γυνή γυναικός ἡ woman (1:14 19x) [gyn-]
Δ 1139 F1 δαιμονίζομαι (4a) I am demon-possessed (0x)
1140 B2 δαιμόνιον -ου τό demon, deity (17:18 1x) [daimonic]
1144 G2 δάκρυον -ου τό tear, weeping (20:19 2x)
1161 A1 δέ (postpos.) but, and, (often untranslated) (1:5 558x) A&G 170
1162 E1 δέησις -εως ἡ prayer (0x)
1163 A2 δεῖ (<δεῖν only in 3 sg.) it is necessary (1:16 22x)
1166 C2 δείκνυμι (7b) I show, point out (7:3 2x) [deictic]
1173 E2 δεῖπνον -ου τό dinner, supper (0x)
1176 D1 δέκα (indecl.) ten (25:6 1x) [deka-]

1186 D1 δένδρον -ου τό tree (0x) [rhodadendron]
1188 B2 δεξιός -ά -όν right (hand or side) (2:25 7x) [dextral]
1189 D2 δέομαι (2b) I pray, ask, beg (4:31 7x)
1194 E2 δέρω (4e) I beat, strike (5:40 3x)
1198 E2 δέσμιος -ου ὁ prisoner (16:25 6x)
1199 D2 δεσμός -οῦ ὁ bond, fetter (16:26 5x)
1203 G2 δεσπότης -ου ὁ lord, master, owner (4:24 1x) [despot]

1205 F2   δεῦτε   come! come on!   (0x)
1208 C1   δεύτερος -α -ον   second (7:13 5x) [Deuteronomy]
1209 B2   δέχομαι (1a)   I take, receive (3:21 9x)

1210 C1   δέω (1b)   I bind, tie (9:2 12x)
1220 E2   δηνάριον -ου τό   denarius, a laborer's day's wage (0x)
1223 A1   διά + gen.   through, during, by means of (1:2 54x) [diameter]
1223 A1   διά + acc.   on account of, because (2:26 20x) A&G 178ff
1228 C2   διάβολος -ος -ον   slanderous (10:38 2x) [diabolical]
1242 C2   διαθήκη -ης ἡ   will, testament, covenant (3:25 2x)A&G 182
1247 C2   διακονέω (1b)   I serve, minister (6:2 2x)
1248 C2   διακονία -ας ἡ   service, ministry (1:17 8x) [diaconate]
1249 D1   διάκονος -ου ὁ/ἡ   servant, helper (0x) [deacon]
1252 E1   διακρίνω (4e)   I separate, differentiate, judge (10:20 4x) A&G 184

1256 F1   διαλέγομαι (1a)   I discuss, reason with (17:2 10x)[dialectic]
1258 H2   διάλεκτος -ου ἡ   language of a region (1:19 6x) [dialect]
1260 E2   διαλογίζομαι (4a)   I consider, reason, argue (0x)
1261 F1   διαλογισμός -οῦ ὁ   thought, opinion, dispute (0x)
1263 E2   διαμαρτύρομαι (1a)   I charge, testify (2:40 9x)
1266 F2   διαμερίζω (4a)   I divide, distribute (2:3 2x)
1271 F2   διάνοια -ας ἡ   understanding, mind, purpose (0x)
1295 H1   διασῴζω (4a)   I bring safely through, save (23:24 5x)
1299 E2   διατάσσω (4b)   I order, direct, command (7:44 5x)
1302 D1   διατί (used in Text.Rec. for διὰ τί) why? (5:3 1x)

1304 G2   διατρίβω (1a)   I stay/remain with (12:19 8x) [diatribe]
1308 F1   διαφέρω (8)   I carry through/about, differ (13:49 2x)
1312 H2   διαφθορά -ᾶς ἡ   destruction, corruption (2:27 6x)
1319 D2   διδασκαλία -ας ἡ   teaching, instruction (0x)
1320 B2   διδάσκαλος -ου ὁ   teacher (13:1 1x)
1321 B1   διδάσκω (6)   I teach (1:1 16x) [didactic]
1322 C2   διδαχή -ῆς ἡ   teaching, instruction (2:42 4x)
1325 A1   δίδωμι (7a)   I give (1:26 35x) A&G 191ff
1330 C1   διέρχομαι (8)   I go through, come/go (8:4 21x)
1342 B1   δίκαιος -α -ον   upright, just, righteous (3:14 6x)

1343 B1   δικαιοσύνη -ης ἡ   uprightness, justice, righteousness (10:35 4x) A&G 195
1344 C2   δικαιόω (1b)   I justify, show justice, vindicate (13:39 2x)
1345 G2   δικαίωμα -ατος τό   regulation, righteous deed, requirement (0x)
1350 F2   δίκτυον -ου τό   net (0x)
1352 B2   διό   wherefore, for this reason (10:29 10x)
1360 D2   διότι   because, therefore (13:35 5x)
1372 E2   διψάω (1b)   I thirst, long for (0x)
1375 G2   διωγμός -οῦ ὁ   persecution (8:1 2x)
1377 C1   διώκω (1a)   I hasten, persecute, drive away, pursue (7:52 9x)
1380 B2   δοκέω (1b)   I think, suppose, seem (12:9 9x) [docetic]

1381 D2   δοκιμάζω (4a)   I examine, approve (0x)
1388 G1   δόλος -ου ὁ   deceit, cunning (13:10 1x)
1391 A2   δόξα -ης ἡ   glory, splendor (7:2 4x) [doxology] A&G 202f
1392 B2   δοξάζω (4a)   I praise, glorify (3:13 5x)
1398 D1   δουλεύω (1a)   I serve as/am a slave (7:7 2x)
1401 A2   δοῦλος -ου ὁ   slave (2:18 3x)
1404 F1   δράκων -οντος ὁ   dragon, serpent (0x) [dragon]
1410 A1   δύναμαι (7a)   I can, am able (4:16 21x)
1411 A2   δύναμις -εως ἡ   power, might, strength (1:8 10x) [dynamic]
1415 C2   δυνατός -ή -όν   powerful, strong, able (2:24 6x)

E

1417 A2 δύο dat.pl. δυσί two (1:10 14x) [duo-]
1427 B1 δώδεκα indecl. twelve (6:2 2x) [Dodecanese]
1431 G1 δωρεά -ᾶς ἡ gift (2:28 4x)
1435 E1 δῶρον -ου ὁ gift (0x) [Dorothea 'gift of God']

1437 A1 ἐάν if (2:21 8x) A&G 210f
1438 A1 ἑαυτοῦ -ῆς -οῦ (unused in nom.) self (1:3 21x) A&G 211
1439 F1 ἐάω (1b) I let, permit (5:38 7x)
1448 C1 ἐγγίζω (4a) I approach, come near (7:17 6x)
1451 C2 ἐγγύς near, short time (1:12 3x)
1453 A2 ἐγείρω (4e) I raise, lift up (3:7 14x) A&G 213f
1458 H2 ἐγκαλέω (1b) I accuse, bring charges against (19:38 6x)

1459 G2 ἐγκαταλείπω (2a) I abandon, forsake (2:27 2x)
1473 A1 ἐγώ (for oblique forms v. εμου) I (7:7 44x) [ego]
1484 A2 ἔθνος -ους τό people, nation (2:5 43x) [ethnic]
1485 F2 ἔθος -ους τό habit, custom, usage (6:14 7x) [ethic]
1488 A1 εἰ if, whether (1:6 36x) A&G 217ff
1492 A1 εἶδον (8) I saw, perceived (2:30 49x) see also οἶδα
1497 G1 εἴδωλον -ου τό false god, image, idol (7:41 2x)
1501 G1 εἴκοσι indecl. twenty (1:15 2x)
1504 D2 εἰκών -όνος ἡ image, form, likeness (0x)
1510 A1 εἰμί (7a irreg.) I am (1:7 276x) A&G 221ff

(2036)A1 εἶπον (8) I said (1:7 124x) A&G 225ff
1515 B1 εἰρήνη -ης ἡ peace, order, health (7:26 7x) [irenic]
1519 A1 εἰς + acc. into, in, toward, to (1:10 295x) A&G 227ff
1520 A1 εἷς μία ἕν one (1:22 21x) [henotheism]
1521 G2 εἰσάγω (1a) I bring/lead in (7:45 6x) [isagogics]
1525 A1 εἰσέρχομαι (8) I enter, come/go in (1:13 32x)
1531 E1 εἰσπορεύομαι (1a) I come/go in (3:2 4x)
1534 F1 εἶτα then, next (0x)
1535 B2 εἴτε if, whether (0x)
1537 A1 ἐκ see ἐξ + gen. from, out of (1:18 84x) A&G 233ff

1538 B1 ἕκαστος -η -ον each, every (2:3 11x)
1540 E1 ἑκατόν indecl. hundred (1:15 1x) [hecatomb]
1543 D2 ἑκατοντάρχης -ου ὁ centurion (10:1 13x) A&G 236
1544 B1 ἐκβάλλω (4e) I drive out, remove (7:58 5x)
1563 B1 ἐκεῖ there (9:33 22x)
1564 D1 ἐκεῖθεν from there, thence (13:4 4x)
1565 A1 ἐκεῖνος -η -ο that person/thing (1:19 22x)
1577 A2 ἐκκλησία -ας ἡ assembly, congregation, church (5:11 23x) [ecclesiastical]
1581 G2 ἐκκόπτω (3) I cut off/down (0x)
1586 D2 ἐκλέγομαι (1a) I choose, select (1:2 7x)

1588 D2 ἐκλεκτός -ή -όν chosen, select, choice (0x) [eclectic]
1601 F1 ἐκπίπτω (1a) I fall off/from, lose, fail, run aground (12:7 5x)
1605 F1 ἐκπλήσσω (4b) I astonish, amaze (13:12 1x)
1607 C2 ἐκπορεύομαι (1a) I come/go out/away (9:29 3x)
1614 E1 ἐκτείνω (4e) I stretch out, extend, speak at length (4:30 3x)
1623 F1 ἐκτός outside (26:22 1x)
1632 E1 ἐκχέω (2b) I pour out, (pass.) abandon myself (2:17 3x)
1632 G1 ἐκχύνομαι (listed separately in Morgenthaler) see ἐκχέω
1636 F2 ἐλαία -ας ἡ olive tree (0x)
1637 G1 ἔλαιον -ου τό (olive) oil (0x)

1646 F1 ἐλάχιστος -η -ον smallest, least (0x)
1651 E1 ἐλέγχω (1a) I bring to light, expose, convict (0x)
1653 C2 ἐλεέω (1b) I have mercy on, pity (0x)

1654 F1 ἐλεημοσύνη -ης ἡ kind deed, alms (3:2 8x) [eleemosynary]
1656 D1 ἔλεος -ους τό mercy, compassion (0x)
1657 G1 ἐλευθερία -ας ἡ freedom, liberty (0x)
1658 D2 ἐλεύθερος -α -ον free, not bound (0x)
1679 C2 ἐλπίζω (4a) I hope, hope for (24:26 2x)
1680 B2 ἐλπίς -ίδος ἡ hope, expectation (2:26 8x)
1683 C2 ἐμαυτοῦ -ῆς (unused in nom.) myself (20:24 4x)
1684 E1 ἐμβαίνω (5a) I go/step in, embark (21:6 1x)
1689 G1 ἐμβλέπω (1a) I look at (22:11 1x)
1699 B1 ἐμός -ή -όν my, mine (0x) §23.31

1700 A1 ἐμοῦ ἐμοί ἐμέ (μου μοι με) me, my (cf. #1473 ἐγώ) (1:8
             139x) §23.1f
1702 F1 ἐμπαίζω (4a) I ridicule, deceive (0x)
1715 C1 ἔμπροσθεν in front, ahead, forward; + gen. before (18:17 2x)
1718 G2 ἐμφανίζω (4a) I make visible, reveal, make known (23:15 5x)
1722 A1 ἐν + dat. in, on, among, with, by, etc. (1:3 275x) A&G 257ff
1766 G2 ἔνατος -α -ον (sometimes listed as ἔννατος) ninth (3:1 2x)
1731 G1 ἐνδείκνυμι (7b) I show (0x)

1746 D1 ἐνδύω (1a) I dress, clothe, put on (12:21 1x)
1752 D1 ἕνεκα + gen. because of, on account of, for (19:32 3x)
1754 D2 ἐνεργέω (1b) I work, operate, produce (0x) [energy]
1763 F1 ἐνιαυτός -οῦ ὁ year (11:26 2x)
1766 G2 ἔννατος see ἔνατος ninth
1777 G2 ἔνοχος -ος -ον subject to, liable (0x)
1781 F1 ἐντέλλομαι I command (1:2 2x)
1785 B2 ἐντολή -ῆς ἡ command(ment), order, precept (17:15 1x)
1799 B1 ἐνώπιον + gen. before, in the presence of (2:25 13x) A&G 270
1803 F1 ἕξ indecl. six (11:12 3x) [hexameter]

1806 F2 ἐξάγω (1a) I lead/bring out (5:19 8x) [exegete]
1807 H1 ἐξαιρέω (1b) I take out, set free, deliver (7:10 5x)
1821 F1 ἐξαποστέλλω (4e) I send out/away/forth (7:12 7x)
1831 A1 ἐξέρχομαι (8) I come/go out/away, retire (1:21 29x)
1832 C2 ἔξεστι(ν) (impers.) it is permitted/possible (2:29 4x)
1839 E1 ἐξίστημι (7a) I displace, amaze, confuse, lose my mind (2:7 8x)
1843 G2 ἐξομολογέομαι (1b) I confess, admit (19:18 1x)
1848 G1 ἐξουθενέω (1b) I despise, contemn, reject (4:11 1x)
1849 A2 ἐξουσία -ας ἡ freedom/ability to act, authority (1:7 7x)
1854 B2 ἔξω outside, out; + gen. outside (4:15 10x)
1855 F1 ἔξωθεν from the outside, outside (0x) A&G 279
1859 D1 ἑορτή -ῆς ἡ festival, feast (0x)

1860 B2 ἐπαγγελία -ας ἡ promise, pledge (1:4 8x)
1861 E2 ἐπαγγέλλομαι (4e) I announce, promise, profess (7:5 1x)
1868 G1 ἔπαινος -ου ὁ praise, approval (0x)
1869 E1 ἐπαίρω (4e) I lift/hold up, rise up, put on airs (1:9 5x)
1870 G1 ἐπαισχύνομαι (4e) I feel/am ashamed (0x)
1883 E1 ἐπάνω above, over; + gen. on, over (0x)
1887 E1 ἐπαύριον tomorrow, on the next day (10:9 10x)
1893 D1 ἐπεί when, after, since, because (0x)
1894 G1 ἐπειδή forasmuch as, because (13:46 3x)
1899 E2 ἔπειτα then, thereupon, next (0x)

1905 B2 ἐπερωτάω (1b) I ask, inquire of, ask for (5:27 2x)
1909 A1 ἐπί + gen. on, at, before, in the time of (2:19 28x) A&G 285
1909 A1 ἐπί + dat. on, in, over, during, etc. (2:26 28x) A&G 286

1909 A1 ἐπί + acc. across, on, up to, against, for (1:8 110x) A&G 287ff
1910 H2 ἐπιβαίνω (5) I go upon, mount, board (20:18 5x)
1911 E1 ἐπιβάλλω (4e) I throw over, lay/put upon (4:3 4x)
1921 C1 ἐπιγνώσκω (6) I know (exactly), recognize, learn (3:10 13x)
1922 D2 ἐπίγνωσις -εως ἡ knowledge, recognition (0x)
1929 G2 ἐπιδίδωμι (7a) I give to (15:30 2x)
1934 F1 ἐπιζητέω (1b) I seek for (12:19 3x)

1937 E2 ἐπιθυμέω (1b) I eagerly desire (20:33 1x)
1939 C2 ἐπιθυμία -ας ἡ desire, longing, passion (0x) A&G 293
1941 C2 ἐπικαλέω (1b) I call, name, call upon (1:23 20x)
1949 E1 ἐπιλαμβάνομαι (5b) I take hold of, grasp, take interest in (9:27 7x)
1961 E1 ἐπιμένω (4e) I stay, remain, continue, persevere (10:48 6x)
1966 H3 ἐπιουσα -ης ἡ following (day) (7:26 5x) from ἔπειμι
1968 G1 ἐπιπίπτω (1a) I fall upon, approach eagerly (8:16 6x)
1980 G1 ἐπισκέπτομαι (3) I inspect, visit (6:3 4x)
1987 F1 ἐπίσταμαι (7a) I understand, know (10:28 9x) [epistemology]
1992 D2 ἐπιστολή -ῆς ἡ letter (9:2 5x) [epistle]

1994 C2 ἐπιστρέφω (1a) I turn, return (3:19 11x)
2004 G2 ἐπιτάσσω (4b) I enjoin, order (23:2 1x)
2005 G2 ἐπιτελέω (1b) I bring to an end, fulfill (0x)
2007 C1 ἐπιτίθημι (7a) I lay/put upon, inflict, give (6:6 14x)
2008 D1 ἐπιτιμάω (1b) I rebuke, censure, punish (0x)
2010 E1 ἐπιτρέπω (1a) I allow, permit, order (21:39 5x)
2032 E1 ἐπουράνιος -ος -ον heavenly (0x)
2033 B1 ἑπτά (indecl.) seven (6:3 8x) [heptad]
2038 C2 ἐργάζομαι (4a) I work, am active, do, perform (10:35 3x)
2040 E2 ἐργάτης -ου ὁ worker, workman, laborer (19:25 1x)

2041 A2 ἔργον -ου τό work, deed, manifestation (5:38 10x) [erg]
2036 A1 ἔπω see εἶπον I said (following #1536)
(3004)B1 ἐρῶ (8) I shall say (23:5 7x) usually listed under λέγω
2048 C1 ἔρημος -ος -ον desolate, desert (1:20 9x) [hermit]
2064 A1 ἔρχομαι (8) I come/go (1:11 54x) A&G 310f
2065 B2 ἐρωτάω (1b) I ask (a question), request (1:6 7x)
2068 B2 ἐσθίω (8) I eat, consume (27:35 1x); cf. φάγομαι #5315
2078 B2 ἔσχατος -η -ον last, least (1:8 3x) [eschatology]
2081 F2 ἔσωθεν from inside, within (0x)
2087 B1 ἕτερος -α -ον other (1:20 17x) [heterodox]

2089 B1 ἔτι yet, still (2:26 5x)
2090 C1 ἑτοιμάζω (4a) I prepare, keep ready (23:23 1x)
2092 E1 ἕτοιμος -η -ον ready, prepared (23:15 2x)
2094 C1 ἔτος -ους τό year (4:22 11x)   [evangelize]
2097 C1 εὐαγγελίζω (4a) I bring good news, proclaim, preach (5:42 15x) ↑
2098 B1 εὐαγγέλιον -ου τό good news, gospel (15:7 2x) [evangel]
2106 D2 εὐδοκέω (1b) I am well pleased, consent, approve (0x)
2112 B1 εὐθέως at once, immediately (9:18 9x)
2117 B2 εὐθύς at once, immediately (10:16 1x)
2127 C1 εὐλογέω (1b) I speak well of, praise, bless (3:26 1x)

2129 E2 εὐλογία -ας ἡ praise, blessing (0x) [eulogy]
2135 H1 εὐνοῦχος -ου ὁ eunuch (8:27 5x) [eunuch]
2147 A2 εὑρίσκω (6) I find, discover (4:21 35x) [heuristic]
2150 E2 εὐσέβεια -ας ἡ piety, godliness, religion (3:12 1x)
2165 F1 εὐφραίνω (4e) I rejoice, gladden (2:26 2x)
2168 C2 εὐχαριστέω (1b) I am thankful, give thanks, pray (27:35 2x) [eucharist]

2169 E2 εὐχαριστία -ας ἡ thankfulness, thanksgiving, the Lord's
Supper (24:3 1x) [eucharist]

2186 D2 ἐφίστημι (7a) I stand by, approach, am present (4:1 11x) A&G 330

2190 C2 ἐχθρός -ά -όν hostile, hated; enemy (2:35 2x)

2192 A1 ἔχω (1a) I have, hold, keep (1:12 44x) A&G 332ff

2193 A2 ἕως until, while; + gen. until, as far as (1:8 22x) A&G 334

Z 2198 A2 ζάω (1b) I live (1:3 12x) A&G 336f

2205 E1 ζῆλος -ου ὁ zeal, ardor, jealousy, envy (5:17 2x); also
ζῆλος -ους τό [zeal]

2206 F2 ζηλόω (1b) I am zealous/jealous, envy (7:9 2x)

2212 A2 ζητέω (1b) I seek, look for, investigate (9:11 10x)

2213 H3 ζήτημα -ατος τό question, issue, debate (15:2 5x)

2219 F1 ζύμη -ης ἡ yeast, leaven (0x)

2222 A2 ζωή -ῆς ἡ life, livelihood (2:28 8x) [zoölogy] A&G 340ff

2226 D2 ζῷον -ου τό living thing, being (0x)

2227 G1 ζῳοποιέω (1b) I make to live, keep alive (0x)

H 2228 A1 ἤ or (1:7 27x)

      C1 ἤ than (4:19 8x)

2232 D2 ἡγεμών -όνος ὁ prince, governor (23:24 6x) [hegemony]

2233 D1 ἡγέομαι (1b) I lead, guide, think, consider (7:10 4x)

2235 B2 ἤδη now, already, by this time (4:3 3x)

2240 D1 ἥκω irreg., perf. for pres. I have come, am present (0x)

(2064) ἦλθον (8) I came; usually listed under ἔρχομαι #2064

2246 C2 ἥλιος -ου ὁ sun (2:20 4x) [heliocentric]

2248 A1 ἡμεῖς ἡμῶν ἡμῖν ἡμᾶς we, us (1:17 128x); cf. ἐγώ #1473 and also
##2249, 2254, 2257 in NEGC

2250 A1 ἡμέρα -ας ἡ day (1:2 94x) [hemerobaptist, ephemeral] A&G 346

θ 2281 B1 θάλασσα -ης ἡ sea (4:24 10x) [thalassic]

2288 A2 θάνατος -ου ὁ death (2:24 8x) [thanatophobia]

2289 G1 θανατόω (1b) I kill, deliver to be killed (0x)

2290 G1 θάπτω (3) I bury (2:29 4x) §13.24

2296 C1 θαυμάζω (4a) I wonder, marvel, admire (2:7 5x) [thaumaturgy]

2300 D2 θεάομαι (1b) I look at, behold, am noticed (1:11 3x)

2307 B2 θέλημα -ατος τό will, what is willed (13:22 3x)

2309 A1 θέλω (4e) I wish, will, like (2:12 14x)

2310 E2 θεμέλιος -ου ὁ/-ον τό foundation (stone) (16:26 1x)

2316 A1 θεός -οῦ ὁ God, god (1:3 166x) [theology] A&G 357f

2323 C1 θεραπεύω (1a) I serve, care for, heal (4:14 5x) [therapeutic]

2325 D2 θερίζω (4a) I reap, harvest (0x)

2326 F1 θερισμός -οῦ ὁ harvest (0x)

2334 B2 θεωρέω (1b) I see, look at, behold (3:16 14x) [theory]

2342 C1 θηρίον -ου τό beast, animal (10:12 3x) [theriomorphic]

2344 E1 θησαυρός -οῦ ὁ storehouse, treasure (0x) [thesaurus]

2346 G2 θλίβω (1a) I press, oppress, become restricted (0x)

2347 C1 θλίψις -εως ἡ oppression, affliction, tribulation (7:10 5x)

2359 E2 θρίξ τριχός ἡ (§13.24) hair (27:34 1x) [trichology]

2362 B2 θρόνος -ου ὁ throne, dominion (2:30 2x) [throne]

2364 D1 θυγάτηρ -τρος ἡ daughter (2:17 3x)

2372 E1 θυμός -οῦ ὁ passion, anger, wrath (19:28 1x)

2374 C2 θύρα -ας ἡ door (3:2 10x)

2378 D1 θυσία -ας ἡ sacrifice, offering (7:41 2x)

2379 D2 θυσιαστήριον -ου τό altar (0x)

2380 F1 θύω (1a) I sacrifice, kill (10:13 4x)

I   2390 D1   ἰάομαι (1b)   I heal, cure (9:34 4x)
    2396 D1   ἴδε   listen! behold! see! (0x)
    2398 A2   ἴδιος -α -ον   one's own (1:7 16x) [idiom] A&G 370f
    2400 A1   ἰδού   behold! see! look! (1:10 23x)
    2409 C2   ἱερεύς -έως ὁ   priest (4:1 3x) [hierarchy]
    2411 B1   ἱερόν -οῦ τό   sanctuary, temple (2:46 25x)

    2425 C1   ἱκανός -ή -όν   sufficient, considerable, large, many (8:11 18x)
    2440 B2   ἱμάτιον -ου τό   garment, cloak, clothing (7:58 8x)
    2443 A1   ἵνα   that, in order that (2:25 12x) A&G 377ff
        A2   ἵνα μή   lest (4:17 3x)
    2462 E1   ἵππος -ου ὁ   horse (0x) [hippodrome]
    2476 A2   ἵστημι (7a)   I set, place, establish, stand (1:11 35x) A&G↑382f
    2478 D1   ἰσχυρός -ά -όν   strong, mighty (0x)
    2480 D1   ἰσχύω (1a)   I am strong, able, powerful (6:10 6x)
    2479 G2   ἰσχύς -ύος ἡ   strength (0x)
    2486 D2   ἰχθύς -ύος ὁ   fish (0x) [ichthyology]

K   2504 B1   κἀγώ (§15.52)   and I (8:19 4x)
    2509 E1   καθάπερ   just as (0x)
    2511 C2   καθαρίζω (4a)   I make clean, cleanse (10:15 3x) [catharsis]
    2513 D1   καθαρός -ά -όν   clean, pure (18:6 2x)
    2518 D2   καθεύδω (1a)   I sleep (0x)
    2521 B1   κάθημαι (7a)   I sit, stay, reside (2:2 6x) [cathedral]
    2523 C1   καθίζω (4a)   I cause to sit, seat, set, appoint (2:3 9x)
    2525 D2   καθίστημι (-στάνω) (7a/5a)   I bring, appoint, ordain (6:3 5x)
    2531 A2   καθώς   just as, as, how (2:4 11x) A&G 392
    2532 A1   καί   and, even (1:1 1108x) Note A&G 392ff!

    2537 C1   καινός -ή -όν   new (unused, unknown) (17:19 2x) [cenozoic] A&G 394f
    2540 B1   καιρός -οῦ ὁ   time (point in or period of) (1:7 9x) A&G 395f
    2545 F2   καίω   I burn, light (0x)
    2546 G2   κἀκεῖ (§15.52)   and there, there also (14:7 5x)
    2547 G2   κἀκεῖθεν (§15.52)   and from there, and then (7:4 8x)
    2548 D2   κἀκεῖνος -η -ο (§15.52)   and that one, he also (5:37 3x)
    2549 G1   κακία -ας ἡ   depravity, wickedness (8:22 1x)
    2556 B2   κακός -ή -όν   bad, evil, harm (9:13 4x) [cacophony]
    2559 H2   κακόω (1b)   I harm, mistreat, make angry (7:6 5x)
    2560 E2   κακῶς   badly, wickedly; ἔχω κ. I am ill (23:5 1x)
    2563 F2   κάλαμος -ου ὁ   reed, staff, rod, pen (0x)

    2564 A2   καλέω (1b)   I call, name, address (1:12 18x) A&G 399f
    2570 B1   καλός -ή -όν   beautiful, good, noble (0x) A&G 401
    2573 C2   καλῶς   well, beautifully, right(ly) (10:33 3x)
    2579 E1   κἄν (§15.52)   and if, even if, if only (5:15 1x)
    2586 F1   καπνός -οῦ ὁ   smoke (2:19 1x)
    2588 A2   καρδία -ας ἡ   heart (2:26 20x) [cardiac]
    2590 B2   καρπός -οῦ ὁ   fruit (2:30 1x) [endocarp]
    2596 B1   κατά + gen.   down from, toward, against, throughout (4:26 16x) [cata-]
    2596 A1   κατά + acc.   along, over, through, toward, by (2:10 74x)
    2597 B1   καταβαίνω (5)   I come down, descend (7:15 19x)
    2602 G1   καταβολή -ῆς ἡ   foundation, beginning, sowing (0x)

    2605 E1   καταγγέλλω (4e)   I proclaim (3:24 10x)
    2609 H1   κατάγω (1a)   I lead/bring down (9:30 7x)
    2617 F1   καταισχύνω (4e)   I dishonor, disgrace, shame (0x)
    2618 F2   κατακαίω (4c)   I burn up/down, consume (19:19 1x)
    2621 F2   κατάκειμαι (7a)   I lie down, recline, am sick (9:33 2x)
    2632 E2   κατακρίνω (4e)   I condemn (0x)
    2638 F1   καταλαμβάνω (5b)   I obtain, understand (4:13 3x)

2641 D1 καταλείπω (2a)   I leave behind, neglect, leave over (2:31 5x)
2647 E1 καταλύω (1a)   I throw down, destroy, demolish, halt (5:38 3x)

2657 F1 κατανοέω (1b)   I perceive (7:31 4x)
2658 F1 καταντάω (1b)   I arrive at, come to (16:1 9x)
2673 D1 καταργέω (1b)   I make ineffective, abolish, nullify (0x)
2675 F1 καταρτίζω (4a)   I put in order, restore, repair (0x)
2680 G1 κατασκευάζω (4a)   I make ready, build, equip (0x)
2716 D2 κατεργάζομαι (4a)   I achieve, accomplish, conquer (0x)
2718 E2 κατέρχομαι (8)   I come down (8:5 12x)   A&G 423f
2722 E1 κατέχω (1a)   I hold back/down, restrain, possess, head for (27:40 1x) ↑
2723 D2 κατηγορέω (1b)   I accuse, reproach (22:30 9x)
2730 C1 κατοικέω (1b)   I dwell, live, inhabit (1:19 20x)

2744 C2 καυχάομαι (1b)   I boast, glory (0x)
2745 G1 καύχημα -ατος τό boast, boasting (0x) A&G 426
2746 G1 καύχησις -εως ἡ boasting, reason for boasting (0x) A&G 427
2749 D2 κεῖμαι (7a)   I lie, recline (0x)
2753 D1 κελεύω (1a)   I command, order, urge (4:15 17x)
2756 E1 κενός -ή -όν empty, without basis/truth/power/result (4:25 1x)
2768 G1 κέρας -ατος τό horn (0x)
2770 E2 κερδαίνω (4e)   I gain, spare myself, avoid (27:21 1x)
2776 B1 κεφαλή -ῆς ἡ head (4:11 5x) [cephalic]
2784 B2 κηρύσσω (4b)   I announce, proclaim, preach (8:5 8x)

2798 G1 κλάδος -ου ὁ branch (0x)
2799 C1 κλαίω (4c)   I weep, cry, bewail (9:39 2x)
2806 F1 κλάζω/κλάω (4a)   I break (bread) (2:46 4x)
2808 E2 κλείω (1a)   I shut, lock, bar (5:23 2x)
2812 E2 κλέπτης -ου ὁ thief (0x) [cleptomaniac]
2813 F1 κλέπτω (3)   I steal (0x)
2816 E1 κληρονομέω (1b)   I inherit, acquire (0x)
2817 F1 κληρονομία -ας ἡ inheritance, possession (7:5 2x)
2818 E2 κληρονόμος -ου ὁ heir (0x)
2819 G1 κλῆρος -ου ὁ lot, share, portion (1:17 5x) [clerical] A&G 436

2821 G1 κλῆσις -εως ἡ call(ing), invitation, station (0x)
2822 G2 κλητός -ή -όν called, invited (0x)
2836 D2 κοιλία -ας ἡ body-cavity, belly, womb (3:2 2x) [coele-]
2837 E1 κοιμάομαι (1b)   I (fall a)sleep, die (7:60 3x)
2839 F1 κοινός -ή -όν common, together (2:44 5x) A&G 438f
2840 F1 κοινόω (1b)   I make common, profane (10:15 3x)
2842 E1 κοινωνία -ας ἡ fellowship, communion, sharing (2:42 1x) A&G 439f
2844 G2 κοινωνός -οῦ ὁ companion, one sharing (0x)
2853 F2 κολλάομαι (1b)   I unite, cling to, join with (5:13 5x) [colloid]
2865 G1 κομίζω (4a)   I bring, carry, get, receive, recover (0x)

2872 D2 κοπιάω (1b)   I become weary, tired, toil (20:35 1x)
2873 E1 κόπος -ου ὁ trouble, difficulty, labor, toil (0x)
2885 G2 κοσμέω (1b)   I put in order, adorn (0x)
2889 A2 κόσμος -ου ὁ world, universe, adornment (17:24 1x) [cosmic]
2895 G1 κράβαττος -ου ὁ bed (5:15 2x)
2896 B2 κράζω (4a)   I cry out, scream (7:57 11x)
2902 C1 κρατέω (1b)   I apprehend, grasp, hold (back/fast) (2:24 4x)
2904 F2 κράτος -ους τό power, might (19:20 1x) [autocrat]
2909 E1 κρείσσων -ων -ον (/κρείττων) more prominent/useful, better (0x)
2917 D1 κρίμα -ατος τό dispute, decision, decree (24:25 1x) [criminal]

2919 A2 κρίνω (4e) I separate, judge, consider (3:13 21x) A&G 452f
2920 C1 κρίσις -εως ἡ judging, judgment, condemnation (8:33 1x) [crisis]
2923 E1 κριτής -οῦ ὁ judge (10:42 4x) [critic]
2926 E1 κρυπτός -ή -όν hidden, secret (0x) [crypt, cryptogram]
2928 E1 κρύπτω (3) I hide, conceal (0x)
2936 E2 κτίζω (4a) I create (0x)
2937 E1 κτίσις -εως ἡ creation (act/result), authority (0x)
2962 A1 κύριος -ου ὁ lord, master, sir, Lord (1:6 107x) [Kyrie] A&G 459ff
2967 D2 κωλύω (1a) I hinder, forbid, refuse (8:36 6x)
2968 D1 κώμη -ης ἡ village, small town or its people (8:25 1x)

2974 F1 κωφός -ή -όν dumb, mute (0x)
Λ 2980 A1 λαλέω (1b) I speak, give sound (2:4 60x) [glossolalia] A&G 464
2983 A1 λαμβάνω (5b) I take, receive (1:8 29x) A&G 465f
2992 A2 λαός -οῦ ὁ people (2:47 48x) [laity, layman] A&G 467f
3000 D2 λατρεύω (1a) I serve (cult), worship (7:7 5x)
3004 A1 λέγω (1a) I say, tell (1:3 102x) [lecture]
3022 D1 λευκός ή -όν white, bright (1:10 1x) [leukemia]
3027 E2 λῃστής -οῦ ὁ robber, highwayman, insurrectionist (0x)
3029 F2 λίαν very (much), exceedingly (0x)
3037 B2 λίθος -ου ὁ stone (4:11 2x) [neolithic, lithograph]

3041 G1 λίμνη -ης ἡ lake, pool (0x)[limnetic]
3042 F2 λιμός -οῦ ὁ hunger, famine (7:11 2x)
3049 C1 λογίζομαι (4a) I reckon, calculate (19:27 1x) [logistics]
3056 A1 λόγος -ου ὁ word, message, matter (1:1 65x) [dialogue] A&G 478ff
3062 B2 λοιπός -ή -όν remaining, rest; finally (2:37 6x) A&G 481
3076 D1 λυπέω (1b) I grieve, am sad (0x)
3077 E2 λύπη -ης ἡ grief, sorrow, pain
3087 F2 λυχνία -ας ἡ lampstand (0x)
3088 F1 λύχνος -ου ὁ lamp (0x)
3089 C1 λύω (1a) I loose, untie, set free, abolish (2:24 6x)

M 3101 A1 μαθητής -οῦ ὁ learner, disciple (6:1 28x)
3107 B2 μακάριος -α -ον blessed, happy, fortunate (20:35 2x)
3112 G2 μακράν far, far away (2:39 3x)
3113 F1 μακρόθεν from afar (0x)
3114 G2 μακροθυμέω (1b) I have patience, delay (0x)
3115 F1 μακροθυμία -ας ἡ patience, endurance (0x)
3122 F2 μάλιστα most of all, especially (20:38 3x)
3123 B1 μᾶλλον more, rather (4:19 7x) A&G 490
3129 D1 μανθάνω (5b) I learn, find out (23:27 1x) [polymath]
3140 B1 μαρτυρέω (1b) I am a witness, bear witness (6:3 11x) [martyr] A&G 493f

3141 C2 μαρτυρία -ας ἡ testimony, testifying (22:18 1x)
3142 D2 μαρτύριον -ου τό testimony, proof (4:33 2x)
3144 C2 μάρτυς -υρος ὁ witness (person) (1:8 13x) [martyr]
3162 D1 μάχαιρα -ης ἡ sword (12:2 2x)
3173 A1 μέγας μεγάλη μέγα large, great, rich (2:20 31x) [mega-] A&G 498f
3187 C1 μείζων -ων -ον larger (compar. of μέγας #3173) (0x) A&G 498f
3195 A2 μέλλω (1a irreg.) I am about to (+ inf.) (3:3 34x) A&G 501f
3196 C2 μέλος -ους τό member, part, limb (0x)
3199 G2 μέλει (impers.) it is a care, concern (18:17 1x)   A&G 503f
*3303 A2 μέν (postpos.) on the one hand, but (often not translated) (1:1 47x) ↑

*Strong and NEGC skip from #3202 to #3303 without explanation.

3306 A2 μένω (4e) I remain, stay, wait (5:14 13x)
3307 F1 μερίζω (4a) I divide, separate (0x) [-mer, polymer]
3309 E1 μεριμνάω (1b) I am anxious, concerned (0x)
3313 C1 μέρος -ους τό part, share (2:10 7x) A&G 506f [-mer]
3319 B2 μέσος -η -ον middle, midst (1:15 10x) [Mesolithic] A&G 508f
3326 A1 μετά + gen. with, among (1:26 36x) [meta-] A&G 509ff
3326 A2 μετά + acc. after, behind (1:3 29x) A&G 511
3327 G1 μεταβαίνω (5a irreg.) I depart (18:17 1x)
3340 C2 μετανοέω (1b) I change my mind, repent (2:38 5x)
3341 D2 μετάνοια -ας ἡ change of mind, repentance, conversion (5:31 6x)
3343 H1 μεταπέμπω (1a) I send for, summon (10:5 9x)
3354 G1 μετρέω (1b) I measure, apportion (0x) [metric]

3358 F1 μέτρον -ου τό quantity, measure (0x)
3360 E1 μέχρι + gen. until, as far as, up to (10:30 2x)
3361 A1 μή not (1:4 65x); note usage, A&G 517ff!
3366 B2 μηδέ and not, but not, not even (4:18 2x) A&G 519
3367 B1 μηδείς μηδεμία μηδέν no, nobody/-thing (4:17 21x) A&G 519f
3371 D2 μηκέτι no longer, never again (4:17 3x)
3376 E1 μήν μηνός ὁ month, new moon (7:20 5x) [mensual]
3379 D1 μήποτε lest, never, whether (5:39 2x) A&G 521
3383 C2 μήτε and not, neither, nor (23:8 8x)
3384 B1 μήτηρ μητρός ἡ mother (1:14 4x) [matriarch]

3385 E2 μήτι interrog. part. expecting negative answer (10:47 1x)
3397 E2 μικρόν -οῦ τό a little, insignificant (0x) [micron] A&G 523
3398 C2 μικρός -ά -όν small (8:10 2x) [micro-]
3403 D2 μιμνῄσκομαι (6) I call to mind, remember, mention (10:31 2x)
3404 C2 μισέω (1b) I hate, detest (0x) [misogynist]
3408 D1 μισθός -οῦ ὁ pay, wages, reward (1:18 1x)
3418 G2 μνῆμα -ατος τό tomb, memorial, grave (2:29 2x)
3419 C1 μνημεῖον -ου τό memorial, monument, tomb (13:29 1x)
3421 D2 μνημονεύω (1a) I remember, mention (20:31 2x) [mnemonic]
3431 F1 μοιχεύω (1a) I commit adultery (0x)

3440 B2 μόνον only (8:16 8x)
3441 C1 μόνος -η -ον only, alone (0x) [mono-]
3450 A1 μου μοι με me, my (listed also under 3165, 3427 in NEGC)
3464 F1 μύρον -ου τό ointment, perfume (0x) [myrrh]
3466 D1 μυστήριον -ου τό mystery, secret rite (0x) A&G 531f
3474 F2 μωρός -ά -όν foolish, stupid (0x) [moron]

N 3483 C2 ναί yes, indeed (5:8 2x)
3485 C1 ναός -οῦ ὁ temple (17:24 3x)
3495 G1 νεανίσκος -ου ὁ young man, servant (2:17 4x)
3498 A2 νεκρός -ά -όν dead (3:15 17x) [necropolis, necrology]

3501 D2 νέος -α -ον new, fresh, young (16:11? 1x?) [neo-] A&G 537f
3507 D1 νεφέλη -ης ἡ cloud (1:9 1x) [nephelometer]
3516 F1 νήπιος -α -ον infant, immature Christian (0x)
3520 H1 νῆσος -ου ἡ island (13:6 6x) [Peloponnesus]
3522 D2 νηστεύω (1a) I fast (13:2 2x)
3528 D1 νικάω (1b) I conquer, overcome (0x) [Nike]
3538 E1 νίπτω (3) I wash, wash myself (0x)
3539 F1 νοέω (1b) I understand, perceive (0x) [noetic]
3543 E2 νομίζω (4a) I think, consider; have in common use (7:25 7x) A&G 543
3551 A2 νόμος -ου ὁ law, Torah, scripture (6:13 17x) [Deuteronomy]

3554 G1 νόσος -ου ἡ disease, illness (19:12 1x)

3563 D2 νοῦς νοός νοΐ νοῦν ὁ understanding, mind (0x)
3566 E2 νυμφίος -ου ὁ bridegroom (0x) [nymph, bride]
3568 A2 νῦν now, at the present time (2:33 25x) A&G 547f
3570 E1 νυνί now (22:1 2x) A&G 548
3571 B2 νύξ νυκτός ἡ night (5:19 16x)

Ξ 3579 G2 ξενίζω (4a) I receive as a guest, surprise (10:6 7x)
3581 F1 ξένος -η -ον strange, stranger (17:18 2x) [xenophobia]
3583 E2 ξηραίνω (4e) I dry, dry out, wither (0x)
3586 E1 ξύλον -ου τό wood, tree, gallows/cross (5:30 4x) [xylophone]

Ο 3588 A1 ὁ ἡ τό, τοῦ τῆς τοῦ, pl. οἱ αἱ τά def.art. the (1:1 2688x) A&G 551-555
3592 G2 ὅδε ἥδε τόδε this (one) (15:23 2x) A&G 555
3598 A2 ὁδός -οῦ ἡ road, way (1:12 20x) [odometer]
3599 F2 ὀδούς ὀδόντος ὁ tooth (7:54 1x) [orthodontist]
3606 E2 ὅθεν from where, whence, from which (14:26 3x)
(1492)A1 οἶδα (8; perf. used as pres.) I know (2:22 19x) A&G 558f
3614 B1 οἰκία -ας ἡ house (4:34 12x) [economy]
3617 F2 οἰκοδεσπότης -ου ὁ master of the house (0x)
3618 C2 οἰκοδομέω (1b) I build (up) (7:47 4x)
3619 E1 οἰκοδομή -ῆς ἡ building, construction (0x) A&G 561f

3623 G2 οἰκονόμος -ου ὁ steward, manager, treasurer (0x) [economics]
3624 A2 οἶκος -ου ὁ house, dwelling, family (2:2 25x) A&G 562f
3625 E2 οἰκουμένη -ης ἡ world, inhabited earth (11:28 5x) [ecumenic]
3631 C2 οἶνος -ου ὁ wine (0x)
3634 F1 οἷος -α -ον of what sort, such as (0x)
3641 C1 ὀλίγος -η -ον few, little, brief (12:18 10x) [oligarchy]
3650 A2 ὅλος -η -ον whole, entire (2:2 19x) [holo-, whole]
3660 D1 ὀμνύω (1a) ὄμνυμι (7b) I swear, take an oath (2:30 1x)
3661 G1 ὁμοθυμαδόν with one purpose/mind (1:14 10x)
3664 C1 ὅμοιος -α -ον like, similar (17:29 1x) [homeopathic]

3666 E2 ὁμοιόω (1b) I make like, compare (14:11 1x)
3668 C2 ὁμοίως so, in the same way, similarly (0x)
3670 D2 ὁμολογέω (1b) I promise, admit, confess, declare (7:17 3x)
3686 A1 ὄνομα -ατος τό name (1:15 60x) [onomatopoea] A&G 573-77
3689 G2 ὄντως really, certainly, in truth (0x) [ontology]
3694 C2 ὀπίσω behind, back; + gen. behind, after (5:37 2x) A&G 578
3699 B1 ὅπου where, in so far as, since (17:1 2x)
3700 K ὀπτάνομαι (from stem *οπ usually under ὀράω #3708) I appear
3700 B2 ὄπτομαι (3) sometimes listed as base for ὤφθην, see ὀράω
3704 B2 ὅπως how, in what way, that (3:20 14x) A&G 580
3705 F2 ὅραμα -ατος τό vision, that which is seen (7:31 11x)

3708 A2 ὁράω (1b) I see, notice; (pass.) appear (7:44 16x); note: fut. ὄψομαι
           and 1 aor.pass. ὤφθην are from *οπ, hence the count is inaccurate.
3709 C2 ὀργή -ῆς ἡ anger, wrath (0x) [orgy]
3710 H1 ὁρίζω (4a) I determine, appoint, designate, define (2:23 5x)
3727 G2 ὅρκος -ου ὁ oath (2:30 1x)
3735 B2 ὄρος -ους τό mountain (1:12 3x) [orography]
3739 A1 ὅς ἥ ὅ, οὗ ἧς οὗ who, which, what (1:4 217x) [who] A&G 587ff
3745 A2 ὅσος -η -ον as/how great/far/much/many/long (2:39 17x) A&G 590
3748 A2 ὅστις ἥτις ὅ τι whoever, whatever (3:23 24x) A&G 590f
3752 A2 ὅταν whenever, when, since (23:25 2x) A&G 592
3753 A2 ὅτε when, while, as long as, until (1:13 10x) A&G 592
3754 A1 ὅτι that, "quote," so that, because (1:5 120x) A&G 592ff

3757 D2 οὗ where (1:13 8x)

3756 A1 οὐκ οὐ οὐχ (when not proclitic οὔ) not, no (1:5 110x) §13.3511 A&G 594f
3759 C1 οὐαί woe, alas! (0x)
3761 A2 οὐδέ and not, nor, neither, not even (2:27 12x) A&G 595f
3762 A1 οὐδείς οὐδεμία οὐδέν no one, nobody/-thing (4:12 25x) A&G 596
3763 E2 οὐδέποτε never (10:14 3x)
3765 C1 οὐκέτι no more, no longer/further (8:39 3x)
3767 A1 οὖν (postpos.) therefore, then, however (1:6 62x) A&G 597
3768 D2 οὔπω not yet (0x)
3772 A1 οὐρανός -οῦ ὁ heaven (1:10 26x) [uranium] A&G 598ff

3775 C2 οὖς ὠτός τό ear, hearing (7:51 5x) [otoscope]
3777 B1 οὔτε neither, nor (2:31 14x)
3778 A1 οὗτος αὕτη τοῦτο this (1:5 237x) A&G 600ff
3779 A1 οὕτως/οὕτω thus, in this manner, so (1:11 27x)
3780 B2 οὐχί not, no, by no means (5:4 [2:7 in Nestle] 3x) A&G 603
3784 C2 ὀφείλω (4e) I owe, am indebted (17:29 1x)
3788 A2 ὀφθαλμός -οῦ ὁ eye (1:9 7x) [ophthalmic]
3789 F1 ὄφις -εως ὁ snake, serpent (0x) [ophiology]
3793 A2 ὄχλος -ου ὁ crowd, multitude, populace (1:15 22x) [ochlocracy
3798 F1 ὀψία -ας ἡ evening (0x)

Π 3804 E2 πάθημα -ατος τό suffering, misfortune (0x) [pathology]
3811 F1 παιδεύω (1a) I train, discipline, instruct (7:22 2x) [pedagogy]
3813 B2 παιδίον -ου τό child (0x) [pediatrics]
3814 F1 παιδίσκη -ης ἡ maid, servant-girl (12:13 2x)
3816 D2 παῖς παιδός ὁ/ἡ youth, son, servant (3:13 6x) A&G 609f
3820 E1 παλαιός -ά -όν old, antiquated (0x) [paleolithic] A&G 610
3825 A2 πάλιν back, again, anew (10:15 6x) [palingenesis] A&G 611f
3841 G2 παντοκράτωρ -ορος ὁ the Almighty, omnipotent One (0x)
3842 C1 πάντοτε always, at all times (0x)
3844 B1 παρά + gen. from (the side of), by (2:33 13x) A&G 614f[para-]
3844 B2 παρά + dat. at/by (the side of), near (9:43 8x) A&G 615
3844 B2 παρά + acc. by, at, to, because, against (4:35 9x) A&G 616

3850 B2 παραβολή -ῆς ἡ comparison, parable (0x) [parabola] A&G 617f
3853 C2 παραγγέλλω (4e) I command, instruct, direct (1:4 10x)
3854 C2 παραγίνομαι (1a) I arrive, am present, appear (5:21 20x)
3855 G2 παράγω (1a) I pass by, go away, disappear·(0x) A&G 619
3860 A2 παραδίδωμι (7a) I hand over, deliver, transmit, permit (3:13 13x)
3862 F1 παράδοσις -εως ἡ tradition, transmission (0x)
3868 F2 παραιτέομαι (1b) I ask for, request; decline (25:11 1x) A&G 621f
3870 A2 παρακαλέω (1b) I call to my side, summon, exhort, implore, comfort,
             encourage (2:40 22x) [Paraclete] A&G 622f
3874 D1 παράκλησις -εως ἡ encouragement, exhortation, appeal (4:36 4x)

3880 C1 παραλαμβάνω (5b) I take with/along, receive (15:39 6x)
3885 G2 παραλυτικός -ή -όν paralytic, lame (0x) [paralytic]
3900 E1 παράπτωμα -ατος τό transgression, sin, false step (0x)
3908 E1 παρατίθημι (7a) I place beside/before, set, give over (14:23 4x)
3916 E1 παραχρῆμα at once, immediately (3:7 6x)
3918 D2 πάρειμι (7a irreg.) I am present, have come (10:21 5x) A&G 629f
3925 G2 παρεμβολή -ῆς ἡ camp, barracks, headquarters (21:34 6x)
3928 C2 παρέρχομαι (8) I go/pass by, pass, pass away (16:8 2x)
3930 E2 παρέχω (1a) I offer, present, grant, bring about (16:16 5x)
3933 E2 παρθένος -ου ἡ young woman, virgin (21:9 1x) [Parthenon]

3936 C1   παριστάνω (5a)   I place beside, present, offer (1:3 13x)
3952 D2   παρουσία -ας ἡ   presence, advent, coming (0x) [Parousia]
3954 C2   παῤῥησία -ας ἡ   frankness, outspokenness, boldness (2:29 (4x)
3955 H1   παῤῥησιάζομαι (4a)   I speak freely, boldly (9:27 7x)
3956 A1   πᾶς πᾶσα πᾶν   every, all, the whole (1:1 170x) [pan-] A&G 636f
3957 D1   πάσχα τὸ (indecl.)   Passover, Paschal (12:4 1x) [Paschal]
3958 C1   πάσχω (6; stem *παθ/πνθ?)   I suffer, experience (1:3 5x)
3960 G2   πατάσσω (4b)   I strike, hit (7:24 3x)
3962 A1   πατήρ πατρός ὁ   father (1:4 35x) [paternal, patristic]
3973 E2   παύω (1a)   I stop, cease, halt (5:42 6x)

3982 B2   πείθω (2a)   I convince, persuade, conciliate (5:36 17x)
3983 D2   πεινάω (1b)   I hunger, desire (0x)
3985 C2   πειράζω (4a)   I try, tempt, test (5:9 5x)
3986 D2   πειρασμός -οῦ ὁ   test, trial, temptation (20:19 1x)
3992 B1   πέμπω (1a)   I send (10:5 11x)
3996 G2   πενθέω (1b)   I am sad, grieve, mourn over (0x)
4002 C1   πέντε (indecl.)   five (4:4 5x) [pentagon]
4008 D2   πέραν   on the other side (0x) [Perea]
4012 A1   περί + gen.   about, concerning, regarding (1:3 64x) A&G 650
4012 C2   περί + acc.   around, near, about (10:3 7x) [perimeter]   A&G 650f
4016 D2   περιβάλλω (4e)   I throw around, put on, clothe (12:8 1x)
4043 B1   περιπατέω (1b)   I walk around, go about, walk, go (3:6 8x)

4052 C2   περισσεύω (1a)   I am rich,   (3s) it is more than enough (16:5 1x) A&G 656
4053 E2   περισσότερος -α -ον   greater, more (0x)
4056 G1   περισσοτέρως   far more, far greater, especially (0x)
4058 G2   περιστερά -ᾶς ἡ   pigeon, dove (0x)
4059 E1   περιτέμνω (5a)   I cut off/around, circumcise (7:8 5x)
4061 C2   περιτομή -ῆς ἡ   circumcision, the Jews (7:8 3x) A&G 658
4071 F1   πετεινόν -οῦ τὸ   bird (10:12 2x)
4073 E2   πέτρα -ας ἡ   rock, stone (0x) [petrify, petroleum]
4077 G1   πηγή -ῆς ἡ   spring, fountain (0x)
4084 F2   πιάζω (4a)   I take hold of, seize (3:7 2x)

(4130)D2   πίμπλημι (7a)   I fill, fulfill (2:4 9x); see πλήθω.
4095 B1   πίνω (5a)   I drink (9:9 3x)
4098 B1   πίπτω (1a, stem *πετ)   I fall (down) (1:26 9x)
4100 A1   πιστεύω (1a)   I believe (2:44 37x) A&G 665ff, esp. ¶2aα-δ
4102 A1   πίστις -εως ἡ   faith, trust, faithfulness (3:16 15x) A&G 668f
4103 B2   πιστός -ή -όν   trustworthy, faithful, trusting (10:45 4x)
4105 C2   πλανάω (1b)   I lead astray, wander, deceive (0x) [planet]
4106 G2   πλάνη -ης ἡ   wandering, delusion, deception (0x)
4118 B2   πλείων -ων -ον, gen. -ονος   more (2:40 19x?), usually s. πολύς
4124 G2   πλεονεξία -ας ἡ   greediness, avarice, covetousness (0x)
4127 D2   πληγή -ῆς ἡ   blow, stroke, wound (16:23 2x) [plague]

4128 C2   πλῆθος -ους τὸ   number, multitude (2:6 16x) [plethora] A&G 674
4129 F2   πληθύνω (4e)   I increase, multiply (6:1 5x)
4130 D2   πλήθω s. πίμπλημι (7a)   I fill, fulfill (2:4 9x)
4133 C2   πλήν   only, nevertheless, in any case, however (8:1 4x)
4134 E1   πλήρης -ης -ες   filled, full, complete (6:3 8x)
4137 B1   πληρόω (1b)   I make full, fill, complete, fulfill (1:16 16x)
4138 E1   πλήρωμα -ατος τὸ   that which fills or makes full, fulness (0x)
4139 E1   πλησίον   near; + gen. near; subst. ὁ neighbor (7:27 1x)
4143 B2   πλοῖον -ου τὸ   ship, boat (20:13 19x)
4145 D1   πλούσιος -ία -ιον   rich, wealthy (0x)

4147 F2   πλουτέω (1b)   I am rich (0x)

4149 D2 πλοῦτος -ου ὁ wealth, riches (0x) [plutocrat]
4151 A1 πνεῦμα -ατος τό wind, breath, spirit (1:5 70x) A&G 680ff
4152 D1 πνευματικός -ή -όν pertaining to spirit, spiritual (0x) [pneumatic]
4159 D1 πόθεν from where? whence? how? in what way? (0x)
4160 A1 ποιέω (1b) I do, make, bring into being (1:1 68x) [poet]
4164 G2 ποικίλος -η -ον of various kinds, manifold (0x)
4165 G1 ποιμαίνω (4e) I tend sheep (20:28 1x)
4166 E1 ποιμήν -ένος ὁ sheep herder, shepherd (0x)
4169 C2 ποῖος -α -ον of what kind? what? (4:7 3x)

4171 E1 πόλεμος -ου ὁ war, battle, strife (0x) [polemic]
4172 A2 πόλις -εως ἡ city-state, city (4:26 42x) [metropolis]
4178 E1 πολλάκις many times, often, frequently (26:11 1x)
4183 A1 πολύς πολλή πολύ much, many, great (1:3 46x) [poly-]
4190 B1 πονηρός -ά -όν sick, evil, wicked (17:5 8x)
4198 A2 πορεύομαι (1a) I go, proceed, travel (1:10 37x)
4202 D1 πορνεία -ας ἡ fornication, unlawful sexual union (15:20 3x)
4204 F2 πόρνη -ης ἡ prostitute, harlot (0x)
4205 G2 πόρνος -ου ὁ fornicator, immoral person (0x) [pornography]
4214 D1 πόσος -η -ον how great? how much? how many? (21:20 1x)

4215 E1 ποταμός -οῦ ὁ river, stream (16:13 1x) [Mesopotamia]
4218 D1 ποτέ at some time or other, once, at times (0x)
4219 E1 πότε when? until when? (0x)
4221 C2 ποτήριον -ου τό cup (0x)
4222 E2 ποτίζω (4a) I give/cause to drink, water (0x) [potion]
4226 C1 ποῦ where? at which place? to what place? (0x)
4228 B1 πούς πόδος ὁ foot (2:35 19x) [podiatry, decapod]
4229 G1 πρᾶγμα -ατος τό deed, event, thing, task (5:4 1x) [pragmatic]
4238 C2 πράσσω (4b) I do, accomplish (3:17 13x)
4240 G1 πραΰτης -ητος ἡ gentleness, humility, courtesy (0x)

4245 B2 πρεσβύτερος -ου ὁ older, elder (2:17 18x) [presbyter]
4250 F1 πρίν, πρίν ἤ before, formerly (2:20 3x)
4253 C1 πρό + gen. before, in front of, above (5:36 7x) [pro-]
4254 E1 προάγω (1a) I lead/bring out, go before, lead (12:6 3x)
4263 C1 πρόβατον -ου τό sheep (8:32 1x)
4286 F2 πρόθεσις -εως ἡ setting forth, plan, purpose (11:23 2x) [prothetic]
4314 K   πρός + gen. to the advantage of, for (27:34 1x)
4314 H2 πρός + dat. near, at, by, in addition to (0x)
4314 A1 πρός + acc. towards, for, on behalf of, against (1:7 133x)
4327 F1 προσδέχομαι (1a) I welcome, receive, look for (23:21 2x)

4328 E2 προσδοκάω (1b) I wait/look for, expect (3:5 5x)
4334 B1 προσέρχομαι (8) I come/go to, approach (7:31 10x)
4336 B1 προσεύχομαι (1a) I pray (1:24 16x)
4335 C2 προσευχή -ῆς ἡ prayer, place of prayer (1:14 9x)
4337 D2 προσέχω (1a) I pay attention to, heed, take care (5:35 6x)
4341 C2 προσκαλέω (1b) I summon, call, invite (2:39 9x)
4342 G2 προσκαρτερέω (1b) I adhere to, persist in, hold fast (1:14 6x)
4352 B2 προσκυνέω (1b) I worship, do reverence to (7:43 4x) [proskynesis]

4355 F2 προσλαμβάνω (5b) I receive, partake, take as associate (17:5 6x)
4369 E1 προστίθημι (7a) I add, put to (2:41 6x) [prosthesis]

4374 C1 προσφέρω (8) I bring (to), offer (7:42 3x)
4383 B1 πρόσωπον -ου τό face, countenance (2:28 11x) A&G 728f

4387 G1 πρότερος -α -ον former, earlier, superior (0x)
4394 E1 προφητεία -ας ἡ prophecy, gift of prophecy (0x)
4395 D1 προφητεύω (1a) I prophesy, proclaim, foretell (2:17 4x)
4396 A2 προφήτης -ου ὁ prophet (2:16 30x) [prophet]
4404 F2 πρωΐ early (in the morning) (28:23 1x)
4412 B2 πρῶτον at first, in the first place (3:36 5x) [proton]
4413 A2 πρῶτος -η -ον first, earliest, foremost (1:1 11x) [proto-]
4438 C2 πτωχός -ή -όν begging, poor, beggarly (0x)

4439 G2 πύλη -ης ἡ gate, door (3:10 3x)
4440 E1 πυλών -ῶνος ὁ gate, entrance (10:17 5x) [pylon]
4441 G1 πυνθάνομαι (5b) I inquire, ask, learn (4:7 7x)
4442 B1 πῦρ πυρός τό fire (2:3 4x) [pyrotechnics, pyre]
4453 D2 πωλέω (1b) I sell (4:34 3x)
4454 F2 πῶλος -ου ὁ young animal, young donkey (0x)
4458 F1 πως (no accent) somehow, in some way, perhaps (27:12 1x)
4459 A2 πῶς how? in what way? (2:8 9x)

P 4461 E2 ῥαββί/ῥαββεί Rabbi (0x)
   4464 G1 ῥάβδος -ου ἡ rod, staff, stick (0x)

4487 B1 ῥῆμα ῥήματος τό word, saying, matter, thing (2:14 14x)
4491 E2 ῥίζα -ης ἡ root (0x)
4506 E2 ῥύομαι (1a) I save, rescue, deliver, preserve (0x)

Σ 4521 B2 σάββατον -ου τό Sabbath, week (1:12 10x) A&G 746
   4531 E2 σαλεύω (1a) I shake, agitate, overthrow (2:25 4x)
   4536 G1 σάλπιγξ -ιγγος ἡ trumpet (0x)
   4537 F2 σαλπίζω (4a) I (sound the) trumpet (0x)
   4561 A2 σάρξ σαρκός ἡ flesh (2:17 3x) [sarcophagus]
   4566 C2 σατάν ὁ (indecl.), σατανᾶς -ᾶ ὁ adversary, Satan (5:3 2x)
   4572 C1 σεαυτοῦ -ῆς (not used in nom.) yourself (sg.) (9:34 3x)

4576 G2 σέβομαι I worship, revere (13:43 8x)
4578 F1 σεισμός -οῦ ὁ earthquake, shaking (16:26 1x) [seismic]
4592 B1 σημεῖον -ου τό sign, mark, miracle (2:19 13x)
4594 C1 σήμερον today, this very day (4:9 9x)
4624 D1 σκανδαλίζω (4a) I cause to fall/stumble, shock (0x) [scandalize]
4601 G2 σιγάω (1b) I am silent, hold my peace (12:17 3x)
4621 F1 σῖτος -ου ὁ wheat, grain (7:12 2x)
4623 G2 σιωπάω (1b) I keep silent, become quiet (18:9 1x)
4625 E2 σκάνδαλον -ου τό temptation to sin, offense (0x) [scandal]
4632 D2 σκεῦος -ους τό vessel, jar, dish (9:15 5x)

4633 D2 σκηνή -ῆς ἡ tent, booth, Tabernacle (7:43 3x) [scene]
4653 E1 σκοτία -ας ἡ darkness, gloom (0x) [scotopia]
4655 D1 σκότος -ους τό darkness, gloom (2:20 3x)
4674 D1 σός σή σόν (§23.31) your, yours (sg.) (5:4 3x) A&G 766
4678 B2 σοφία -ας ἡ wisdom (6:3 4x) [philosophy]
4680 D2 σοφός -ή -όν clever, wise, skillful (0x) [sophomore]
4687 B2 σπείρω (4e) I sow, scatter (0x)
4690 C1 σπέρμα -ατος τό seed, descendants (3:25 4x) [sperm]
4697 F2 σπλαγχνίζομαι (4a) I feel sympathy with/for (0x)
4698 G1 σπλάγχνον -ου τό, usually pl. τά σπλάγχνα bowels, affections
         (1:18 1x) A&G 770

4704 G1 σπουδάζω (4a) I am zealous/eager, I hurry (0x)
4710 F2 σπουδή -ῆς ἡ haste, speed, eagerness (0x)
4716 D1 σταυρός -οῦ ὁ stake, cross (0x)

4717 C1 σταυρόω (1b) I crucify, put on the stake (2:36 2x)
4735 D1 στέφανος -ου ὁ wreath, crown (0x) [Stephan]
4739 G2 στήκω (used in pres. and impf., formed from ἵστημι) I stand firm (0x)

4741 F1 στηρίζω (4a) I fix, strengthen, confirm, establish (18:23 1x)
4750 B1 στόμα -ατος τό mouth (1:16 12x) [stoma]
4755 G2 στρατηγός -οῦ ὁ chief magistrate, captain (4:1 8x)
4757 D1 στρατιώτης -ου ὁ soldier (10:7 13x)

4762 E1 στρέφω (1a) I turn, return, change (7:39 3x)
4771 A1 σύ σοῦ σοί σέ (§23.13) you (sg.) (1:24 137x) also enclitic
4802 G2 συζητέω (1b) I discuss, dispute (6:9 2x)
4808 E2 συκῆ -ῆς ἡ fig tree (0x)
4815 E2 συλλαμβάνω (5b) I seize, grasp, conceive (1:16 4x) A&G 784
4851 E1 συμφέρω (8) I bring together, help; it is profitable (19:19 2x)
4862 A2 σύν + dat. with (1:14 52x) [syn- sym- syl]
4863 B1 συνάγω (1a) I gather, bring together, lead to (4:5 11x)
4864 B2 συναγωγή -ῆς ἡ place of assembly, meeting (6:9 19x) [synagogue]
4889 G2 σύνδουλος -ου ὁ fellow-slave (0x)

4892 D2 συνέδριον -ου τό high council (4:15 14x) [Sanhedrin]
4893 C2 συνείδησις -εως ἡ consciousness, conscience (23:1 2x) A&G 794
4904 F1 συνεργός -ός -όν fellow-worker, helper (0x)
4905 C2 συνέρχομαι (8) I come together, assemble, travel with (1:6 16x)
4912 F2 συνέχω (1a) I hold together, constrain, stop (7:57 3x)
4920 D1 συνίημι (7a irreg. A&G 797) I understand (7:25 4x)
4921 E2 συνίστημι (7a)/συνιστάνω (5a) I bring together, present, establish (0x)
         A&G 798
4969 G2 σφάζω (4a) I slaughter, murder (0x)
4970 G1 σφόδρα very mucy, extremely, greatly (6:7 1x)
4972 E2 σφραγίζω I seal, attest (0x)

4973 E2 σφραγίς -ίδος ἡ seal, stamp, that which attests (0x)
4977 G2 σχίζω (4a) I split, rend (14:4 2x) [schism]
4982 A2 σῴζω (4a) I save, rescue, preserve (2:21 13x)
4983 A2 σῶμα -ατος τό body (9:40 1x) [somatic]
4990 D2 σωτήρ σωτῆρος ὁ savior, deliverer (5:31 2x) [soteriology]
4991 C1 σωτηρία -ας ἡ deliverance, salvation, preservation (4:12 6x)

T 5007 F1 τάλαντον -ου τό talent (measure of weight/money) (0x)
  5013 F1 ταπεινόω (1b) I humble, humiliate (0x)
  5015 E1 ταράσσω (4b) I shake together, stir up, trouble (15:24 3x)
  5030 G2 ταχέως quickly, without delay (0x)

5035 E1 ταχύ quickly, without delay (14:2 1x) [tachometer]
5037 A1 τε (encl.) and, both (1:1 140x)
5043 B1 τέκνον -ου τό child (2:39 5x)
5046 E1 τέλειος -α -ον complete, perfect, having attained the purpose (0x)
         [teleology]
5048 D2 τελειόω (1b) I bring to an end, accomplish, fulfill (20:24 1x)
5053 G1 τελευτάω (1b) I die (2:29 2x)
5055 D1 τελέω (1b) I bring to an end, complete, accomplish (13:29 1x)
5056 C1 τέλος -ους τό end, conclusion, goal (0x)
5057 D2 τελώνης -ου ὁ tax-collector (0x)
5059 E2 τέρας -ατος τό portent, omen, wonder (2:19 9x)

5062 D2 τεσσαράκοντα (indecl.) forty (1:3 8x)
5064 C1 τέσσαρες -ες -α (pl. only) four (10:11 6x)
5067 G2 τέταρτος -η -ον one-fourth, quarter (10:30 1x)

5083 B1 τηρέω (1b) I keep watch over, keep, hold, observe (12:5 8x)
5087 A2 τίθημι (7a) I put, place, serve, remove (1:7 23x) A&G 823f
5088 E1 τίκτω (1a, stem τεκ, *τιτεκω > τικτω) I bear, give birth to (0x)
5091 D2 τιμάω (1b) I estimate, set a price on, honor (28:10 1x)
5092 C1 τιμή -ῆς ἡ price, value, honor, compensation (4:34 6x)
5093 F1 τίμιος -α -ον valuable, precious, respected (5:34 2x)
5100 A1 τις τι, gen. τινός (§23.34, encl.) any/some -one/thing (2:45 112x)
5101 A1 τίς τί, gen. τίνος (§23.5) who? which? what? (1:11 55x)

5108 B2 τοιοῦτος -αύτη -οῦτον of such a kind, such (16:24 4x)
5111 E2 τολμάω (1b) I dare, have courage (5:13 2x)
5117 B1 τόπος -ου ὁ place, position, region (1:25 18x) [topography]
5118 G2 τοσοῦτος -αύτη -οῦτον so great/strong/much (5:8 2x)
5119 A2 τότε at that time, then, thereupon (1:12 21x)
---- E1 τουτέστι(ν) found in some texts for τουτ᾽ εστι(ν)
5132 E2 τράπεζα -ης ἡ table, meal, bank (6:2 2x)
5140 B2 τρεῖς τρεῖς τρία (pl. only) three (5:7 12x)
5143 E1 τρέχω (8) I run (0x)
5144 G1 τριάκοντα (indecl.) thirty (0x)

5151 F2 τρίς three times, thrice (10:16 2x) [trisagion, tricycle]
5154 C1 τρίτος -η -ον third (2:15 4x) [tritium]
5158 F1 τρόπος -ου ὁ manner, way, kind, guise (1:11 4x) [-trope]
5160 E2 τροφή -ῆς ἡ nourishment, food (2:46 7x) [atrophy]
5177 F2 τυγχάνω (5b) I meet, attain, find, happen to be (19:2 5x)
5179 E2 τύπος -ου ὁ mark, copy, figure (7:43 3x) [type]
5180 F1 τύπτω (3) I strike, beat (18:17 5x)
5185 B2 τυφλός -ή -όν blind (13:11 1x)
5198 F2 ὑγιαίνω (4e) I am healthy/sound (0x) [hygiene]
5199 G1 ὑγιής -ής -ές healthy, sound (4:10 1x)

5204 B1 ὕδωρ ὕδατος τὸ water (1:5 7x) [hydro-]
5207 A1 υἱός -οῦ ὁ son (2:17 21x) A&G 841ff
5210 A1 ὑμεῖς ὑμῶν ὑμῖν ὑμᾶς (§23.14) you (pl.) (1:5 121x) NEGC 5209 5213 5216
5212 G2 ὑμέτερος -α -ον belonging to you, your (27:34 1x)
5217 B1 ὑπάγω (1a) I go away, go (0x)
5218 E2 ὑπακοή -ῆς ἡ obedience (0x)
5219 D2 ὑπακούω (1a) I obey, follow, hear (6:7 2x)
5221 G2 ὑπαντάω (1b) I go to meet (16:16 1x)
5225 B2 ὑπάρχω (1a) I exist, am present, am (2:30 25x)
5228 A2 ὑπέρ + gen. for, in behalf of (5:41 7x) A&G 846f
5228 E1 ὑπέρ + acc. above, beyond (26:13 1x) A&G 847 [hyper-]

5257 D2 ὑπερέτης -ου ὁ servant, helper, assistant (5:22 4x)
5259 A2 ὑπό + gen. by (2:24 38x) A&G 850f
5259 B2 ὑπό + acc. under, below (2:5 3x) A&G 851 [hypo-]
5266 G2 ὑπόδημα -ατος τὸ sandal, footwear (7:33 2x)
5270 G1 ὑποκάτω under, below (0x)
5273 E1 ὑποκριτής -οῦ ὁ pretender (0x) A&G 853 [hypocrite]
5278 E1 ὑπομένω (4e) I remain, stay, wait (17:14 1x)
5281 C2 ὑπομονή -ῆς ἡ patience, endurance, stedfastness (0x)
5290 C2 ὑποστρέφω (1a) I turn back, return (1:12 11x)
5293 C2 ὑποτάσσω (4b) I subject, become subject (0x) [hypotaxis][
5302 E2 ὑστερέω (1b) I come too late, miss, am in need, lack, fail (0x)

5305 F1 ὕστερος -α -ον the latter, in the second place (0x)[hysteron]
5308 G1 ὑψηλός -ή -όν high, exalted, proud (13:17 1x)
5310 F1 ὕψιστος -η -ον highest, most exalted (7:48 2x)

5312 D2 ὑψόω (1b) I lift up, exalt (2:33 3x)

Φ 5315 B1 φάγω (8) I eat (9:9 6x), usually s. ἐσθίω # 2068

5316 C2 φαίνω (4e) I shine, appear, am revealed (0x) [epiphany]

5318 D2 φανερός -ά -όν visible, clear, evident, plain (4:16 2x)

5319 C1 φανερόω (1b) I reveal, make known, become known (0x)

5339 G2 φείδομαι (1a) I spare, refrain from (20:29 1x)

5342 B2 φέρω (8) I bear; carry, endure (2:2 10x) [Christopher]

5343 C2 φεύγω (2a) I flee, escape, seek safety (7:29 2x) [refuge]

5346 B2 φημί (7a irreg.) I say, affirm (2:38 24x)

5357 F2 φιάλη -ης ἡ bowl (0x) [vial, phial]

5368 D1 φιλέω (1b) I love, like (0x)

5384 D1 φίλος -η -ον beloved, dear; friend (10:24 3x) [philosophy]

5399 B1 φοβέομαι (1b) I am afraid, fear (5:26 14x) [phobia] A&G 870f

5401 C1 φόβος -ου ὁ causing fear, fear, fright, reverence (2:43 5x)

5407 F2 φονεύω (1a) I murder, kill (0x)

5426 D1 φρονέω (1b) I think, set my mind on (28:22 1x)

5429 F1 φρόνιμος -ος -ον sensible, thoughtful, wise (0x)

5438 C1 φυλακή -ῆς ἡ guarding, guard, prison (5:19 16x)

5442 C2 φυλάσσω (4b) I watch, guard, keep, guard against (7:53 8x)

5443 C2 φυλή -ῆς ἡ tribe, nation (13:21 1x) [-phyle]

5449 F2 φύσις -εως ἡ natural endowment, nature (0x) A&G 877

5452 G1 φυτεύω (1a) I plant (0x) [phytogenesis]

5455 C1 φωνέω (1b) I produce a sound, speak loudly (9:41 4x) [phone]

5456 A2 φωνή -ῆς ἡ sound, noise, voice (2:6 27x) [phonetic]

5457 B1 φῶς φωτός τό light (9:3 10x) [photography, photometer]

5461 G1 φωτίζω (4a) I shine, illuminate, enlighten, reveal (0x)

X 5463 B1 χαίρω (4e) I rejoice, am glad (5:41 7x)

5479 B2 χαρά -ᾶς ἡ joy, gladness (8:8 4x) A&G 883f

5483 D2 χαρίζομαι (4a) I give freely, remit, pardon (3:14 4x)

5485 A2 χάρις -ιτος ἡ graciousness, grace, favor (2:47 17x) [charity]

5486 E1 χάρισμα -ατος τό gift, favor freely bestowed (0x) [charism]

5495 A2 χείρ χειρός ἡ hand (2:23 45x) [chiropractice] A&G 888

5501 G1 χείρων -ων -ον gen. -ονος worse, more severe (0x)

5503 D1 χήρα -ας ἡ widow (6:1 3x)

5506 D2 χιλίαρχος -ου ὁ commander of 1,000, tribune (21:31 21x)

5505 D2 χιλιάς -άδος ἡ thousand (4:4 1x) [chiliasm]

5507 G1 χίλιοι -αι -α (pl. only) thousand (0x)

5509 G1 χιτών -ῶνος ὁ tunic, shirt (9:39 1x)

5519 F2 χοῖρος -ου ὁ young pig, swine (0x)

5526 E2 χορτάζω (4a) I feed, eat my fill, am satisfied (0x)

5528 E2 χόρτος -ου ὁ grass, hay (1 Cor. 3:12) (0x)

5530 G1 χράομαι (1b) I use, deal with, employ (27:3 2x)

5532 C1 χρεία -ας ἡ need, necessity (2:45 5x)

5544 G2 χρηστότης -ητος ἡ goodness, kindness, uprightness (0x)

5550 B2 χρόνος -ου ὁ time, period of time (1:6 17x) [chronology]

5553 F1 χρυσίον -ου τό gold, gold ornaments (3:6 2x)

5557 E1 χρυσοῦς -ῆ -οῦν golden (0x) [chrysanthemum]

5560 F1 χωλός -ή -όν lame, crippled (3:2 3x)

5561 D1 χώρα -ας ἡ region, country, land (8:1 8x) [epichoristic]

5564 G2 χωρίον -ου τό piece of land, field, surrounding region (1:18 7x)

5562 G2 χωρέω I go, go out, go forward, contain, grasp (0x) A&G 897f

5563 F1 χωρίζω I separate, go away (1:4 3x)

	5565	C1	χωρίς separately, apart; + gen. separated from (0x)
Ψ	5574	F2	ψεύδομαι (1a) I lie, deceive (5:3 2x) [pseudo-]
	5578	G1	ψευδοπροφήτης -ου ὁ false prophet (13:6 1x)
	5579	G2	ψεῦδος -ους τό lie, falsehood (0x)
	5583	G2	ψεύστης -ου ὁ liar (0x)
	5590	A2	ψυχή -ῆς ἡ life-principle, life, soul (2:27 15x) [psyche]
Ω	5599	E2	ὦ O! (1:1 4x)
	5602	B2	ὧδε here, in this place, hither (9:14 2x)
	5610	A2	ὥρα -ας ἡ hour, short period (2:15 11x) [horologe]
	5613	A1	ὡς as, like, while, when, after (1:10 65x) A&G 905ff
	5615	E1	ὡσαύτως similarly, in the same way (0x)
	5616	C2	ὡσεί as, something like, about (1:15 6x)
	5618	C1	ὥσπερ just as (2:2 3x) A&G 908
	5620	B1	ὥστε for this reason, so that, in order that (1:19 8x)
	5623	E2	ὠφελέω (1b) I help, aid, am of use to (0x)

[A note on word-counts is in order. Authorities differ, for (1) the various
editions of the text have different readings at many points; (2) different men
count forms of the same basic word in different ways; and (3) errors creep in.
For example, Morgenthaler gives the total as 5,436 words, but lists 5,438 (without numbering them). Strong's Concordance (followed by the New Englishmen's
Greek Concordance) skips from 3202 to 3303, and numbers the nom., gen., dat., and
acc. of certain pronouns separately. One wonders why the comparative πρεσβύτερος
is numbered, when νεώτερος is not, or why the neuter forms of some nouns are numbered separately as adverbs, while improper prepositions are not so listed; or
why the oblique singular forms are listed under ἐγώ while the plural forms are
not (although in both cases they are not derived from ἐγώ). I have tried to eli-
minate some of the inconsistencies, but am aware that I have not eliminated all
of them. I have omitted all proper names, since they can usually be recognized
on sight. I have included all words occurring 10 times or more in the NT and 5
times or more in Acts.]

Group 1 (Lesson 4)

3588 A ὁ ἡ τὸ the (def.art.)
3303 A μέν (postpos.) on the one hand, but; often not translated
4012 A περί + gen. about, concerning, with respect to
3450 A μου μοι με me, my (cf. #1700)
5037 A τε (encl.) and, both
2532 A καί and, even
 891 C ἄχρι + gen. until, as far as
1223 A διά + gen. through, during, by means of
3326 A μετά + acc. after, behind
1722 A ἐν + dat. in, on, among, with, by, etc.

Group 2 (Lesson 5)

3056 A ὁ λόγος -ου word, message, matter [dialogue]
 652 B ὁ ἀπόστολος -ου messenger, delegate [apostle]
2316 A ὁ θεός -ου God, god [theology]
4413 A πρῶτος -η -ον first, earliest, foremost [prototype]
3739 A ὅς ἥ ὅ who, which, what [who]
2250 A ἡ ἡμέρα -ας day [ephemeral]
  40 A ἅγιος -α -ον holy, sacred [hagiographa]
 932 A ἡ βασιλεία -ας kingship, kingdom [basilica]
1860 B ἡ ἐπαγγελία -ας promise, pledge
1438 A ἑαυτοῦ -ῆς -οῦ (not used in nom.) self, oneself

Group 3 (Lesson 6)

 575 A ἀπό + gen. from [apostate]
3361 A μή not
3754 A ὅτι that, so that, because, "quote"
1161 A δέ (postpos.) but, and (often untranslated)
3756 A οὐκ οὐ οὐχ not, no
3767 A οὖν therefore, then, however
1488 A εἰ if, whether
4314 A πρός + acc. towards, for, on behalf of, against [prosthetic]
2228 A ἤ or, than
1909 A ἐπί + acc. across, on, up to, against, for [epicenter]

Group 4 (Lesson 7)

3507 D ἡ νεφέλη -ης cloud [nephelometer]
3788 A ὁ ὀφθαλμός -οῦ eye [ophthalmic]
3772 A ὁ οὐρανός -οῦ heaven [Uranus]
1849 A ἡ ἐξουσία -ας freedom/ability to act, authority
2540 B ὁ καιρός -οῦ time (point in or period of)
2962 A ὁ κύριος -ου lord, master, Lord, sir [Kyrie]
5550 B ὁ χρόνος -ου time, period of time [chronology]
 846 A αὐτός -ή -ό self, same; 3d sg. pron. (except nom.) [automatic]
3778 A οὗτος αὕτη τοῦτο this
1700 A ἐμοῦ ἐμοί ἐμέ me, my

Group 5 (Lesson 8)

3735 B τὸ ὄρος -ους mountain [orography]
1135 A ἡ γυνή γυναικός woman [gynecology]
3384 B ἡ μήτηρ μητρός mother [maternal]
1411 A ἡ δύναμις -εως power, might, strength [dynamic]
3144 C ὁ μάρτυς -υρος witness (person) [martyr]
3962 A ὁ πατήρ πατρός father [paternal]
3956 A πᾶς πᾶσα πᾶν every, all, the whole [panchromatic]

4151 A τὸ πνεῦμα -ατος wind, breath, spirit [pneumatic]
 435 A ὁ ἀνήρ ἀνδρός male, man [androgynous]
5204 B τὸ ὕδωρ ὕδατος water [hydroelectric]

Group 6 (Lesson 9)

3319 B μέσος -η -ον middle, midst [Mesopotamia]
3793 A ὁ ὄχλος -ου crowd, multitude, populace [ochlophobia]
3686 A τὸ ὄνομα -ατος name [onomatopoea]
1124 B ἡ γραφή -ῆς scripture [Hagiographa]
4750 B τὸ στόμα -ατος mouth [stoma]
1248 C ἡ διακονία -ας service, ministry [diaconate]
4521 B τὸ σάββατον -ου Sabbath, week
3598 A ἡ ὁδός -οῦ road, way [odometer]
  80 A ὁ ἀδελφός -οῦ brother [Philadelphia]
1093 A ἡ γῆ γῆς earth, ground, land [geometry]

Group 7 (Lesson 10)

2078 B ἔσχατος -η -ον last, least [eschatology]
3753 A ὅτε when, while, as long as, until
4862 A σύν + dat. with [syn-, sym- syl-]
 129 B τὸ αἷμα -ατος blood [haemoglobin]
1537 A ἐξ ἐκ + gen. from, out of [exit, exodus]
5620 B ὥστε for this reason, so that, in order that
1063 A γάρ (postpos.) for, so
1565 A ἐκεῖνος -η -ο that person/thing
2048 C ἔρημος -ος -ον desolate, desert [hermit]
2087 B ἕτερος -α -ον other [heterodox]

Group 8 (Lesson 11)

 908 D τὸ βάπτισμα -ατος baptism [baptism]
 386 C ἡ ἀνάστασις -εως resurrection, rise
1520 A εἷς μία ἕν one [henotheism]
4183 A πολύς πολλή πολύ much, many, great [polysyllabic]
 235 A ἀλλά but, yet, rather
1473 A ἐμοῦ ἐμοί ἐμέ (μου μοι με) me, my
5210 A ὑμεῖς ὑμῶν ὑμῖν ὑμᾶς you (pl.)
1519 A εἰς + acc. into, in, toward, to [eisagogic]
2193 A ἕως until, while; + gen. until, as far as
2248 A ἡμεῖς ἡμῶν ἡμῖν ἡμᾶς we, us

Group 9 (Lesson 12)

4771 A σύ σοῦ σοί σέ (σου σοι σε) you (sing.)
3326 A μετά + gen. with, among [meta-]
5117 B ὁ τόπος -ου place, position, region [topography]
2398 A ἴδιος -α -ον one's own [idiom]
5613 A ὡς as, like, while, when, after
5101 A τίς τίς τί (τίνος) who? which one? what?
2400 A ἰδού behold! see! look!
3779 A οὕτω(ς) thus, in this manner, so
5119 A τότε at that time, then, thereupon
1451 C ἐγγύς near, short time

Group 10 (Lesson 14)

4160 A ποιέω (1b) I do, make, bring into being [poet]
 756 B ἄρχω (1a) I rule, ἄρχομαι I begin [monarch]
1321 B διδάσκω (6) I teach [didactic]

3004 A λέγω (8) I say, tell [lecture]
3936 C παριστάνω (5a) I place beside, present, show, offer
2198 A ζάω (1b) I live
3958 C πάσχω (6) I suffer, experience [pathology (stem παθ]
1163 A δεῖ (only in 3d sing.) it is necessary
1831 A ἐξέρχομαι (8) I come/go out/away, retire
1125 A γράφω (1a) I write, record [autograph]

Group 11 (Lesson 15)

3853 C παραγγέλλω (4e) I command, instruct, direct
 191 A ἀκούω (1a) I hear [acoustic]
 907 B βαπτίζω (4a) I baptize [baptize]
4905 C συνέρχομαι (8) I come together, assemble, travel with
2065 B ἐρωτάω (1b) I ask, request
2036 A εἶπον (8) I said
1510 A εἰμί (7a) I am
1097 A γινώσκω (6) I know, comprehend [Gnosis, know]
5087 A τίθημι (7a) I put, place, serve, remove
2983 A λαμβάνω (5b) I take, receive

Group 12 (Lesson 16)

4130 D πίμπλημι (7a) I fill, fulfill
2980 A λαλέω (1b) I speak, give sound [glossolalia]
 991 A βλέπω (1a) I see, look at
1869 E ἐπαίρω (4e) I lift/hold up, rise up, put on airs
 816 F ἀτενίζω (4a) I gaze upon, look intently at
4198 A πορεύομαι (1a) I go, proceed, travel
2476 A ἵστημι (7a) I set, place, establish, stand
2064 A ἔρχομαι (8) I come/go
2300 D θεάομαι (1b) I look at, behold, am noticed
5290 C ὑποστρέφω (1a) I turn back, return

Group 13 (Lesson 17)

1839 E ἐξίστημι (7a) I displace, amaze, confuse, lose my mind
2296 C θαυμάζω (4a) I wonder, marvel, admire [thaumaturgy]
2564 A καλέω (1b) I call, name, address
2192 A ἔχω (1a) I have, hold, keep
1525 A εἰσέρχομαι (8) I enter, come/go in
 305 B ἀναβαίνω (5a) I go up, ascend
4336 C ἡ προσευχή -ῆς prayer, place of prayer
 450 A ἀνίστημι (7a) I raise, rise, get up
1096 A γίνομαι (1a) I come to be, become
4137 B πληρόω (1b) I make full, fill, complete, fulfill

Group 14 (Lesson 18)

5342 B φέρω (8) I bear, carry, endure [Christopher]
4815 E συλλαμβάνω (5a) I seize, grasp, conceive
1632 E ἐκχέω (2b) I pour out, (pass.) abandon myself
2730 C κατοικέω (1b) I dwell, live, inhabit
2521 B κάθημαι (7a) I sit, stay, reside [cathedral]
2523 C καθίζω (4a) I cause to sit, seat, set, appoint
1941 C ἐπικαλέω (1b) I call, name, call upon
4336 B προσεύχομαι (1a) I pray
1325 A δίδωμι (7a) I give
4098 B πίπτω (1a) I fall, fall down

Group 15 (Lesson 19)

4561 A ἡ σάρξ σαρκός flesh [sarcophagus]
5207 A ὁ υἱός -οῦ son
2364 D ἡ θυγάτηρ -τρος daughter
4245 B ὁ πρεσβύτερος -ου elder, (adj.) older [presbyter]
1401 A ὁ δοῦλος -ου slave [hyperdulia]
5059 E τὸ τέρας -ατος portent, omen, wonder
4942 B τὸ σημεῖον -ου sign, mark, miracle
2246 C ὁ ἥλιος -ου sun [helium, heliocentric]
4655 D τὸ σκότος -ους darkness, gloom
4396 A ὁ προφήτης -ου prophet [prophet]

Group 16 (Lesson 20)

1492 A οἶδα (8) I know
5495 A ἡ χείρ χειρός hand [chiropractice]
 337 D ἀναιρέω (8) I take away, destroy
3089 C λύω (1a) I loose, untie, set free, abolish
2288 A ὁ θάνατος -ου death [thanatophobia, euthanasia]
1415 C δυνατός -ή -όν powerful, strong, able
2443 A ἵνα that, in order that; ἵνα μή lest
1799 B ἐνώπιον + gen. before, in the presence of
1188 B δεξιός -ά -όν right (hand/side) [dextral, ambidextrous]
2902 C κρατέω (1b) I apprehend, grasp, hold (back/fast) [autocrat]

Group 17 (Lesson 21)

1223 A διά + acc. on account of, because
2588 A ἡ καρδία -ας heart [cardiac]
2089 B ἔτι yet, still
1680 B ἡ ἐλπίς -ίδος hope, expectation
5590 A ἡ ψυχή -ῆς life-principle, life, soul [psyche, psychology]
3761 A οὐδέ and not, nor, neither, not even
1909 A ἐπί + gen. on, at, before, etc.
2222 A ἡ ζωή -ῆς life, livelihood [zoölogy]
4383 B τὸ πρόσωπον -ου face, countenance
1832 C ἔξεστι(ν) (impersonal verb) it is permitted/possible

Group 18 (Lesson 22)

5225 B ὑπάρχω (1a) I exist, am present, am
1909 A ἐπί + dat. on. in. over. during. etc.
2590 B ὁ καρπός -οῦ fruit [endocarpal]
2362 B ὁ θρόνος -ου throne, dominion [throne]
1492 A εἶδον (8) I saw, perceived
3568 A νῦν now, at the present time
5312 D ὑψόω (1b) I lift up, exalt
3844 B παρά + gen. from (the side of), by [paradigm]
3954 C ἡ παῤῥησία -ας frankness, outspokenness, boldness (or παρρησία)
4531 E σαλεύω (1a) I shake, agitate, overthrow

Group 19 (Lesson 23)

2190 C ἐχθρός -ά -όν hostile, hated, enemy
 302 A ἄν -soever (often impossible to translate)
4228 B ὁ πούς ποδός foot [tripod, podiatry]
4717 C σταυρόω (1b) I put on the stake, crucify
3062 B λοιπός -ή -όν remaining, rest; finally
3340 C μετανοέω (1b) I change my mind, repent
 859 E ἡ ἄφεσις -εως release, pardon

 266 A   ἡ ἁμαρτία -ας   sin [hamartiology]
5043 B   τὸ τέκνον -ου   child
3745 A   ὅσος -η -ον   as/how   great/far/much/many/long

Group 20   (Lesson 24)

  93 D   ἡ ἀδικία -ας   unrighteousness, wrongdoing
5618 C   ὥσπερ   just as
2531 A   καθῶς   just as, as, how
5259 B   ὑπό + acc.   under, below [hypodermic]
3780 B   οὐχί   not, no, by no means
4459 A   πῶς   how? in what way?
2596 A   κατά + acc.   along, over, through, toward, by [catalog]
1065 C   γε (encl.)   yet, at least
1437 A   ἐάν   if
4341 C   προσκαλέω (1b)   I summon, call, invite

Group 21   (Lesson 25)

5259 A   ὑπό + gen.   by
3757 D   οὗ   where
1577 A   ἡ ἐκκλησία -ας   assembly, congregation, church [ecclesiastical]
2036 A   εἶπον (8)   I said
4487 B   τὸ ῥῆμα -ατος   word, saying, matter, thing
3650 A   ὅλος -η -ον   whole, entire [holo-, holocaust]
3624 A   ὁ οἶκος -ου   house, dwelling, family
3777 B   οὔτε   neither, nor
1100 B   ἡ γλῶσσα -ης   tongue, language [isogloss, glossolalia]
4442 B   τὸ πῦρ πυρός   fire [pyre, pyrotechnics]

Group 22   (Lesson 26)

1263 E   διαμαρτύρομαι (4e)   I charge, testify
3870 A   προσκαλέω (1b)   I call to my side, summon, exhort, implore, comfort,
            encourage [Paraclete]
1074 C   ἡ γενεά -ᾶς   family, descent, race [genealogy]
4369 E   προστίθημι (7a)   I add, put to [prosthesis]
5100 A   τις τις τι (τινὸς) (encl.)   any/some-one/thing
1322 C   ἡ διδαχή -ῆς   teaching, instruction [didactic]
1012 F   ἡ βουλή -ῆς   purpose, decision
 740 A   ὁ ἄρτος -ου   bread, loaf
5401 C   ὁ φόβος -ου   causing fear, fear, fright, reverence [phobia]
4100 A   πιστεύω (1a)   I believe

Group 23   (Lesson 28)

 154 B   αἰτέω (1b)   I ask, request, demand
3195 A   μέλλω (1a)   I am about to (+ inf.)
2836 D   ἡ κοιλία -ας   body-cavity, belly, womb [coele-]
 941 D   βαστάζω (4a)   I take up, carry, endure
2374 C   ἡ θύρα -ας   door
1531 E   εἰσπορεύομαι (1a)   I come/go in, enter
4328 E   προσδοκάω (1b)   I wait/look for, expect
4982 A   σῴζω (4a)   I save, rescue, preserve
1538 B   ἕκαστος -η -ον   each, every
5456 A   ἡ φωνή -ῆς   sound, noise, voice [phonetic]

Group 24   (Lesson 29)

4043 B   περιπατέω (1b)   I walk around, go about, walk, go
1453 A   ἐγείρω (4e)   I raise, lift up

5615 C ὡσεί as, something like, about
1484 A τὸ ἔθνος -ους people, nation [ethnic]
 537 C ἅπας -ασα -αν the whole, all, everybody/-thing
5610 A ἡ ὥρα -ας hour, short period [horologe]
4118 B πλείων -ων -ον (πλείονος) more (often listed under πολύς)
5485 A ἡ χάρις -ιτος graciousness, grace, favor [charity]
5160 E ἡ τροφή -ῆς nourishment, food [atrophy]
2992 A ὁ λαός -οῦ people [laity, layman]

Group 25 (Lesson 30)

1921 C ἐπιγνώσκω (6) I know (exactly), recognize, learn
 611 A ἀποκρίνομαι (4e) I answer, reply)
3816 D ὁ/ἡ παῖς παιδός youth, son, servant
1392 B δοξάζω (4a) I praise, glorify
3816 D ὁ/ἡ παῖς παιδός youth, son, servant [pedagogue]
3860 A παραδίδωμι (7a) I hand over, deliver, transmit, permit
 720 C ἀρνέομαι (1b) I deny, refuse, repudiate
2919 A κρίνω (4e) I judge, separate, consider
 630 B ἀπολύω (1a) I set free, pardon
2411 B τὸ ἱερόν -οῦ sanctuary, temple

Group 26 (Lesson 31)

1342 B δίκαιος -α -ον upright, just, righteous
5483 D χαρίζομαι (4a) I give freely, remit, pardon
5532 C ἡ χρεία -ας need, necessity
 615 B ἀποκτείνω (4e) I kill
3498 A νεκρός -ά -όν dead [necrology, necropolis]
4102 A ἡ πίστις -εως faith, trust, faithfulness
2334 B θεωρέω (1b) I see, look at, behold [theory]
4238 C πράσσω (4b) I do, accomplish
 758 C ὁ ἄρχων -οντος ruler, prince, official [monarch, oligarch]
5154 C τρίτος -η -ον third [tritium, trito-Isaiah]

Group 27 (Lesson 32)

1994 C ἐπιστρέφω (1a) I turn, return
3704 B ὅπως how, in what way, that
 649 A ἀποστέλλω (4e) I send away [apostle]
1209 B δέχομαι (1a) I take, receive
 165 A ὁ αἰών -ῶνος long time, age, eon, world, eternity [eon, aeon]
3748 A ὅστις ἥτις ὅ τι (neut. always two words) whoever, whatever
2605 E καταγγέλλω (4e) I proclaim
1242 C ἡ διαθήκη -ης will, testament, covenant
4690 C τὸ σπέρμα -ατος seed, descendants [sperm]
 694 D τὸ ἀργύριον -ου silver, money [argyrol, argent]

Group 28 (Lesson 33)

4412 B πρῶτον at first, in the first place [proton]
2127 C εὐλογέω (1b) I speak well of, praise, bless [eulogy]
2186 D ἐφίστημι (7a) I stand by, approach, am present
2409 C ὁ ἱερεύς -έως priest [hierarchy, hieroglyph]
1911 E ἐπιβάλλω (4e) I throw over, lay/put on
2235 B ἤδη now, already, by this time
 706 E ὁ ἀριθμός -οῦ number [arithmetic]
5505 D ἡ χιλιάς -άδος, group of 1,000 [chiliasm, kilometer]
4002 C πέντε (indecl.) five [pentagon, pentapolis]
4863 B συνάγω (1a) I gather, bring together, lead to [synagogue]

Group 29   (Lesson 34)

243 A   ἄλλος -η -ο   other [allopath]
4169 C   ποῖος -α -ον   of what kind? what?
4594 C   σήμερον   today, this very day
350 E   ἀνακρίνω (4e)   I question, examine, judge
444 A   ὁ ἄνθρωπος -ου   man, human being [anthropoid]
772 D   ἀσθενής -ής -ές   weak, feeble [asthenia]
3037 B   ὁ λίθος -ου   stone [neolithic, lithography]
2776 B   ἡ κεφαλή -ῆς   head [cephalic]
3762 A   οὐδείς οὐδεμία οὐδέν   no one, nobody/-thing
4991 C   ἡ σωτηρία -ας   deliverance, salvation, preservation [soteriology]

Group 30   (Lesson 35)

2323 C   θεραπεύω (1a)   I serve, care for, heal [therapeytic]
2753 D   κελεύω (1a)   I command, order, urge
1854 B   ἔξω   outside, out; + gen. outside
4892 D   τὸ συνέδριον -ου   council, high council [Sanhedrin]
565 A   ἀπέρχομαι (8)   I go away, depart
240 A   ἀλλήλων (pl.gen., no nom.)   one another
5318 D   φανερός -ά -όν   visible, clear, evident, plain
1410 A   δύναμαι (7a)   I can, am able
3371 D   μηκέτι   no longer, never again
3367 B   μηδείς μηδεμία μηδέν   no, nobody/-thing

Group 31   (Lesson 36)

3123 B   μᾶλλον   more, rather
2147 A   εὑρίσκω (6)   I find, discover [heuristic, eureka!]
2094 C   τὸ ἔτος -ους   year
2756 E   κενός -ή -όν   empty, without basis/truth/power/result
935 A   ὁ βασιλεύς -έως   king [basilica]
2596 B   κατά + gen.   down from, toward, against, throughout [cata-]
225 A   ἡ ἀλήθεια -ας   truthfulness, truth
518 C   ἀπαγγέλλω (4e)   I report, announce
142 A   αἴρω (4e)   I take/lift up, take away
2281 B   ἡ θάλασσα -ης   sea [thalassic, thalassocracy]

Group 32   (Lesson 37)

1614 E   ἐκτείνω (4e)   I stretch out, extend, speak at length
1189 D   δέομαι (2b)   I pray, ask, beg
3844 B   παρά + acc.   by, at, to, because, against [parabola]
4172 A   ἡ πόλις -εως   city-state, city [metropolis, politician]
3366 B   μηδέ   and not, but not, not even
1122 B   ὁ γραμματεύς -έως   secretary, clerk, scribe
749 A   ὁ ἀρχιερεύς -έως   high priest
1085 D   τὸ γένος -ους   race, descendants, people [genocide]
4128 C   τὸ πλῆθος -ους   number, multitude [plethora]
3004 B   ἐρῶ (8)   I shall say (usually listed under λέγω)

Group 33   (Lesson 38)

591 C   ἀποδίδωμι (7a)   I give away/out/up, return, reward
3142 D   τὸ μαρτύριον -ου   testimony, proof
3614 B   ἡ οἰκία -ας   house [economia]
4453 D   πωλέω (1b)   I sell
5092 C   ἡ τιμή -ῆς   price, value, honor, compensation
3874 D   ἡ παράκλησις -εως   encouragement, exhortation, appeal
3173 A   μέγας μεγάλη μέγα   large, great, rich [megalopolis, mega-]

(3700)B ὄπτομαι (8) I see (sometimes listed as base for ὤφθην, see ὁράω)
1110 E γνωστός -ή -όν known, remarkable, intelligible [Gnostic]
3313 C τὸ μέρος -ους part, share

Group 34 (Lesson 39)

  68 C ὁ ἀγρός -οῦ field [agronomy, agriculture]
4566 C ὁ σατάν (indecl.) adversary, Satan
3306 A μένω (4e) I remain, stay, wait
1586 D ἐκλέγομαι (1a) I choose, select [eclectic]
3916 E παραχρῆμα at once, immediately
  27 B ἀγαπητός -ή -όν beloved
  37 D ἁγιάζω (4a) I sanctify, consecrate
  50 D ἀγνοέω (1b) I do not know, am ignorant [agnostic]
  79 D ἡ ἀδελφή -ῆς sister
166 B αἰώνιος -α -ον eternal, ages ago

Group 35 (Lesson 41)

5140 B τρεῖς τρεῖς τρία (pl. only) three [triad]
3483 C ναί yes, indeed
3985 C πειράζω (4a) I try, tempt, test
  189 D ἡ ἀκοή -ῆς hearing, listening, ear
  264 C ἁμαρτάνω (5a) I sin, do wrong
1302 D διατί why?
  514 C ἄξιος -α -ον worthy, equal in value [axiology]
4674 D σός σή σόν you, yours (sing.)
  571 D ἄπιστος -ος -ον unbelievable, unbelieving
  680 C ἅπτω (3) I light, touch, hold

Group 36 (Lesson 42)

5111 E τολμάω (1b) I dare, have courage
4337 D προσέχω (1a) I pay attention to, heed, take care
  169 C ἀκάθαρτος -ος -ον unclean, impure [catharsis]
2205 E ὁ ζῆλος -ου (τὸ ζῆλος -ους) zeal, ardor, jealousy, envy [zeal]
  769 D ἡ ἀσθένεια -ας sickness, weakness, timidity [asthenia]
  782 B ἀσπάζομαι (4a) I greet, welcome
  906 A βάλλω (4e) I throw, place, put [ballistics, parabola]
  987 C βλασφημέω (1b) I revile, blaspheme [blaspheme]
1121 E τὸ γράμμα -ατος letter, document [telegram, grammatical]
1127 D γρηγορέω (1b) I am awake/alert

Group 37 (Lesson 43)

2808 E κλείω (1a) I shut, lock, bar
  32 A ὁ ἄγγελος -ου messenger, angel [angel]
3571 A ἡ νύξ νυκτός night [nocturnal]
  455 B ἀνοίγω (1a) I open
5438 A ἡ φυλακή -ῆς guarding, guard, prison [prophylactic]
3854 C παραγίνομαι (1a) I arrive, am present, appear
  71 B ἄγω (1a) I lead, bring
5257 D ὁ ὑπηρέτης -ου servant, helper, assistant
1176 D δέκα (indecl.) ten [Decalogue, Decapolis]
1344 C δικαιόω I justify, show justice, vindicate

Group 38 (Lesson 44)

1905 B ἐπερωτάω (1b) I ask, inquire of, ask for
1014 C βούλομαι (1a) I wish, want, desire
5399 B φοβέομαι (1b) I am afraid, fear [phobia]
1360 D διότι because, therefore

1564 D ἐκεῖθεν from there, thence
1679 C ἐλπίζω (4a) I hope, hope for
1683 C ἐμαυτοῦ -ῆς (unused in nom.) myself
1752 D ἕνεκα + gen. because of, on account of, for
1785 B ἡ ἐντολή -ῆς command(ment), order, precept
 868 F ἀφίστημι I mislead, withdraw, keep away

Group 39 (Lesson 45)

4337 D προσέχω (1a) I pay attention to, heed, take care
4253 C πρό + gen. before, in front of, above [profess, procephalic]
3586 E τὸ ξύλον -ου wood, tree, gallows/cross [xylophone]
4990 D ὁ σωτήρ -τῆρος savior, deliverer [soteriology]
3341 D ἡ μετάνοια -ας change of mind, repentance, conversion
3982 B πείθω (2a) I convince, persuade, conciliate
1320 B ὁ διδάσκαλος -ου teacher
2068 B ἐσθίω (8) I eat, consume
2090 C ἑτοιμάζω (4a) I prepare, keep ready
2307 B τὸ θέλημα -ατος will, what is willed

Group 40 (Lesson 46)

3694 C ὀπίσω behind, back; + gen. behind, after
2548 D κἀκεῖνος (crasis) and that one, he also
.622 B ἀπόλλυμι (7a) I destroy, ruin, lose, perish
 863 A ἀφίημι (7a) I let go, send away, remit
5185 B τυφλός -ή -όν blind
2041 A τὸ ἔργον -ου work, deed, manifestation [erg, energy]
2647 E καταλύω (1a) I throw down, destroy, demolish, halt
3379 D μήποτε lest, never, whether
1194 E δέρω (4e) I beat, strike
5463 B χαίρω (4e) I rejoice, am glad

Group 41 (Lesson 47)

4129 F πληθύνω (4e) I increase, multiply
3101 A ὁ μαθητής -οῦ learner, disciple
5503 D ἡ χήρα -ας widow
1427 B δώδεκα (indecl.) twelve [Dodecanese]
2641 D καταλείπω (2a) I leave behind, neglect, leave over
1247 C διακονέω (1b) I serve, minister [diaconate]
5132 E ἡ τράπεζα -ης table, meal, bank [trapezoid]
3140 B μαρτυρέω I am a witness, bear witness [martyr]
2033 B ἑπτά (indecl.) seven [heptad]
4134 E πλήρης -ης -ες filled, full, complete

Group 42 (Lesson 48)

4864 B ἡ συναγωγή -ῆς place of assembly, meeting [synagogue]
2480 D ἰσχύω (1a) I am strong, able, powerful
3551 A ὁ νόμος -ου law, Torah, scripture [Deuteronomy, agronomy]
1484 A τὸ ἔθνος -ους people, nation [ethnic]
1439 F ἐάω (1a) I let. permit
3973 E παύω (1a) I stop, cease, halt [pause]
2097 C εὐαγγελίζω (4a) I bring good news, proclaim, preach [evangelize]
4678 B ἡ σοφία -ας wisdom [philosophy]
2525 D καθίστημι (7a; καθιστάνω 5a) I bring, appoint, ordain
1485 F τὸ ἔθος -ους habit, custom [ethic]

Group 43 (Lesson 49)

1391 A ἡ δόξα -ης glory, splendor [doxology]

```
1166 C   δείκνυμι (7b)   I show, point out [deictic]
 599 A   ἀποθνήσκω (5)   I die
 968 F   τὸ βῆμα -ατος   tribunal, judicial bench [bema]
1398 D   δουλεύω (1a)   I am a slave, serve as a slave
1473 A   ἐγώ  I  [ego, egocentric]
3000 D   λατρεύω (1a)   I serve (cult), worship
4061 C   ἡ περιτομή -ῆς   circumcision, the Jews
4059 E   περιτέμνω (5a)   I cut off/around, circumcise
2007 C   ἐπιτίθημι (7a)   I lay/put upon, inflict, give
```

Group 44   (Lesson 50)

```
2347 C   ἡ θλίψις -εως   oppression, affliction, tribulation
2233 D   ἡγέομαι (1b)   I guide, lead, think, consider
1208 C   δεύτερος -α -ον   second [Deuteronomy, deuterocanonical]
2597 B   καταβαίνω (5a)   I come down, descend
 837 D   αὐξάνω (5a)   I grow, increase, cause to grow [auxanometer]
5219 D   ὑπακούω (1a)   I obey, follow, hear
5346 B   φημί (7a)   I say, affirm
1080 B   γεννάω (1b)   I beget, bear
1417 A   δύο (pl.dat. δυσί(ν))   two [duo-]
2537 C   καινός -ή -όν   new (unused, unknown) [cenozoic]
```

Group 45   (Lesson 51)

```
1448 C   ἐγγίζω (4a)   I approach, come near
3376 E   ὁ μήν μηνός   month, new moon [mensual]
2378 D   ἡ θυσία -ας   sacrifice, offering
4374 C   προσφέρω (8)   I bring (to), offer
4633 D   ἡ σκηνή -ῆς   tent, booth, lodging, Tabernacle [scene]
5179 E   ὁ τύπος -ου   mark, copy, figure [type]
4352 B   προσκυνέω (1b)   I worship, do reverence to [proskynesis]
1299 E   διατάσσω (4b)   I order, direct, command
5062 D   τεσσαράκοντα (indecl.)   forty
2309 A   θέλω (1a)   I wish, will, like  [monothelite]
```

Group 46   (Lesson 52)

```
  91 D   ἀδικέω (1b)   I act unjustly, do wrong, hurt
3543 E   νομίζω (4a)   I think, consider, have in common use
4920 D   συνίημι (7a)   I understand
1515 B   ἡ εἰρήνη -ης   peace, order, health [irenic]
4139 E   πλησίον  near; + gen.  near; ὁ πλησίος -ου  neighbor
5343 C   φεύγω (2a)   I flee, escape, seek safety [refuge]
3618 C   οἰκοδομέω (1b)   I build, build up
3705 F   τὸ ὅραμα -ατος   vision, that which is seen
3708 A   ὁράω (1b, 8)   I see, notice; (pass.) I appear
3775 C   τὸ οὖς ὠτός   ear, hearing [otoscope]
```

Group 47   (Lesson 54)

```
2896 B   κράζω (4a)   I cry out, scream
1544 B   ἐκβάλλω (4e)   I drive out, remove
2440 B   τὸ ἱμάτιον -ου   garment, cloak, clothing
2837 E   κοιμάομαι (1b)   I (fall a)sleep, die
5561 D   ἡ χώρα -ας   region, country, land [epichoristic]
4133 C   πλήν   only, nevertheless, in any case, however
4334 B   προσέρχομαι (8)   I come/go to, approach
4762 E   στρέφω (1a)   I turn, return, change
 321 D   ἀνάγω (1a)   I lead/bring up, sail
3485 C   ὁ ναός -οῦ   temple
```

Group 48   (Lesson 55)

1330 C   διέρχομαι (8)   I go through, come, go
2718 E   κατέρχομαι (8)   I come down
2784 B   κηρύσσω (4b)   I announce, proclaim, preach
5479 B   ἡ χαρά -ᾶς   joy, gladness
3398 C   μικρός -ά -όν   small [microscope, microbe]
2425 C   ἱκανός -ή -όν   sufficient, considerable, large, many
3408 D   ὁ μισθός -οῦ   pay, wages, reward
4395 D   προφητεύω (1a)   I prophesy, proclaim, foretell
 686 C   ἄρα   so then, indeed
5443 C   ἡ φυλή -ῆς   tribe, nation [phyle, phylon]

Group 49   (Lesson 56)

3768 D   οὔπω   not yet
3440 B   μόνον   only
(2064)A   ἦλθον (8)   I came (s. ἔρχομαι #2064)
1377 C   διώκω (1a)   I hasten, persecute, drive away, pursue
5442 C   φυλάσσω (4b)   I watch, guard, keep, guard against
5055 D   τελέω (1b)   I bring to an end, complete, accomplish [teleological]
3419 C   τὸ μνημεῖον -ου   memorial, monument [mnemonic]
3908 E   παρατίθημι (7a)   I place beside/before, set, give over
3606 E   ὅθεν   from where, whence, from which
1535 B   εἴτε   if, whether

Group 50   (Lesson 57)

2968 D   ἡ κώμη -ης   village, small town, the people of a town
 314 C   ἀναγινώσκω (6)   I read, read aloud
4263 C   τὸ πρόβατον -ου   sheep
2920 C   ἡ κρίσις -εως   judging, judgment, condemnation [crisis]
2098 B   τὸ εὐαγγέλιον -ου   good news, gospel [evangel]
4202 D   ἡ πορνεία -ας   fornication, unlawful sexual union [pornography]
5015 E   ταράσσω (4b)   I shake together, stir up, trouble
3880 C   παραλαμβάνω (5b)   I take with/along, receive
4052 C   περισσεύω (1a)   I am rich; (impers.) it is more than enough
3928 C   παρέρχομαι (8)   I go/pass by, pass, pass away

Group 51   (Lesson 58)

2967 D   κωλύω (1a)   I hinder, forbid, refuse
3765 C   οὐκέτι   no more, lo longer/further
1699 B   ἐμός -ή -όν   my, mine
3930 E   παρέχω (1a)   I offer, present, grant, being about
4127 D   ἡ πληγή -ῆς   blow, stroke, wound [plague]
5108 B   τοιοῦτος -αύτη -οῦτον   of such a kind, such
1198 E   ὁ δέσμιος -ου   prisoner
1199 D   ὁ δεσμός -οῦ   bond, fetter
3022 D   λευκός -ή -όν   white, bright [leukemia]
3699 B   ὅπου   where, insofar as, since

Group 52   (Lesson 59)

1992 D   ἡ ἐπιστολή -ῆς   letter [epistle]
1210 C   δέω (1b)   I bind
5457 B   τὸ φῶς φωτός   light [photography, photometer]
5315 B   φάγομαι (8)   I eat [sarcophagus]
4095 B   πίνω (5a)   I drink
2212 A   ζητέω (1b)   I seek, look for, investigate
 308 D   ἀναβλέπω (1a)   I look up, see again, gain sight
2556 B   κακός -ή -όν   bad, evil, harm [cacophony]

2513 D   καθαρός -ά -όν   clean, pure [catharsis]
1715 C   ἔμπροσθεν   in front, ahead; + gen.   before

Group 53   (Lesson 60)

5602 B   ὧδε   here, in this place, hither
4632 D   τὸ σκεῦος -ους   vessel, jar, dish
2112 B   εὐθέως   at once, immediately
1859 D   ἡ ἑορτή -ῆς   festival, feast
1131 E   γυμνός -ή -όν   stripped, naked [gymnasium]
4851 E   συμφέρω (8)   I bring together, help; (impers.) it is profitable
2040 E   ὁ ἐργάτης -ου   worker, workman, laborer
3049 C   λογίζομαι (4a)   I reckon, calculate [logistics]
2372 E   ὁ θυμός -οῦ   passion, anger, wrath
4143 B   τὸ πλοῖον -ου   ship, boat

Group 54   (Lesson 61)

1949 E   ἐπιλαμβάνομαι (5b)   I take hold of, grasp, take interest in
1607 C   ἐκπορεύομαι (1a)   I come/go out/away
3986 D   ὁ πειρασμός -οῦ   test, trial, temptation
5048 D   τελειόω (1b)   I bring to an end, accomplish, fulfill [teleology]
3421 D   μνημονεύω (1a)   I remember, mention [mnemonic]
2872 D   κοπιάω (1b)   I become weary / tired, I toil
3107 B   μακάριος -α -ον   blessed, happy, fortunate
1563 B   ἐκεῖ   there
2390 D   ἰάομαι (1b)   I heal, cure
4572 C   σεαυτοῦ -ῆς (unused in nom.)   yourself (sing.)

Group 55   (Lesson 62)

  18 A   ἀγαθός -ή -όν   good
 770 C   ἀσθενέω (1b)   I am sick, weak, in need [asthenia]
2799 C   κλαίω (4c)   I weep, cry, bewail
4983 A   τὸ σῶμα -ατος   body [somatic]
5455 C   φωνέω (1b)   I produce a sound, speak loudly [phonetic]
1543 D   ὁ ἑκατοντάρχης -ου   centurion
 156 D   ἡ αἰτία -ας   cause, reason, charge, accusation
3844 B   παρά + dat.   at/by (the side of), near [parable]
3141 C   ἡ μαρτυρία -ας   testimony, testifying
2010 E   ἐπιτρέπω (1a)   I allow, permit, order

Group 56   (Lesson 63)

4012 C   περί + acc.   around, near, about [perimeter]
3992 B   πέμπω (1a)   I send
4757 D   ὁ στρατιώτης -ου   soldier
1887 E   ἐπαύριον   tomorrow, on the next day
1089 E   γεύομαι (1a)   I taste, ccome to know
5064 C   τέσσαρες -ες -α (pl. only)   four
 746 B   ἡ ἀρχή -ῆς   beginning; ruler, rule [archetype, monarch]
2342 C   τὸ θηρίον -ου   beast, animal [theriomorphic]
3763 E   οὐδέποτε   never
3825 A   πάλιν   back, again, anew [palingenesis]

Group 57   (Lesson 64)

2117 B   εὐθύς   at once, immediately
2511 C   καθαρίζω (4a)   I make clean, cleanse [cathartic]
4440 E   ὁ πυλών -ῶνος   gate, entrance [pylon]
1252 E   διακρίνω (4e)   I separate, differentiate, judge

3918 D πάρειμι (7a) I am present, have come
5384 D φίλος -η -ον beloved, dear; friend [philosophy]
3660 D ὀμνύω or ὄμνυμι (1a 7b) I swear, take an oath
4214 D πᾶσος -η -ον how great? how much? how many?
5506 D ὁ χιλίαρχος -ου commander of 1,000, tribune
2723 D κατηγορέω (1b) I accuse, reproach

Group 58 (Lesson 65)

1352 B διό wherefore, for this reason
3360 E μέχρι + gen. until, as far as, up to
3522 D νηστεύω (1a) I fast
3403 D μιμνήσκομαι (6) I call to mind, remember, mention
2573 C καλῶς well, beautifully, right(ly)
2038 C ἐργάζομαι (4a) I work, am active, do, perform
1343 B ἡ δικαιοσύνη -ης uprightness, justice, righteousness
4893 C ἡ συνείδησις -εως consciousness, conscience
2560 E κακῶς badly, wickedly; ἔχω κακῶς I am ill
3383 C μήτε and not, neither, nor

Group 59 (Lesson 66)

1228 C διάβολος -α -ον slanderous; ὁ δ. the Devil [diabolical[
2923 E ὁ κριτής -οῦ judge [critic]
4103 B πιστός -ή -όν trustworthy, faithful, trusting, believing
1961 E ἐπιμένω (4e) I stay, remain, continue, persevere
3670 D ὁμολογέω (1b) I promise, admit, confess, declare
 203 D ἡ ἀκροβυστία -ας foreskin, circumcision
1107 D γνωρίζω (4a) I make known, know [ignore]
1186 D τὸ δένδρον -ου tree [rhodadendron]
1249 D ὁ/ἡ διάκονος -ου servant, helper [deacon]
1656 D τὸ ἔλεος -ους mercy, compassion

Group 60 (Lesson 68)

3625 E ἡ οἰκουμένη -ης the inhabited earth, world [ecumenical, oecumenical]
3752 A ὅταν whenever, when, since
2917 D τὸ κρίμα -ατος dispute, decision, decree [criminal]
 417 C ὁ ἄνεμος -ου wind [anemometer]
2570 B καλός -ή -όν beautiful, good, noble
2168 C εὐχαριστέω (1b) I am thankful, give thanks, pray [eucharist]
1893 D ἐπεί when, after, since, because
2396 D ἴδε listen! see! behold!
2478 D ἰσχυρός -ά -όν strong, mighty
3076 D λυπέω (1b) I grieve, am sad

Group 61 (Lesson 69)

 190 B ἀκολουθέω (1b) I follow
 227 D ἀληθινός -ή -όν true, dependable, genuine
1380 B δοκέω (1b) I think, suppose, seem [docetic]
3162 D ἡ μάχαιρα -ας sword
3957 D τὸ πάσχα (indecl.) Passover, Paschal [paschal]
4016 D περιβάλλω (4e) I throw around, put on, clothe
5083 B τηρέω (1b) I keep watch over, keep, hold, observe
5091 D τιμάω (1b) I honor, revere, value
5426 D φρονέω (1b) I think, set my mind on
3466 D τὸ μυστήριον -ου mystery, secret rite [mystery]

Group 62 (Lesson 70)

```
  59 C  ἀγοράζω (4a)  I buy, purchase
1601 F  ἐκπίπτω (1a)  I fall off/from, lose, fail, run aground
 281 A  ἀμήν  verily, truly [Amen]
 473 D  ἀντί + gen.  instead of [anticlimax]
1746 D  ἐνδύω (1a)  I dress, clothe, put on
2240 D  ἥκω (perf. for pres.)  I have come, am present
3641 C  ὀλίγος -η -ον  few, little, brief [oligarchy]
4218 D  ποτέ  at some time or other, once, at times
3528 D  νικάω (1b)  I conquer, overcome [Nike]
3441 C  μόνος -η -ον  only, alone [monologue, monotone]
```

Group 63 (Lesson 71)

```
  25 A  ἀγαπάω (1b)  I love
  26 A  ἡ ἀγάπη -ης  love [Agape]
 721 C  τὸ ἀρνίον -ου  lamb
 737 C  ἄρτι  now, just now
 975 C  τὸ βιβλίον -ου  book, scroll [bibliography, Bible]
5565 C  χωρίς  separately, apart; + gen.  separated from
5056 C  τὸ τέλος -ους  end, conclusion, goal [teleology]
3668 C  ὁμοίως  so, in the same way, similarly
3850 B  ἡ παραβολή -ῆς  comparison, parable [parabola]
3813 B  τὸ παιδίον -ου  child [pediatrics]
```

Group 64 (Lesson 72)

```
1653 C  ἐλεέω (1b)  I have mercy on, I pity [eleeomosynary]
1939 C  ἡ ἐπιθυμία -ας  desire, longing, passion
2744 C  καυχάομαι  I boast, glory
3196 C  τὸ μέλος -ους  member, part, limb
3404 C  μισέω (1b)  I hate, detest [misogynist]
3631 C  ὁ οἶνος -ου  wine
3709 C  ἡ ὀργή -ῆς  anger, wrath [orgy]
3759 C  οὐαί  woe! alas!
3842 C  πάντοτε  always, at all times
4438 C  πτωχός -ή -όν  begging, poor, beggarly
```

Group 65 (Lesson 73)

```
1060 D  γαμέω (1b)  I marry, get married [monogamy, bigamy]
2008 D  ἐπιτιμάω (1b)  I rebuke, censure, punish
3501 D  νέος -α -ον  new, fresh, young [neophyte, neo-]
4105 C  πλανάω (1b)  I lead astray, wander, deceive [planet, planetary]
4221 C  τὸ ποτήριον -ου  cup
4624 D  σκανδαλίζω (4a)  I cause to fall, stumble, shock [scandalize]
5281 C  ἡ ὑπομονή -ῆς  patience, endurance, stedfastness
5293 C  ὑποτάσσω (4b)  I subject, become subject [hypotaxis]
5316 C  φαίνω (4e)  I shine, appear, am revealed [epiphany]
4145 D  πλούσιος -α -ον  rich, wealthy
```

Group 66 (Lesson 74)

```
 228 D  ἀληθινός -ή -όν  true, dependable, genuine
 268 C  ἀμαρτωλός -ός -όν  sinful, sinner
 601 D  ἀποκαλύπτω (3)  I reveal, disclose [apocalyptic]
 792 D  ὁ ἀστήρ -έρος  star [astral, astronomy]
 936 D  βασιλεύω  I am/become king, I rule
4152 D  πνευματικός -ή -όν  pertaining to spirit, spiritual [pneumatic]
```

3187 C μείζων -ων -ον larger (compar. of μέγας #3173)
1118 D οἱ γονεῖς -έων (pl.) parents [theogony, cosmogony]
3129 D μανθάνω (5b) I learn, find out [polymath (stem *μαθ, Class 5b)]
4226 D ποῦ where? at which place? to which place?

Group 67 (Lesson 75)

4687 B σπείρω (4e) I sow, scatter
4716 D ὁ σταυρός -οῦ stake, cross
5217 B ὑπάγω (1a) I go away, go
5319 C φανερόω (1b) I reveal, make known, become known
4159 D πόθεν from where? whence? how? in what way?
4735 D ὁ στέφανος -ου crown, wreath [Stephan]
5368 D φιλέω (1b) I love, like [Philhellenic]
1319 D ἡ διδασκαλία -ας teaching, instruction
1381 D δοκιμάζω I examine, approve
1504 D ἡ εἰκών -όνος image, form, likeness [ikon, iconoclast]

Group 68 (Lesson 76)

1588 D ἐκλεκτός -ή -όν chosen, select, choice [eclectic]
1658 D ἐλεύθερος -α -ον free, not bound
1754 D ἐνεργέω (1b) I work, operate, produce [energy]
1922 D ἡ ἐπίγνωσις -εως knowledge, recognition
2106 D εὐδοκέω (1b) I am well pleased, consent, approve
2226 D τὸ ζῷον -ου living thing, being
2232 D ὁ ἡγεμών -όνος prince, governor [hegemony]
2325 D θερίζω (4a) I reap, harvest
2379 D τὸ θυσιαστήριον -ου altar
2486 D ὁ ἰχθύς -ύος fish [ichthyology]

Group 69 (Lesson 77)

2518 D καθεύδω (1a) I sleep
2716 D κατεργάζομαι (4a) I achieve, accomplish, conquer
2673 D καταργέω (1b) I make ineffective, abolish, nullify
2723 D κατηγορέω (1b) I accuse, reproach [category]
2749 D κεῖμαι (7a) I lie, recline
3563 D ὁ νοῦς νοός understanding, mind [nous]
3952 D ἡ παρουσία -ας presence, advent, coming [Parousia]
3983 D πεινάω I hunger, desire
4149 D ὁ πλοῦτος -ου wealth, riches [plutocrat, Plutus]
4337 D προσέχω (1a) I pay attention to, heed, take care

Group 70 (Lesson 78)

4680 D σοφός -ή -όν clever, wise, skillful [sophomore, sophistry]
5057 D ὁ τελώνος -ου tax-collector
 430 E ἀπέχομαι (1a) I endure, bear
5015 E ταράσσω (4b) I shake together, stir up, trouble
2092 E ἕτοιμος -η -ον ready, prepared
 318 E ἡ ἀνάγκη -ης necessity, compulsion, distress
1435 E ὁ δῶρον -ου gift
1684 E ἐμβαίνω (5a) I go/step in, embark
3570 E νυνί now
5278 E ὑπομένω (4e) I remain, stay, wait

Group 71 (Lesson 79)

1140 B τὸ δαιμόνιον -ου demon, deity [demonic, daimonic]
2889 A ὁ κόσμος -ου world, universe, adornment [cosmic]
3664 C

3664 C ὅμοιος -α -ον like, similar [homeopathic]
3784 C ὀφείλω I owe, am indebted
4190 B πονηρός -ά -όν sick, evil, wicked
1651 E ἐλέγχω (1a) I bring to light, expose, convict
1883 E ἐπάνω above, over; + gen. on, over
2032 E ἐπουράνιος -ος -ον heavenly
2344 E ὁ θησαυρός -οῦ storehouse, treasure [thesaurus]
2462 E ὁ ἵππος -ου horse [hippodrome]

The following index is designed to help the student locate any word quickly in either the Arndt & Gingrich Lexicon or the Moulton & Geden Concordance, by using the numbering of the New Englishman's Greek Concordance. First, determine the number of the word (using either NEGC or Strong's Concordance). Locate that number (or the nearest number to it) in the adjoining column for either A&G or M&G. E.g. ἱλαστήριον, NEGC #2435, will be found on p. 376 in A&G (NEGC #2432 = A&G 376 and NEGC #2441 = A&G 377).

A&G	NEGC	M&G	A&G	NEGC	M&G	A&G	NEGC	M&G	A&G	NEGC	M&G	A&G	NEGC	M&G
1	1			217	40	67	441		102	676		130	900	
	2	1	35	222		68	445		103	684			905	137
2	12	2	36	226	41		446	75		686	104	131	907	138
3	19	4		228	42	69	447		104	690		132	908	139
4	22		37	231			451	77		696	105		913	140
5	26	6	38	236	43	70	453			706	106	133	916	
6	27	7	39	241	44		456	78	106	707		134	927	141
	28	8		244	46	71	457		107	715		135	934	143
7	31		40	245		72	463			720	107	136	936	144
8	33	10	41	256	47		470	79	108	722			940	145
9	38	11	42	265		73	474			727	108	137	943	
10	41	14	43	267	49	74	483		109	728		138	950	
11	48			268	50		484	80	110	738	109		954	146
12	54		44	269		75	491			741	110	139	958	
	58	15		278	51	76	505	81	111	745			968	147
13	61		45	279		77	513		112	747	111	140	970	
	69	16		282	52		515	82		750	112	141	977	148
14	70		46	287		78	516			754	113	142	986	
	72	17		292	53	79	521	83	113	757			989	149
15	74		47	296		80	530			759	114	143	992	150
16	81	21	49	302		81	537	84	114	762		144	995	
17	88			303	55	82	544	85		767	115		1000	151
	92	22		304	56	83	555		115	770		145	1009	
18	95			306	57		562	86		773	116	146	1015	152
	102	23	50	307		84	568	87	116	779		147	1026	
10	104		51	313		85	571	88		783	117		1028	153
20	110			315	58	88	576	89	117	787		148	1037	
	116	24	52	317		89	583			793	118		1042	153
21	120		53	322	59	90	592	90	118	799			1047	154
22	129	25	54	332		91	600	91	119	809		149	1050	
	130	26	55	339			601	92		811	119		1057	155
23	131			340	60	92	603		120	822		150	1059	
24	143	27	56	350			611	93		833	120	151	1063	156
	151	28		354	61	93	612	95	121	834			1064	157
25	154		57	358			616	96	122	842		152	1065	
26	157		58	367		94	619		123	847	130		1072	158
	158	29		374	62	95	623	97		849	131	153	1073	
27	166	30	59	376			630	98	124	852		154	1078	
28	167	31	60	387	63	96	631			860	132		1080	159
	170	32	61	391			638	99	125	862		155	1081	160
29	174			395	64	97	639		126	864	133	156	1088	
30	186		62	396		98	649			866	134		1092	161
	187	33	63	403			650	101	127	874			1094	163
31	191	34		409	65	99	652			881	135	157	1095	
32	192	38	64	416			653	102	128	888			1096	164
	200	39		425	66	100	655			892	136	159	1097	170
33	201		65	428		101	663		129	894		161	1098	172
34	212		66	436	69		670	103		896	136		1101	173

A&G	NEGC	M&G	A&G	NEGC	M&G	A&G	NEGC	M&G	A&G	NEGC	M&G	A&G	NEGC	M&G
162	1102		198	1354			1581	318	282	1871			323	2128	
163	1109	174		1360	221	242	1587			1880	352			2134	402
164	1115		199	1365			1589	319	283	1884			324	2136	
	1119	175	200	1374	222	243	1598			1894	353		325	2147	
165	1123	176	201	1381	223		1605	320	284	1895			326	2148	
166	1126	179	202	1383		244	1608			1905	354			2149	404
167	1132			1384	224		1615	321	285	1906			327	2156	
	1136	182	203	1392	226	245	1616		289	1910	364			2158	405
168	1138			1393	227	246	1626		290	1912	365		328	2166	
	1139	182	204	1394			1628	322	291	1922	366			2169	406
	1141	183	205	1402	229	247	1633		292	1926			329	2170	
169	1144		206	1409			1638	323		1934	367		330	2174	
	1153	184		1411	231	248	1643		293	1937				2182	407
170	1160		207	1412	233	249	1652	324	294	1942	368		331	2187	
	1162	185	208	1416		250	1658	325	295	1949			332	2191	408
171	1163			1419	235	251	1668			1951	369		334	2193	415
	1164	186	209	1424			1671	326	296	1959			336	2194	416
172	1167			1428	236	252	1680	327	297	1968				2197	417
	1170	187	210	1435	237	253	1681			1969	370		337	2199	418
173	1177			1436	237		1684	328	298	1973				2200	419
	1182	188	211	1438	240	254	1690		299	1984			338	2203	
174	1189	189		1439	244		1699	329		1986	371		339	2210	
175	1198		212	1440		255	1701		300	1987				2213	421
	1199	190		1447	245		1705	330	301	1993			340	2215	
176	1207	191	213	1449		256	1707			1995	372			2222	422
	1210	192	214	1454	247		1716	331	302	2001			341	2223	423
177	1211		215	1460		257	1717		303	2008	373		342	2224	
178	1218	193	216	1470		261	1723	333		2012	374			2227	424
180	1224	200		1473	247		1729	334	304	2014				2228	424
181	1228			1474	255	262	1731		305	2023			343	2229	
	1229	201		1480	256		1739	335		2032	375			2231	425
182	1241			1485	258	263	1742		306	2033			344	2232	
	1243	202	220	1491	270	264	1748			2034	376			2236	426
183	1245		221	1500			1754	336	307	2039			345	2238	
	1249	203		1506	271	265	1755			2040	377			2244	427
184	1250			1510	271	266	1764	337	308	2042	379		346	2245	
	1257	204	225	1511			1774	338	309	2042	380		348	2251	432
185	1259			1512	288	267	1775		310	2060			349	2260	
	1265	205		1513	297	268	1782			2064	381			2265	433
186	1267		226	1514			1785	339	311	2065	388			2270	434
	1280	206	227	1516	298	269	1788		312	2066	389		350	2271	
187	1282		229	1519			1790	340	313	2069	391			2280	434
188	1293			1520	299	270	1797		314	2079	392		351	2282	435
	1295	207	231	1521	303		1800	341	315	2086			352	2289	437
189	1304		232	1528	306	271	1805			2088	393		353	2297	438
	1309	208	233	1533			1807	342	316	2090	394		354	2301	
190	1312			1536	307	272	1813			2091	395			2304	439
191	1321	209	236	1538	308	273	1822	343	317	2094			355	2308	
	1322	210		1539	309	274	1832	345		2095	396		356	2310	442
	1323	211	237	1545	310	275	1833	346	318	2098	397		357	2313	
193	1326	215		1551	311	276	1840			2099	398		358	2317	457
	1327	216	238	1555		277	1844		319	2101			359	2319	
194	1333			1564	312		1845	347		2107	399		360	2326	458
	1339	217		1565	313	278	1850	348	320	2108				2335	459
195	1343	218	239	1566	315	279	1855	349	321	2113			361	2336	
196	1344	219		1568	316	280	1860	350		2117	400		362	2343	460
197	1345		240	1572		281	1864		322	2124			363	2348	461
	1350	220	241	1578	317		1865	351		2125	401		364	2356	

AEG	NEGC	M&G	A&G	NEGC	M&G	A&G	NEGC	M&G	A&G	NEGC	M&G	A&G	NEGC	M&G
	2358	462	401	2566		442	2853		486	3097		530	3442	
365	2363	463		2571	521	443	2857		487	3102	611		3452	658
366	2373		402	2573			2860	554		3107	612	531	3455	
	2374	464		2574	522	444	2867		488	3108			3467	659
367	2379	465	403	2577			2874	555	489	3113	613	533	3469	
368	2382		404	2585	523	445	2876		490	3121		533	3470	
	2383	465	405	2589	525	446	2886			3123	614	534	3476	660
	2385	466	406	2592			2889	556	491	3125			3481	661
369	2391	467		2593	526	448	2890	557		3127	615	535	3484	
370	2397		409	2597	531		2895	558	492	3132			3486	662
371	2399	469		2598	532	449	2897		493	3138	616	536	3488	
372	2401	471	410	2600			2900	559		3141	617	537	3499	663
373	2411	472		2608	533	450	2903		494	3142			3501	664
	2413	473	411	2609			2909	560	495	3143	618	538	3503	
374	2415		412	2619		451	2910		496	3145		539	3510	
	2418	474		2621	534	452	2918			3150	619		3517	665
	2420	475	413	2630		453	2920	562	498	3168			3518	
	2424	475		2637	535	454	2921			3171	620	540	3526	
	2425	485	414	2639			2924	563	499	3174	622	541	3529	666
375	2426	486	415	2642		455	2926		500	3178		542	3535	
376	2432			2648	536	456	2932		501	3189	623	543	3541	
377	2441	487	416	2656			2936	564	502	3196	625		3542	667
379	2444	495	417	2665	537	457	2938		503	3197		544	3549	
	2447	496	418	2671		458	2945		504	3304	628	545	3552	669
380	2450		419	2676	538		2950	565	505	3307	629	546	3557	
	2454	498	420	2687		459	2956		506	3308			3561	670
	2455	499		2702	539	461	2963	574		3312	630	547	3564	
381	2456		421	2703		462	2964		507	3314		548	3570	672
	2463	500	422	2711			2969	575	508	3317		549	3572	673
382	2471		423	2718	540	463	2971		509	3320	631		3578	673
	2475	501	424	2723			2975	575	511	3327	636	550	3579	
383	2477	503		2724	541	464	2979		512	3328			3584	674
384	2479		425	2728		465	2981	578		3336	637	551	3585	
	2480	504		2733	542	466	2984	581	513	3339			3588	674
385	2484		426	2735		467	2986		514	3342		555	3589	683
	2490	505	427	2745			2990	582		3343	638		3594	684
	2492	506		2746	543	468	2995	584	515	3346		556	3595	
386	2493		428	2750		469	3002		516	3352		557	3599	685
	2498	507		2754	544	471	3005	597		3356	639	558	3607	
	2504	507	429	2757		472	3009		517	3360		559	3609	686
387	2505	508	430	2763		473	3014			3364	646	560	3615	687
	2510	509		2769	545		3015	598	519	3365	647	561	3619	688
388	2511		431	2774		474	3024			3367	648	562	3622	
389	2514			2777	546		3027	599	520	3368		563	3625	689
	2517	510	432	2782		475	3034			3369	649	564	3626	690
390	2521			2785	547		3038	600	521	3378		565	3632	
	2522	511	433	2787		476	3040			3380	650		3635	691
391	2524	512		2793	548		3045	601	522	3385	651	566	3639	
392	2530		434	2798		477	3050		523	3395		567	3642	
394	2533	514		2802	549	478	3054			3398	652		3646	692
395	2538	515	435	2808		480	3057	605	524	3402			3651	693
396	2541	516		2814	550	481	3062		525	3405	653	568	3652	
396	2541		436	2817			3065	606	526	3413		569	3661	
397	2545		437	2822	551	482	3069			3416	654		3662	694
	2548	517	438	2833		483	3077		527	3422	655	570	3665	
398	2550			2837	552		3078	607	528	3429			3668	695
399	2557	51·8	439	2840		484	3084			3436	656	571	3669	
400	2565	520	440	2843	553		3090	608	529	3438		572	3672	
			441	2846		485	3092	608		3441	657		3677	696

A&G	NEGC	M&G	A&G	NEGC	M&G	A&G	NEGC	M&G	A&G	NEGC	M&G	A&G	NEGC	M&G
573	3678		621	3861	756	663	4086			4287	852		4568	889
577	3687	699	622	3869		664	4092		714	4292		753	4572	
578	3691		623	3871	757		4096	804	715	4299			4576	890
	3695	700		3874	758	665	4099	805		4305	853	754	4580	
579	3696		624	3876		668	4101	808	716	4308		755	4589	
580	3700	701	625	3881	759	670	4103		718	4315	860	756	4593	891
581	3706	702	626	3888		671	4104	811		4319	861		4595	892
582	3709	703		3895	760		4105	812	719	4325		757	4601	
583	3710		627	3898		672	4107		720	4333		758	4609	
	3714	704	628	3907			4114	813		4335	863		4610	893
584	3718			3909	761	673	4116		721	4337	864	759	4614	
585	3726		629	3914			4121	814	722	4338			4616	894
	3733	705	630	3919		674	4127			4342	865	760	4623	
586	3735			3923	762		4129	815	723	4343			4626	895
587	3738	706	631	3926		675	4131		724	4353	866	761	4627	
589	3740	712	632	3931		676	4135	816	725	4359		762	4633	
590	3744			3934	763	678	4138	817		4360	867		4637	896
	3747	713	633	3936		679	4141		726	4368		763	4639	
591	3749	715	634	3938			4144	818	727	4375	868	764	4648	
592	3752			3942	764	680	4148	819	728	4380			4654	897
	3753	717	635	3949		685	4152	824	729	4384		765	4656	
	3754	718	636	3955	765	686	4155			4385	869	766	4666	
594	3755		638	3957	778	687	4160			4387	870		4672	898
	3757	719	639	3958		689	4161	831	730	4393		767	4679	899
595	3758	720	640	3959		690	4164			4396	871	768	4681	
	3759	721		3961	779	691	4167		731	4397	872	769	4688	900
596	3762	723	642	3963	783		4170	832	732	4401			4691	901
	3763	725		3969	784	692	4173	834		4402	873	770	4694	
597	3766	726		3973	785	693	4176			4413	874	771	4704	
598	3769		643	3974		694	4182		734	4414	875		4705	902
	3770	727	644	3975	786	696	4184	838	735	4423		772	4715	
600	3773	730	645	3983	787	697	4189			4431	876	773	4718	903
	3776	731	646	3985			4190	839	736	4435		774	4729	904
602	3779	737		3987	788	698	4192		737	4441		775	4737	
	3780	740	647	3988			4193	840		4442	877	776	4742	905
603	3781		648	3993	789	699	4199	841	738	4443		777	4748	
	3785	741		4001	790		4201	842		4444	878		4751	906
604	3786		649	4006		700	4203		739	4454		778	4753	
	3789	742		4009	791	701	4212		740	4458			4757	907
605	3790		650	4011			4213	843		4459	879	779	4763	
606	3794	744	651	4013	795	702	4220	844		4460	880		4770	908
	3797	745	652	4017		703	4225			4474	881		4772	914
607	3802	745	653	4025			4227	845	742	4476		780	4774	915
608	3807			4027	796		4229	846	743	4488	882	781	4780	
609	3812	746	654	4031		704	4230		744	4497			4790	926
	3815	747	655	4044	797	705	4235			4502	883	782	4791	
610	3817		656	4048			4239	847	745	4507		783	4798	
611	3823			4050	798	706	4241		746	4518	884	784	4809	
612	3824		657	4053		707	4246	848		4522	885	785	4820	
	3828	749		4056	799		4250	849	747	4523			4823	916
613	3835		658	4059		708	4251		748	4532		786	4827	
614	3842	750		4062	800	709	4255	850		4538	886	787	4842	
616	3845	752	659	4063		710	4264		749	4542			4843	925
617	3847		660	4072			4267	851	750	4555		788	4852	
618	3851		661	4075	802	711	4271			4560	887	789	4860	
	3852	753	662	4080		712	4278		752	4562			4863	917
619	3855	754		4084	803	713	4286			4563	888	791	4865	918

A&G	NEGC	M&G	A&G	NEGC	M&G	A&G	NEGC	M&G
792	4873			5141	960	871	5400	
	4875	919	834	5147		872	5402	
793	4885			5153	961		5407	994
	4890	920	835	5158		873	5413	
794	4892			5161	962		5425	995
795	4901		836	5165		874	5426	
	4902	921	837	5177		875	5432	
796	4906			5179	963	876	5439	996
	4911	922	838	5180		877	5444	997
797	4913			5186	964	878	5451	
798	4921	923	839	5188			5456	998
799	4924			5191	964	879	5457	999
800	4932		840	5199		880	5458	1000
	4936	926		5201	965	881	5462	
801	4937		841	5205			5463	1000
802	4950			5206	966	882	5464	1001
	4953	927	843	5208	970	883	5473	
803	4960		844	5214			5477	1002
804	4973			5218	971	884	5480	
	4975	928	845	5219		885	5484	1003
805	4977			5221	972	887	5486	1005
806	4983	929	846	5226		888	5494	
807	4984	931	847	5229	974	889	5496	1007
808	4987		848	5233			5503	1008
809	4992	932		5236	975	890	5504	
810	4998		849	5243			5510	1009
	5000	932	850	5252		891	5516	
811	5005			5257	976	892	5524	
	5008	933	851	5260	978		5529	1010
812	5012		852	5264		893	5532	
813	5016	934		5267	979		5537	1011
814	5028		853	5273		894	5538	
	5036	935		5279	980	895	5546	
815	5037		854	5280			5548	1018
816	5044	936	855	5288	981		5553	1019
817	5047		856	5294	982	897	5556	
	5048	937	857	5303			5562	1020
818	5049			5309	983	898	5563	
820	5057	938	858	5311		899	5566	
821	5065	939	859	5314	983		5567	1021
	5069	940	860	5317	984	900	5576	
822	5080		861	5321			5581	1022
823	5084	941		5325	985	901	5586	
824	5088	942		5331	986	902	5591	1023
825	5092	943	862	5333		903	5594	
826	5094		863	5343	987		5596	1024
	5096	944		5344	988		5598	1024
827	5100		864	5345		904	5604	1025
	5101	949		5349	989	905	5611	1026
828	5102	954	865	5351		907	5614	1031
829	5109	955	866	5357		908	5617	1032
830	5117			5363	990		5621	1033
831	5118	956	867	5369		909	5624	
	5119	957	868	5377	991			
	5121	958	869	5385				
832	5132		870	5395				
	5134	959		5396	992			
833	5140			5398	993			

SUBJECT INDEX

1

2